Christianity:
the One, the Many

Christianity:
the One, the Many

**What Christianity Might Have Been
and Could Still Become**

Volume 2 of 2

John F. Nash

Author of *Quest for the Soul* and
The Soul and Its Destiny

To order additional copies of this book, contact:
Xlibris Corporation
1-888-795-4274
www.Xlibris.com
Orders@Xlibris.com
43074

Table of Contents

Volume 2

Introduction to Volume 2

The One and the Many

Christianity: the One, the Many is an interpretive history of Christianity that conveys the richness of the Christian experience. The book presents little-known facts and interesting personal stories about prominent Christians as well as the large-scale history of the medieval church and the Catholic, Protestant, and Eastern Orthodox churches that developed from it. It discusses the Gnostic alternative to early mainstream Christianity, the Celtic church of the British Isles, the Cathars of 12th-century France, the Evangelical movements, the Pentecostal movement of early 20th-century America, and most other major and minor denominations. This book also presents a bold new vision of Christianity, a new appreciation of what Christianity has been in the past and what it can offer today and tomorrow. All religious texts are to some degree the personal testimonies of their authors, but the hope is that this one will inspire many modern seekers and clarify their religious options.

The new vision honors both the transcendent unity of Christianity and the natural diversity of the spiritual paths within it. In accordance with Eastern Orthodox tradition, the larger unity is referred to as the *Ekklesia*, understood as an archetype expressing the totality of the Christian experience—the totality of responses to Jesus Christ. The Ekklesia is envisioned as a great "cathedral" into which all sincere Christians are invited to a communion of worship and service.

An attempt is made to define "a Christian." Based on the premise that any definition must be guided by Jesus' example of inclusiveness, criteria are proposed that include: expressing the divine presence in our lives, engaging in worship, following truth wherever it may lead, loving our neighbor as ourselves, and growing in perfection as guided by higher purpose. The broad inclusiveness of the criteria is balanced by the realization that certain types of behavior might disqualify individuals and groups from membership in the Ekklesia.

On the assumption that actions are more powerful than creeds, the spiritual paths are identified by what people *do*, rather than what they *believe*. Seven broad paths are discussed:

- **Devotion**: the approach to God through prayer, worship, artistic expression, and mysticism
- **Ceremony**: the approach to God through ritual, liturgy, and the sacraments
- **Knowledge**: the approach to God through the pursuit and sharing of truth
- **Service**: the approach to God through helping our neighbor and making the world a better place
- **Healing**: the approach to God through alleviating pain and nurturing the fullness of life
- **Activism**: the approach to God through the pursuit of peace and justice
- **Renunciation**: the approach to God through self-discipline, the reordering of priorities, and surrender to the divine will.

Like the Ekklesia, the seven paths are archetypes, and the descriptors: "Devotion," "Ceremony," and so forth, have larger meanings than they have in everyday usage. As a reminder of those expanded meanings, the descriptors are capitalized and in a few cases italicized.

Conceptually, the seven paths are not new. They are fundamental to Christianity, linking the faithful both to God and to the world, and we show how they were exemplified by outstanding Christians in history. But they are presented here in a new way. Some of us may be drawn to a single path; others may want to explore more than one—perhaps all of them, although that would dilute what we could hope to achieve. The seven paths represent ideals, and we have the opportunity to express them to the extent of our ability. Studying the paths will help us make choices of emphasis and perhaps will give direction to our own spiritual journeys.

Outline of the Book

Volume 1

Volume 1 covered the life of Jesus Christ, the birth of Christianity, the rise to power of the medieval "catholic" church, the Gnostic and Celtic alternatives, Christianity's early fragmentation in the east, and the development of the Eastern Orthodox churches.

We examined what we know of Jesus' life, death and resurrection, along with the political and cultural context in which those events occurred. We also examined some of the many stories, myths and legends that expressed people's experience of Christ. Our conclusion was that no clear-cut proof can be offered that Jesus ever lived, or proof that he did or said any of the things attributed to him. The evidence we have is all, to some degree, ambiguous. But in that ambiguity there is opportunity for faith. It seems clear that *something* profound happened 2,000 years ago to transform human consciousness, and we suggested that the reality of Jesus was demonstrated more clearly by his impact on the lives of Christians than by historical or scriptural evidence. The larger impact of Jesus' life is more apparent, and more important, than the details over which scriptural scholars, historians and skeptics may argue. However, we also concluded that sacred scripture is as meaningful, profound and relevant today as it was for people in the early church.

The Christianity of apostolic times was not a unified experience or a coherent body of beliefs and religious practices; nor was diversity introduced by corruption of a pristine unity and coherence. Diversity was there from the very beginning, reflecting spontaneous responses to the richness of Christ's life and teachings. Early Christianity was a melting pot of widely differing religious forms, all of which could have developed into major, complementary movements. But those forms were not allowed to develop in mutual harmony. Instead, stark choices were made, and a Darwinian struggle for survival ensued, in which weaker movements were overcome by stronger ones.

The Judaic Christianity of Palestine, led by James the brother of Jesus, was abandoned in favor of a new Hellenic Christianity preached by the apostle Paul to the people of the Roman Empire. But substantial diversity existed even within Pauline Christianity, and Christian communities operated autonomously. Afraid that diversity and spontaneity were getting out of hand, a group of dedicated but ambitious men sought to impose centralized control and to channel the Christian experience into standardized beliefs and practices. The institutional "catholic" church that dominated Christianity until the 10th century traced its origins back to that group. In our historical survey we saw how the church seized the political initiative in late antiquity and cemented relationships with secular powers. We studied the church's growing organizational structure: the episcopacy, the eastern patriarchates, and the papacy, all of which were modeled on administrative precedents in the Roman Empire.

The roles of the clergy in the institutional church changed over the first few centuries. We examined the transition from gender-inclusive liturgical leadership to exclusive leadership by celibate males and the equally important transition from presbyters, or elders, to priests empowered to perform the "sacrifice" of the Mass. Christian doctrine evolved from Paul and John the Evangelist, to the church fathers, to the ecumenical councils, and finally to professional theologians. We criticized the practice of resolving theological disagreements by up-or-down vote that permanently divided valuable insights into "orthodox" and "heretical." We studied the evolution of forms of worship, including devotion and sacramental rituals. We recognized the unique contribution made by the monastic system and the religious orders—in which women enjoyed opportunities not available elsewhere in the church and played important leadership roles. We paid tribute to the great flowering of sacred architecture, art and music which continued through the Renaissance and beyond.

Weaker competitors to the institutional church were soon suppressed, but Gnosticism was a formidable adversary, and the church fathers invested considerable energy in their campaign against it. Although classical Gnosticism lost the competition to represent Christianity, its basic forms survived and found new expression in the neo-Gnostic Manichaeans, Bogomils and Paulicians of eastern Europe and Asia and in the Cathars of western Europe. Eventually the Cathars were exterminated by the Roman church in the first large-scale act of religious genocide. Meanwhile, the Celtic church of the British Isles developed outside the Roman Empire and, for a while, outside the control of the mainstream church. As a result it acquired distinctive beliefs, practices and cultures—including strong links to nature and patterns of communal living—that have not entirely been lost.

Other branches of Christianity found themselves outside the main Christian corpus as the result of doctrinal disputes—in some cases tinged by political rivalries. As a religious alternative Arianism may have been short-lived, though it offered a theology that still finds broad support today. The Assyrian Church and its missionary creation, the Thomas Church of India, survived, as also did the Coptic Church of Egypt and its partners in the Oriental Orthodox Communion. The Assyrian ("Nestorian") Church and the Oriental churches were regarded as holding polar opposite positions on the nature and personhood of Christ. Rome and Constantinople claimed to occupy a middle position between those extremes. But it is not certain that those depictions were accurate or that the "middle ground" was the right one.

Volume 1 concluded with a study of the Great Schism of the 11th century and the separate evolution of the Eastern Orthodox Churches. The fortunes of the Greek church were tied closely to those of the Byzantine Empire, and when the empire went into decline, Greek Orthodoxy lost its power base. However the Russian Orthodox Church, initially an offshoot of its Greek parent, rose to ascendancy and launched the Orthodox tradition onto a new, rich spiritual journey. We extended the study of Eastern Orthodoxy to more recent times because of its relevance to modern Christianity. The Greek and Russian churches are of major importance to our theme, providing a glimpse of what Christianity might have been like if the dice had rolled a different way in the early Middle Ages. Eastern Orthodoxy has a great deal to offer as we look toward the future of Christianity as a whole.

Throughout Volume 1 we saw evidence that all seven spiritual paths were exemplified by the lives of prominent Christians, including the greatest saints. We also saw glimpses of the overarching archetype of the Ekklesia. For all its faults, the "catholic" church of the Middle Ages may represent the best *organizational* expression of the Ekklesia that has yet been achieved. By the end of Volume 2 we shall see that a more perfect manifestation of the Ekklesia may be achieved, not through an all-powerful organization but through the subjective communion of Christians united in common purpose despite their natural diversity in beliefs and practices.

Volume 2

Volume 2 focuses most directly on western Christianity, though important aspects of the eastern traditions are discussed when they impact our story. Divided into three parts, this volume takes us from the high Middle Ages to the present, and into the future.

Part IV: *The Western Church*, traces the path taken by western Christianity from the dawn of the second millennium to the Reformation. The high Middle Ages and Renaissance were times of crisis but also times of great opportunity and progress. Despite early fragmentation in the east and the more serious Great Schism, the western church was still united and subject to the centralized authority of Rome. However the Roman church went into decline as the result of internal corruption and failure to meet the needs of the faithful. When the Reformation came it simply gave expression to widespread perceptions of the church's irrelevance. Protestantism was a complex set of religious initiatives. We shall study the forms it took in Germany, Switzerland, and the British Isles, and the Catholic response in the Counter-Reformation.

Part V: *Christianity in the Modern World*, studies the development of Christianity since the Reformation. Context is provided by a brief study of the political, scientific, philosophical and social challenges that faced Christianity from the 17th century onward. Four chapters are devoted to a study of Christianity's response to those challenges: the growth of Evangelical and charismatic Christianity; the emergence of modern esoteric Christianity; the polarities of liberalism and fundamentalism; and important changes occurring within mainstream denominations. Our evaluation of contemporary mainstream Christianity is purposefully expanded to include developments in Eastern Orthodoxy.

Part VI: *The Future of Christianity*, explores in detail the vision of the Ekklesia and the seven spiritual paths—expressions of the One and the Many. The dual format provides the basis on which we evaluate Christianity's current and future place in the world and examine the options available to religious seekers in the 21st century. The Ekklesia is studied from both a theoretical and also a practical standpoint. In that connection we also attempt to define a Christian. Our study of the spiritual paths identifies their broad characteristics, historical precedents, and comments on their practice in the modern world.

Each chapter ends with a "Reflections" section providing commentary on the topics and integrating them into the book's larger themes. These sections and the whole of Part VI are written in a normative style that contrasts with the more descriptive style of the rest of the book.

Terminology

In accordance with traditional Christian usage I have used "Jesus" and "Christ" more or less interchangeably, though in places I discuss their possible distinction. In a departure from convention, I use "Mary of Nazareth" rather than "the Virgin Mary" to avoid an unnecessary doctrinal statement. Biblical quotations are from the King James Bible except where otherwise noted. In conformity with customary practice, the *Acts of the Apostles* will be referred to simply as *Acts*, even though other cited texts have titles such as the *Acts of Thomas* and *Acts of Peter*; the latter will always be spelled out in full.

"The Great Schism" refers here to the 11th-century split between east and west, not to the conflict between popes and antipopes two centuries later. For brevity, the Church of Rome will be referred to as "Catholic," rather than "Roman Catholic," except where obvious confusion would result, for example, with Anglo-Catholicism. The lower case, "catholic" refers to the unified church of the Middle Ages. Hinduism and Buddhism are referred to as "Asian" rather than "eastern" to avoid confusion with Oriental and Eastern Orthodox Christianity.

Except where a proper name or title is involved, capitalization is used sparingly. But judgments still have to be made, and the results are rarely satisfying, even to an author. In direct quotes I have tried to preserve original authors' (or translators') styles as well as national spelling conventions, such as "judgement" and "saviour." The practice of capitalizing descriptors of the seven paths has already been mentioned.

Consistent with modern usage, dates are designated as "CE" (Common Era) or "BCE" (before the Common Era) rather than "BC" (before Christ) or "AD" (*anno Domini*). Dates of people's lives include the following abbreviations: "b." (born) "d." (died), "r." (reigned or held office), and "c." (*circa* or about). Periods in history have always been somewhat ill-defined, and nobody would claim that delineations are precise; but a rough consensus has emerged, and the following designations are used for convenience of reference. "Late antiquity" refers to the period from the first to the fourth century CE. The "early Middle Ages" extended from the fourth to the tenth century, the "high Middle Ages" from about 1000 to 1300, and the "late Middle Ages" from 1300 to 1500. The "early modern age"—which encompassed the Renaissance—ran from about 1500 to 1800, and the "modern age" from 1800 onward. We have tried to adhere to these conventions.

Acknowledgements

Several hundred books and articles are referenced in this work, and I am in great debt to their authors for what they have taught me. Internet resources greatly facilitated the research, and I gratefully acknowledge use of material graciously provided on websites, including the *Ante-Nicene Fathers, New Advent Catholic Encyclopedia, Christian Classics Ethereal Library, Early Christian Writings, Gnostic Society Library*, and *Internet Classics Archive*. All applicable references are cited. Also I wish to express my debt to the innumerable lecturers, preachers, colleagues and friends who generously shared their insights. I have learned much from discussions with John A. Shuck, pastor of the First Presbyterian Church of Elizabethton, Tennessee.

I am indebted to Donna Brown, Nancy Seifer, B. Harrison Taylor, Christine Tipton, and Martin Vieweg who provided valuable feedback on the manuscript. Finally I record my sincere thanks to Sylvia Lagergren who not only spent countless hours reviewing the manuscript but whose love, encouragement and sacrifice made the work possible. Remaining weaknesses in the book are mine alone.

The Author

John Francis Nash, Ph.D., was born in the United Kingdom before World War II and moved to the United States in the 1960s. He earned his doctorate from the University of London and holds other degrees from British, Belgian and American institutions. A varied career led him from scientific research and business to higher education, before he "retired" to freelance writing and teaching in philosophy, religion, and spiritual healing.

Dr. Nash has published 12 books and roughly 150 scholarly articles, papers, and other contributions to the literature of multiple fields. His most recent books, both published in 2004, were *Quest for the Soul* and *The Soul and its Destiny*. Recent articles include "The Trinity and Its Symbolism," "Esoteric Healing in the Orthodox, Roman and Anglican Churches" and "The Power and Timelessness of Ritual." He founded and serves as editor-in-chief of *The Esoteric Quarterly*, an online peer-review journal of esoteric philosophy (www.esotericstudies.net/quarterly). He has given numerous presentations and conducted workshops in the United States and Europe. Further information can be found on his website: www.uriel.com.

Part IV
The Western Church

Perhaps I had better pass over our divines in silence and not stir this pool or touch this fair but unsavory plant, as a kind of men that are supercilious beyond comparison, and to that too, implacable; lest setting them about my ears, they attack me by troops and force me to a recantation sermon, which if I refuse, they straight pronounce me a heretic. For this is the thunderbolt with which they fright those whom they are resolved not to favor. And truly, though there are few others that less willingly acknowledge the kindnesses I have done them, yet even these too stand fast bound to me upon no ordinary accounts; while being happy in their own opinion, and as if they dwelt in the third heaven, they look with haughtiness on all others as poor creeping things and could almost find in their hearts to pity them; while hedged in with so many magisterial definitions, conclusions, corollaries, propositions explicit and implicit, they abound with so many starting-holes that Vulcan's net cannot hold them so fast, but they'll slip through with their distinctions, with which they so easily cut all knots asunder that a hatchet could not have done it better, so plentiful are they in their new-found words and prodigious terms. Besides, while they explicate the most hidden mysteries according to their own fancy—as how the world was first made; how original sin is derived to posterity; in what manner, how much room, and how long time Christ lay in the Virgin's womb; how accidents subsist in the Eucharist without their subject.

Desiderius Erasmus. *The Praise of Folly.*[1]

Chapter 13
Western Christianity in Crisis

Age of Transition

The Germanic migrations that changed the face of Europe in the fifth century were followed by the Muslim conquests of the seventh century and the Viking invasions of the ninth and tenth centuries. Within 10 years of Mohammed's death in 632 CE, Arab armies swept across the Middle East, conquering large areas of the Byzantine Empire. Damascus fell in 635, Jerusalem in 638, and Alexandria four years later. Constantinople barely survived a siege of 674-678 and another in 717-718, saved according to defenders by the intercession of Mary Theotokos.[2]

Muslin armies moved across north Africa and attacked the Iberian Peninsula in 711. Within seven years they had conquered most of what are now Spain and Portugal. The Moors—Arabs and north-African Berbers—settled the peninsula, which they called *Al-Andalus*,[3] and established their capital at Cordoba. Their armies even crossed the Pyrenees and advanced into France until they were stopped at the battle of Poitiers in 732 by Charles Martel, father of the Carolingian dynasty. Under the emir Abd al-Rahman, Moorish Spain enjoyed its golden age. Scholarship, literature, poetry and architecture flourished, and Muslim scholars provided a major channel through which Greek philosophy returned to western Europe after the Dark Ages. Moreover, Muslims, Jews and Christians lived together in relative harmony. There were restrictions; Christians were not permitted to proselytize, and Christian men were not permitted to marry Muslim women; and persecution did erupt later. But during the golden age, religious and ethnic toleration was the norm.

Viking raids began at the end of the eighth century, and we have already discussed their impact on the British Isles. The Vikings also ravaged parts of continental Europe, contributing to the downfall of the Carolingian empire. By the end of the ninth century Viking colonies stretched from Greenland to the Urals. The Vikings were fierce warriors but they also demonstrated their ability to assimilate into local cultures: Danes in England, Norwegians in Normandy, and Swedes in Rus'. In the two latter cases the Norsemen drew upon their traditional military ethos to contribute important traditions of their own. The

Normans established the orders of Christian knights of western Europe; and descendents of the Swedish colonists in Rus' provided the famous Veringian Guard in Constantinople.

Growing divisions within Christianity came to a head in 1054 with the Great Schism and the mutual excommunications of Pope Leo IX and Patriarch Michael Cerularius of Constantinople. Less than 50 years later the crusades were in full swing. They succeeded in expelling the Moors from Spain and converting pagans in the Baltic, but they failed to liberate the Holy Land from the Muslims. As a direct consequence of the crusades, the Byzantine Empire was so fatally weakened that it too fell under Muslim control. Ultimately the kings of Europe benefited the most, wresting control away from both the nobility and the church. In the aftermath of the crusades, powerful nation states emerged in Europe, and the maritime nations set out to colonize the Americas and south Asia.

The Church of Rome was in decline, and the Reformation would bring about the wholesale fragmentation of western Christianity. On the other hand, the high Middle Ages—defined roughly as the 11th through 13th centuries—saw a great intellectual revival; and the Renaissance would begin in the 15th century, laying the foundations on which the modern age would eventually be built. Those very positive developments will be discussed in the next chapter. Here we look at the challenging political and religious developments in Europe and the eastern Mediterranean during the same general period.

The Crusades

The crusades were highly organized military campaigns directed against the enemies of Christianity. Or perhaps we should say the enemies of *mainstream* Christianity because, from time to time, they were directed against internal enemies; as we saw in Chapters 10 and 11 the institutional church was willing to take up arms against fellow Christians. However, the main thrust was against the Muslims who held Palestine.

The Middle East

Muslims regarded both Christians and Jews as "people of the Book" and, for the most part, exercised religious tolerance in the territories they occupied. After the conquest of Jerusalem Umar al-Faruq, caliph and former companion of Mohammed, invited Jewish families to return to the city and live there.[4] But in 1009 the eccentric Fatamid caliph al-Hakim ordered the destruction of the Church of the Holy Sepulcher, considered the holiest shrine in Christendom.[5] Byzantine Emperor Alexius I appealed for western help to recapture the Holy Land which had previously lain within his jurisdiction; he also hoped that the west would help defend what remained of his empire from Seljuk Turks.[6]

Pope Urban II launched the first crusade in 1095, and the following year a large army led by French nobles set off for the Middle East. The crusade was amazingly successful; between 1097 and 1098 the crusaders took Edessa, Antioch, Tripoli, and finally Jerusalem. Sadly, in the course of taking Jerusalem, virtually all its inhabitants—Muslims, Jews, and even eastern Christians—were massacred. That kind of mass atrocity may have been new to the Church Militant in the late-11th century, but it was repeated in 1209 when the entire Christian population of Béziers was massacred during the Albigensian Crusade. The French nobles established the "crusader states" of *Outremer* ("Across the Sea") and installed themselves as counts and kings. In 1100 Baldwin I became the first king of "Jerusalem," a relatively large kingdom extending beyond the ancient city. Genoese and Florentine merchants, flocked to the crusader states, and generations of other Europeans would call Outremer home. The Knights Templar and Knights Hospitaler exerted considerable influence in the region, becoming more than just military orders.

Over time, Muslim forces reconquered much of the territory they had lost. Edessa was taken in 1144; and the city of Jerusalem fell to the Ayyubid sultan Saladin in 1187. Further crusades were launched in the attempt to defend the Christian states and repel Muslim attacks. Some were partially successful; others complete fiascos. The third crusade, led by three of Europe's most powerful monarchs: Richard I ("the Lionhearted") of England, Philip II of France, and the Holy Roman Emperor Frederick I Barbarossa, created much fanfare but ended in disaster. Frederick drowned before reaching the Holy Land. Richard (1157-1199) captured Cyprus and turned it into another crusader state; and in 1191 he and Philip relieved Acre which was under siege by Saladin's army. Richard marched on to Jerusalem but, realizing that he could not take the city, left for Europe, only to be seized on his way home by King Leopold V of Austria and held for ransom.

The fourth crusade set out to conquer Egypt; instead, in 1204, it sacked Constantinople, capital of the Byzantine Empire and center of Orthodox Christianity. For more than 50 years western emperors sat on the imperial throne and Latin bishops were appointed to the patriarchate of Constantinople.[7] Frankish nobles divided up the Balkans and Aegean Islands into fiefdoms. The saintly king Louis IX led the seventh (1248) and eighth (1270) crusades, both of which were total failures. Louis himself was captured in Egypt, released upon payment of a large ransom, but died in Tunis. The kingdom of Jerusalem survived, stripped of its capital, for more than a century. In one form or another, Outremer held on until 1291 when Acre, the last crusader stronghold, fell to Muslim forces. The crusade adventure in the Middle East lasted roughly 200 years.

The Iberian Peninsula

As early as the 720s the Visigoth nobleman Pelaya led a rebellion against the Moors of Al-Andalus and established the Christian kingdom of Asturias in the extreme north of Spain; an expanded Asturias was later divided into León and Castile. Charlemagne's son Louis the Pious made another small dent in Moorish Spain when he conquered Barcelona in 801. A larger-scale campaign to retake the Iberian Peninsula from the Moors began after 1000. It took more than four centuries and might not have succeeded at all but for internal divisions within the Islamic empire and the fragmentation of Al-Andalus into small kingdoms. King Alfonso VI of León scored the first major victory when he occupied Toledo in 1085. Portugal traces its origins as an independent kingdom to a victory over the Muslims at Ourique in 1139 and subsequent formal secession from León. King James 1 of Aragon conquered Valencia 1237, and by 1250 the Muslims had been driven from most of the country. However Granada, in the far south, survived as a vassal state of Castile for another three centuries. The armies of Ferdinand II of Aragon and Isabella I of Castile finally brought Granada under Christian control in 1492.[8] The reconquest of the Iberian Peninsula took roughly 770 years.

Portugal remained a separate kingdom, but Ferdinand and Isabella unified the rest of the Iberian Peninsula under a single monarchy which became Spain as we know it today. They also initiated a systematic purge of non-Christians; Muslims and Jews were given the option of conversion to Christianity or expulsion from Spain. Many Muslims retreated to North Africa, and Jews fled to Africa, Eastern Europe, and even Palestine.[9] A group of Jewish scholars settled at Safed (Tzfat) in Galilee and founded the great center of Qabalistic scholarship. Those who submitted to conversion—and in some cases their children and grandchildren—were harassed, denied full participation in the church, and even subjected to outright persecution on suspicion of heresy. Regarded as only half-hearted Christians, they became favorite targets of the Spanish Inquisition. To his credit Ignatius Loyola (1491-1556), Spanish soldier and founder of the Society of Jesus, regarded Jewish blood as an asset; both his own secretary and his successor as Father General of the Order, Diego Laynez, were of Jewish descent. But, after his death, attempts were made to erase any mention of Laynez' heredity in official Jesuit history.[10]

In addition to the religious and ethnic cleansing, the monarchs and clergy of both Spain and Portugal embarked on a process of reform to instill a high degree of piety, strict observance of religious practices, and a zealous missionary spirit. That spirit valued the "purification" and expansion of Christendom above virtually all other virtues, including compassion, justice, and respect for life; the same ruthless policy would be applied in Spanish and Portuguese colonies in the Americas and south Asia.

The Baltic Countries

Unable to contribute much to the war effort in Outremer, the Teutonic Knights returned to Europe. In 1226 they accepted an invitation from Duke Konrad I of Masovia, Poland, to subdue the pagan tribes that threatened his northern borders. The campaign took 50 years and resulted in great bloodshed; but upon its conclusion, the pope and the Holy Roman Emperor authorized the knights to administer the Prussian territories, which included parts of present-day Poland and most of Estonia, Latvia and Lithuania. Emboldened by their success in Christianizing the Baltic, the knights devised a plan to convert the Russians to Latin Christianity; fortunately they abandoned the plan before further harm could be done.

Under Teutonic rule many new cities were founded in Prussia, and large numbers of immigrants came from western Europe. However the 14th century was marred by continual military conflict with its neighbors. In 1410 the Knights were defeated at the Battle of Grunwald by a combined Polish-Lithuanian army, and the northern territories of Prussia were annexed and divided among Poland, Russia and Sweden. Teutonic rule of the southern territories ended when the order's grand master Albrecht of Brandenburg converted to Lutheranism in 1525. Prussia became a duchy, the first Protestant state in Europe.

The alliance between Poland and Lithuania began in 1386 when Grand Duke Jogaila of Lithuania converted to Christianity and married Queen Jadwiga of Poland. Subsequently, the two nations merged into a single kingdom, the largest in Europe. Poland-Lithuania, Silesia and Transylvania offered religious toleration—a rare commodity of that era. By the end of the 16th century those nations would provide a haven for many radical groups persecuted by Catholic or Protestant authorities elsewhere in Europe.

Changing Political and Social Environment

Regardless of what they achieved, or failed to achieve, the crusades brought the ruling classes of Europe together in collaborative endeavors of unprecedented proportions. Leadership of the crusades shifted from nobles to kings. Not incidentally, by the time end of the crusades, Europe was ruled by powerful monarchs. Also a new merchant class gained power, further eroding the influence of the nobility. None of those developments benefited the institutional church.

Challenge to the Social Order

During the Middle Ages society rested on three pillars, or "estates": the church, the nobility, and the peasantry. The church's religious and political power depended on the cooperation of the Holy Roman Emperor and the kings and nobles of

Europe. The aristocracy provided the military power necessary to maintain social stability and, when necessary, to defeat religious enemies. Like the church, the aristocracy was structured on hierarchical lines, with vassals and fiefs holding land in exchange for the payment of taxes and agreement to provide military service as and when demanded by their liege-lords.

By medieval times the cities established by the Romans had largely been depopulated and had fallen into serious disrepair. The mass of the people lived on large estates owned by the nobility or the church. They worked the land, providing food for the other two estates and—what was left—for themselves. The three estates were believed to be divinely ordained. If you were born a farm laborer, that was the station to which God had appointed you; if you were born a king, you were divinely ordained to rule. Society was ordered by "the Great Chain of Being," and to violate it was not only a social or political offense but also a grave sin against God.

However city states emerged, notably in the north of Italy. Venice, Florence and Genoa grew rich during the crusades from the transportation of troops and supplies across the Mediterranean and also from opportunities to trade with Outremer, the Byzantine Empire, and the Islamic world. New port cities grew up around the Mediterranean and along the Atlantic seaboard. Trade, in turn, spawned industries like textile manufacturing and banking. Rich merchants and bankers in Florence and elsewhere would become patrons of the arts, making possible the cultural upsurge of the Italian Renaissance. In many cases the new city states acquired partial or even complete political independence. The new merchant class did not fit comfortably into the three-estate model of medieval society, and eventually it became powerful enough to challenge the political power of the church and nobility. The cities witnessed the first stirrings of democratic, secular government.

The rebirth of cities in Europe in the high Middle Ages had an important effect on the relative influence of major units of Christianity. The bishops, whose dioceses were centered on the cities, gained both political influence and proximate sources of revenue. The monasteries, located primarily in rural areas, lost influence and posed less of a competitive threat. On the other hand, the new mendicant orders, like the Franciscans and Dominicans, gained significantly in power. Without a fixed base they could serve the population wherever it might be located. Their presence in the cities provided for easy comparisons between their own discipline and learning and the laxity and ignorance of the secular clergy; their austerity also provided for easy comparison with the opulence of the ecclesiastical hierarchy. In the end, the mendicant orders would pose a more serious threat to the bishops than the monasteries ever had.

War and Pestilence

The 14th century—conventionally considered the beginning of the late Middle Ages—was a very bad time for Europe. People feared that the end of the world was imminent. An unusually cold spell caused the Baltic Sea, which normally was navigable year-round, to freeze over twice during the century's first decade. Flooding and earthquakes, which destroyed the city of Basel and many other places, added to people's misery. In 1337 the Hundred Years' War broke out between England and France. England lost its territories on the European mainland; while France, technically the victor, was devastated. More seriously, from the viewpoint of European civilization, the age of chivalry came to an end, and warfare took on a more brutal character. Before the war ended, Joan of Arc was captured by Duke of Burgundy and sold to the English; subjected to a mock trial by Bishop Pierre Cauchon, she was burned at the stake in 1431.

The Black Death struck in 1346, borne by rats on a ship docked at Marseilles, France. It was caused by a single virus but took several forms, the most common being the bubonic plague. Since the gestation period was several days, many other people could be infected before symptoms appeared. Then death came quickly; in the words of Florentine author Giovanni Boccaccio, victims "ate lunch with their friend and dinner with their ancestors in paradise." The plight of ordinary people was acute:

> [D]eluded by hope or constrained by poverty, they stayed in their quarters, in their houses where they sickened by thousands a day, and, being without service or help of any kind, were, so to speak, irredeemably devoted to the death which overtook them. Many died daily or nightly in the public streets; of many others, who died at home, the departure was hardly observed by their neighbors, until the stench of their putrefying bodies carried the tidings; and what with their corpses and the corpses of others who died on every hand the whole place was a sepulchre.[11]

The plague ravaged cities and villages. At its peak, 500-600 people in Venice died every day. The plague spread quickly, crossing the English Channel to reach London by 1348, and Scotland, Wales and Ireland the following year:

> Sometimes it came by road, passing from village to village, sometimes by river, as in the East Midlands, or by ship, from the Low Countries or from other infected areas . . . Few settlements were totally depopulated, but in most others whole families must have been wiped out, and few can have been spared some loss, since the plague killed indiscriminately, striking at rich and poor alike.[12]

Within four years more than one-third of the population of Europe was dead, and in some areas the death-rate was far higher. Moreover, the plague returned almost every generation for at least 150 years, often after bad harvests undermined nutritional levels. Not surprisingly, with the great loss of life, particularly among the peasant classes, the economy collapsed. Finally, law and order broke down. People turned against one another, and survivors of the plague were exposed to robbery, murder and rape. In several countries peasants revolted against their landowners. Jews were blamed for the plague, exacerbating long-standing patterns of anti-Semitism; pogroms were launched, and in several German cities, including Worms and Mainz, entire Jewish populations were expelled.[13]

Emergence of Powerful Nation States

The European political scene continually changed through conquests and more particularly through strategic marriages. One of the most important royal dynasties to emerge during the late Middle Ages was the Hapsburg family. The Hapsburgs originally came from Alsace and northern Switzerland in the 10th century; three centuries later they gained control of Austria, Bohemia and Hungary. In 1438, the Hapsburg Albert II was elected Holy Roman Emperor; and from then the family supplied more emperors than any other. Hapsburg possessions reached their greatest extent under Charles V (1500-1558), grandson of Ferdinand and Isabella of Spain. By 1520, holding the offices of king of Spain and Holy Roman Emperor, he controlled a huge swath of Europe from the Netherlands to Sicily; he also controlled the Spanish colonies in the Americas. The flow of wealth from the New World sustained Hapsburg dynastic ambitions for centuries.

Charles V was nominal ruler over the sprawling Hapsburg possessions; but, stretched so thin, he was never able to focus attention on individual trouble spots. Wars erupted with France, he invaded Italy in the 1520s, and constant threats came from the Ottoman Turks in the east. Turkish forces led by Suleiman the Magnificent conquered the Balkans and Hungary and in 1529 lay siege to Vienna. Those distractions had important consequences for the imperial heartland of Germany. The empire had already splintered into semi-autonomous states under Frederick Barbarossa in the 12th century. Under Charles it splintered further until Germany consisted of some 300 jurisdictions whose rulers owed no more than superficial allegiance to imperial authority. Although the Hapsburgs remained staunchly Catholic, the Reformation succeeded because the principalities of northern Germany felt free to defy imperial opposition and embrace the new forms of Christianity.

Meanwhile, powerful monarchies were emerging in other parts of Europe. Henry VII of England (1457-1509), who came to the throne in the aftermath of the War of the Roses, asserted control over his nobles to an unprecedented degree.

His successor, Henry VIII, annexed the neighboring principality of Wales and turned Ireland into a kingdom under English rule.[14] The centralized authority the two kings built would play an important role in the English Reformation. Francis I of France (1494-1547) embarked on bold foreign initiatives, including the exploration of Canada and the first attempt to reach an accommodation with the Ottoman Turks to secure the balance of power in Europe. Francis was also a great humanist and patron of the arts; what became the distinctive French culture of the Renaissance owed much to his reign.

The rise of powerful nation states signaled changes to the social order that left many people feeling unsettled. One response was the growing popularity of utopian literature. English statesman Thomas More published his *Utopia* in 1515; inspired by Plato's *Republic*, it envisioned an ideal society which had eradicated poverty and misery, which went to war only if attacked, and where there were few laws (and no lawyers). Later utopian works included Italian satirist Trajano Boccalini's *Parnassus Comparisons*, published in 1612, and Italian philosopher Tommaso Campanella's *The City of the Sun*, published in 1623. More was executed for treason by King Henry VIII; Boccalini officially died from colic, but according to some reports was murdered in his bed; Campanella was investigated by the Inquisition and spent 27 years in a Spanish prison.[15] Notions of utopianism appeared in the Rosicrucian Manifestos of 1614-1616, which will be discussed in Chapter 18. They would appear again in the Fruitlands community of American Transcendentalist Amos Bronson Alcott (1799-1888), in the communes of the 1960s, and in today's intentional communities.

The powerful monarchs of the 15th and 16th centuries claimed to rule by divine right invested in their dynasties; but in the 17th century the principle began to emerge that sovereignty might reside in the state—or even in the people.[16] In the American, and more particularly the French, Revolutions we find clear applications of that principle. State identity would be expressed even more strongly in the nationalistic movements of the 19th and 20th centuries. The shifting locus of sovereignty had important implications for institutional Christianity.

The Rise of Colonialism

Portuguese colonies were established on the Pacific coast of South America and also in south Asia. Spain established much larger colonies in eastern South America, the Caribbean, and North America. Pope Alexander VI (r. 1492-1503) drew the north-south line through the Americas dividing the Portuguese and Spanish spheres of influence. The papacy also gave the two nations authority and responsibility for the Christianization of their colonial possessions. In due course France also became a colonial power, with settlements in Newfoundland.

The Roman church had received the command to teach "all nations," but it struggled with the question of how far its responsibilities extended. The church fathers discussed the status of the "monsters" believed to inhabit the regions beyond the ends of the earth. Augustine took an inclusive view: "Whoever is born anywhere as a human being . . . however strange he may appear to our senses in bodily form or colour or motion or utterance, or in any faculty . . . let no true believer have any doubt that such an individual is descended from the one man who was first created."[17] If they were descended from Adam and Eve presumably they were human beings, capable of salvation. No monsters were actually found by the explorers,[18] but in 1512 Pope Julius II found it necessary to issue an official declaration certifying that Native American were true human beings, even though they were not mentioned in the Bible. Perhaps they were descended from Babylonians who somehow managed to survive the flood and made their way to America; or perhaps they were descended from the lost tribes of Israel.

Spain was by far the more successful colonial power, amassing enormous wealth not only from exploitation of the mineral resources of the conquered lands but also from plunder. Indigenous populations were slaughtered, enslaved, and/or forcibly converted to Christianity. However many missionaries tried to protect native people, often coming into conflict with brutal, unprincipled colonists. The Jesuits established missions on the fringes of the Spanish colonies of Chile, Peru and Paraguay and repelled repeated attacks by Portuguese slave traders. At their peak the missions housed 100,000 people; indigenous people were taught trades and crafts as well as principles of self-government. Had they survived the missions might have evolved into an independent nation; however in 1767 King Charles III of Spain expelled the Jesuits from South America. Soon thereafter the missions were destroyed, and many native people were sold into slavery.[19] Six years later the Society of Jesus was suppressed worldwide in a vendetta reminiscent of the suppression of the Knights Templar in the 14th century; the Jesuits were not restored until 1814.

Decline of the Western Church

The crusades drained resources and distracted the western church from its responsibilities to the faithful. The papacy itself went into decline after 1300. However the seeds of western Christianity' decline were sown before the church celebrated its first millennium. Problems existed at every level in the church, from local parishes to the papal court.

Failure of Pastoral Care

The performance of the medieval secular clergy left much to be desired. Men of a saintly disposition and with the right connections were drawn to the religious orders;

the nobility saw abbotships and bishoprics as good career options. Ordination to the priesthood was just a prerequisite for higher office; sons of ambitious parents were often ordained as children to launch them onto a fast track to promotion. Serving as a parish priest was rarely considered a fitting vocation for the privileged.

Wealthy families sometimes endowed churches and provided a "living" to parish clergy. In the very rare cases where the living was substantial, appointment to those churches was eagerly sought-after; positions might be filled on the basis of patronage—or for a fee—from the lower levels of the aristocracy or "landed gentry."[20] More typically, parish clergy were recruited from the ranks of the peasantry. Their lot was meager; viewed from above, by both the nobility and the episcopacy, they were regarded with patronizing contempt.

The medieval parish priest, institutional Christianity's representative in direct contact with the faithful, typically was uneducated and poorly trained:

> The great majority of priests were too ignorant to prepare a sermon, and barely understood the Latin liturgical forms. A Synod of Aix, 802, prescribed that they should learn the Athanasian and Apostles' Creed, the Lord's Prayer with exposition, the Sacramentarium or canon of the mass, the formula of exorcism, the commendatio animae, the Penitential, the Calendar and the Roman cantus; they should learn to understand the homilies for Sundays and holy days as models of preaching, and read the pastoral theology of Pope Gregory. This was the sum and substance of clerical learning.[21]

Liturgical Latin was learned by rote, with little or no understanding of its meaning. That mattered little to the faithful who understood even less. In any event the Mass was normally celebrated behind a screen, separating the chancel from the nave, and the faithful could neither see nor hear the priest. People were forced to attend church services; perhaps they enjoyed the fellowship, but they could scarcely have been inspired by the services.

The problem of incompetent clergy was a major incentive for the creation of mendicant religious orders. Friars were trained and supervised by their own superiors, separate from the episcopacy. Not surprisingly, relations between secular clergy and friars were strained. Parish priests resented the friars, while the latter looked down on the secular clergy. Preaching was the friars' main function, providing effective teaching—at least in major cities—for the first time. However sermons were still preached in Latin; when Meister Eckhart preached in German he was accused of "confusing the simple people."[22] The Protestant reformers resolved to place new emphasis on preaching and to make sermons the centerpiece of Sunday worship services; moreover the reformers had the good sense to preach in the vernacular.

Inadequate supervision compounded problems of moral laxity among the secular clergy. That problem was not new. A passage in *Isaiah* shows that clerical excesses predated Christianity: "the priest and the prophet have erred through strong drink, they are swallowed up of wine."[23] And, in the first century CE, the *Didache* warned against false prophets, including those motivated by money and ones who do not practice what they preach; their sin "shall not be forgiven."[24] Problems increased during the Middle Ages to the point where confidence in the clergy was seriously undermined.

Men sometimes became priests to evade military service;[25] but they were rarely drawn to the parish clergy by materialistic ambition, as were many of their bishops. Poverty was so pervasive that many priests were driven to poaching, smuggling, or other illegal activities just to survive. More serious, from the standpoint of their public image, was sexual immorality. When celibacy was imposed throughout the western church in the 12th century, many priests struggled to live up to its demands. They kept "housekeepers" or satisfied their physical drives in other ways. In small communities the priest's behavior was often common knowledge, and people questioned his ability to celebrate the Mass or administer the sacraments. Clergy might be able to perform their sacerdotal functions satisfactorily despite personal weaknesses;[26] but appearances are important, and even suspicions of immorality could undermine trust.[27] The faithful might need the priest and fear him, but they were unlikely to see him as a source of inspiration or solace.

People turn to religion in times of crisis, and the need for pastoral case increased dramatically during the Black Death. Tthe plague brought out the best and the worst among the clergy. Dedicated priests, monks and nuns worked under the most appalling conditions to offer care for the sick or administer the last sacraments; their task was overwhelming: "[T]imes without number it happened, that as two priests, bearing the cross, were on their way to perform the last office for some one, three or four biers were brought up by the porters in rear of them, so that, whereas the priests supposed that they had but one corpse to bury, they discovered that there were six or eight, or sometimes more."[28] Through contact with the sick and dying, clergy were particularly exposed to the disease and suffered disproportionately. In Montpellier, France, only seven of 140 Dominican friars survived. Less dedicated priests abandoned their congregations and fled.

Preachers said the Black Death was God's will: people were being punished for their sins. But they could not identify what sins could have attracted such terrible punishment. The faithful wanted answers, but the clergy had none. People prayed to God, begged for forgiveness, and died by the tens and hundreds of thousands.

Worldliness of the Episcopacy

As soon as Christianity became the official religion of the Roman Empire, bishops became public figures of influence and prestige. During the Middle Ages senior members of the church hierarchy wielded even greater power and influence, in some cases exercising direct civil authority.[29] Some city-states in Lombardy were ruled by bishops serving as vassals to the king.[30] Positions in the hierarchy were filled almost exclusively by the nobility; in some areas, that was even legislated.[31] In the rigidly stratified society of the time, to rise above one's birth-station was virtually impossible. The notion that individuals of exceptional merit but low birth might be promoted to leadership positions in religion—or, for that matter, the military or government—was incomprehensible. However belonging to the nobility, with its tradition of wealth and privilege, did not automatically translate into saintliness; nor did it necessarily equip a man to handle the responsibilities of episcopal office.

In the Holy Roman Empire bishops were appointed by the pope. The practice promoted good relations between Rome and the dioceses and preserved effective centralized control. Appointees were loyal and committed to the goals and wellbeing of the church—except perhaps when corrupt popes sat on the throne of Peter. However, the practice was widely resented; local rulers often perceived bishops as outsiders. One notorious case involved the famous Nicholas of Cusa. Pope Nicholas V raised him to the rank of cardinal and in 1450 named him bishop of Brixen in the Tyrol; however Archduke Sigmund of Austria opposed Nicholas' appointment and incarcerated him. Sigmund was excommunicated and eventually capitulated, but not before Nicholas' death.

Elsewhere ecclesiastical appointments were usually made by secular authorities. The latter practice may have reduced centralized control; but it had certain advantages. Rulers were familiar with local conditions and could identify promising candidates; moreover, bishops often functioned as secular bureaucrats, serving both church and state.[32] Conscientious rulers could appoint educated, saintly men with good administrative skills who would enjoy local support. Frequently the monasteries were tapped for suitable candidates, and many abbots found their way into the episcopacy. Unfortunately, rulers were not always conscientious and did not always have the interests of the church at heart. Bishoprics were regarded as instruments of political patronage or could be sold for a fee.[33] They were good investments for anyone looking for a lifetime of relative luxury and few demands. A bishopric might offer suitable placement for the younger son of a nobleman who would not inherit the family estates. Bishops typically received taxes from their parishes and in some cases enjoyed grants or endowments from rich aristocrats. As with all persons in positions of authority, occasionally they might see opportunities to collect gratuities or bribes.

Few bishops or prelates of the Middle Ages felt the desire to emulate the poverty of Jesus, the socialism of the early Christians,[34] or the asceticism of the desert fathers. They expected to live in luxury, comparable with the standards of their upbringing or of their peers in secular positions. In return, many bishops did virtually nothing, not even live in their dioceses. Some held multiple bishoprics, like a portfolio of investments. Historian Philip Schaff related an example from 15th-century Spain: "Gonzalez de Mendoza, while yet a child, held the curacy of Hita, at twelve was archdeacon of Guadalajara, one of the richest benefices of Spain, and retained the bishopric of Seguenza during his successive administrations of the archbishoprics of Seville and Toledo."[35] His contemporary, the Italian Giuliano della Rovere, who later became Pope Julius II, held no fewer than eight bishoprics; how much attention he could possibly have devoted to any of them is open to question. Most importantly the bishops rarely gave their clergy the support so urgently needed. Given the worldliness and indifference of the bishops, it is no wonder that parish clergy lacked meaningful supervision.

History has not focused on personal moral failure in the episcopacy to the same degree as it has on the papacy; but records show that, from time to time, bishops and archbishops violated their sacred trust. As early as 600 CE the Celtic saint Columban wrote to Pope Gregory I complaining of lax morals among the Frankish bishops.[36] In 742 Boniface, "apostle of the Germans," sought Pope Zacharias' advice on what to do with bishops who "are shiftless drunkards, addicted to the chase, who march armed into battle and shed with their own hands the blood of Christians and heathens alike."[37] In the 10th century Hatto, archbishop of Mainz, is reputed to have lured hungry peasants into a barn and set light to it, whereupon, according to legend, hoards of mice ran out and pursued Hatto to his death.[38] Of the Gonzalez de Mendoza mentioned earlier, we learn: "[He] was a gallant knight and, in 1484, when he led the army which invaded Granada, he took with him his bastard son, Rodrigo, who was subsequently married in great state in the presence of Ferdinand and Isabella to Ferdinand's niece."[39]

In the early 16th century, the bishop of Winchester operated brothels in the London suburb of Southwark; King Henry VIII eventually closed the brothels for fear of the newly identified disease of syphilis.[40] In 16th-century Scotland: "Bishops lived openly in concubinage and married their daughters into the ranks of the nobility. In the marriage document, certifying the nuptials of Cardinal Beaton's eldest daughter to the Earl of Crawford, 1546, the cardinal called her his child. On the night of his murder, he is said to have been with his favorite mistress, Marion Ogilvie."[41] The shock of the Reformation provoked stricter discipline within the Roman church. But it was still recorded that Cardinal Andreas of Austria (1558-1600), son of the emperor Ferdinand II and governor of the Netherlands, had two illegitimate children.

Decline of the Papacy

In 1305 King Philip IV of France lobbied successfully for the election of the new pope, the Frenchman Clement V. Soon thereafter he pressured Clement to seek "refuge" in Avignon from political instability in Rome.[42] Thus began what came to be known as the "Babylonian captivity," and it lasted almost exactly as long as the one in the sixth century BCE. At Philip's insistence Clement suppressed the Knights Templar, allowing Philip to seize their wealth. Both Philip and Clement died in 1314, but the papal court remained in Avignon for a further 63 years. A total of seven popes spent their days there, serving French political interests.

The Avignon popes had little power, but they lacked none of the amenities to which pontiffs were accustomed. Indeed the papal court rose to new heights of opulence and sank to new lows of corruption. To pay for lavish lifestyles new sources of revenue were needed, particularly because income was no longer flowing from the Papal States. Simony became a way of life; everything was for sale; ecclesiastical offices were offered to the highest bidder, and bishops or abbots were removed from office if a better offer came along.

Pope Clement VI (r.1342-1352) formalized the sale of indulgences that would inflame Martin Luther 174 years later.[43] Indulgences have to be understood in relation to the doctrine of purgatory.[44] The normal way to reduce the time to be spent in purgatory, and the associated suffering, was by performing good works while still on earth. However, at the pope's discretion, it could also be reduced by drawing upon the "treasury of merit" accrued by the saints and particularly by the martyrs of the early church. An "indulgence" was a document authorized by the pope stating the equivalent period of good works. In short, by purchasing an indulgence a person bought relief from purgatorial suffering.[45] Whether or not indulgences benefited the recipients, they greatly benefited the church. But the income from indulgence sales was still not enough to meet papal needs, so taxes on the faithful were raised too. Needless to say, both the sales of indulgences and the taxation continued beyond the Avignon period.

The renowned mystic Catherine of Siena persuaded Gregory XI to return to Rome in 1377, just one year before he died. Unfortunately the restoration of the papacy to its traditional home did not restore its power and prestige. Upon Gregory's death the papal schism erupted. The cardinals elected Pope Urban VI in 1378; however they soon regretted their decision, claiming that he was insane. Certainly Urban was abrasive and erratic; but the real reason for wanting to replace him may have been that he initiated ecclesiastical reforms which upset influential French bishops. A majority of the cardinals held a second conclave, deposed Urban, and elected a new pope, Clement VII. Urban rejected the conclave as illegal and declared Clement an usurper or "antipope."[46] He raised an army, and forced Clement to flee—back to Avignon. There were now two popes, each with his own administrative structure, each demanding allegiance from bishops, kings and ordinary people, and each excommunicating supporters of the other. The nations of Europe lined up on one side or the other: France, Castile, Aragon and Scotland supported the Avignon pope, while Germany, Scandinavia, England and Portugal supported Rome.

After the schism dragged on for 20 years, a council of bishops met in 1409 at Pisa, Italy, to try to restore unity. It deposed the current pope Gregory XII in Rome, and the antipope Benedict XIII in Avignon, and appointed a third man, Alexander V. Unfortunately, neither Gregory nor Benedict would resign, so there were now three popes. The schism was finally ended when Holy Roman Emperor Sigmund convened the Council of Constance in 1414. The council deposed all three contenders and elected Pope Martin V (r.1417-1431).[47] It acted with courage and decisiveness on that issue; unfortunately the Council of Constance is also remembered for its betrayal and execution of the Bohemian priest Jan Hus.

Although the schism was resolved, the papacy was seriously weakened. The bishops claimed that they, rather than the pope, held ultimate power; after all they had put Martin on the throne. The "conciliar movement," as was called, posed a real threat to papal supremacy. In a ploy to regain the upper hand, popes secured the support of powerful secular rulers by ceding to them greater authority to make ecclesiastical appointments. The kings of France and Spain secured that important right; and the Holy Roman Emperor would also have done so, but for ongoing tensions with Rome. Another factor that helped the papal cause was the continuing threat from the Ottoman Turks in the East. The fall of Constantinople in 1453 and subsequent invasion of the Balkans shocked the western church into rallying around the bishop of Rome. Had not Leo the Great saved Rome in the fifth century?

The papacy's recovery of power was marked by a declaration by the Council of Florence (1438-1445):

> [T]he holy Apostolic see and the Roman pontiff holds the primacy over the whole world; . . . the Roman pontiff himself is the successor of the blessed Peter Prince of the Apostles and the true Vicar of Christ, and the head of the whole Church, and the father and teacher of all Christians, and . . . to him in blessed Peter the full power of feeding, ruling and governing the universal Church was given by our Lord Jesus Christ, and this is also recognized in the acts of the ecumenical council and in the sacred canons.[48]

Thus the pope once again claimed to be the ruler of both the western and eastern churches, even though the latter refused to recognize his authority. The conciliar movement continued intermittently until the Fifth Lateran Council (1512-1517). By then some of the most unsuitable men were serving as popes and the western church would soon confront its greatest challenge: the Reformation.

Moral Failure

The example of Pope John XII in the tenth century might have had a sobering effect on the moral climate of later pontificates; but memories fade, and scandals in the papal court reached a new peak in the 16th century.

Rodrigo Borgia, nephew of another pope, is rumored to have bribed his way to election in 1492 as Alexander VI. Alexander already had several illegitimate children, four by a Roman woman, Vannozza dei Cattani. One of them was the infamous Lucrezia Borgia; another, Cesare, was appointed archbishop of Valencia at age 16 and went on to become a major player in papal affairs. After his election, the pontiff proceeded to have a tryst with a 19 year-old married woman, Giulia Farnese. Among the orgies Alexander arranged was the "Banquet of Chestnuts," in which guests fornicated with naked prostitutes crawling on the floor; reportedly the pope gave a prize for the greatest virile endurance.[49] After Alexander's death, attributed to poisoning, his successor, Pius III, forbade the celebration of a requiem Mass, explaining: "It is blasphemous to pray for the damned." For all his failings, Alexander was reckoned to be an able administrator and generous patron of the arts. Giulia Farnese's brother, referred to in the papal court as "Cardinal Petticoat" for his notorious womanizing, became Pope Paul III in 1534. He is remembered for launching the Counter-Reformation and convening the Countil of Trent, but he delayed his ordination to finish an affair that bore him four illegitimate children.

Leo X (r.1513-1521), second son of Lorenzo de Medici, was ordained a priest at age seven and created a cardinal at 14. Elected pope, he reportedly told his brother: "Since God has given us the papacy, let us enjoy it." But another quote popularly attributed to him: "How well we know what a profitable superstition this fable of Christ has been for us," comes from a fictional work.[50] In addition to personal extravagance, Leo X donated huge sums to charity, embarked on an ambitious building program, and became the patron of artist Raphael. To pay for his excesses he offered political and religious offices for sale; and by the end of his reign more than 2,000 offices had been sold, bringing in revenue of 3 million ducats. Leo also sold indulgences on an unprecedented scale. The Reformation erupted during his reign—not least because of the indulgence scandal—and it was Leo who excommunicated Martin Luther in 1521.

Those popes bore a terrible responsibility for their moral failures; but responsibility also lay with the cardinals who elected them. The College of Cardinals was a corrupt, inbred group of men, indifferent to their responsibilities to the church and unworthy to hold the offices with which they were entrusted.

Grassroots Religious Movements

The stresses of the times, failure of pastoral care, and revulsion against the behavior of bishops, prelates and popes forced many people to do what had previously been unthinkable: to question the authority of the institutional church. Many people grumbled but remained within the framework of Roman Christianity, others were expelled from the church, and still others turned away to seek God elsewhere. In reaction to the oppressive structure of a church which had become disconnected from people's spiritual needs, grassroots movements arose to meet the needs of the laity. People sought a simple religion of the heart, anticipating the Evangelical movements of the 16th and 17th centuries. There was no overt rejection of orthodox doctrine; the beliefs of the peasantry and even many urban dwellers had never been more than rudimentary. However those movements did tap into the substratum of pagan folk-religion that had survived beneath the gloss of Christianity.

Flagellants

The stresses of the high Middle Ages caused many people to believe that only the harshest forms of penance could assuage an obviously angry God—or if the end times were approaching could increase their odds of favorable judgment. A popular form of penance, for women as well as man, was self-flagellation. Looking back with today's psychological perspectives, we can detect a desire to relieve the pent-up anger and frustration that many people felt.

Flagellation, recalling Christ's scourging at the pillar, was often prescribed as a penance for serious sins. Count Raymond VII of Toulouse was flogged in front of Notre-Dame Cathedral in 1229 in exchange for the annulment of an excommunication order. Self-flagellation was encouraged in monasteries as a means to subdue the flesh. The 11th-century Peter Damianus, a friend of Hildegard of Bingen, popularized a practice in which a monk would recite the Psalter, accompanying each psalm with a hundred lashes with a leather thong to his bare back.[51] The entire Psalter corresponded to 15,000 lashes. Many monks flogged themselves to death, but one Dominicus Loricatus managed to recite the Psalter twenty times in one week before he died of exhaustion.[52]

Many laypeople took up self-flagellation in the 13th century. Bands of men organized themselves into sodalities each with its patron saint; Mary Magdalene— the penitent Magdalene of Gregorian origin—appeared on at least one of their banners.[53] Flagellants beat themselves with whips in public displays of penitence.

Large bands would march from place to place, encouraging others to join them and mocking any who declined. They would work themselves into a frenzy, sometimes destroying property along the way or attacking Jews and other minorities.

The flagellant movement spread across Europe, reaching a peak in 1260, when Cistercian monk Joachim of Fiore prophesied the world would end; and it reached another peak at the time of the Black Death. The 14th-century French historian Jean Froissart described a procession he witnessed:

> In the Year of Grace 1349, the penitents went about, coming first out of Germany. They were men who did public penance and scourged themselves with whips of hard knotted leather with little iron spikes. Some made themselves bleed very badly between the shoulders and some foolish women had cloths ready to catch the blood and smear it on their eyes, saying that it was miraculous blood. While they were doing penance, they sang very mournful songs about the nativity and passion of Our Lord.[54]

Self-flagellism in the Dominican and Franciscan Orders was endorsed by the church, but Pope Alexander IV banned the sodalities in 1261. Many people ignored the ban, until Innocent VI (1352-1362) excommunicated participants and clergy who accompanied them on their marches. Even then, its role in private penance remained within the popular consciousness. A 1663 painting by the French artist Elisabetta Sirani Besançon shows a bare-breasted Mary Magdalene scourging herself with a knotted cord.[55]

Beguines

Of much gentler disposition were the *Beguines*, mentioned briefly in Chapter 6. Their founder is thought to have been Marie of Oignies (1167-1213) who was born in Nivelles, in what is now Belgium.[56] The Beguines were lay women who lived in urban communal houses. Although they did not take formal vows, they adopted a simple, austere lifestyle; they also committed themselves to celibacy at least while they remained within their communities—which most did for life. Typically the Beguines cared for the poor in their neighborhoods, supporting themselves by working as artisans, primarily in textiles, or by teaching or nursing. Many communities were located near hospitals or leper colonies. Within a few decades the movement had spread from the Low Countries to France, Germany, and parts of Italy.

Each communal house, or Beguinage, was autonomous and had little contact with others. As a result religious observances varied significantly from one community to another; however communal devotions were uniformly popular, and most Beguines also spent time in private prayer and study. The Beguines were widely respected by the general public, but they came under attack from both craft guilds and ecclesiastical authorities. The guilds resented their work as artisans because it undermined long-standing monopolies. Many bishops resented them because the Beguine communities had been founded without church approval and, for the most part, operated without episcopal oversight. The Beguines lay outside the accepted framework of the religious orders.

At times Beguines attained the protection of powerful individuals, like King Louis IX of France and Cardinal Jacques de Vitry.[57] In 1233 Pope Gregory IX gave the Beguines a measure of recognition, and Clement IV (r.1265-1268) instructed the Dominican Order to provide them with spiritual advisers. As part of his responsibilities as Dominican provincial in Saxony, and later vicar-general in Bohemia, Meister Eckhart took several communities under his wing—and learned much from them.[58] At other times the Beguines came under intense fire from individual bishops, and in the early 14th century opposition became widespread. The church was alarmed by the proliferation of lay groups, including the flagellant sodalities, and was reluctant to tolerate the existence of another large group outside its control. Also the Beguines were sometimes confused with women's communities established by the Cathar church in the south of France.

Whether the Beguines embraced beliefs that differed from official church teachings is unclear. Most likely they paid little attention to theological issues; and even if dissenting views were expressed it is unlikely that they spread significantly. Nevertheless, when the Council of Vienne—the same council that condemned the Knights Templar—formally condemned the Beguines in 1312, it chose heresy to justify its action. Pope Clement V issued a vitriolic decree addressing women "commonly known as Beguines" who "as if insane" discussed the Trinity and the divine essence, and "led simple people into error."[59] Reacting against a public outcry in their defense, Clement's successor John XXII issued another decree in 1318 which attempted to distinguish "good" Beguines, who stayed in their houses and refrained from discussing theological issues, from "bad" Beguines who evidently did otherwise and had to be silenced. Church authorities evidently found it hard to distinguish good from bad, however; and within a few years, most Beguinages had been closed.

Faced with mounting persecution, some Beguines left to join recognized religious orders. The famous Mechtild of Magdebourg (1207-1282) was a Beguine and the first German mystic to write in the vernacular. But, as she neared death, she entered the monastery of Helfta where the nuns helped her complete *The Flowing Light of the Godhead*, a book that influenced Dante's *Paradiso*. Others, like the Frenchwoman Marguerite de Porete (1250-1310), were outspoken in their criticism of the church and went to the stake.[60] Not all Beguine communities were eradicated, and a few still operate today. Less numerous than the Beguines, but with similar goals and following a similar lifestyle, was the male confraternity of the Beghards.

Waldensians

The origins of the Waldensians are not known with certainty. The most likely explanation is that they were founded by Peter Waldo (c.1160-1218) of Lyons, France, the son of a prosperous merchant. Waldo, whose life recalled Francis of Assisi's, had a powerful conversion experience in 1173;[61] he became a lay preacher, gave away his money, and dedicated himself to a life of poverty. Waldo attracted a group of followers who became known as the "Poor Men of Lyons." The simplicity of their message and commitment to emulate the poverty of Jesus struck a chord among people appalled by the materialism of the institutional church. The ranks of the Poor Men grew rapidly, and soon they attracted women and whole families. By then known as the Waldensians, they spread to the Piedmont area of Italy.[62] Alternative names were Vaudois, Valdenses and Valdesi.

Initially Peter Waldo attempted to work from within the church. In 1179 he asked Pope Alexander III to recognize the Poor Men as a religious order. Rejected, he appealed to the Third Lateran Council, but the council also refused. The Poor Men were perceived as having links with their contemporaries, the Cathars; Lyon was not that far from Languedoc. Certainly the Poor Men shared many Cathar values, and their histories have certain parallels. But the Waldensians never embraced neo-Gnostic dualism; in many respects they were forerunners of the Methodists and Presbyterians.[63] Notwithstanding, the archbishop of Lyons condemned Waldo and his followers, and in 1184 Pope Lucius III excommunicated them. The Waldensians became a sect outside the Roman communion—the first "Protestant" denomination.

The Waldensians proceeded to reject church teachings and the traditional sacraments in favor of sole reliance on the authority of scripture. Waldensian scholars translated portions of the Bible into French. The issue of vernacular translations of scripture would crop up time and time again. As we have seen, the eastern churches encouraged translation into vernacular languages, but the fourth-century Latin *Vulgate* became the standard version in the Latin church.[64] From then on, few vernacular translations appeared. The Venerable Bede translated *John* into Old English in 735, and translations of the complete gospels were available by the mid-10th century.[65] Clandestine French versions of the whole Bible circulated among the nobility in the high Middle Ages. But ecclesiastical attitudes progressively hardened, and church authorities increasingly opposed all vernacular translations.[66] They feared that people would interpret scripture for themselves, without clerical guidance.

After the excommunication order the Waldensians faced the full force of the Inquisition. Many members suffered torture and death,[67] though it is not known whether Peter Waldo himself met that fate. Others fled into the Italian Alps. In the late 15th century Catholic armies attacked the Waldensians in their mountain strongholds, and eventually the remaining sect members were driven out of Italy into Switzerland. After the Reformation some Waldensians embraced Calvinism; one of their members, a relative of John Calvin, translated the entire Bible into French. Others preserved their distinctive religion. In 1689, under an agreement with the Duke of Savoy, a number of Waldensian families returned to Italy; but their stay was short-lived. When the Waldensians finally won emancipation in Italy in 1848, they had endured more than six centuries of persecution.

Seventeenth-century English poet John Milton wrote an impassioned sonnet in memory of the Waldensians's persecution in northern Italy:

> Avenge O Lord thy slaughter'd Saints, whose bones
> Lie scatter'd on the Alpine mountains cold,
> Ev'n them who kept thy truth so pure of old
> When all our Fathers worship't Stocks and Stones,
> Forget not: in thy book record their groanes
> Who were thy Sheep and in their antient Fold
> Slayn by the bloody Piemontese that roll'd
> Mother with Infant down the Rocks. Their moans
> The Vales redoubl'd to the Hills, and they
> To Heav'n. Their martyr'd blood and ashes sow
> O're all th' Italian fields where still doth sway
> The triple Tyrant [the pope]: that from these may grow
> A hunder'd-fold, who having learnt thy way
> Early may fly the Babylonian woe.[68]

In 1856 some Waldensian families emigrated from Italy to South America and founded a church in Uruguay. Others founded settlements in the United States in the 1890s, including the one at Valdese, North Carolina. The modern Waldensians share values espoused by Peter Waldo, though not all claim him as their founder.

Friends of God

Something of the attitudes and lifestyle of the Cathars and Waldensians reappeared in a German group called the Friends of God. Two main factors contributed to the group's formation. One factor was the prevailing fear that the end of the world was imminent. Another was political; in the early 14th century a dispute broke out between Pope John XII and the emperor Louis IV. John demanded that Louis abdicate; when he refused, the pope excommunicated him and withdrew the church's support from the region. Feeling that the church had abandoned them, the people turned to one another and formed an association for mutual support. The Friends of God had no central authority, no dogma, no prescribed form of worship, and no political affiliation. However members shared a desire to seek truth and spirituality through personal experience. They set up "Brotherhood Houses" where groups of Friends could meet and in some cases live communally.

The group's name and inspiration came from a mysterious layman known as "The Friend of God from the Oberland." *Oberland* means "high country" and in that context referred to the Alps. The Friend had undergone four years of rigorous ascetic training, during which he had experienced a number of visions; finally he was told: "Only now have you trodden the right path of love. You have passed your time of probation."[69] In 1339 he made contact with Johannes Tauler, a Dominican priest and renowned preacher in Strasburg.[70] Tauler had continued preaching in defiance of Rome's prohibition. The Friend of God supplied Tauler with a number of prayers and rules for the spiritual life. The Friend emphasized practical spirituality; one of his precepts was: "Never trust a virtue which has not been put into practice." When the Black Death struck, Tauler stayed in Strasburg, ministering to the sick and burying the dead.

Tauler served as confessor to a wealthy man, Rulman Merswin. Merswin had a number of mystical experiences, and he too was visited by the Friend of God from the Oberland. Merswin bought an island in the River Ill, near Strasburg, and built a retreat house and chapel there for the Friends.[71] The retreat center, which became known as the House of St. John of Green Island, opened in 1367, six years after Tauler's death. The Friends of God were officially recognized as a branch of the Knights of St. John of Jerusalem, later the Knights of Malta. That affiliation gave the group protection from diocesan authorities who might have brought heresy charges. Johannes Tauler wrote a number of books which influenced the Protestant Reformers. Martin Luther commented on his works: "Never in either Latin or German language have I found more wholesome, purer teaching nor any that more fully agrees with the Gospel."[72]

Brethren of the Common Life

The Brethren of the Common Life were founded by the Dutchman Geert de Groote (1340-1384), also known by his Latin name Gerardus Magnus. The Brethren promoted *Devotio Moderno* ("Modern Devotion"), a commitment to personal spirituality free from the formality and materialism of institutional Christianity; however they took no vows. Like its companion order, the Sisters of the Common Life, the Brethren lived communal lives of poverty and simple piety. Communities, similar to those of the Beghards and Beguines, sprang up throughout the Netherlands and Germany. The movement was opposed by the religious orders but attracted secular clergy to its ranks. Eventually it won the protection of Pope Eugenius IV and became one of the few grassroots movements of the period to escape persecution.

The Brethren dedicated their work to preaching, education and literature. Many of the communities supported themselves by copying manuscripts or, after invention of the printing press, printing books. De Groote died of the plague at age 44, but his successors founded the monastery of Windesheim in the Netherlands, which became the main center of Common Life activities. At its peak in 1500 the school at Windesheim enrolled 2,000 students. Thomas à Kempis (1380-1471) may have become a Brother, though he later joined an Augustinian monastery.[73] The *Imitation of Christ*, one of the best-known works of Christian piety, is attributed to Kempis. Other graduates of Common Life schools were Nicholas of Cusa and the Dutch pope Adrian VI.

John Wycliffe

Englishman John Wycliffe (c.1325-1384), a contemporary of Julian of Norwich, was an ordained priest and, for a while, master of Balliol College, Oxford. He studied the natural sciences and mathematics; but his main interests were theology and ecclesiastical politics, and for his views on the latter topics Wycliffe became embroiled in controversy. Wycliffe claimed that the Mass had no basis in scripture and that Christ was not physically present in the Eucharist. He also argued that "the church" was the body of the faithful, not the ecclesiastical hierarchy, and its only rightful head was Christ. Because of their worldliness, he declared, the popes had forfeited any right to serve as his temporal representatives; indeed, "It is supposed, and with much probability, that the Roman pontiff is the great Antichrist." In 1377—the very year that the Avignon exile ended and one year before the papal schism began—Pope Gregory XI sent a papal bull to the archbishop of Canterbury denouncing 18 of Wycliffe's theses as heretical.

Meanwhile, Wycliffe had emerged as a champion of national sovereignty and a strong critic of Roman interference. Church ownership of land, in his view, was unjust and ecclesiastical taxes burdensome on the poor. The church had abused its stewardship, and the state would be justified in confiscating its property. That opinion was well received by nobles who were interested in sharing the spoils. When Wycliffe was ordered to answer to a synod of bishops in London to face the charges in the papal bull, powerful individuals came forward to protect him, including John of Gaunt, son of King Edward III.[74] As Wycliffe continued to write polemical books, the list of heresy charges steadily grew; after his death the Council of Constance identified 45 heresies, including: "The Roman Church is the synagogue of Satan" and "God ought to obey the devil."[75]

Wycliffe organized the "Poor Priests" who, like the Poor Men of Lyon, preached the life of austere piety.[76] As ecclesiastical hostility increased, many of his Poor Priests were arrested. But Wycliffe himself had sufficient support to be left unharmed; he died of natural causes in 1383, still holding his pastor's living in Leicestershire. Wycliffe had also attracted large numbers of ordinary followers who became known as "Lollards," a derogatory Dutch term implying that they muttered their prayers. By the 1390s the Lollards had evolved into an organized group urging religious reform, and that triggered their downfall. Religious reform movements were perceived as a threat to the state; criticism of the church could easily spill over into criticism of the civil order. To meet that threat and to curry ecclesiastical favor King Henry IV moved against the Lollards. In 1401 several of its members were burned at the stake;[77] others were reabsorbed into the mainstream church, while a few went underground in the hope that a more tolerant environment would develop. Unfortunately, the Reformation was more than a century away.

Wycliffe is best remembered for his translation of the Bible. Anticipating the position of the Protestant reformers, he believed that scripture was the only source of legitimate authority; but English people's only contact with scripture was through Jerome's Latin *Vulgate*. In an act of great audacity, comparable with that of the Waldensians on the continent of Europe, Wycliffe translated the New Testament into English to meet the needs of ordinary people. Along with a translation of the Old Testament by his friend Nicholas of Hereford, it was published in 1388, four years after Wycliffe's death. The archbishop of Canterbury reacted by denouncing Wycliffe as a "pestilent wretch of damnable heresy who, as a complement of his wickedness, invented a new translation of the Scriptures into his mother tongue."[78]

Distribution of Wycliffe's and Hereford's Bible was still limited by the laborious process of manual copying; Johannes Gutenberg did not invent his printing press until 1440.[79] Nevertheless, it was the only complete English version until the Tyndale Bible appeared in the 1520s.[80] To evade the English censors, William Tyndale (c.1484-1536) published his influential translation in the Netherlands. Unfortunately, Tyndale was arrested in Antwerp by agents of the Holy Roman Emperor. Convicted of heresy, he was strangled and then his body was burned at the stake. The King James Bible, published nearly a century after the Reformation, drew upon the Wycliffe/Hereford and Tyndale translations.

Jan Hus

Jan Hus (1369-1415) was born into a poor Bohemian family. But he was fortunate to receive an education, and after his ordination as a priest, he became dean of philosophy and eventually rector at the University of Prague. Hus came into contact with the teachings of John Wycliffe at the turn of the 15th century. Anne, sister of King Wenceslaus of Bohemia and wife of Richard II of England, admired Wycliffe and had sent copies of his books back to Bohemia. Hus disagreed with Wycliffe over the real presence in the Eucharist; he only insisted on the faithful's right to receive communion "under both kinds."[81] But Hus agreed with Wycliffe on many other issues, including the people's right to read the Bible in the vernacular. He preached at the Bethlehem Chapel in Prague in his native Czech language and became renowned for his fiery sermons. Like Wycliffe, Hus began to challenge the wealth and worldliness of the church, which owned roughly half the land in Bohemia and imposed stiff taxes. His views drew strong support from the peasants of Bohemia and even from some members of the aristocracy.

Aside from the controversies over ecclesiastical and theological issues, Hus became embroiled in political disputes. One was a struggle for supremacy between ethnic Czechs and the many Germans who had settled in Bohemia; the other was the ongoing papal schism. Although the Bohemian king had encouraged neutrality in the schism, Hus found himself at odds with Archbishop Zbynek of Prague over the Council of Pisa's attempts to resolve the schism and institute church reform. Hus and his followers supported Alexander V, the new pope appointed by the council, while Zbynek and the German faction continued to support the Roman contender Gregory XII.

As controversy intensified, ecclesiastical authorities made determined efforts to silence Hus. Twice he was excommunicated, and finally he was summoned to appear before the Council of Constance to explain his pro-Wycliffe views.[82] Despite a promise of safe conduct by the emperor, Hus was arrested, brought to trial on charges of heresy, and burned at the stake in 1415. Reportedly his dying words were: "in 100 years, God will raise up a man whose calls for reform cannot be suppressed." Exactly 102 years later, Martin Luther nailed his 95 Theses to the church door in Wittenberg. News of Hus's death, and the execution of his disciple Jerome the following year, provoked outrage in Bohemia. With the support of both aristocracy and peasantry, his followers rebelled against papal authority. Clergy were assaulted, church lands were seized, and the Hussites prepared to defend themselves against a German crusade sent to crush them. During 12 years of war, which became a struggle for Bohemian independence as much as a defense of the Hussite cause, successive attacks were resisted.

The Hussite movement eventually divided into mutually hostile factions. The moderate Utraquist faction eventually won limited recognition by Rome and permission to receive communion under both kinds. Radical Hussites, who leaned toward Wycliffe more than to Hus himself, organized the *Unitas Fratrum* ("Unity of Brethren") in 1457. Unitas can be regarded as an early Protestant denomination, predating Lutheranism by 70 years. Among its most famous members was the Czech educational reformer Jan Amos Comenius (1592-1670). Unitas supporters were forced to leave Bohemia during the Counter-Reformation but reorganized in Germany. The Moravian Church, which remains a significant force in the United States, is a distant descendant of the Brethren. In 1999 Pope John Paul II apologized for the betrayal and execution of Jan Hus but did not lift the charges of heresy against him.

Reflections

During the course of the Middle Ages, the epicenters of Christian activity moved steadily away from the Mediterranean. In a transition that some have regarded as of profound significance,[83] Germanic, Nordic and Slavic ethnic groups began to take control of Christianity. The rise of the Holy Roman Empire and conversion of the peoples of Scandinavia and Russia permanently changed the face of Christianity. Eventually, missionaries would take Christianity still farther afield, and innovative forms of Christianity would develop in North America and elsewhere.

Christianity achieved a great deal during the Middle Ages, and we shall examine the work of the great mystics and theologians in more detail in the next chapter. The church's failure lay in the administrative and governance structures that had been built so carefully on Roman imperial foundations. As early as the ninth century the mission of western institutional Christianity was getting lost in the corruption and worldliness of the papacy and episcopacy. Problems mounted, and after 1300 the papacy went into a political and moral decline from which it never fully recovered. Meanwhile, strong ruling dynasties in Europe emerged, establishing political structures that would last until modern times. Long-standing relationships between church and state, between monarchy and aristocracy, and between urban and rural societies were permanently changed.

Rome's exaggerated sense of global mission made the crusades not only possible but inevitable. The crusades were the first great multinational endeavor in history, and the deployment of resources on so large a scale was a tribute to papal leadership and to the religious fervor of secular rulers. But despite early successes, the crusades failed both in terms of their own objectives and in terms of Rome's position in Christendom. The inability to drive Muslim rulers from the eastern Mediterranean destroyed any hope of Christian control over its holy sites. And any pretense that the crusades enjoyed divine support was shattered by the atrocities committed in Christ's name. Sadly, institutional Christianity would continue to perpetrate atrocities against people of all faiths, including its own. Eastern Orthodox Christians continue to feel the pain of the Fourth Crusade and still find it hard to trust the Catholic Church. Politically, the crusades were a disaster for the papacy. They boosted the confidence of the European monarchs, leading to a power struggle that Rome could not win.

Western Christendom may have been affected little by the Great Schism, but the Avignon captivity, the papal schism, and the scandals of the papal court did irreparable harm. Rome's political adventures and the self-absorption of senior church officials distracted attention from its charge to serve the spiritual needs of the faithful. Failures in pastoral care were not new, but they became critical in the difficult times of the 14th century. It would be easy to blame the parish clergy, but the real cause was the breakdown of spiritual leadership at higher levels in the hierarchy. Reform was urgently needed, but the need was ignored—and would continue to be ignored by the Roman church until the latter part of the 16th century. By that time the situation had spun out of control, and the Reformation would permanently divide western Christianity.

The episcopacy proclaimed itself successor of the apostles; and the papacy regarded itself as the successor of Peter, prince of the apostles. Those lofty claims should have attracted the most worthy men to ecclesiastical office and inspired them to the heights of saintliness. Saintly men did serve. But too many office-holders were corrupt, ambitious, cynical individuals who lived lives of aristocratic opulence, indifferent to their pastoral responsibilities. The bishops and popes of the period do not come across in a good light. Christianity's failure during the Middle Ages—and possibly at other times—can justifiably be laid at their feet.

Abandoned by their church, the people of Europe were left alone to face the horrors of the Black Death and the continental-wide disruption that accompanied it. Not surprisingly many people turned away from the institutional church to explore alternative religious forms. Most of the grassroots movements were short-lived, but they encouraged larger-scale reform, they influenced the subsequent development of western Christianity, and they continue to inspire us. We shall see later in the book that today's small Christian communities have much in common with those late-medieval movements. Also, a case could be made that the early 21st century mirrors the 14th century in its uncertainty and disillusionment with institutional religion.

It would naïve to believe that the grassroots movements of the late Middle Ages were composed entirely of sincere, simple people seeking God. Their ranks probably included individuals with personal, political or anarchical motives. Reports from the period indicate that violence and pillaging were not uncommon; and the flagellants were not the only ones who went on anti-Semitic rampages. However we have to conclude that a large proportion of the movements' members were drawn to lives of prayer, renunciation, service and activism. The flagellants obviously took renunciation to unhealthy extremes; but the

Beguines, the Waldensians, and the Brethren of the Common Life demonstrated a simplicity of lifestyle comparable to the monastic state, and they also engaged in meritorious works of service. John Wycliffe and Jan Hus were brave activists, drawing attention to what was wrong within the Roman church. They inspired the Protestant reformers to do the same—with more lasting results.

---

1   Desiderius Erasmus. *The Praise of Folly*, 1511. (Transl: J. Wilson.) Project Gutenberg.

2   The siege began on August 15, the feast of the Assumption, and ended on August 15 the following year.

3   Al-Andalus was the Arabic form of "Vandal," referring to the Vandals or Goths who had ruled Spain since the fall of the Roman Empire. In turn, Al-Andalus was the basis of the name "Andalusia."

4   Most Jews had been expelled by the previous Byzantine Christian rulers.

5   Al-Hakim was notorious for his add behavior; in addition to killing most of his officials, he once ordered all Egyptian men to work at night and sleep during the day. The Church of the Holy Sepulcher was rebuilt by his successor with Byzantine help.

6   At that time there were two main Muslim groups: the Fatamids, who ruled Palestine, north Africa and Spain, and the Seljuks whose main base was in Asia Minor and Mesopotamia.

7   Byzantine forces, which had been driven to Nicaea, eventually retook the city; but Constantinople fell to the Ottoman Turks in 1453.

8   Frederick II was king of Aragon, and Isabella I was queen of Castille. They married in 1469, uniting the two kingdoms.

9   Jews from Spain came to be known as Sephardic Jews.

10   Christopher Hollis. *The Jesuits: a History*. Barnes & Noble, 1968, pp. 93-94.

11   Giovanni Boccaccio. *Decameron*. (Transl: M. Rigg.) Campbell, 1921, Vol. 1, p. 11

12   James Bolton. "The World Upside Down." *Black Death in England* (Ormrod & Lindley, eds.) 1996, p. 27.

13   Geog Dehn (ed.). Introduction to: *The Book of Abramelin: a New Translation*. (Transl: S. Guth). Ibis Press, 2006, p. xxii.

14   Following the 13th-century Anglo-Normal invasion, Wales became a fief of the English king; and the English pope Adrian IV granted King Henry II the lordship of Ireland. Three centuries later Henry VIII annexed Wales, incorporated it into England, and outlawed the Welsh language. His action in making Ireland a kingdom, far from giving it greater autonomy, brought it firmly under English control.

15   Campanella's release was finally secured by Pope Urban VIII, whereupon he became the pope's astrological advisor. He ended his days in the convent of Saint-Honoré in Paris.

16   That principle arose during the English Civil War when parliament confronted royal sovereignty.

[17] Augustine. *City of God*, book 10, §14. (Transl: M. Dodd.) Modern Library, 1950.

[18] In view of the atrocities perpetrated by the Conquistadors, it has been suggested that they should have looked within themselves.

[19] Richard O'Mara. "The Jesuit Republic of South America." *Virginia Quarterly Review*, Spring 1999. See also the comment in: Christopher Hollis. *The Jesuits: A History*. Barnes & Noble, 1968, pp. 78-79

[20] "Livings" remained common in the Church of England to our own times. Insights into their role in the church society were provided by the novels of Jane Austen (1775-1817). Austen was the daughter of an Anglican parson.

[21] Philip Schaff. *History of the Christian Church*, Revised Edition. Charles Scribner, 1910, vol. IV, ch. 10, §93. Evidently that particular problem was not confined to the lowest ranks of the clergy. Schaff added: "there was hardly a Western bishop or pope in the middle ages who was able to study the divine oracles in the original."

[22] Matthew Fox. *Passion for Creation*. Inner Traditions, 1980/2000, pp. 14-15.

[23] *Isaiah* 28:7. The passage goes on to describe the situation in more graphic terms.

[24] *Didache*, 11. (Transl: Roberts-Donaldson.) Early Christian Writings.

[25] Under feudal laws every able-bodied man was liable to be called to military duty by his local lord; and in the event of a war the probability of being killed in action or dying from injuries was high. To become a priest, however poor, might be an option worth considering.

[26] The argument could be made that God often chose weak people to be instruments of divine purpose. Ideally, a religious vocation would imply saintliness, but this was not necessarily the case.

[27] Realistically, it was not always possible for the faithful to make accurate judgments of clerical morality. Some clergy no doubt were accused unfairly; others may have concealed grave moral weaknesses under a façade of saintliness.

[28] Giovanni Boccaccio. *Decameron*. (Transl: M. Rigg.) Campbell, 1921, Vol. 1, p. 11

[29] Muslim leaders often delegated rule of Christian populations to bishops, metropolitans or patriarchs.

[30] Source: "Lombardy." *New Advent Catholic Encyclopedia*.

[31] In several dioceses in the Holy Roman Empire, admission to the episcopacy was expressly limited to the nobility. See: Schaff, *History of the Christian Church*, vol. VI, ch. 9, §73

[32] In Scandinavia, the establishment of stable, unified kingdoms had to await the coming of Christianity which provided an episcopal structure to support the national institutions.

[33] After Constantinople passed under Turkish rule, appointments to the patriarchate were taxed, and patriarchs were often deposed so that another tax would become payable.

[34] *Acts* 2:32-37; 4:32.

[35] Schaff, *History of the Christian Church*, vol. VI, ch. 9, §73.

[36] J. F. T Kelly. "The Irish Monks and the See of Peter." *Monastic Studies*, 14, 1983, pp. 207-223.

37 Boniface. Letter to Pope Zacharias, 742. *Correspondence of St. Boniface*. Medieval Sourcebook.

38 The legend was immortalized in Robert Southey's poem "God's Judgment on a Wicked Bishop."

39 Schaff, *History of the Christian Church*, vol. VI, ch. 9, §73.

40 Diarmaid MacCulloch. *The Reformation*. Penguin Books, 2003, p. 632.

41 Schaff. *History of the Christian Church*, vol. VI, ch. 9, §73.

42 Law and order broke down in Rome due to a dispute between rival political factions, but it is unclear whether the pope's safety was ever threatened.

43 Clement VI. Papal Bull: *Unigenitus*, 1343.

44 Purgatory was a state of temporal suffering in which souls made restitution for—or from an alternative viewpoint cleansed themselves of—sins already forgiven by the sacrament of penance.

45 In cases of financial hardship, indulgences were occasionally given to worthy recipients. See for example: MacCulloch, *The Reformation*, p. 122.

46 Clement was not the first antipope. That honor goes to Hippolytus (217-235) or possibly to the earlier Natalius (c.200). A total of 42 antipopes "reigned" through the mid-15th century. Source: *Catholic Encyclopedia* and other references. There have been several more in recent times.

47 At that time the contenders were John XXIII, Benedict XIII, and Pope Gregory XII. Subsequent popes took the names Benedict XIII and most recently John XXIII, based on the argument that the antipopes' names were invalid.

48 Source: *Catholic Encyclopedia*. Encyclopedia Press, 1913-1990.

49 William Manchester. *A World Lit Only by Fire*. Little, Brown & Co., 1992, p. 79.

50 The quote derives from *The Pageant of the Popes*, a satirical play by the former Carmelite monk John Bale.

51 Schaff, *History of the Christian Church*, vol. V, ch. 16, §135.

52 Dominicus also wore an iron *cuirass*, or breastplate, under his clothes.

53 Susan Haskins. *Mary Magdelan: Myth and Metaphor*. Riverhead Books, 1993, p. 143.

54 Quoted in: Geoffrey Brereton (ed.) *Jean Froissart, Chronicles*. Penguin, 1968, pp. 111-112.

55 Musée des Beaux-Arts et d'Archéologie, Besançon, France.

56 Marie of Oignies, beatified but never canonized, is revered as the patron of women in labor.

57 Margaret W. Labarge. *A Small Sound of the Trumpet*. Beacon Press, 1986, pp. 116-117.

58 Fox, *Passion for Creation*, pp. 35ff.

59 Clement V. Bull: *Cum de Quibusdam Mulieribus*, 1312. (Transl: unknown.)

60 During her trial Marguerite was accused of being a Beguine, but it is not certain that she was.

61 Waldo's conversion was documented by an anonymous chronicler who wrote in 1218 or thereabouts. See: J. H. Robinson (ed.). *Readings in European History*. Ginn, 1905, pp. 381-383.

62   Some authorities claim that Waldensians were already settled in Italy when the Lyons contingent arrived. If true, that would imply that Waldo was not their founder.

63   In 1895 Waldensian settlers in North Carolina formally allied themselves with the Presbyterian Church.

64   It will be recalled that, at about the same time, Ulfilas translated the Bible into Gothic, and it became a favored version among western Arians.

65   The Lindisfarne gospels, glossed into Old English by Aldred (d.968), are the oldest surviving English translations.

66   In 1486, Archbishop Berthold of Mainz threatened to excommunicate anyone who translated or circulated translations of sacred books, especially the Bible, without his permission. See: Schaff, *History of the Christian Church*, vol. VII, ch. 1, §6.

67   In the 12th century the suppression of heresy was the still responsibility of local bishops. Establishment of the Holy Office of the Inquisition in 1231 provided additional resources, and these were used against the Waldensians.

68   John Milton. *On the Late Massacre in Piedmont*. Sonnet XVIII, 1655.

69   William Rath. *The Friend of God*. Hawthorn Press, 1991, p. 32.

70   The early spelling of *Straßburg*, or Strassburg, was changed to Strasburg during a period of French occupation.

71   Rath, *The Friend of God*, pp. 33ff.

72   Paul M. Allen. Introduction to: Rudolf Steiner. *Mysticism at the Dawn of the Modern Age*. SteinerBooks, 1900/1960, p. 36.

73   Thomas à Kempis wrote a biography of Geert de Groote.

74   Williston Walker. *A History of the Christian Church*. Revised edition. Charles Scribner, 1959, pp. 268-269.

75   Council of Constance, session VIII, May 4, 1415. It is unclear whether he ever made the latter statement.

76   Walker. *A History of the Christian Churc*, pp. 269-270.

77   *Ibid.*, p. 270.

78   *Ibid.*

79   The "Gutenberg Bible," published in the 1450s, was in Latin.

80   King Henry VIII broke with Rome 14 years later.

81   Harold O. J. Brown. *Heresies: Heresy and Orthodoxy in the History of the Church*. Hendrickson, 1984, p. 299. As noted in Chapter 8, the practice of giving communion "under one kind"—the consecrated bread only—was justified by the doctrine of transubstantiation.

82   Walker. *A History of the Christian Church*, p. 272

83   Theosophists view the ethnic shift as a necessary transition from the fourth to the fifth subrace.

Chapter 14
Renewal and Synthesis

Despite the dismal times in Europe in the 14th and 15th centuries, western civilization was poised for a great leap forward. The seeds of a major expansion of consciousness had been planted in the early and high Middle Ages. The great blossom that grew from those seeds, the Renaissance, transformed the European mindset. Western intellectual, artistic and spiritual life was permanently changed, and the groundwork was laid for the scientific revolution of the 17th century and the intellectual revolution of the 18th. The transformation came partly from the renewal and revitalization of native traditions that had fallen into decay during the "Dark Ages" and partly from an influx of ideas from outside Europe. The Renaissance was a time of great optimism, but western Christianity was not in a good position to share in that optimism. The institutional church was rapidly losing its power and influence. Emphasis began to shift from ecclesiastical institutions to the faithful in religious matters and to secular institutions in intellectual, social and political matters.

Intellectual Revival

To place the renewal and synthesis in their proper context, we must step back momentarily to the dawn of the Middle Ages. Alexandria's 700-year reign as the world's greatest center of scholarship ended in 400 CE with the destruction of the famous library and the murder of the female mathematician Hypatia. Augustine of Hippo, last of the western church fathers, died in 430. By the mid-fifth century the heartland of the former Roman Empire was sinking into intellectual stagnation. But European scholarship was not totally extinguished.[1] The Roman scholar Anicius Boethius translated Aristotle's logical treatises into Latin in the sixth century, laying groundwork for the Aristotelian revival of the 11th. He also did work of far-reaching importance in the areas of music theory and esthetics. Even Plato's academy in Athens survived as a center of Neoplatonic study until 526. Most importantly, scholarship flourished in Celtic Ireland, Anglo-Saxon England, and Moorish Spain.

The revival of scholarship on the continent of Europe began in the eighth and ninth centuries. Charlemagne (742-814), king of the Franks and first Holy Roman Emperor, established schools of classical education whose teachers were known as *scholastici* (Latin: "of the school") giving their name to the scholasticism of later centuries.[2] The great Carolingian schools were the first centers of higher education in the modern sense. Scholars were recruited from throughout the empire as well as from England and Ireland to staff the school at the imperial capital of Aachen. Alcuin of York was invited to Aachen in 781. Fifteen years later he was appointed abbot of the famous monastery of St Martin at Tours, where he established a school, library and scriptorium. Under Alcuin's leadership the scriptorium achieved the notable level of productivity of three complete Bibles per year.

Charlemagne's grandson Charles the Bald invited the Irish scholar John Scotus Eriugena (810-c.877) to his court. John reintroduced the Greek technique of dialectic as a basis for examining complex philosophical issues. Under Bishop Fulbert (c.957-1028), the cathedral school of Chartres attained an intellectual preeminence that would last 200 years. One of its chancellors, the 12th-century Breton scholar Bernard of Chartres, was revered as the greatest Platonist of his time. The equally renowned John of Salisbury served as the city's bishop.

The schools of the Carolingian tradition did not operate outside the structure of church authority; nor were the scholastici intentionally hostile to church doctrine. But intellectual integrity sometimes led to disputes with the bishops. John Scotus displeased the authorities when he argued against biblical literalism and stressed the importance of bringing reason to bear in interpreting sacred texts.[3] In so doing he anticipated modern Biblical criticism by nine centuries. Another scholar who incurred official displeasure was Fulbert's student Berengar of Tours (999-1088). He was denounced for heresy for opposing Radbertus Paschasius' teachings on the transubstantiation of the Eucharist.[4] Berengar claimed that Radbertus and his supporters—who included the church hierarchy—had argued their case by sophistry rather than logic.

Aristotelian Revival

The schools of Aachen and Chartres retained their traditional Platonic orientation, filtered through Neoplatonism and the writings of Augustine.[5] However the Aristotelian revival that would facilitate the rise of scholasticism was already on the horizon. Islamic scholars translated the works of Aristotle and other Greek writers into Arabic and brought them to Europe in the 11th and 12th centuries. Translation into Latin quickly followed, largely through the work of James of Venice and his contemporary, Robert Grosseteste, bishop of Lincoln. Grosseteste (c.1175-1253) wrote a commentary on Aristotle; but he is also remembered for his treatises on science and esthetics. He asserted that light was the first creative impulse, and that to understand light was to understand creation; but he placed mathematics ahead of light because light obeyed the laws of mathematics.

Albertus Magnus (1200-1280) initiated the study of Aristotelian philosophy at the University of Paris, which by the 13th century had supplanted Chartres as the foremost center of learning in Europe. But he met with considerable opposition from ecclesiastical authorities who remained committed to Platonist tradition. At times the study of Aristotle was banned by church edict; and as late as 1277 Bishop Stephen Tempier of Paris condemned 219 Aristotelian theses as heretical, citing their "naturalism" and "rationalism."[6] Both Albertus and his famous student Thomas Aquinas were affected by the condemnation, and at one point Albertus had to explain that his interest was purely academic and not a statement of belief. "I expound," he was forced to write, "I do not endorse, Aristotle." Opposition to the Aristotelian revival was not confined to France. Grosseteste's most famous student, Roger Bacon, was imprisoned in England when his Franciscan superiors found "suspected novelties" in his work.

Thomas Aquinas (1225-1274) was born into a noble family in Aquino, in the south of Italy. At the age of six his parents entrusted his education to the Benedictine monks of Monte Casino. By age 20 he resolved to join the newly founded Order of Friars Preachers, the Dominicans, and traveled to Cologne to study with Albertus Magnus. Aquinas taught at the University of Paris in the 1250s, after which he returned to Italy and spent some time with the papal Curia. Aquinas never abandoned Platonism, which he held in high regard and put to good use; but he integrated Aristotelian philosophy firmly into Christian doctrine. Despite assaults on his work by Tempier and others, his stature in the church, together with growing acceptance of Aristotelianism among other churchmen, protected him from his many conservative critics. More importantly, he was protected from the Inquisition.

Aquinas is often portrayed as a cold, ponderous intellectual, but he also had a great love of scripture, reverence for nature, and understanding of the mystical aspects of religion.[7] Shortly before his death, and before he was able to complete his monumental *Summa Theologica*, he had a visionary experience that undermined confidence in his earlier theological studies: "All that I have written seems to me like so much straw compared to what I have seen and what has been revealed to me." Aquinas' last work may have been the alchemical text: *Aurora Consurgens.*[8]

Despite suspicions concerning his orthodoxy Thomas Aquinas was canonized 49 years after his death; and in 1567 Pope Pius V pronounced him "Angelic Doctor." Aquinas is reckoned to be the greatest theologian since Augustine of Hippo, and arguably the greatest in the history of western Christianity. His work put into more-or-less final form the great body of Christian doctrine that had evolved over the preceding millennium.

Scholasticism

Scholasticism focused the power of intellect on metaphysical issues. Scholastics, also referred to as "schoolmen," were professional scholars and teachers, typically attached to major institutions of learning. They understood that much truth lay beyond the reach of the human mind; but they also asserted that whatever we accepted on faith had to be reasonable and internally consistent. To question authority—so long as it was done responsibly—was not disrespectful; it was to be encouraged. Authoritative pronouncements in scripture, doctrine, and the writings of other scholars were studied and built upon, leading to great advances in theology. In Thomas Aquinas' words: "We study what men have thought in order to discover the truth."[9] Besides Aquinas and Albertus Magnus, the 11th-century Anselm of Canterbury and the 13th-century John Bonaventure[10] and John Duns Scotus[11] are counted among the greatest scholastics.

Scholasticism emphasized dialectic, but it did not ignore semantics and rhetoric. Much of the effort was directed at examining points of apparent conflict among different authorities. For example, an apparent disagreement might be detected between the writings of a church father and the pronouncement of a council of bishops. The two sources would be studied in detail and points of contention noted, along with their supporting arguments. Assumptions would be tested for logical consistency and careful consideration given to possible ambiguity in meaning. An apparent conflict might turn out simply to be a matter of semantics. Scholastic inquiry would have been enhanced further if more attention had been given to difficulties of translation, but at the time few scholars could read Greek or Hebrew. Jerome's Latin *Vulgate* was the standard, and sole, scriptural source. Many of the theological conflicts that divided the east and west were later seen to have been caused by inconsistencies in terminology.

Scholastics believed that it was essential to understand fully the arguments supporting each position and the context in which it was written. A popular technique was disputation (Latin: *disputatio*), an application of dialectic and rhetoric. Scholars were appointed to represent opposing viewpoints and debated before a neutral "jury." Each advocate would produce authoritative support for the superiority of his own position, while trying to undermine his opponent's. Sometimes, to avoid personal bias and to encourage broad understanding, the two scholars would switch sides after the first round of debate and argue the opposing viewpoint. The latter technique recalled the methods promoted by the Sophists of classical Greece. Disputations were often used as an instructional technique. Students would debate among themselves, or a class would debate with the instructor.

Thomas Aquinas used a modified kind of disputation in his own writings. He would defend a certain position eloquently and compellingly—leading cursory readers to conclude that he took that position. But then he might provide an equally eloquent and compelling defense of an opposing position. Only after detailed examination of each would Aquinas express his own opinion.

Once Aristotelian philosophy was accepted, its potential for placing Christian doctrine on a more rational basis soon became apparent. It provided intellectual categories that were not available to the church fathers or to the bishops who wrestled with the great issues of Christology at the ecumenical councils. Among the categories were matter (Greek: *hyle*, υλη), form (*eidos*, ειδος; or *morphe*, μορφη), and causation.[12] Aristotle proposed a fourfold theory of causation: the "material cause" (*hyle*): what something is made of; the "formal cause" (*morphe*): the form that it takes; the "efficient cause" (*kinesis*, κινεσις): what sets it in motion; and the final cause (*telos* (τελος, "end"): the purpose it serves.[13] So great was the theological value attached to Aristotelian concepts that people of the time suggested that God must have arranged for Aristotle to be born in anticipation of the development of Christian doctrine.

During the scholastic period it became popular to suppose that one could prove the existence of God by reason. Two major types of proofs were proposed: *a priori* or *ontological* (Greek: οντως, "really") proofs that involved nothing more than intellect itself, and *a posteriori* proofs that incorporated experience or observation of the world.[14] In turn, the latter can be divided into cosmological and teleological proofs. Anselm of Canterbury devised an ontological proof that was later refined by René Descartes in the 17th century. It contended that the very definition of God as an infinite being mandates that being's existence.[15] Thomas Aquinas offered five cosmological proofs, and the 18th-century naturalist William Paley offered a teleological proof.[16] New proofs for the existence of God continue to be devised.

In the 18th century David Hume, Immanuel Kant, and others would question whether any of the proofs held up to serious philosophical analysis.[17] Perhaps a more serious weakness was that the proofs produced a cold, abstract God which nobody would want to worship. Seventeenth-century Pietists claimed with some justification that scholastics seemed incapable of contemplating what every believer takes to be the real God. The modern view, as articulated by Kant, is that God's existence can neither be proved nor disproved. More-or-less persuasive, *pro* and *con* arguments can be developed; but persuasive to whom? Cynics comment that no believer needs a proof, and no skeptic would ever be convinced by one.

Anselm, whose ontological proof is still widely discussed, found his proof convincing because he already believed in God: "I do not seek to understand so that I may believe; but believe so that I may understand."

Scholastic Heritage

Platonic philosophy, which influenced Christianity for the first millennium, was based on a "top-down" view of reality. Its otherworldliness and its contrast between the eternal and the transient inspired the development of a transcendent theology that focused on the nature of God and the primacy of the human soul. Divine energy flowed from above into people, things and situations on earth. However, the otherworldliness led to a serious dichotomy in the view of human nature: the view that the soul is the only real, worthwhile and "good" part of the human constitution, and the body is "a sort of residence for man . . . sometimes a workshop, sometimes a prison, sometimes a grave."[18] The contempt for the physical body expressed by Augustine and others went much further than Plato would have allowed, but it might never have developed but for his work.

Aristotle took a contrasting, "bottom-up," view of reality. People, things and situations had intrinsic value that stemmed from their nature and function. Although Bishop Tempier's depiction of Aristotelianism as naturalistic and rationalistic may have been exaggerated, it was not entirely inappropriate. Aristotle's naturalism balanced the extreme Platonism, or what people had come to attribute to Plato. Aquinas modified Aristotle's notion of the soul, as something volatile that bubbles up from the physical body,[19] to argue that the soul is real and eternal but still linked inextricably to the body. Even though his formula reduced the high status the soul had enjoyed under Platonism, he hoped to give the body a new, more favorable status. Unfortunately his hopes were never realized. Negative attitudes to the body persisted in both Catholicism and Protestantism until the 20th century, by which time not only Thomism but much of traditional Christianity had been rejected. However, Aquinas' campaign to rescue the human body from corruption may have contributed to new conventions in religious art. We shall consider that later in this chapter.

Interestingly, scholasticism reached the peak of its influence at the very time when the power of the Roman church began to decline. The scholastic mindset would continue to dominate university curricula through the 17th century;[20] but within a generation of Aquinas' death it was already degenerating into endless pedantic arguments over trivia. The sense of excitement that had come from the synthesis of mysticism, naturalism and logic was lost. Dominican priest Meister Eckhart, whose life spanned the 13th and 14th centuries, found scholasticism overly constricting and turned to mysticism. In the 16th century the Council of Trent would reinstate scholasticism as the "official" philosophy of the Catholic

Church. But a new approach to intellectual inquiry was needed, and that would be provided by humanism. The notion that the divine could be apprehended by the intellect would eventually give way to—or return to—a recognition that the Divine must be experienced.

Meanwhile the emphasis on rationality had longer-term consequences, laying a foundation for the scientific and intellectual revolutions of the 17th century onward. Russia took pride in being spared the Aristotelian revival and scholasticism and preserving a more mystically oriented Christianity from the early church. But it did not participate until much later in the intellectual and technological advances that occurred in the west.

Mystics and Mystical Philosophers

Nobody experiences the Divine so profoundly as do the great mystics. Mysticism seeks to establish direct union with God, not through dogma or exoteric religious observances, but in the deepest reaches of one's own being.[21] Institutional Christianity provided monastic environments where it could flourish, but mystics saw no useful role for the church as an intermediary between themselves and God. Indeed, the flowering of mysticism in the high Middle Ages may have been, at least in part, a reaction against the oppressiveness of the church. A 20th-century American spiritual writer commented: "Mysticism always increases when prevailing religious institutions are dogmatically narrow or reactionary . . . The mystic seeks in himself that which he has failed to find in his creed. The moment the search for reality is turned inward, away from forms and toward life itself, the deeper and more beautiful facts of religions become apparent."[22]

We have already discussed the mysticism of Bernard of Clairvaux in the 12th century who, along with much else, encouraged devotion to Mary of Nazareth. Here we study four other great mystics of the medieval period: Hildegard of Bingen, Joachim of Fiore, Francis of Assisi, and Meister Eckhart. Their lives, which spanned more than two centuries, contributed in unique ways to the development of western Christianity, though their work was sometimes unsettling for the institutional church. The four individuals' mysticism was not ungrounded. They were in touch with nature and also capable of profound intellectual discourse. And like Thomas Aquinas and other early scholastics, their work was integrative, bringing together multiple modes of experience. Not unexpectedly the mystics and scholastics interacted and influenced one another; Hildegard and Francis influenced Aquinas, who in turn influenced Eckhart.[23] Moreover, in different ways their contributions influenced the Florentine Renaissance that began a century after Eckhart's death.

Hildegard of Bingen

Few people expressed the mystical path better than Hildegard of Bingen (1098-1179). Her work as an abbess was mentioned in Chapter 6. Hildegard, just a few years younger than Bernard of Clairvaux, was the first of the Rhineland mystics, often singled out as the "Sybil of the Rhine."[24] While still a child at the Benedictine double monastery at Disibodenberg, she learned to read the Psalter and gained a sufficient grasp of Latin to write in a style that could be understood on many levels. Hildegard had the gift of instant comprehension of religious texts:

> This happened in AD 1141 when I was 42 years and 7 months old: A fiery light, of the greatest flashing brightness, coming out of a cloudless sky, flooded my entire mind and so inflamed my whole heart and my whole breast like a flame—yet it was not blazing but glowing hot, as the sun makes anything on which its rays fall hot. And I suddenly experienced the understanding of the exposition of books, that is, of the Psalter, the Gospel, and of the other orthodox volumes of both the Old and the New Testaments.[25]

Hildegard's visions started when she was only three years old and continued for the rest of her life. For many years she shared the visions only with her teacher, Jutta of Sponheim, and with Volmar, a monk who served as her lifelong secretary.[26] However, in middle age Hildegard had a life-changing experience in which God told her to write down everything she observed. She produced many visionary works, including *Scivias* ("Know the Ways of the Lord") and *Liber divinorum operum* ("Book of Divine Works"). Hildegard gave full expression to the inner spiritual life and provided a good example of esoteric Christianity, as it was allowed to develop within the cloister. Some of her teachings could easily have been construed as heretical, though her understanding of Christ and redemption was fully in accord with traditional doctrines. A vision of the ascension was reported thus in *Scivias*: "The Son of God ascends to the Father, who alone with the Son and the Holy Spirit is the utmost excellent height of inexpressible joy and bliss. There the Son appears gloriously to the faithful in the abundance of bright sanctity and blessedness, and they believe in the purity and simplicity of their hearts that he is true God and man."[27]

Hildegard demonstrated an ability to write evocative poetry. One of her antiphons is as follows:

> Most splendid of gemstones! Bright Beauty of the sun! He poured upon you, as a leaping fountain from the heart of the Father, His unique and only Word, through whom he made the primal matter of the world which Eve the woman through into confusion. In your image, Father, this Word created the human being. Therefore, Mary, you are the bright matter through

which the Word breathed all the virtues forth, as once he led forth, in the primal matter of the world, the whole of creation.[28]

Celtic influence on the Rhineland mystics was clear, and Hildegard in particular invoked images from the natural world; for example: "The soul is a breath of living spirit, that with excellent sensitivity, / permeates the entire body to give it life. / Just so, the breath of the air makes the earth fruitful. / Thus the air is the soul of the earth, moistening it, greening it.[29]

Hildegard's love of music may also have begun at Disibodenberg when she heard the monks chanting their daily office. She composed a number of significant liturgical works, including antiphons and plainchant sequences for festivals of the saints and Mary of Nazareth.[30] Her moral play *Ordo Virtutum* ("Play of Virtues"), which may have been performed in her own convent, is often considered the first oratorio. Despite remarkable accomplishments, Hildegard was overwhelmed by a sense of her own inadequacy.

In her writing Hildegard addressed a wide variety of topics. *Liber subtilatum* ("The book of subtleties of the Diverse Nature of Things") discussed the medicinal uses of plants, animals, trees and stones. Lack of personal experience did not deter her from tackling subjects which she believed warranted attention. For example, there is no evidence that she ever violated her vow of chastity, but she managed to write insightfully about the pleasures of sex, including female orgasm.

Hildegard supported the concept of ecclesiastical authority. But she did not hesitate to criticize individual bishops and even popes who fell short of her expectations. She rebuked her own archbishop, telling him that his days were numbered; shortly afterward he was deposed and died. Her advice was sought from far and wide. She was even contacted by the patriarch of Jerusalem who had heard that a "divine force operated in and through her."[31] Hildegard also felt secure enough to lecture secular rulers on their shortcomings; for instance she warned the emperor Conrad III to reform his life.

Despite her air of independence, the unusual range of her insights and teachings, and her ecstatic experiences, Hildegard managed to stay in the church's good graces. She won ecclesiastical approval for condemning the Cathars. She was never canonized, but she had the good fortune to live in an age when the reality of visions was still accepted. Three centuries later, as Joan of Arc discovered, the church had become more rigid and paranoid, and exceptional insights were not taken so lightly.

Joachim of Fiore

Joachim of Fiore (1130-1202) lived during the century separating Hildegard and Francis of Assisi. While on a visit to the Holy Land as a young man, he had a religious experience and decided to become a Cistercian monk. Joachim was appointed abbot of the monastery of Corazzo, Italy, but left to found the abbey of St. John in Fiore with a stricter rule. The new order was approved by Pope Celestine III in 1197.

Joachim devoted much time to private study and scriptural analysis; and as noted in an earlier chapter, he also engaged in a debate over the Trinity. But he is best known for a series of prophecies. One involved the proposition that history could be divided into three epochs: that of the Father, corresponding to the biblical period; that of the Son, corresponding to the period from Jesus' time onward; and a new epoch of the Holy Spirit.[32] In the third epoch the ecclesiastical hierarchy would become unnecessary, and Christianity would function like a worldwide monastic community. Naturally people were interested to know when the new epoch would begin. In Joachim's opinion, it had already begun with the work of Benedict of Nursia, sixth-century father of western monasticism, and it was expected to reach maturity in 1260.[33]

More radical still was the suggestion that the New Testament "gospels of the letter" would be superseded by an esoteric message of Christ that lay hidden behind the literal wording. That "eternal" or "spiritual gospel" was to be preached by two new prophets, and the greater part of humanity would be converted to the new Christianity.[34] Joachim did not identify the two prophets, but later followers speculated that they were Francis and Dominic, founders of the orders of friars

Joachim documented his prophecies and humbly—and naïvely—submitted them to Pope Innocent III. Perhaps it was fortunate that he died before the pope could reply. That most powerful of popes would scarcely have appreciated the suggestion that the hierarchy had become irrelevant. The prophecies attracted considerable attention among the "Spiritual Franciscans" who sought to strengthen the strict rule of poverty prescribed by the order's founder.[35] One of them, Gerardo di Borgo San Donnino, asserted that Joachim's writings themselves constituted the eternal gospel. Rivals of the Franciscans at the University of Paris pressed heresy charges, and Gerardo and other Spirituals were imprisoned. Joachim's writings were condemned by a synod at Arles in 1263. However Joachim continued to exert influence, and his "age of the Spirit" was interpreted in millennial terms. Dante placed Joachim in Paradise in his *Inferno*. Joachim's prediction of an age of the Holy Spirit was gradually forgotten in the west; but, more than 600 years after his death, it would find unexpected favor in 19th-century Russia.[36]

Francis of Assisi

The individual we know as Francis of Assisi (c.1182-1226) was born Giovanni di Bernardone; Francis, or Francesco, was a nickname. The son of a wealthy merchant in Assisi, north of Rome, he received a good education and served as a soldier. Captured by enemy forces, he had a profound religious experience while in prison. Upon his release, Francis rejected his family's wealth to become a beggar.

While praying in a church near Assisi, Francis had a vision in which Christ told him to "repair my house which is falling into ruins." Believing that it referred to the building, he set about rebuilding the church and several other others in the area. However it soon became clear that his charge was to minister to people. He preached in the streets and attracted a band of followers who cared for the poorest and sickest people in the community, including lepers. In 1209 a reluctant Pope Innocent III granted Francis petition to found a religious order that came to be known as the Order of Franciscan Friars Minor. Its motto was "Leave all and follow me." Two years later, the companion Order of Poor Clares was founded for women.

Like Hildegard, Francis developed a great love of nature, and the relationship became the topic of numerous legends. In one he preached to a large flock of birds; in another he tamed a wolf that terrorized the town of Gubbio. Despite living in abject poverty, Francis and his companions were the most cheerful of men, singing as they traveled around the country. Francis composed a number of songs, including the famous *Canticle of Brother Sun*:

> Most High Almighty Good Lord, Yours are praise, glory, honor and all blessings; To You alone! Most High, do they belong, and no man is worthy of speaking Your Name!
>
> Be praised, Lord, with all Your creatures, and above all our Brother Sun, who gives us the day by which You light our way, and who is beautiful, radiant and with his great splendor is a symbol to us of You, O Most High!
>
> And be praised, Lord, for our Sister Moon and the Stars. You created them in the heavens bright, precious and beautiful!
>
> And be praised, Lord, for our Brother the Wind and for the air and the clouds and for fair weather and for all other through which You sustain Your creatures.
>
> And be praised, Lord, for our Sister Water, so useful, and humble, and chaste!
>
> And be praised, my Lord, for our Brother Fire, through whom You light up the night and who is handsome, joyful, robust, and strong!
>
> And be praised, my Lord, for our Sister, Mother Earth, who supports and carries us and produces the diverse fruits and colorful flowers and trees!

Praise and bless the Lord and give thanks to Him and serve Him with great humility!

Be praised, my Lord, for our Sister, bodily Death from whom no living man can escape!

Woe only to those who die in mortal sin; but blessed are those who have done Your most holy will; for the second death can cause them no harm!

In 1223, while at prayer on Mount Alvernia, Francis received the stigmata, the marks of Christ's wounds on his body. He was the first known individual to be so recognized, though several later instances of stigmata were documented. Francis died three years later and was canonized in 1228.

The Franciscan Order became a rival of the Dominican Order of Friars Preachers, founded in 1215. Together, the two orders ably typified the new concept of religious life in which members worked in the world rather than in the cloister. Both left their indelible marks on the development of Christianity.

Meister Eckhart

Johann Eckhart von Hochheim (c.1260-1327) entered the Dominican order the year after Thomas Aquinas died. He became highly respected as a teacher and preacher. In the 1310s, upon completion of his master's degree at the University of Paris, Eckhart was appointment to the chair once held by Aquinas and gained the title "Meister Eckhart." At the height of his fame he was appointed in 1320 to a professorship at the University of Cologne. In Paris he became thoroughly acquainted with the scholasticism of Albertus Magnus and Aquinas, both of whom he greatly admired. But scholasticism had already passed its peak, and Eckhart felt that it had placed too much emphasis on scripture and reason and not enough on the inspiration of the Holy Spirit. Accordingly he turned to mysticism and an additional source of knowledge. He is regarded as the last of the Rhineland Mystics.

Following the 12th-century theologian Peter Lombard and perhaps influenced by Qabalistic teachings, Eckhart conceived of a Godhead that overshadowed the three persons of the trinity. Furthermore, Eckhart leaned toward the Neoplatonic concept of emanation in which the universe is an outpouring of the divine essence. As a result all things are equally divine: "In their first outflow angels, men, and all creatures flow from God equal . . . . If one takes a fly in God, it is nobler in God that the highest angel is in itself."[37] Moreover, such divinity is ontologically necessary: "What help is it to me that Mary is full of grace, if I am not also full of grace? And what help is it to me that the Father gives birth to his Son unless

I too give birth to him?"[38] That kind of deification of man placed Eckhart closer to Eastern Orthodox teachings than to western tradition. Like the Gnostics he believed that the human entity contains a divine spark which, like Christ, was not created but existed from all eternity. The divine content gave the soul both preexistence and an ability to function independently of the body. In contrast, Aquinas taught that the soul is created sometime between conception and birth and requires the resurrection of the body in order to regain wholeness.

Meister Eckhart eloquently expressed the optimism that had pervaded the Celtic church. God does not look down on a corrupt, Augustinian world, wracked by sin; instead God sees his creation and rejoices. Quoting from *Isaiah* Eckhart preached: ""Rejoice, heaven and earth!" . . . For God has sheer delight and laughter over a good deed. For all other deeds that do not take place in praise of God are quite like ashes in God's sight. "Rejoice, heaven and earth!" God has consoled his people."[39]

Like many other prominent thinkers before and after his time, Meister Eckhart was accused of heresy. An inquiry by his own Dominican Order failed to find fault with his teachings, but rivals in the Franciscan Order persisted in their charges. He offered to retract any teachings that were at variance with church dogma; but that was not enough. The Avignon pope John XXII formally declared that "someone by the name of Eckhart from Germany, a doctor of sacred theology . . . was led astray by that Father of Lies who often turns himself into an angel of light in order to replace the light of truth with a dark and gloomy cloud of the senses."[40] John identified 17 propositions as heretical and a further 11 as "evil-sounding" and "very rash." The main thrust of the charges was that in defending God's presence in the world Eckhart was a pantheist, though today we would describe him more accurately as a *panentheist*, which carries a very different connotation. Taking issue with his belief in the deification of man, one of the 17 charges quoted Eckhart as saying: "We shall all be transformed totally into God and changed into him. In the same way, when in the sacrament bread is changed into Christ's Body, I am so changed into him that he makes me his one existence, and not just similar."[41]

Meister Eckhart died shortly before the papal bull was issued and never learned of the condemnation. Despite the charges Eckhart influenced many later thinkers, including Martin Luther, 16th-century mystic Jacob Böhme, and 18th-century Anglican churchman William Law. Eckhart'a views have been shown to resonate with systems of thought ranging from Marxism to Zen.[42] The modern theologian Matthew Fox, who left the Dominican Order, is a great admirer of Eckhart, seeing in his work the foundations of modern creation spirituality. Recently efforts have been made to secure a formal rescission of the heresy charges.

The Renaissance

W hat we customarily call "the Renaissance" was actually the third of three renaissances that spanned a period of some 800 years. The first was the "Carolingian renaissance" of the eighth and ninth centuries, and the second was the great synthesis of intellectual and mystical pursuits in the 12th and 13th centuries.

Italian Renaissance

Some historians date the beginning of the Renaissance to the year 1300, pointing to the work of poet Dante Alighieri (1265-1321) and his close contemporary, the artist Giotto di Bondone.[43] Certainly it was significant that both men were natives of the city-state of Florence, and there is little doubt that the Renaissance started there. But a more meaningful date of origin lies between 1380 and 1420, when the Albizzi family took control of Florence.

The Albizzis sought ways to revive the economy of Florence after the continental economic depression that followed the Black Death, a war with Milan, and widespread social problems. The strategy they adopted was based on the belief that the Greek and Latin classics—pre-Christian sources—contained the lessons needed to lead a moral and effective life in society. The Albizzis encouraged a return to the educational standards of classical Greece and Rome and a revival of the seven liberal arts of arithmetic, geometry, astronomy, music, grammar, logic and rhetoric. The hope was that by studying the political and social life of antiquity Florence could achieve the power and success of Athens or Rome. The elite families of Florence built new schools and hired secular tutors to teach their children classical wisdom and communication skills. Both were needed for participation in the political process, to allow future citizens to play their proper role in society.

Whether or not educational reform was responsible, by 1415 the Florentine economy was booming. The new prosperity allowed the Albizzis, and even more the Medici family that rose to power in 1434, to become great patrons of the arts. The Renaissance soon spread to Milan, Venice, and other cities. The celebrated artist, architect and engineer, Leonardo da Vinci (1452-1519), worked in Florence, Milan and Rome.

Religious motifs continued to dominate artistic creation. During the Middle Ages the church was the primary patron, and some great works were produced. But, mindful of the icon controversy of the eighth and ninth centuries, ecclesiastical authorities closely monitored artistic subjects and style. Christ, Mary of Nazareth, and the saints were portrayed as idealized, almost mythical, figures. That was entirely consistent with the Platonic outlook that attached higher value to the ideal than to its shadow in the physical world. Typical depictions of the crucifixion showed no pain either in the body of Christ or on the faces of his attendant followers. In contrast, Renaissance artists began to depict religious figures as real people displaying real pain, fear, joy or ecstasy. Artists, sculptors and architects imitated works of the classical era, but soon they developed styles of their own, experimenting with color, light, line and perspective.

Rich patricians like the Medicis of Florence, the Viscontis and Sforzas of Milan, and the doges of Venice became generous patrons, commissioning religious art as well as other works. Often the figures looked *very* real—like the sponsors or the artists themselves. Notwithstanding, art lovers could identify with the works and their emotions, and the works had great devotional impact. Furthermore, the human body was no longer considered shameful. Not only David but also Mary Magdalene could be depicted partially or even totally nude.[44] Michelangelo's fresco "The Creation of Adam," in the Sistine Chapel, portrays God the Father with his arm around a nude female figure.[45] The flesh was no longer considered concupiscent but had spiritual as well as esthetic value. Only Jesus and Mary of Nazareth continued to be depicted clothed.

Lorenzo de Medici, "the Magnificent," died in 1492, and the Florentine Renaissance quickly came to an end. In 1497 the crazed Dominican friar Girolamo Savaranola burned the books and artwork of Florence in the town square, only to be burned himself the following year. An epidemic of syphilis brought back all-too-vivid memories of the plague. And the army of King Charles VIII of France invaded northern Italy in 1494, devastating Florence and the other city states.

The center of the Renaissance moved to Rome, wooed by the largess of the Medici popes Leo X and Clement VII. During the next several decades Raphael Sanzio (1483-1520) and Michelangelo Buonarroti (1475-1564) did their greatest work. But in 1527 the Hapsburg army of Emperor Charles V, which had already laid northern Italy to waste, sacked Rome. Not long thereafter, the Counter-Reformation ushered in a new age of austerity within the Roman church. By 1550 the Italian Renaissance was essentially over, though construction of the basilica of St. Peter's in Rome continued through the end of the century. Fortunately, the new culture and humanism had already spread to northern Europe. By 1700 the Renaissance had reached England and Scandinavia.

Rise of Humanism

Humanism was the great intellectual achievement of the Renaissance. Dante Alighieri (1472-1629) is often said to have been the first humanist, and certainly he admired the classics. But most historians regard the author and poet Francesco Petrarch (c.1304-1374) as the father of humanism.[46] Petrarch was born in Arezzo, near Florence, and he too grew up to have a great love of the classics, though he never learned Greek. Another influential humanist was his friend Giovanni Boccaccio (1313-1375), historical novelist and author of *Decameron*, an exposé of life in 14th-century Italian society.

The educational reforms already mentioned spurred a more general interest in scholarship. Libraries were searched for manuscripts of the classical writers, and scholars began translating and studying them. Texts by Cicero, Virgil, and others were studied not just for their literary value but as a way to return liturgical Latin to the quality of its classical origins.[47] The goal was largely achieved, though it widened the gulf between Latin and the vernacular Romance languages to the point where ordinary people in Italy and elsewhere could no longer understand the liturgy.

The humanists' motto was *sapientia et eloquentia*, "wisdom and eloquence." Eloquentia was to be gained by studying and imitating the impeccable Latin of the classical writers, as distinct from the "vulgar" Latin of the medieval church. It would give educated people the power of persuasion in both oral and written communications. Rhetoric had not been ignored during the scholastic era, but it took second place to dialectic; humanism reversed the priorities.

Several other characteristics distinguished humanism from scholasticism. First, its focus was much broader. Humanism addressed a whole range of issues beyond theology, including the nature, aspirations and behavior of humanity—hence the name "humanism." That is not to say that humanism, as the term came to be used later, was opposed to religion. Most of the great Renaissance humanists were devout Christians, and it was not long before a humanist would become pope. Enea Silvio Piccolomini of Siena (1405-1464) was crowned poet laureate by the Emperor Frederick in 1442. He became a cardinal in 1456 and, two years later, was elected Pope Pius II. Pius was not an outstanding scholar, but he had wide literary interests and some literary talent; he is the only pope known to have written not only an autobiography but also an erotic novel. It was said of him, in admiration, that his "character reflected almost every tendency of the age in which he lived."

Education and scholarship had long been church monopolies, subordinated to the glory of God and the advancement of Christianity. Now education was valued for its social benefits. And scholarship, patronized by wealthy families, like the Albizzis and Medicis, was valued in and of itself. Cosimo de Medici founded the Platonic Academy in Florence for the study of classical Greek and Neoplatonic thought.[48] That gave humanists important new freedom to study issues that might embarrass the institutional church. For example, in 1440 the Italian humanist Lorenzo Valla demonstrated that the *Donation of Constantine* was a forgery.[49] The humanists also developed new, rigorous standards of scholarship. Scholars were beginning to have access to scriptural texts in Latin, Greek and Hebrew and were able to perform comparative analysis. In some cases church doctrine was shown to rest on dubious translations or obscure scriptural passages.

One of the classical topics studied was the Pythagorean musical scale, described in Plato's *Timaeus*,[50] and the closely related topic of sacred geometry. Both affirmed the harmony of divine creation, which should be imitated in order to bring that harmony into human affairs. In 1525 Francesco di Borgio (1439-1502) dedicated his monumental work *De Harmonia Mundi* ("On the Harmony of the Universe") to Pope Clement VII. The church became so enamored of the elegance of the Pythagorean scale that later attempts to introduce tempered scales would be condemned as blasphemous.[51]

A final, important characteristic of both humanism and the Renaissance in general was their optimism. The notion that man was created in the image of God was interpreted to mean that man's creativity reflected divine creativity. Through art, music, literature and intellectual pursuits, people were discovering and expressing their divine potential. A new age had dawned that would carry humanity to ever greater heights. The feeling was captured particularly well by the Florentine nobleman Giovanni Pico della Mirandola (1463-1494) in his book: *Oration on the Dignity of Man*. But in an ironic metaphor for the dashing of hopes, Giovanni Pico died the very year that Florence was overrun by the French army.

Erasmus

By the end of the 16th century humanism spread from Italy to northern Europe, contributing to the momentum for reform in the church. One of the greatest humanists was the Dutch theologian Gerhard Gerhardson[52] (c.1466-1536) who adopted the persona of "Desiderius Erasmus." Born in or near Rotterdam, Erasmus entered a monastery and was ordained a priest in his 20s. Despite deep affection for another monk, he detested the monastic life and escaped as soon as he could. Erasmus declined to seek the comfortable life of a university lecturer, for which his education and ordination equipped him. Instead he became an independent scholar, supported by his writing and by gifts from wealthy patrons, who included high churchmen as well as aristocrats. He traveled extensively throughout Europe, spending time in France, Italy, and Henry VIII's England. Erasmus died in Basel, Switzerland, two decades after the start of the Reformation.

Erasmus attracted to him many of the great minds of his times. But he is remembered not only for his ideas but also for his writing style—a style that, in the best humanist tradition, captured the *eloquentia* of the classics. Erasmus learned Greek so he could read the works of the church fathers and could study early scriptural manuscripts. He devoted many years to a translation and critical analysis of the New Testament. Published in several editions from 1516 to 1535, he dedicated the work to Pope Leo X. Erasmus' scriptural analysis, based on multiple sources, is regarded as one of the first examples of modern biblical exegesis.

Erasmus became an iconoclast of everything that could be questioned in Europe's institutions of power. Not surprisingly the church was a major target. Still sore from his early experiences as a monk he was particularly scathing in his depictions of the monastic system and clerical celibacy. He did much to promote the virtue of marriage, though his own sex drive seems to have been entirely sublimated. Erasmus criticized many of the religious observances of his time, particularly those that involved emotion, which he distrusted; for him, piety should be quiet, reflective, and under the full control of the mind. That austere style of religion would later appeal to John Calvin. Erasmus also had harsh words for theologians:

> Perhaps it would be wise to pass over the theologians in silence. That short-tempered and supercilious crew is unpleasant to deal with . . . They will proclaim me a heretic. With this thunderbolt they terrify the people they don't like. Their opinion of themselves is so great that they behave as if they were already in heaven; they look down pityingly on other men as so many worms.[53]

Erasmus was equally scathing about the Marian cult that had grown up in popular Catholicism since the writings of Bernard of Clairvaux in the 12th century.[54] In his view it was offensive to project onto Mary titles from the *Song of Songs* and the wisdom literature of Hellenic Judaism and pagan titles like Star of the Sea. Moreover, he determined that Mary should be described as "gracious" rather than "full of grace."[55] His attack on the Marian cult would inspire generations of Protestant teachers intent of ridding Christianity of anything resembling a goddess. The Reformation was in full swing during the latter part of his life. But Erasmus declined to join the Protestant cause, in part because he could not accept Luther's denial of freewill. He remained an independent voice. Despite his criticism of traditional Christianity he never formally severed his links with Catholicism: "I will put up with this Church until I see a better one, and it will have to put up with me, until I better become."[56] But Rome was not so generous. When the Index of Prohibited Books was instituted in 1559, Erasmus' writings were among its first listings.

Confluence of Traditions I

The late Middle Ages and Renaissance were times when multiple cultural, religious and intellectual traditions came together to produce new synthesis and a new western worldview. Ideas flowed in from various Christian and non-

Christian sources. Here we discuss just a few of them and examine how they influenced the development of western Christian thought. This section is headed "Confluence of Traditions I" because another important confluence occurred in the 19th century; it will be discussed in Chapter 18.

Eastern Orthodox Treasures

The crusaders from western Europe who sacked Constantinople in 1204 were impressed by the richness of the Byzantine capital and brought back a vast horde of treasure, including sacred art. But they did not bring back much of eastern Christianity's teachings. There is somewhat more evidence that the Knights Templar acquired significant knowledge of Sufism and other religions from the Middle East. However claims that the round Templar churches were inspired by Islamic architecture have to confront the more likely explanation that they were modeled after the Church of the Holy Sepulcher in Jerusalem.

Large numbers of Orthodox scholars did come to western Europe during the crusaders' occupation of Constantinople, the tenuously reestablished Byzantine Empire, and finally the new Turkish regime. A prominent visitor was the Greek philosopher and esotericist Georgius Gemistos, also known as Plethon. Gemistos was an Orthodox delegate to the Council of Florence in 1438-1439; but he stayed on and taught at the Florentine Academy.[57] The Byzantine scholars brought with them a wealth of classical, religious and scientific texts, and most importantly their own expertise. For example Gemistos was an authority on Zoroaster and Plato. That influx of knowledge was one of the major channels through which the Greek classics were rediscovered in the west. On religious topics, the interaction between eastern and western scholars was particularly fruitful because Greek theology had not been influenced by scholasticism and represented a form of Christianity closer to the patristic age.

The émigrés from Constantinople also brought with them sacred and scholarly texts in Arabic. During the high Middle Ages Islamic scholars had led the world in science and mathematics, and now the knowledge became available to the west—at a particularly opportune time. By the 15th century Islamic scholarship had gone into decline, while in the west the scientific revolution was on the horizon, and the work of the Arabs would soon be put to good use.

Qabalah and Hermeticism

During the Moorish period many Jewish scholars had settled in Spain and southern France. A major subject of study was the Qabalah (Hebrew: קבלה, "tradition"), a system of metaphysical symbolism whose roots may go back to Zadokite priests in the Jewish temple.[58] In the 12th century Jewish scholars compiled and published two influential books: the *Bahir* ("Brilliance") and the *Sepher Yetzirah* ("Book of

Formation/Creation"). Even more influential was the monumental *Sepher Zohar* ("Book of Splendor"), compiled by Moses de León and published around 1290. The medieval Qabalah was essentially a composite of an ancient oral tradition in Judaism and Neoplatonic mystical philosophy.

The Qabalah presented views of God and the created universe that contrasted with both Christian doctrine—save for the work of Meister Eckhart—and the teachings of rabbinic Judaism.[59] It affirmed the Neoplatonic concept of divine emanation, postulating that the divine essence cascades down through a sequence of 10 *sephiroth*, which the Safed scholars arranged in the form of a glyph called the "tree of life."[60] Sephiroth, the plural of the Hebrew word *sephirah* (ספירה, "number") can be viewed either as differentiations of the divine essence or as the vessels into which it is poured. Important sephiroth for our purposes are: No. 1, *Kether* (כתר, "the crown"); No. 6, *Tiphareth* (תפארת, "beauty" or "harmony"); and No. 10, *Malkuth* (מלכות, "the kingdom"). The divine essence descends from its most sublime form in Kether to its most concretized form in Malkuth. In response, seekers must raise their consciousness through the sephiroth to attain union with God. Clearly, the descent into matter and subsequent return to spirit recalls a Platonic view of the soul's destiny.

Hermeticism had a quite different lineage. It refers to a body of philosophical, alchemical, magical and astrological teachings of Egyptian, Persian, and possibly Chaldean origin. Greek texts from the first-to-third centuries CE had been preserved in Constantinople and brought to Europe by the Byzantine scholars. The texts purported to contain the secret wisdom of one Hermes Trismegistus. That Hermes, "Thrice-Great Hermes," was a mythical figure representing a conflation—and embellishment—of the Egyptian Thoth and Greek demigod Hermes. Hermeticism, even more than the Qabalah, overlapped with Gnostic thought. Its appeal was enhanced by a widely held belief during the Renaissance that wisdom came originally from the east, perhaps from sources predating both Hebrew and Greek traditions.[61] The notion that *Matthew*'s three wise men came from the east played into the belief.

Qabalistic and Hermetic teachings came to the attention of important European scholars, including Marsilio Ficino, Giovanni Pico, John Reuchlin, and Giordano Bruno. Ficino (1433-1499), a priest and head of the Florentine Academy, who had earlier translated several of Plato's works into Latin, translated a number of Hermetic texts and published them as the *Corpus Hermeticum*. Ficino's colleague and Florentine nobleman, Giovanni Pico, who has already been mentioned, translated a number of Qabalistic manuscripts and wrote several works of his own. Neoplatonic influence on the Qabalah and Hermeticism increased as the synthesis of systems of thought increased throughout the Renaissance.

Qabalistic teachings fed a prevailing fascination for occult teachings, but the scholars also saw their potential relevance to Christian theology. Ficino, Pico, and their followers considered that the Qabalah and Hermeticism were part of the ageless wisdom on which all religion and philosophy rested.[62] Giovanni Pico asserted that Christianity, in particular, was founded largely on Qabalistic teachings: "No science can better convince us of the divinity of Jesus Christ than magic and the Qabalah."[63] Reuchlin (1455-1522), a German scholar and pioneer in the study of the Hebrew language, wrote an influential book *On the Art of the Kabbalah*, arguing that works of Jewish mysticism reflected classical traditions and supported Christian doctrine.

With the work of those individuals, the "Christian Qabalah," or "Hermetic Qabalah," was born, though the latter term was of dubious validity.[64] Of particular interest was the sephirah Tiphareth, the mediator between Kether and Malkuth. Christian Qabalists identified it with Jesus Christ, the mediator between the Godhead and humanity and the restorer of harmony after the disruption of the fall of Adam. The divine essence poured down on humanity through Christ, and through Christ we must seek "redemption" in the form of union with God. However, even Malkuth, which could be identified with the physical world, was divine. The world was not corrupt but simply the farthest removed from the level of pure divinity in Kether. Similarly, humanity might be estranged from God but was potentially divine and capable of a different kind of redemption from the one customarily taught by the church. That new view of redemption had much in common with the Eastern Orthodox notion of *theosis*, or "deification." We have already noted that Meister Eckhart found that concept appealing.

Qabalistic teachings took a more sensitive attitude to good and evil than did orthodox Christianity.[65] Qabalists viewed morality not as an absolute but as a question of balance. Certain actions produce imbalance and call for complementary actions to restore balance. For example, aggressiveness needs to be balanced by kindness and generosity; otherwise it harms the actor as well as others. However, excessive generosity may need to be balanced by prudent withholding of bounty so that recipients can develop a sense of values. The resolution of opposites would be illustrated well in Edmund Spenser's *Faerie Queene* by Dame Concord and her twin sons Love and Hate.[66]

Another man who helped bridge the gap between Christianity and other world religions was Cardinal Egidio Antonini da Viterbo (c.1465-1532). Also known as "Giles of Viterbo," he was prior-general of the Augustinian Order and later Latin Patriarch of Constantinople. A humanist scholar, deeply interested in Qabalah, he believed that Hebrew was the only true sacred language and is reported to have searched the Hebrew scriptures for hidden meanings.[67] Egidio was proficient in several other ancient languages and studied the *Qur'an* in the original Arabic. As head of the Augustinian Order, Egidio may have met Martin Luther when he was a monk.

Despite the involvement of monks and even cardinals, the church viewed studies of the Qabalah, Christianized or otherwise, with considerable suspicion. On the one hand there was a sense that the Qabalah might provide a means to win Jews to Christianity; but, on the other, there was fear that it might be a "Trojan horse" that would bring down the church.[68] The Qabalistic studies represented an unusual interest in Judaism during a period of blatant anti-Semitism. Giovanni Pico was questioned by the Inquisition, but his noble rank—and perhaps his early death— protected him from what might have been a full-blown attack on his orthodoxy. John Reuchlin, one of the few Christian Qabalists outside Italy, opposed a proposal by the Dominicans of Cologne to burn all Jewish books within the Holy Roman Empire. The Inquisition sent him to Rome and, despite the support of Cardinal Egidio, he was fined for heresy; later he secured the protection of a German prince. The outspoken Giordano Bruno (1548-1600)—in a terrible reenactment of the betrayal of Jan Hus by the Council of Constance in 1417—was lured to Rome on a promise of safe conduct and burned at the stake.

A century after Ficino and Pico, a Franciscan friar named Chrysostomus of Capranica suggested to the emperor Ferdinand II that he might achieve victory over the Turks by invoking the Aramaic/Hebrew name of Jesus, *Yeshuah* (יהשוה), which consisted of the Tetragrammaton (יהוה), the four-letter Hebrew name of God, augmented by the letter *shin* (ש).[69] Interest in the Qabalah and Hermeticism surfaced again in the work of Protestant visionary Jakob Böhme and artist-poet William Blake (1757-1827). The late 18th-century English diarist Ambrose Serle related the three highest sephiroth in the tree of life to the Father, Son and Holy Spirit.[70] The Qabalistic trinity had much in common with the one proposed by the Neoplatonist Plotinus.

Natural Philosophy

The term "science" was unknown at the time of the Renaissance. The study of nature was referred to as "natural philosophy," and it had strong links with religion. Importantly, it included alchemy and magic. Study of the physical and nonphysical worlds was integrated and holistic, quite unlike the reductionism of the 19th century in which academic disciplines became walled cities. Serious study of natural philosophy began as early as the 13th century,[71] while vestiges of the holistic, Renaissance attitude to science continued through the 18th century.

Alchemy was a leading science of the Renaissance—one that expressed all the integrative, non-dualistic vision of the times. Today, it is either dismissed as the futile attempt to turn base metals into gold or explained away as "primitive chemistry," "primitive Jungian psychology," or "sex magic, a western version of Tantra." Alchemy may have included some of those things, but it went much further; alchemy was the "spiritualization of matter and the materialization of spirit."[72] Certainly it had to do with transmutation, and there is evidence that the transmutation of metal occasionally was achieved.[73]

The real goal was a more important: "For the alchemist . . . power over matter and energy is only a secondary reality . . . The material results are only a pledge of the final result, which is spiritual . . . the transmutation of man himself . . . his fusion with the divine energy."[74] It seems unlikely that anyone whose primary goal was the production of gold for purposes of amassing wealth would succeed, though the Avignon pope John XXII reportedly did so before outlawing the study of alchemy.[75] Significantly, the Christian Qabalists assigned lead to the lowest sephirah, Malkuth, and gold to the central sephirah, Tiphareth, which they associated with Christ. Hence, the transmutation of lead into gold was, among other things, a metaphor for raising the human consciousness to Christ. Even at the time of the Renaissance, it was recognized that alchemical transmutation had implications for the Eucharist.[76]

Magic was a broad field that included the healing arts, mathematics, and even technology; for example, clock design was regarded as a branch of magic. The saying, "It works like magic" had a literal meaning. From medieval times, the church had not been totally opposed to magic; after all, it was magi who followed the star to Bethlehem. Rather, it took the sensible approach of distinguishing different types of magic according to their purpose. Well into the Renaissance, Gabriel Naudé (1600-1653), librarian to two cardinals, identified "divine magic," "religious magic," "natural magic," and "witchcraft."[77] But by then attitudes were hardening, not least because of the influx of Hermetic texts which persuaded church leaders that all forms of magic were linked to dangerous forms of paganism. Although individual churchmen and even cardinals continued to dabble, the practice of magic became a pursuit of rich nobles—in rooms off-limits to ecclesiastical visitors—and secret societies.

Technology overlapped with art. Aristotle had spoken of "servile" or "mechanical arts": those like painting and sculpture that involved manual labor, contrasted with the more highly favored "liberal arts" of poetry, rhetoric and music. The decorative arts were still trying to shake off those "servile" associations in the high Middle Ages[78] when art became a topic of scholastic interest. The scholastics scoffed that art tried to imitate nature but only succeeded in creating lifeless forms.[79] However technology came to the rescue; the moving and "speaking" sculptures that graced palace gardens[80] were intended, at least in part, to show that art could indeed come to life. The overlap between art and technology was expressed by Leonardo da Vinci (1452-1519)—Renaissance man *par excellence*—who engaged in both. Besides producing a large artistic output, including the famous painting of the Last Supper, Leonardo made important observations in mechanics, anatomy, and optics. He also developed designs of many mechanical devices and consulted on issues of military engineering. Rejecting any concept of servility, Leonardo believed that painting reflected, to a high degree, divine creation.

Mathematics was regarded as a bridge between rational thought and mysticism. The eminent mathematician John Dee (1527-1608) was accused of sorcery not only because of his occult work but also because of his mathematics. In the introduction to his English translation of Euclid's geometry he complained of being regarded as "a companion of the helhounds [sic], a caller and a conjurer of wicked and damned spirits."[81]

Reflections

The Aristotelian revival of the high Middle Ages provided intellectual tools that allowed the reasonableness and consistency of doctrine to be tested in new ways. Using those tools the great theologians of the scholastic age refined doctrinal formulations of the seven ecumenical councils. However medieval Christianity is remembered not only for its intellectual attainments but also for the blossoming of the monastic life and the insights of its great mystics. Similarly the Renaissance was not just another intellectual revival but a larger expansion of consciousness. Its impact on western culture was profound. Sacred art became richer, more accessible, and more "human." Renaissance music, itself of timeless excellence, fed directly into the Baroque style of the 18th century, arguably the greatest in western civilization.

The Renaissance was marked by a new synthesis of science, metaphysics, art and scholarship. That synthesis was served by a more balanced Platonic/Aristotelian world-view that took root after scholasticism had run its course. To be sure, humanism was more Aristotelian than Platonic in outlook, focusing on humanity's intrinsic value rather than its higher realities, and Aristotelian influence was evident in Renaissance art. But Platonic ideals inspired utopian literature and influenced Renaissance metaphysics—an influence that became explicit in studies at the Florentine Academy and in the later work of the Cambridge Platonists. Platonism's influence declined once again in the modern age, but it is preserved in the modern esoteric Christianity that took shape during the Renaissance and perhaps in modern science.[82]

Institutional Christianity's response to the Renaissance was mixed. The church embraced Renaissance music, art and architecture. The Baroque art which followed would become almost a monopoly of the Church of Rome, its rich sensuality contrasting with the increasing austerity of Protestant Europe. Renaissance and Baroque music was embraced by both Catholics and Lutherans but rejected by Calvinists. Rome's attitude to humanism was mainly skeptical, and the church took an understandably strong dislike for Erasmus. Institutional Christianity—Catholic and Protestant—showed surprisingly little interest in the synthesis of Christian and non-Christian metaphysics which could have mounted a major challenge to doctrinal foundations. Fortunately, for the church's sake, the new metaphysics was studied by relatively small groups of people and its conclusions were not widely publicized. However the church would learn to its cost the consequences of ignoring the new physical sciences. By the 17th century, when the western world-view was forever changed and traditional church teachings seriously threatened, science had acquired unstoppable momentum.

The Renaissance was a period of great optimism for artists, scientists, intellectuals, and the emerging merchant classes. The Dark Ages were over, and Europe was moving forward in exciting new ways. As historian Philip Schaff put it: "The air was stirred by the spirit of progress and freedom. The snows of a long winter were fast, melting before the rays of the vernal sun. The world seemed to be renewing its youth; old things were passing away, all things were becoming new."[83] But he added, "Pessimists and timid conservatives took alarm at the threatened overthrow of cherished notions and institutions, and were complaining, fault-finding and desponding."[84]

Foremost among those pessimists and timid conservatives were religious leaders, particularly Catholic leaders. "Progress" was not an exciting concept for an institutional Christianity whose mindset was still medieval. Expansion through missionary activity took a high priority, but otherwise the church was committed to eternal stasis. Suggestions of progress also contrasted with the obvious fact of the church's declining power. From the Renaissance onward institutional Christianity—Roman and Protestant—lost control of the intellectual and cultural life of Europe. European culture would become increasingly secular, and scholarly inquiry would expand into many fields previously off-limits. The new freedoms would be expressed to the full in the Enlightenment.

---

1. Some modern scholars feel that "Dark Ages" refers more to our lack of knowledge of the period than to a dearth of scholarship.

2. Manly Palmer Hall. *Pathways of Philosophy*. Philosophical Research Society, 1947, pp. 46ff. The teachers were known variously as *magisteri*, or *doctores*, *scholastici*.

3. Deidre Carabine. *John Scottus Eriugena*. Oxford University Press, 2000, pp. 18-20

4. This eucharistic controversy was discussed in Chapter 7.

5.   By that time few scholastics knew Greek and had to rely on Latin translations of
     Plato and Aristotle.
6.   Anton C. Pegis. *Introduction to Saint Aquinas*. Modern Library, 1948, p. vii. See
     also: Matthew Fox. *Passion for Creation*. Inner Traditions, 1980/2000, p. 20.
7.   Matthew Fox. *Sheer Joy*. Tarcher/Putnam, 1992, pp. 19-27. We saw in an earlier
     chapter that Aquinas also contributed to the theory of esthetics.
8.   *Aurora Consurgens* was published anonymously. But its style and its author's extensive
     knowledge of scripture and theology persuade many scholars to attribute it to Aquinas.
     See the translation and commentary by Marie-Louise von Franz, Inner City Books,
     2000.
9.   See: Anton C. Pegis. *Introduction to St. Thomas Aquinas*. Modern Library, 1948, p. xv.
10. John's father was Giovanni di Fidanza. The origins of the name Bonaventure are unclear.
11. John Duns Scotus, born in Duns, Scotland, is not to be confused with the ninth-
     century Irishman John Scotus Eriugena. John Duns, a Franciscan friar, studied and
     lectured at the universities of Oxford, Paris and Cologne.
12. Importantly, Aristotle's notion of form was different from Plato's. Aristotle's form
     was not Plato's idealized Form (capitalized) that overshadowed physical reality but
     a quality of the thing itself, inseparable from the object to which it referred.
13. Aristotle. *The Metaphysics*. (Transl: Hugh Lawson-Tancred.) Penguin Books, 1998.
14. Ontological proofs can be traced back to Parmenides in ancient Greece.
15. Formally, Anselm defined God is "that than which no greater can be conceived."
     In Cartesian terms, existence is more perfect than nonexistence; therefore the most
     perfect conceivable being must exist. Mathematicians Gottfried Wilhelm Leibniz
     (1646-1716) and Kurt Gödel (1906-1978) would offer their own ontological proofs
16. Teleological proofs invoke the concept of Aristotle's final cause.
17. David Hume. *Dialogues Concerning Natural Religion*, 1779; and *The Natural History
     of Religion*, 1757. Immanuel Kant. *The Critique of Pure Reason*, 1781/1787.
18. Anton C. Pegis. *Introduction to Saint Aquinas*. Modern Library, 1948, p. xvii.
19. John Nash. *Quest for the Soul*. 1stBooks Library, 2004, pp. 57-58.
20. Even Harvard College, founded in Cambridge, Massachusetts, in 1639 retained a
     scholastic curriculum for many years.
21. The church tried to offset its loss of control by insisting that mystics ground their inner
     life firmly on scripture. See for example: Thomas Merton. *Bread in the Wilderness*.
     New Directions, 1953.
22. Manly P. Hall. *The Mystical Christ*. Philosophical Research Society, 1951, pp.
     11-12. Perhaps the Essenes flourished because of a similarly repressive climate in
     post-Maccabean Judaism.
23. Matthew Fox. *Sheer Joy*. Tarcher/Putnam, 1992, p. 9.
24. The last Rhineland mystic is usually reckoned to be Meister Eckert.
25. Hildegard of Bingen. *Scivias*, 3. (Transl: A. Führkötter & A. Carlevaris.) Turnhout, 1978.
26. Skeptics have attributed Hildegard's visions to visual hallucinations associated with
     the migraine from which she suffered. Common symptoms of migraine include
     sickness, paralysis and blindness, followed by a period of euphoria—all of which
     she reported.

27. Hildegard of Bingen. *Scivias,* 17. *Hildegard Selected Readings*. (Transl: M. Atherton.) Penguin Books, 2001, p. 20.

28. Hildegard of Bingen. Antiphon "O Splendidissima Gemma." *Symphonia*. (Transl: M. Atherton.) *Hildegard Selected Readings*. Penguin Books, 2001, p. 117. In identifying Mary with "bright matter", Hildegard draws on the similarity between the Latin words for "mother" and "matter."

29. Quoted in: Gabriele Uhlein. *Meditations with Hildegard of Bingen*. Bear & Co., 1983, p. 61. Source not provided. In speaking of the soul as breath she seemed to recall the earliest meanings of the Hebrew words *nephesh* and *ruach*.

30. *Sequences* were lengthy settings of scriptural texts used in the Mass. Many were in use at one time, but only four survive in the modern Roman liturgy.

31. Philip Schaff. *History of the Christian Church*. Charles Scribner's Sons, 1910, ch. 8, sect. 67.

32. Joachim argued that the three ages could also be associated with Peter, Paul and John.

33. Schaff, *History of the Christian Church*, ch. 8, sect. 67.

34. *Ibid.*

35. Attempt to strengthen the asceticism of the Franciscans—or at least to oppose efforts to make the order more lax—began even before the death of Francis of Assisi. Persecution of the Spirituals continued well into the 14th century.

36. Nikolai Berdyaev. *The Russian Idea*. (Transl: R. French.) Lindisfarne Press, 1947/1992, p. 66.

37. Meister Eckhart. Sermon 12: *Who Hears Me*. Bernard McGinn (ed.). Meister Eckhart: Teacher and Preacher. Paulist Press, 1986, pp. 267-271. The enumeration of the sermons varies from one edition to another.

38. Meister Eckhart. Sermon 5: *How All Creatures*. Matthew Fox (ed.). *Passion for Creation*. Inner Traditions, 1980/2000, p. 93.

39. Meister Eckhart. Sermon 10: *A God Who Rejoices*. Fox, *Passion for Creation*, p. 151.

40. John XXII. Bull: *In Agro Dominico*, prologue, 1329. (Transl: B.d McGinn, E. Colledge, & B. McGinn.)

41. *Ibid.*

42. Fox, *Passion for Creation*, pp. 2-3

43. Others date the beginning of the Renaissance at 1453, when Constantinople fell to the Ottoman Turks.

44. Michelangelo's totally nude David did raise some Florentine eyebrows at the turn of the 16th century. During the Renaissance it become common to depict Mary Magdalene with bare breasts; and in the 19th century William Etty and Marius Vasselon painted completely nude Magdalenes.

45. The female figure is thought to be the Sophia, or Divine Wisdom, who, according to *Proverbs* 8:22-30, was present at the creation. See the discussion by Susanne Schaup in: *Sophia*. Nicholas-Hays, 1997, p. 7.

46. Interestingly, both Dante and Petrarch idealized women: Dante the dead Beatrice, and Petrarch Laura. They two writers seem to have been influenced by the Troubadour tradition of an earlier century.

47. In some cases the quality of Latin had become so poor as to cast serious doubts on the efficacy of the sacraments.

48. For a discussion of some of the Academy's activities see: Désirée Hirst. *Hidden Riches: Traditional Symbolism from the Renaissance to Blake*. Eyre & Spottiswoode, 1964, pp. 15-43.

49. The *Donation* purported to give the pope temporal control of what had been the western Roman Empire.

50. Plato. *Timeus* 31C.

51. Stuart Isacoff. *Temperament*. Alfred Knopf, 2001.

52. Or in Dutch, "Gerrit Gerritzoons."

53. Desiderius Erasmus. *The Praise of Folly*, 1509. (Transl: J. Wilson.) Medieval Sourcebook.

54. See for example: Bernard of Clairvoix. *Sermons on the Blessed Virgin*.

55. Diarmaid MacCulloch. *The Reformation*. Peguin Books, 2003, p. 100

56. Quoted in *Ibid.*, p. 152.

57. See for example: Christopher Bamford. Introduction to *"Freemasonry" and Ritual Work*. Steinerbooks, 2007, p. xxxvi-xxxvii.

58. See for example: Leonora Leet. *The Secret Doctrine of the Kabbalah.*" Inner Traditions, 1999, pp. 5-8. "Qabalah" comes closest to transliterating the original Hebrew, but a variety of other forms is in common use, including: "Kabbalah," "Kabala," and even "Cabala."

59. For a general introduction to Qabalistic teachings see: Arthur E. Waite. *The Holy Kabbalah*. Citadel, (undated, c.1910); Dion Fortune. *The Mystical Qabalah*. Weiser, 1935/1998; Aryeh Kaplan. *Sefer Yetzirah: the Book of Creation*. Weiser, 1977.

60. Meister Eckhart, who also favored the theory of emanation, may have been influenced by Qabalistic teachings.

61. Hirst, *Hidden Riches: Traditional Symbolism from the Renaissance to Blake*, pp. 16-18.

62. D. P. Walker. *The Ancient Theology*. Cornell University Press, 1972; Jerome Friedman. *The Most Ancient Testimony: Sixteenth-Century Christian-Hebraica in the Age of Renaissance Nostalgia*. Ohio University Press, 1983.

63. Quoted in: C. J. M. Hopkins. *The Practical Kabbalah*. Godsfield Press, 2001, p. 10.

64. "Hermetic" has no inherent association with Christianity. Hermeticism influenced the Qabalah regardless of any influence on Christian esotericism.

65. John Nash. "Duality, Good and Evil, and the Approach to Harmony." *The Esoteric Quarterly*. Fall 2004, pp. 15-26.

66. Edmund Spenser. *The Faerie Queene*, Book VI, canto 10. London, 1596. We can also see parallels with the Bogomil doctrine of Jesus and his brother Satanael.

67. Diarmaid MacCullough. *The Reformation*. Penguin Books, 2003, p. 91. See also: John O'Malley. "Historical Thought and the Reform Crisis of the Early Sixteenth Century." *Theological Studies*, vol. 28, 1967, pp. 531-548.

68. Hirst, *Hidden Riches: Traditional Symbolism from the Renaissance to Blake*, pp. 110-111.

69. Ken Gewertz. *Mystical Encounters*. Harvard University Exhibit, 1996. Chrysostomus nay have drawn his inspiration from the 1557 work of another Franciscan who wrote under the pseudonym Archangelus of Burgonovo.

70. Ambrose Serle. *Essays Upon Some Remarkable Names and Titles of Jesus Christ*, 1799. Quoted in: Désirée Hirst. *Hidden Riches: Traditional Symbolism from the Renaissance to Blake*. Eyre & Spottiswoode, 1964, pp. 282-283. A trinity can be extracted from the tree of life in more than one way, all of them revealing important correspondences, but none completely satisfying in its symbolism. See: John Nash. "The Trinity and Its Symbolism." *Esoteric Quarterly*, Spring 2005, pp. 33-46.

71. For example, Franciscan friar Roger Bacon studied optics and even described a method for making gunpowder.

72. Bamford, Introduction to *"Freemasonry" and Ritual Work*, p. xxxv.

73. Individuals believed to have achieved the transmutation include: Raymond Lully (1233-1313), Nicholas Flamel (1330-1418), Basil Valentine (c. 1413), Alexander Seton (d. 1604), Eirenaeus Philalethes (b. 1612), Lascaris (c. 1700), Sehfeld (early 18th century), the Count of Sainte-Germain (1710-1784?), Jean Julien Fulcanelli (1877-1932), and R. A. Schwaller de Lubicz (1887-1961). Scientists who, while not themselves alchemists, reportedly observed successful transmutation include: Jakob Zwinger (16th century), Wolfgang Dienheim (late 16th century), Jean-Baptiste van Helmont (b. 1577) and Johann Friedrich Schweitzer (b. 1625). See for example: Kenneth R. Johnson. *The Fulcanelli Phenomenon*. Neville Spearman, 1980, p. 25; Jacques Sadoul. *Alchemists and Gold*. Neville Spearman, 1970, pp. 59-187.

74. Louis Pauwels & Jacques Bergier. *The Morning of the Magicians*. Avon, 1960, p. 118.

75. Jacques Sadoul. *Alchemists and Gold*. Neville Spearman, 1970, pp. 76-77.

76. Bamford, Introduction to *"Freemasonry" and Ritual Work*, pp. xxxvi-xxxvii.

77. Gabriel Naudé. *Apology for Great Men Suspected of Magic*, 1625. Quoted in: Frances Yates. *The Rosicrucian Enlightenment*. Routledge, 1972, p. 146.

78. In the city-states of northern Italy where craft guilds held sway, the "mechanical arts" were highly esteemed because of those societies' focus on labor. See for example: Frederick Hartt. *History of Italian Renaissance Art*. Prentice-Hall, 1987, p. 16.

79. Umberto Eco. *Art and Beauty in the Middle Ages*. Yale University Press, 1986, pp. 95-96.

80. See for example: Yates, *The Rosicrucian Enlightenment*, pp. 16ff.

81. See for example: Nicholas H. Clulee. *John Dee's Natural Philosophy: Between Science and Religion*. Routledge, 1988.

82. Some commentators see Platonic concepts in particle physics and elsewhere.

83. Schaff, *History of the Christian Church*, vol. VII, ch. 1, §1.

84. *Ibid.*

Chapter 15
The Reformation

The reform movements of the 14th and 15th centuries remained small or failed entirely in their efforts to change the institutional church. Perhaps the environment was not yet conducive to enduring change. But the need for reform remained as pressing as ever. The year 1500 had great symbolic significance, and its approach fostered the expectation that great changes were afoot. When 1500 passed without incident people looked to 1530, the 1,500th anniversary of the crucifixion and resurrection. Some thought that the end of the world was imminent, but a more widespread belief was that a great prophet would arise to bring a new message to humanity. Even the pope was nominated as a possible candidate. As the Reformation got underway, people pointed to one or other of the reformers. It was unclear who should wear the mantle, but anticipation of important new revelation lent weight to what all the reformers had to say.

The German Reformation

The Protestant Reformation officially started on Halloween 1517, a century after Jan Hus' death. On that day Martin Luther (1483-1546), an Augustinian monk and professor at the University of Wittenberg, Germany, nailed his Ninety-Five Theses to the door of the Castle Church in Wittenberg. He wanted to make a strong statement and provoke debate, but his action was less disrespectful of ecclesiastical property than might be supposed; the church door routinely served as a bulletin board for university faculty. Wittenberg was uniquely suited to play its pivotal role in the Reformation. The university, the first in Germany to be founded by a secular ruler, had been endowed 15 years earlier by the elector Frederick III of Saxony. Frederick was one of the seven electors of the Holy Roman Emperor, and political power gave him special prominence and freedom. Also, the city of Wittenberg was home to a printing firm that would publish many of Luther's early writings.

Martin Luther

Martin Luther grew up in a well-to-do peasant family in Saxony, the son of an authoritarian father. Pressed to better himself, he enrolled in law studies at the

University of Erfut. According to legend, when a bolt of lightning narrowly missed him on his way to class, Luther resolved to enter a monastery. In 1508 he was ordained into the priesthood and soon started teaching theology at Wittenberg. In the monastery he embarked on a program of intense prayer, fasting, and self-flagellation;[1] he also made several pilgrimages. But obsessed with his own sinfulness he was unable to find inner peace.[2] Soon he concluded that salvation could not be secured through "good works." Rather, it depended totally on divine grace and our faith in its efficacy. That principle came to be known as "justification through faith."

Like many others of his time, Luther was convinced that the church had lost its original integrity. He was particularly critical of the sale of indulgences. Indulgence sales had become a common method of capital fundraising, and in the early 16th century major funding was needed to construct St. Peter's basilica in Rome. Pope Leo X contracted with the Jakob Fugger Bank of Germany to administer the program in the Holy Roman Empire. The bank had already loaned money to Luther's own archbishop, Albrecht von Brandenburg, to buy his third bishopric. So the parties agreed that locally collected revenue would be split between Rome and the archbishop, allowing Albrecht to pay off his loan.

For Luther the final straw came when Fugger's indulgence salesman, a Dominican friar named Johann Tetzel, arrived at Wittenberg. Tetzel is reported to have sung a promotional jingle: "As soon as the money clinks in the casket, the soul springs free from the fires of purgatory!"[3] In his zeal to raise money, Tetzel seems to have exaggerated and distorted the church's teachings. Indulgences were supposed to reduce a soul's time in purgatory for sins already forgiven;[4] but Tetzel allegedly told people that they could forgive sin. An amusing story circulated that a thief asked Tetzel whether he could buy forgiveness for future sins as well as for past ones. Tetzel said yes, but it would cost him a thousand gold pieces. The thief paid the money, took the indulgence, and then stole back the money from Tetzel.[5]

Between 1617 and 1620 Luther preached and wrote a number of polemical works. At that time he had no ambition to found a new branch of Christianity; his goal was simply to rid the church of what he considered materialism and corruption. Luther was argumentative and temperamental. But he had enormous self-confidence, believing that he could reform the church single-handedly through his own powers of persuasion.

The Ninety-Five Theses, "for the purposes of eliciting truth" would probably have attracted little attention outside the university had Luther not sent a copy to Archbishop Albrecht, who in turn forwarded it to Rome. Upon learning of the incident, church authorities initially dismissed Luther as a "drunken heretic." Later, when they took him more seriously, they overreacted. The authorities summoned Luther to Rome to face charges of challenging the power of the papacy. Fortunately, the elector Frederick intervened to keep Luther safely in Germany; Rome had to act cautiously because Frederick was a candidate for emperor. But gaining secular protection only emboldened Luther. When served with a papal bull in 1520, demanding that he retract 41 "heretical" statements or face excommunication, Luther's response was to burn it, exclaiming: "I submit to no laws of interpreting the word of God." He accused the pope of being the Antichrist and urged the princes of Germany to depose him.[6]

Luther could snub Rome, but he could not disobey his own emperor. In 1521 Charles V convened the Diet of Worms and commanded Luther to attend, with a guarantee of safe passage. When asked by the papal delegate whether he would retract the teachings in his books, Luther reportedly replied:

> Unless I am convicted by Scripture and plain reason—I do not accept the authority of popes and councils, for they have contradicted each other—my conscience is captive to the Word of God. I cannot and will not recant anything, for to go against conscience is neither right nor safe . . . Here I stand. I can do no other. God help me. Amen.[7]

The diet, or imperial general assembly, voted to condemn Luther and revoked the safe passage. However Luther had already left and was spirited away to safety at Frederick's Wartburg Castle in Eisenach.[8] He stayed there for some time in disguise and under an assumed name. When he felt safe to do so, Luther returned to Wittenberg and, ironically, moved into the very building that previously housed the Augustinian priory. As the political situation became more stable, Luther traveled to many locations in Germany. By that time the new Christian denomination of "Lutheranism"—a term that he did not relish—had taken hold.

Martin Luther had tapped into anticlerical and anti-Roman sentiment to win popular support as well as the endorsement of secular rulers. Unfortunately, his ideas were twisted and found unexpected outlets. Upon returning to Wittenberg, he was appalled to discover that his followers had gutted the liturgy of the Mass, smashed sacred art, and outlawed music in the churches—actions that gave a preview of the Calvinist Protestantism that would emerge a generation later. Even more embarrassing for Luther, when German peasants rose in revolt in 1524, his teachings were turned into a manifesto for social revolution. Although he came from a peasant background, Luther supported the social structure as God-given. He quickly distanced himself from the revolt and sided with the nobility, a stance that earned his movement the label *magisterial Reformation*. The revolt was crushed within a year with great loss of life.

Luther's teachings stirred nationalistic sentiments, and his diatribes against the papacy evoked suspicions—still echoed in political circles today—that

Catholicism eroded national sovereignty. Many north-German princes took advantage of their autonomy within the empire to declare Lutheranism the official religion in their jurisdictions. Each prince became the head of a separate Lutheran church. No doubt the princes genuinely supported Luther's efforts to reform Christianity, but a favorable side-effect was that they could seize church property and the income it generated. Any semblance of church-state separation came to an end, and from then on the fusion of religious and secular authority became a conspicuous feature of European Protestantism.

Most southern princes remained loyal to Rome, with the result that a pattern of tensions, partly political and partly religious, developed between the two regions of Germany. The Catholic emperor Charles V would have preferred to suppress Lutheranism in the northern principalities. But he had limited power and was distracted by constant crises elsewhere in the Hapsburg possessions. Most importantly, he needed money from the northern princes to support his military campaigns. In due course north-south tensions would erupt into full-scale war.

Northern princes walked out of the Diet of Speyer in 1529 to protest a vote to enforce the prohibition on Lutheran teachings approved at Worms. They were called "Protestants," giving rise to the term that came to denote all western Christians opposed to the Roman church. The following year, in an attempt to bring harmony, the emperor convened the Diet of Augsburg and ordered both sides to submit statements of belief that might lead to compromise. Luther was unable to attend, but the distinguished scholar Philipp Melanchthon (1497-1560) presented the Lutheran case. He submitted a list of 28 "Articles of Faith and Doctrine," together with a preamble expressing the hope that members of the diet

> may come together, as far as this may be honorably done, and . . . the dissension, by God's help, may be done away and brought back to one true accordant religion; for as we all are under one Christ and do battle under Him, we ought to confess the one Christ, after the tenor of Your Imperial Majesty' edict.[9]

No compromise could be reached, and the mutual animosity continued. However the Articles, which became known as the *Augsburg Confession*, formed a basic statement of Lutheran values, still quoted today.

Luther died at his birthplace of Eisleben in 1546. His final words reportedly were: "Into your hands, I command my spirit. You have saved me, Father, you faithful God."

Luther's Teachings

Salvation, in Martin Luther's view, was *sola gratia* ("by grace alone"), *sola fide* ("by faith alone"), *sola scriptura* ("by scripture alone"), *solus Christus* ("in

Christ alone"), and *soli Deo gloria* ("to the glory of God alone"). The first two principles expressed Luther's doctrine of justification by faith: that salvation is an unmerited gift of God, dependent on faith alone; we shall return to that doctrine shortly. *Sola scriptura* asserted that all necessary revelation was contained in the Bible; it was a direct assault on Rome's claim that Christ invested his authority not in a book but in the church's *magisterium*.

Establishing a concept that would be expanded upon by John Calvin, Luther asserted that scripture was "self-authenticating," requiring no external authority to validate or interpret it. Interestingly, neither Rome nor Luther considered that nature offered a complementary source of revelation, as Meister Eckhart and even Thomas Aquinas had suggested. In any event, *sola scriptura* required that every Christian read the Bible. That had only recently become feasible as the result of three important developments. One was the mass-production of Bibles facilitated by Johann Gutenberg's invention of the printing press; previously only large churches and monasteries could afford one. A second was increasing literacy levels stimulated by the Renaissance.[10] A third was translation of the Bible into the vernacular. Luther defended the use of the vernacular on the grounds that the Holy Spirit had enabled the apostles to speak in multiple languages at Pentecost so that everyone heard the message in his or her own tongue.

Luther's translation of the Bible into German was one of his greatest accomplishments. The work began during his time at Wartburg and continued for the rest of his life. The first edition of his complete Bible appeared in 1534, and the last 12 years later. The Latin *Vulgate* had been translated into Middle High German and Low German as early as the 14th century, but distribution was suppressed in 1486 by Archbishop Berthold of Mainz.[11] Luther almost certainly had access to one or other of those earlier translations, but he also drew directly from the Hebrew and Greek Bibles. His own translation has become a classic, largely because of Luther's own stature; but it is not free from errors or questionable interpretations. Luther's New Testament included all the books of the traditional canon, though he placed *Hebrews*, *James*, *Jude* and *Revelation* in a separate section. He was particularly critical of *Revelation*, commenting: "I can in no way detect that the Holy Spirit produced it."[12] Dionysius of Alexandria and Eusebius of Caesarea would have agreed with him.

The doctrine of justification through faith became the lynchpin of Protestant teachings. It was inspired by Augustine's opinion that humanity was hopelessly mired in sin and, but for the grace of God, was destined to hell. Faith in God's infinite mercy was our only option. The doctrine was based on three passages from *Romans*:

For therein is the righteousness [Greek: *dikaiosune*] of God revealed from faith to faith: as it is written, the just shall live by faith,[13]

But to him that worketh not, but believeth on him that justifieth [*dikaioo*] the ungodly, his faith is counted for righteousness [*dikaiosune*].[14]

[B]eing justified [*dikaioo*] by faith, we have peace with God through our Lord Jesus Christ,[15]

The Greek word *dikaiosune* (δικαιοσυνη) can be translated as either "righteousness" or "justification;" *dikaioo* (δικαιοω) is the corresponding verb.[16] Thus "justification through faith" can also be read as "righteousness through faith." To bolster his case Luther followed a long and hallowed tradition of making subtle changes to scripture; in his German translation of the third passage he added the word "alone," so that it read: "[B]eing justified by faith *alone*, we have peace . . ." Luther toyed with the idea of predestination but would leave it to Calvin to develop the doctrine.

Justification through faith alone implied that good works had no value. To make that argument Luther had to ignore the passage in *James*: "[F]aith without works is dead."[17] He also had to define "good works." Many people assumed that there was no virtue in service or benevolence; the result was growing indifference to the plight of the needy. In Protestant countries that indifference only compounded the impact of suppression of religious orders which had been the principal social-service providers of the Middle Ages. However, in rejecting "good works," Luther may have been referring more directly to asceticism and popular religious practices like pilgrimages and the veneration of relics. Also he conceded that, although good works could not secure salvation, they were the "fruits of faith." In Luther's words: "We are to offer up ourselves for our neighbors' benefit and for the honor of God . . . distributing our works for the benefit of our neighbors."[18] That principle would be affirmed by the authoritative *Book of Concord* published after Luther's death. Some commentators have suggested that the difference between the Lutheran doctrine of justification through faith and the Catholic insistence on faith, hope and charity was largely a matter of semantics; Luther's "faith" already encompassed hope and might also encompass charity.[19]

Martin Luther did not disagree with the greater part of Catholic doctrine. Rather, he challenged the Church of Rome's manipulation of doctrine to boost its power. Along with the other Protestant reformers, he complained that Rome had repositioned itself from a preaching institution to a dispenser of sacraments—in the case of the Eucharist, the dispenser of Christ's body and blood. Luther claimed that it was part of a calculated strategy to make the church the essential intermediary between the faithful and God. His rejection of all but the two or three "dominical" sacraments: baptism, the Eucharist ("Lord's Supper"), and possibly confirmation was motivated more by the desire to break the church's power than by distaste for ritual.

Although he rejected the specific doctrine of transubstantiation, he accepted the real presence in the Eucharist through a "sacramental union" with Christ.[20] His eucharistic formula acknowledged the true presence of Christ "in, with, and under" the bread and wine. An advantage of the formula was that the real presence depended on the faith of the communicant rather than on the power, or morality, of the priest. The formula is sometimes termed *consubstantiation*, but modern Lutherans reject such specificity, preferring to leave the mechanism of the real presence open to individual interpretation.

Luther popularized a doctrine that had been proposed by John Wycliffe more than a century earlier: the "priesthood of all believers." It was based on a verse from *1 Peter*: "[Y]e are a chosen generation, a royal priesthood, an holy nation, a peculiar people."[21] The doctrine was important to the Protestant cause; if everybody was a "priest," people could talk directly to God and the established church was unnecessary. Moreover, the paucity of scriptural or patristic evidence led Luther to doubt that the sacrament of holy orders had been instituted by Christ. He distrusted priests and distrusted even more the mendicant religious orders, like the Franciscans and Dominicans.[22] Luther demonstrated his contempt for celibacy in 1525 by marrying the former nun Katharina von Bora who bore him six children.

Whatever his views about the sacraments and the clergy, Martin Luther had no reservations about the value of the musical liturgy:

> I truly desire that all Christians would love and regard as worthy the lovely gift of music, which is a precious, worthy, and costly treasure given to mankind by God. The riches of music are so excellent and so precious that words fail me whenever I attempt to discuss and describe them . . . . Next to the Word of God, the noble art of music is the greatest treasure in the world. It controls our thoughts, minds, hearts, and spirits.[23]

That was not an isolated expression of his love of music. As a young man Luther sang in the monastery choir, and he learned to play the lute and flute. He was convinced of music's central role in Christian worship. His hymn *Ein' feste Burg ist unser Gott* ("A Mighty Fortress is Our God") is still popular today.[24] Luther insisted that hymns be based on bold melodies and be written in the vernacular so that ordinary people could sing them. One of Luther's largest works, written in 1526, was the *Deutsche Messe* ("The German Mass and Order of Divine Service").[25] Lutheranism would inspire a rich heritage of sacred music, including the north German school of organ music that nurtured composers like Dietrich Buxtehude and Johann Sebastian Bach.

What seems surprising, in view of the direction taken later by Protestantism, was the extent of Luther's devotion to Mary of Nazareth. Not only did he preserve the notion that Mary was the mother of God, as defined by the Council of Ephesus, he even affirmed the doctrine of the immaculate conception: "It is a sweet and pious belief that the infusion of Mary's soul was effected without original sin; so that in the very infusion of her soul she was also purified from original sin and adorned with God's gifts, receiving a pure soul infused by God; thus from the first moment she began to live she was free from all sin."[26]

In the generations after Luther, the notion of scriptural inerrancy became the focus of much debate. Clearly, inerrancy was of major importance if scripture was to be the sole source of religious truth. The Old Testament presented special difficulties in that regard. The Hebrew alphabet contains no vowels; the diacritical marks now known as "vowel points" were medieval inventions.[27] Frequently, the meaning of a Hebrew word could be discerned only from its context. Not surprisingly, disagreements among scholars were common. In the Greek *Septuagint* and more recent translations of the Bible, including Luther's, decisions had been made regarding those words; but could they be relied upon? Did the Holy Spirit oversee the insertion of the vowel points as well as the original Hebrew text? Was the *Septuagint* inerrant as well as the Hebrew Bible, and if so what should be done about obvious inconsistencies between them?[28]

Religious Authority

In the Lutheran churches of northern Germany, and later in Scandinavia, we see considerable tension between Martin Luther's own views and the religious framework that evolved from his reformation. For example, Luther rejected tradition as a major source of church authority, insisting that scripture was the sole source of religious authority. But over time new traditions were established and new structures erected to legislate on matters of belief and religious practice. One section of the *Augsburg Confession* warned against abuses of ecclesiastical power: "There has been great controversy concerning the Power of Bishops, in which some have awkwardly confounded the power of the Church and the power of the sword. And from this confusion great wars and tumults have resulted."[29] Despite that warning and Luther's distrust of the ministry, the Lutheran churches retained an ordained clergy and, in some jurisdictions, even a hierarchical episcopacy. But little attention was paid to the apostolic succession that the Roman church considered so important.[30]

Even though most of the Catholic sacraments had been discarded, sacramental rituals were preserved on a formal or informal basis in Lutheranism. People continued to be married in church, and, even where divorce was permitted, the sanctity of marriage was not to be taken lightly.[31] In 17th- and 18th-century Protestant churches, penance became a matter between the penitent and the whole congregation; after suitable public humiliation sinners were forgiven by the congregation and readmitted to full life in the church.[32]

Luther had little confidence in the power of human reason to penetrate divine mysteries. When Erasmus argued that Luther's denial of human freewill was unreasonable, Luther rejected the relevance of reason.[33] Not surprisingly, Luther criticized the scholastic approach to theological development. But later generations of Lutheran scholars had much more confidence in it. They "produced as many complete works of dogmatics in a few years as the early and medieval church had produced over the course of centuries."[34] The late-16th and 17th centuries were for Protestantism what the 12th and 13th centuries had been for the Roman church. In 1577 a group of theologians began work on a consensus body of doctrine for the new Lutheran churches. Three years later *The Confessions of the Evangelical Lutheran Church* was published. It was signed by representatives of 86 Lutheran churches and 8,000 theologians, an incredible number attesting both to a strong emphasis on theological study and to the willingness to reach agreement. The *Confessions*, now referred to as the *Book of Concord*, remain an important reference.

The *Book of Concord* included a new statement of faith called "The Solid Declaration of the Formula of Concord." It expressed gratitude that Luther had explained and purified "the chief articles of our Christian religion (which under the Papacy had been horribly obscured by human teachings and ordinances)" and had corrected "the papistic errors, abuses, and idolatries."[35] One of the issues addressed was the controversy over good works; some theologians argued that good works were not only of no consequence, as Luther had claimed, but might even be injurious. The "Solid Declaration" offered a principle that would become a standard feature of Protestant teachings, that good works were the natural outcome of faith:

> [I]t is God's will, order, and command that believers should walk in good works; and that truly good works are . . . those which God Himself has prescribed and commanded in His Word; also, that truly good works are done, not from our own natural powers, but in this way: when the person by faith is reconciled with God and renewed by the Holy Ghost.[36]

The *Augsburg Confession* and *Book of Concord* provided religious norms, and Lutheranism was not slow to embrace traditional notions of orthodoxy and heresy. The *Confession* condemned Manichaeans, Valentinians, Arians, Eunomians, Samosatenes, Pelagians, Anabaptists, Donatists, "Mohammedans and all such" as heretics.[37] The inclusion of Anabaptists in the list is interesting because the sect was a product of the Reformation that Luther set in motion. However no centralized authority existed to enforce the newly defined norms. Lutheranism was divided into scores of separate churches, each with its own governing body. German churches typically were governed by synods, while in Scandinavia the older, episcopal style of governance had been preserved. Legislative and judicial responsibility was invested in the respective governing bodies, but routine disciplinary action was often delegated to local congregations. Excommunication of ministers or lay persons was the responsibility of congregations "acting in Christ's name." To quote a modern authoritative statement: "[Christ] desires that a sinner in a congregation be regarded as a heathen and a tax collector and that the dreadful judgment of excommunication be pronounced on him only after manifold private admonitions and the public admonition before and by the congregation have proved themselves fruitless."[38]

Even without strong centralized authority, uniformity of belief was encouraged and, to a large extent, achieved. But the *Augsburg Confession* affirmed tolerance of variations in religious observance: "[I]t is [not] necessary that human traditions, that is, rites or ceremonies, instituted by men, should be everywhere alike."[39] Within Lutheranism there has always been considerable diversity in religious practices. Some churches are more conservative in their liturgies than others. For example the Church of Sweden still preserves Roman styles of the Mass and Eucharist, and crucifixes are common in Swedish churches.

The *Augsburg Confession* codified another important aspect of Lutheran teachings: the doctrine of the "two kingdoms."[40] The doctrine asserted that God works through two agencies on earth: the church was concerned with religion and the state with civil matters. It became one of the underpinnings of the notion of separation of church and state. Ironically, church and state were intimately linked in the principalities of north Germany and in the Scandinavian countries where Lutheranism became state religions. The powerful Lutheran nations of Denmark and Sweden would play critical roles in the Thirty Years' War that pitted Protestant northern Europe against the Catholic Hapsburgs. In due course European emigrants would take Lutheranism to the United States, where it confronted constitutional church-state separation for the first time.

The Swiss Reformation

Ulrich Zwingli

Largely independent of, the events in Wittenberg, another reformation started in Zürich, Switzerland.[41] In 1519, a young priest, Ulrich Zwingli (1484-1531), was appointed to the Grossmünster Church in Zürich which had been founded by Charlemagne. By the time Zwingli learned of Luther's work, he was already planning his own reform movement. His personality was very different from Luther's; he was quiet and studious, a humanist scholar strongly influenced by Erasmus. Zwingli had served as a soldier in a Swiss mercenary army and was a good politician.

Zwingli argued for a return to the "apostolic church." Scripture would serve as the sole authority in Christianity, and anything that could not be traced to the Bible should be stripped away to leave a lean, mean Christianity. Scripture provided a clear and unambiguous standard for belief and morality, and it was to be read literally. When Zwingli started to preach those ideas from the pulpit, the bishop of Constance moved to silence him; but the city government of Zürich supported Zwingli and protected him from disciplinary action.

One of Zwingli's first targets was the Lenten fast. In 1522 a group of men ate a "ritual meal" of sausage.[42] In addition to being a gesture of defiance, it became a lasting symbol of the Swiss Reformation. Another target was the granting of indulgences, and a third was the Mass. In an interesting sign of the new convergence of church and state, in 1525 the Zürich city government banned celebration of the Mass, "much as a city council might today place parking restrictions on its streets."[43]

Zwingli argued that the Eucharist was not the central act of Christian worship, in which the elements were transformed into the body and blood of Christ, but was a purely symbolic and commemorative ritual. Luther was outraged by the suggestion. In 1529 Philip of Hesse invited Zwingli to meet with Luther at his Marburg Castle to try to work out their differences.[44] With an agenda of 15 items, the two men agreed on 14 but could reach no compromise on the Eucharist. Luther regarded Zwingli as a fanatic, out of touch with reality, while Zwingli regarded Luther as a crypto-Catholic. From then on the German and Swiss Reformations took separate paths. Zwingli's spiritual descendents coined the term "Reformed Church" to distinguish it from Lutheranism, which in their view did not carry the Reformation to its logical conclusion.

In contrast to Luther's lifelong commitment to music, Zwingli prohibited organ-playing and even congregational singing during worship services at his church in Zürich. He was a talented musician and author of several hymns, and he did not object to singing *per se*. But, like Augustine of Hippo before him, Zwingli felt that singing had usurped more important elements of collective worship, like preaching. Not until 1598, more than 60 years after Zwingli's death, was hymn-singing restored in Zürich's churches.

Just as Wittenberg provided fertile soil for Luther's Reformation, Switzerland provided a supportive environment for Zwingli's. Switzerland was formally part of the Holy Roman Empire, but the cantons of the Swiss Federation enjoyed substantial independence. Its arch enemies were the Hapsburgs; and the pope's recent support for them angered many Swiss people. Zwingli's teachings met with resistance in the conservative, rural cantons, and he died in a religious war two years after the Marburg meeting. However his teachings won favor in the major cities. Zürich, Bern and Basel had already become officially Reformed Protestant, and Geneva followed suit in 1535. Zwingli's ideas also began to spread further down the Rhine to Strasburg and other centers in Germany.

Radical Reformers

Luther was dismayed that his teachings triggered more extensive religious and social revolutions. The Peasant Revolt was one example, and Zwingli's movement was another. However, many people felt that the "logical conclusion" of the Reformation was a lot more radical than even Zwingli envisioned.

One of the offshoots of the Swiss reform movement was a sect with both religious and social reform ambitions known as *Anabaptists*, or "Rebaptizers." Drawn primarily from the lower strata of society, the Anabaptists insisted on adult baptism, contrasting with the tradition of infant baptism endorsed by Luther and Zwingli as well as by Catholicism. Anyone baptized as a child was rebaptized upon entry to the sect. The Anabaptists who emerged in Zürich in 1525[45] were led by Konrad Grebel, a former Zwingli disciple. Their principal manifesto was the *Schleitheim Confession* of 1527, attributed to one Michael Sattler. It urged the sect to distance itself from a sinful world: "We have been united concerning the separation that shall take place from the evil and the wickedness which the devil has planted in the world, simply in this: that we have no fellowship with them, and do not run with them in the confusion of their abominations."[46] The Anabaptists refused to participate in military service and refused to pay taxes. Some groups practiced the sharing of property and/or polygamy. But the polygamy did not necessarily translate into extreme male dominance. Women played important roles, some even making ecstatic declarations of intimacy with God.[47] Many Anabaptists were suspicious of the charismatic aspect of the movement.

Anabaptist teachings found many supporters throughout Europe. But in an odd turn of events that united Lutherans, Zwinglians and Catholics against a common enemy, the Anabaptists were almost universally hated and persecuted. Less than three months after the *Schleitheim Confession* was published, Catholic authorities executed Sattler in a particularly gruesome manner and drowned his wife. In 1534 Anabaptists seized control of the German city of Münster and turned it into a theocracy. Many of the existing inhabitants fled, including the bishop; but those who stayed were given the choice of conversion to the sect or death. Münster's second "king," Jan Beukels, had sixteen wives, one of whom he beheaded for insubordination.[48] A Catholic army overran the city in 1536 and slaughtered the sect's members.

The Anabaptists were not all extremist fanatics. The Tyrolean Anabaptist Jacob Hutter (d. 1536) formed communities which, inspired by the socialism of the first Christians,[49] practiced complete sharing of property. Known as the Hutterites, the sect flourished in Bohemia and Transylvania. Another sect, the Mennonites—named after the Dutch former-priest Menno Simons (c.1496-1561)—committed themselves to peace, simple living, and service to others. The Mennonites spread in popularity, particularly in the Netherlands. In 1693, a Swiss bishop named Jacob Amman broke from the Mennonite Church, and his followers called themselves the Amish. Some Anabaptists believed, as church fathers Origen and Gregory of Nyssa had, that hell was only a temporary state.[50]

Two other groups of radical reformers, the Radical Spiritualists and the Evangelical Rationalists, were drawn not from the lower classes but from a highly educated elite. The Radical Spiritualists rejected most or all external forms of religion. Silesian nobleman Kasper Schwenkfeld (c.1489-1561) held that the sacraments had been corrupted and recommended that baptism and the Eucharist be suspended until they could be restored to their original purity. Sebastian Franck (1499-1542), a former priest, went further to reject the idea of an external church entirely; he saw clergy, ceremonies and scripture as distractions from true spirituality. Franck spoke of an "invisible church" whose members were nurtured by the Inner Light, the indwelling Holy Spirit. Truth was to be sought, not in doctrine or even in the Bible, but through a personal contact with God. In Franck's and Schwenkfeld's teachings we can see the roots of the esoteric Christianity of Jakob Böhme (1575-1624) and 17th-century Rosicrucianism. Franck's invisible church can also be viewed as a glimpse of the Ekklesia.

Evangelical Rationalists sought to place reason alongside scripture as the primary sources of religious authority. But, instead of embracing the conclusions of scholasticism, they questioned a number of aspects of traditional Christological and trinitarian doctrine. A prominent Evangelical Rationalist was the Italian reformer Lelio Sozzini (1525-1562) who gave his name to *Socinianism*, an early form of antitrinitarianism or Unitarianism. Another was the Spanish scholar Michael Servetus (c.1510-1553). In 1531 Servetus wrote a controversial book, *De Trinitatis Erroribus* ("On the Errors of the Trinity"), for which he was burned at the stake in Geneva. The prosecuting attorney at his trial was John Calvin.

The various radical groups were persecuted throughout western and central Europe, but some found refuge in the religiously tolerant nations of eastern Europe. Anabaptists formed churches in Silesia and Poland. And antitrinitarians organized the Polish Brethren and Unitarian churches in Lithuania and

Transylvania. Modern Unitarianism traces its heritage back to these 16th-century origins. The Netherlands became a haven from persecution in the 17th century; and Mennonite and Amish groups found safety in William Penn's colony of Pennsylvania in the early 18th century.

John Calvin

John Calvin (1509-1564) was not a priest but a middle-class French lawyer and renowned scholar. His skill as a lawyer would be evident in the clarity with which he expressed his ideas. Like Zwingli, Calvin identified with humanist principles, and in 1536 he published a reformist text *Institutes of the Christian Religion*, which he dedicated to King Francis I.[51] The text addressed a wide range of religious, political and social issues. Man's primary responsibility was to God, not to ecclesiastical or hereditary secular authorities. But he disagreed with the Anabaptists' rejection of civil authority, insisting that, "in the sight of God," [it is] not only sacred and lawful, but the most sacred and by far the most honourable, of all stations in mortal life."[52] Calvin's political theory sought a balance between authority and democracy. He warned against tyranny and insisted that rulers were not above the law, but he accepted the contemporary belief that secular rulers derived their authority from God and had a responsibility to proclaim the gospel.

Calvin left no doubt about his contempt for the Church of Rome and was forced to leave France. In 1535 he traveled to Geneva; but the city was experiencing a period of political volatility, and he moved temporarily to Strasburg. During that time, with friends' help, he selected a wife who was "modest, obliging, not haughty, not extravagant, patient, and solicitous for my health."[53] Calvin and his followers were invited back to Geneva in 1541 to found a "new Jerusalem" of Protestant Christianity. He remained there for the rest of his life. Once established, Calvin set about constructing a new religious, political, economic and social order based on the *Institutes*.

The presbyterian style of ecclesiastical governance that Calvin created was a compromise between the hierarchy and democracy. Local congregations were overseen by *presbyteries* which, in turn, were responsible to synods that held legislative and judicial power. Positions on the presbyteries and synods were filled not by appointment, as in episcopal styles of governance, but by election by member congregations. Four categories of ministry were established: doctors, pastors, deacons and elders. Doctors were scholars charged with formulating doctrine, teaching, and training new ministers. Pastors were to preach, administer the sacraments, and provide pastoral care. Deacons oversaw institutional charity, serving the sick and the poor; and elders were to serve as religious police, regulating morals. A consistory council comprised of clergy and laypeople was formed to run the church, enforce moral discipline, and oversee secular government. Among other things the consistory would handle cases of immorality referred to it by the elders. Significantly, the Catholic and Lutheran term "priest" was not included among the four levels of clergy in the Reformed church.

Calvin may have promoted democratic ideals, but he established a theocratic society in Geneva, in which he was virtually a dictator. Calvin appointed himself the only "doctor" to serve in his church hierarchy. He forced the city council to ratify his Ecclesiastical Ordinances of the Church of Geneva. Ironically, Calvin, who shared Luther's belief in the irrelevance of "good works," imposed a strict puritan moral code on the people. Calvin would not tolerate opposition in matters of religion. When, in 1544, close associate Sebastian Castellio disagreed about the interpretation of two passages in scripture, he was banished. Castellio moved to Basel where, under the pseudonym Martinus Bellius, he wrote an influential book, *De Haereticis* ("Concerning Heretics"). It advocated tolerance: "Let us who are Christians not condemn one another, but, if we are wiser than they are, let us also be better and more merciful."[54] Castellio contrasted that viewpoint with what he considered Calvin's bigotry. Later he would strongly protest the execution of Servetus.

Bigotry or not, the absolute certainty and force of logic with which Calvin presented his beliefs and dealt with dissent was appealing to people who lived in an uncertain world. As always, the masses liked to be told what to believe and what to do. Calvin's vision of a new socio-religious order would meet with stiff resistance from the entrenched princely cast of Europe. But Switzerland, a confederation of self-governing cities and cantons, was the ideal environment for the new order to be developed and perfected. In the face of anti-Protestant repression in many parts of Europe people flocked to Geneva, and by the 1550s nearly one-half of the population was foreign-born. The visitors may initially have been moderate Lutherans, but by the time they left they had absorbed the strict Calvinist principles. Upon returning to their own countries, they spread those principles throughout much of Europe.

Despite his autocratic tendencies, Calvin was driven by a sense of mission rather than ego; and he insisted on being buried in an unmarked grave. Importantly, Calvin and his followers did not feel that they had said the last word regarding reform. They adopted the slogan *Ecclesia Reforma, semper reformanda*, "Reformed Church, *always* being reformed."[55]

Reform Doctrine

The Reformed Church in Switzerland produced two statements of doctrine known as the *Helvetic Confessions*. The *Second Confession* of 1562, consisting of 30 articles, became the official creed of the Swiss cantons and was also recognized in Scotland, Hungary, France, and Poland. It won a favorable reception in Holland and England and was subsequently acknowledged as an important, authoritative statement of Protestant theology. The *Second Confession* affirmed scripture as the sole norm of belief, and condemned the use of images in worship, law, gospel and faith. The doctrines of Providence, predestination, the church, ministry and the sacraments were discussed and a number of ancient and contemporary heresies condemned.

Of the seven traditional sacraments, John Calvin retained only baptism and the Eucharist, or "Lord's Supper," referring to the others as "pseudo-sacraments." And in his attacks on Catholicism he complained that the Mass was an "abomination" that "not only profanes, but annihilates the Lord's Supper."[56] Calvin supported Ulrich Zwingli's argument that the Eucharist was symbolic; but he disagreed with the position that it was nothing more than a commemoration of the Last Supper. For Calvin it symbolized something taking place in the present between the recipient and God. After Calvin's death, the influential scholar Isaac Casaubon (1559-1614) criticized the Catholic sacraments on the grounds that they were derived from pagan mystery rites.[57]

Calvin placed great emphasis on divine sovereignty: the notion that God's will could never be frustrated by human action. He asserted: "[T]he will of God is the supreme and primary cause of all things, because nothing happens without his order or permission."[58] But having come to that conclusion, Calvin wrestled, as Augustine of Hippo, Thomas Aquinas, and Martin Luther had done earlier, with the conflict between God's omniscience and human freewill. What possible freedom could human beings have to choose between righteousness and sin if God is omniscient and can foresee the future? Those questions led Calvin to his doctrine of predestination.

Augustine had stated: "Predestination is nothing else than the foreknowledge and foreordaining of those gracious gifts which make certain the salvation of all who are saved."[59] What he meant was debated both before and after the Reformation. At the time, Augustine was engaged in a polemical exchange with the English monk Pelagius. Whereas Pelagius argued that salvation was merited by good works, Augustine contended that good works could not possibly overcome the crushing burden of original sin. He seemed to imply that all souls deserved hell but that God, in his infinite goodness, had chosen a few, the "elect," for salvation. Ironically, in their appeal to Augustine, both Luther and Calvin unintentionally distanced themselves from the notion of the "apostolic church." Augustine was not even born at the time of Constantine's conversion to Christianity, the last of the various dates given for the demise of the apostolic church. Be that as it may, Calvin boldly affirmed belief in divine election and "limited atonement":

God by His eternal goodwill . . . appointed those whom He pleased unto salvation, rejecting all the rest; and . . . those whom He blessed with this free adoption to be His sons He illumines by His Holy Spirit, that they may receive the life which is offered to them in Christ; while others, continuing of their own will in unbelief, are left destitute of the light of faith, in total darkness.[60]

Calvinist doctrine is often summarized by five principles (made famous by the mnemonic TULIP): the Total depravity of humanity, Unconditional election, Limited atonement, Irresistible grace, and the Perseverance of the saints. The first affirmed the belief that, unaided, the whole of humanity deserved hell. The second and third go together; the elect are saved regardless of any action on their part, and Christ's atonement only applied to them. The last two also go together; the elect who have been chosen by God for salvation cannot resist divine grace, and therefore they will keep the faith through all difficulties. If someone sinned, that would prove that he or she never belonged to the elect. Calvin was understandably reluctant to be too explicit about what fraction of humanity was predestined for salvation; but his estimates varied from about one in five to as few as one in 100.[61]

Calvin's position that, through God's mercy, certain souls are saved from the first moment of their existence is referred to as "single predestination." Théodore de Bèze (1519-1605), Calvin's immediate successor in Geneva, acknowledged the almost inescapable corollary that other souls are *condemned* from the first moment of their existence. The latter position is referred to as "double predestination." Bèze explained it in terms of divine justice; the damned went to hell not only because of original sin but also because of actual sins committed as the inevitable consequence of their predestination. They were not condemned *despite* any good works they might perform; they were simply *incapable* of good works; freewill had been lost with the fall of Adam. Perhaps those unfortunate souls could be compared with the *choics*, or "mud people," whom the Gnostic Valentinus wrote off as having no expectation of enlightenment.

A former student of Bèze's, the Dutch theologian Jacob Arminius (1560-1609) urged a more moderate form of predestination in which freewill played a role; but mainstream Calvinists dismissed him as a heretic.[62] Later Protestant reformers rejected the doctrine of predestination altogether, notably John Wesley, the founder of Methodism. Wesley insisted that Christ's atonement was *unlimited*: it applied not just to a favored elect but to everybody. However belief in predestination surfaced in the Jansenist movement in Catholicism.[63]

The Swiss reformers placed more emphasis than the Roman church had on the Judaic origins of Christianity.[64] That emphasis was particularly evident in "covenant theology," first developed by Heinrich Bullinger (1504-1575), Zwingli's successor in Zürich. Bullinger spoke of the covenant between God and humanity through which Christ's redemption has played out through history. Calvin related the covenant firmly to its counterpart in the Old Testament:

> The covenant which God always made with his servants was this, "I will walk among you, and will be your God, and ye shall be my people," (*Lev.* 26:12.) These words, even as the prophets are wont to expound them, comprehend life and salvation, and the whole sum of blessedness. For David repeatedly declares, and with good reason, "Happy is that people whose God is the Lord." "Blessed is the nation whose God is the Lord; and the people whom he has chosen for his own inheritance," (*Psalm* 144:15; 33:12;).[65]

While the Hebrew covenant was restricted to the descendents of Abraham, the new covenant was open to all "whom [God] has chosen."[66] Covenant theology was developed further by successive generations of Reform scholars.

In its fully developed form, covenant theology envisioned three interrelated covenants. The fall of Adam broke the first covenant, and in consequence good works no longer had merit. Christ entered into a second covenant with the Father to serve as the mediator for humanity that was lost in sin. Through his death on the cross Christ instituted a third covenant of grace by which the elect could be saved. Calvinist covenant theology influenced the 19th-century dispensationalist movement of John Nelson Darby.[67] Covenant theology restored a moral imperative which had been placed in doubt by *sola fide*. Just as the covenant with Abraham had imposed responsibilities on the people of Israel, the new covenant imposed moral responsibility on the Christian elect.

Spread of Calvinism

Calvinism spread to Germany, displacing Lutheran allegiance in a number of principalities. It was able to portray itself as the new, dynamic form of Protestantism, compared with the more conservative Lutheranism. In 1559 Frederick III, a staunch Calvinist, became elector of the important state of the Rhine Palatinate.[68] In the 17th century the Palatinate would become the target of devastating attack by Catholic forces in the 30 Years' War. Separately, elector, John Sigismund (1572-1620) of Brandenburg—much of whose population was Lutheran—converted to Calvinism.[69] Brandenburg and Prussia, which he united in 1618, offered considerable religious tolerance. The University of Halle, founded in 1694, would become not only an intellectual center of Reformation thought but, in due course, an important center of the German Enlightenment.

Calvinism infiltrated France, despite anti-Protestant laws. The French Calvinists, or Huguenots, faced ongoing persecution and eventually, for those who did not flee for their lives, genocide. Calvinism gained a strong foothold in Scotland, under the Presbyterian label, and also in the Netherlands where a Protestant rebellion against Spanish control was supported both by the Palatinate and by Elizabethan England. The Dutch Reformed Church was one of the bastions of Calvinism in northern Europe. In turn, colonial activity brought Dutch Calvinism to North America, particularly to the city of New Amsterdam, later renamed New York. It also spread to South Africa; the Afrikaans were the descendents of Dutch Calvinist settlers.

John Calvin cannot be considered the father of Evangelical Christianity, which will be discussed in Chapter 17. Calvinism was theologically based, whereas Evangelicalism was experiential. However Calvinist principles would have a major influence on Baptists and Congregationists, particularly in the United States. In that sense the spread of Calvinism was even greater than the already broad reach of the churches that formally traced their origins back to Calvin.

Reformation in England and Scotland

The English church was founded in 597 CE by Augustine of Canterbury,[70] displacing the Celtic church that, even then, had a long tradition in the British Isles. Canterbury became preeminent among the English bishoprics. When King Henry VIII (1491-1547) first heard about Martin Luther in 1521 he wrote the *Defence of the Seven Sacraments* and dedicated it to Pope Leo X. In gratitude Leo gave Henry the appellation *Fidei Defensor*, "Defender of the Faith." To Rome's dismay, Henry soon set in motion the events that led to the English Reformation.

Times of Uncertainty

By 1526 Henry's wife, Catherine of Aragon, youngest daughter of Ferdinand and Isabella of Spain, had become pregnant seven times but had only born one surviving child: the future Queen Mary I. With no male heir, Henry sent an envoy to Rome to petition for annulment of his marriage on rather flimsy grounds. But at that time Pope Clement VII was virtually a prisoner of the emperor Charles V, Catherine's nephew. Legal wrangling dragged on for three years. Angered by the delays, in 1533 Henry contracted a marriage with Ann Boleyn, sister of a former mistress. The newly appointed archbishop of Canterbury, Thomas Cranmer (1489-1556), who presided over the wedding, declared Henry's previous marriage to Catherine void and validated the new marriage to Ann. Lord Chancellor Thomas Moore refused to recognize it and was beheaded for treason.[71]

Pope Clement excommunicated Henry, whereupon the English parliament passed the Act of Supremacy in 1534, declaring that the king was "Supreme Head in Earth of the Church of England." In itself the claim to be head of a national church was not particularly radical. The kings of France and Spain made similar claims having bargained for a large degree of autonomy in exchange for helping defeat the 15th-century conciliar movement; but they still viewed themselves as being in communion with Rome. Henry did not.

Historians continue to debate the extent to which Henry's reformation built on existing anti-Roman sentiment. Certainly many people resented church corruption, the power of ecclesiastical courts, and the despotic cardinal Thomas Wolsey; the king curried popular favor by disbanding the courts and dismissing Wolsey. However Henry's divorce was widely regarded as a matter of royal prerogative and the break with Rome as political; few people in England felt strongly about either. Henry left the doctrine and observances of the English church largely unchanged, resisting pressure for further reforms from the Lutheran faction that grew up around Cranmer and Ann Boleyn. His *Six Articles* of 1539 reaffirmed belief in transubstantiation, communion under one kind, clerical celibacy, and the sacrament of penance. Viewed from Rome, the Church of England was in schism rather than heresy. But, like his German Protestant counterparts, Henry seized church property and dissolved the monasteries in England, Wales and much of Ireland.[72]

Ann Boleyn was eventually beheaded on trumped-up charges, and Henry went on to marry four more times. One of his later wives was also beheaded. Henry's six wives bore him three surviving children: a son and two daughters. Before the king's death in 1547 parliament ruled that the son by his third wife, Jane Seymour, was the heir apparent.

Edward VI (1537-1553) succeeded to the throne in 1547 when he was nine years old. He was a sickly boy and died before his 16th birthday. During his brief reign the country was ruled by powerful anti-Catholic regents; and with their encouragement Archbishop Cranmer took the first steps to bring the English church into line with European Protestantism. The *Six Articles* were repealed, and a new prayer book was issued. The 1548 *Book of Common Prayer* established a comprehensive liturgy for the Mass and sacraments that preserved more of the old rituals than did Lutheran and Calvinist liturgies. But it was in English, not Latin, and that change provoked outrage among Catholic traditionalists. Rebellion broke out in Cornwall, and, joined by sympathizers from neighboring counties, an informal army of Catholics besieged the city of Exeter. The rebellion was crushed the following year, and a royal decree mandated use of the new Prayer Book throughout the kingdom.[73] Among much else the Prayer Book offered the

Lord's Supper to any man who "openly declared hymselfe to have truly repented, and amended his former naughtie life."[74]

During Edward's reign a number of leading Protestants came to England, including the German Martin Bucer (1491-1551), the Italian Peter Martyr Vermigli (1499-1562), and the Polish Jan Łaski (1456-1531). With the presence of such notables, England might have become the leading Protestant country in Europe; but the reformist agenda was frustrated by the king's untimely death.

Edward was succeeded in 1553 by Mary I (1516-1558), Henry's daughter by Catherine of Aragon and husband of the much-younger King Philip II of Spain. Mary Tudor became England's first female monarch. A staunch Catholic, she called upon the capable Cardinal Reginald Pole (1500-1558), who had spent several years in Rome, to restore England's relationship with the papacy. She also sought to eliminate the major manifestations of Protestantism. In that endeavor she was uncompromising. Archbishop Cranmer went to the stake in 1556; and 300 others were executed during her short reign, earning, earning her the title "Bloody Mary." Mary did not produce an heir; and when she died in 1558 the throne passed to her half-sister Elizabeth, Henry VIII's daughter by Ann Boleyn.

Protestant Stability

Elizabeth I (1533-1603) was a Protestant, and upon her succession she set out to repeal the pro-Catholic reforms initiated by her predecessor. Within a period of eleven years, England had swung from independent Catholic to Protestant, to Roman Catholic, and back to Protestant. In 1559 parliament passed a new Act of Supremacy recognizing the queen as the church's "supreme governor." Four years later the Convocation of Canterbury adopted the *Thirty-Nine Articles* which became the principal confession of the Church of England.[75] The *Articles*, which acknowledged the authority of the Apostles, Nicene and Athanasian Creeds, affirmed belief in the sufficiency of scripture, justification by faith, and the sacraments of baptism and the Lord's Supper. They approved of good works, "the fruit of faith," though good works done before justification were "not pleasant to God." Ironically, the *Articles* also affirmed the Calvinist notion of predestination:

> Predestination to Life is the everlasting purpose of God, whereby (before the foundations of the world were laid) he hath constantly decreed by his counsel secret to us, to deliver from curse and damnation those whom he hath chosen in Christ out of mankind, and to bring them by Christ to everlasting salvation, as vessels made to honour . . . [On the other hand,] curious and carnal persons, lacking the Spirit of Christ, [should] have continually before their eyes the sentence of God's Predestination . . . a most dangerous downfall, whereby the Devil doth thrust them either into

desperation, or into wretchlessness of most unclean living, no less perilous than desperation.[76]

Elizabeth was committed to Protestantism, but she also wanted to heal the religious wounds of the previous two reigns. In what came to be known as the "Elizabethan Settlement," the queen sought to accommodate a variety of traditions into the Church of England. In that effort she was supported by clergyman Richard Hooker who argued for a *via media*, or middle way, between Catholicism and neo-Calvinist Puritanism. The consequences are still apparent today.

The Church of England was now firmly entrenched; and except for one brief period it would remain the state religion until the present.[77] Pope Pius V excommunicated Elizabeth in 1570, describing her as "a heretic and an abettor of heretics" and "a slave of wickedness."[78] He refused to recognize her accession and urged the English people to rise up in rebellion. When that did not happen, the pope authorized King Philip II of Spain—the husband of Elizabeth's predecessor, Mary I—to lead a crusade to restore Catholicism in England. The failure of the crusade will be described in the next chapter.

Upon Elizabeth's death in 1603 James I ascended the throne, uniting England with Scotland of which he was already king. James was a learned man with a liking for literature, poetry and the theater. He was also interested in religion, and in 1611 he commissioned the English translation of the Bible which bears his name.[79] James was generally tolerant of religious diversity, except for Catholics and Unitarians. He also became interested in a variety of esoteric topics; his reign provided a supportive environment for metaphysical poet John Donne and Paracelsian physician Robert Fludd. James lent moral support to the Cambridge Platonists, a group of academic theologians at Cambridge University who combined a commitment to Platonic and Neoplatonic philosophy with openness to Renaissance esoterica.[80]

James had a difficult time managing the conflicting Protestant factions, and he distrusted Puritans because of their increasing political power. He became enamored of the doctrine of the divine right of kings: the notion that kings are anointed by God and are responsible to him rather than to their subjects. Not surprisingly, the crown's relationship with the staunchly Puritan parliament steadily worsened. It deteriorated still further under his successor, Charles I (1625-1649), resulting in civil war, Charles' execution, and overthrow of the monarchy. For eleven years England was ruled as a commonwealth under the "Lord Protector" Oliver Cromwell (1599-1658). The Church of England was dismantled, a Presbyterian style of Christianity was established, and Puritan ideals took root. In a wave of iconoclasm, sacred art was destroyed; stained-glass windows were smashed, statues defaced, and organ pipes were torn from churches.

The monarchy was restored in 1660 under Charles II (1630-1685).[81] Two years later the Church of England was re-established as the state religion. A thread of continuity with the past had been maintained by a group of Anglican churchmen known as the "Caroline Divines," named for the two King Charleses.[82] Inspired by Richard Hooker's *via media*, they tried to stem the tide of Puritanism and preserve some of the doctrines and practices of earlier times. Modern Anglicanism has not always supported their belief in the real presence in the Eucharist, and it rejects the sacrament of penance. But it has preserved the traditional threefold structure of holy orders: bishops, priests and deacons. Although the episcopacy ceased to exist during the commonwealth, the Church of England claims the unbroken apostolic succession of its bishops via Augustine of Canterbury.[83]

Reformation in Scotland

By the time of the Reformation, Scotland had essentially forgotten its earlier tradition of Celtic Christianity. Scotland was a sovereign nation, but through intermarriage its royal family had strong ties to France; and the country was overwhelmingly Catholic. However, in the early 16th century, Protestant ideas began to filter in despite the best efforts of the crown and the church to stop them.

The Protestant Reformation in Scotland was closely linked to the career of John Knox (c.1513-1572). Born in Scotland, he was ordained a priest, studied Augustine of Hippo, converted to Protestantism, and taught at St. Andrew's University. Not long thereafter he was arrested by the authorities and spent 18 months as a French galley slave. Upon his release Knox served as a chaplain in the Church of England during the reign of King Edward VI. In 1554 he paid the first of several visits to Geneva and came into close contact with John Calvin. Knox returned to Scotland in 1559 and, emboldened by the rise of reformist sentiment, he began preaching the Protestant cause. The following year, parliament established Calvinist Presbyterianism as the national Church—or Kirk—of Scotland. Knox was appointed minister of St. Giles Cathedral in Edinburgh. He was of a fiery disposition, and both his preaching and his writing were vibrant, coarse and often ill-tempered. Nevertheless, Knox's *History of the Reformation* is considered a classic.

Clashes were inevitable between John Knox and Queen Mary I of Scotland (1542-1587).[84] The Catholic "Mary Stewart" and Knox met several times and had heated debates; neither managed to convert the other, but Mary is reported to have said: "I fear the prayers of John Knox more than all the assembled armies of Europe." Under pressure from both Protestants and the English, Mary was forced to flee the country, only to be imprisoned for 20 years and eventually executed by the English Queen Elizabeth I. While the English Reformation had been orchestrated by the crown, the Scottish Reformation was accompanied by the overthrow of a reigning monarch—an event of no small concern to other European secular rulers.

Scottish Presbyterians rejected an episcopal style of governance in favor of regional presbyteries headed by "superintendents;" but the term "bishop" was sometimes used for an ordained minister supervising a trainee.[85] Most Presbyterian ministers were poor, lacking the endowments, or "livings," that supported their English counterparts. Enlightenment writer Voltaire offered an unflattering description: "[A] Scotch Presbyterian . . . affects a serious gait, puts on a sour look, wears a vastly broad-brimmed hat, and a long cloak over a very short coat; preaches through the nose, and gives the name of the whore of Babylon to all churches where the ministers are so fortunate as to enjoy an annual revenue of five or six thousand pounds."[86]

The Church of Scotland, which John Knox helped found, accepted none of the compromises with Catholicism crafted by Henry VIII and Elizabeth I in England. When the Scottish parliament approved a *Confession of Faith* in 1560, Mary I refused to sign it. But after she was deposed, it became law in 1567 and served as the doctrinal basis of the Church of Scotland for 80 years. By that time the English Civil War was in progress, and Calvinist parliamentarians and Scottish Presbyterians prepared a joint statement of belief known as the *Westminster Confession of Faith*. The *Westminster Confession* remains a comprehensive standard of Presbyterian beliefs adhered to, at least in part, to the present.

The *Westminster Confession* was ambiguous enough to accommodate some degree of doctrinal pluralism. It affirmed the basic principle of justification through faith but also affirmed the importance of love: "Faith, thus receiving and resting on Christ and His righteousness, is the alone instrument of justification; yet is it not alone in the person justified, but is ever accompanied with all other saving graces, and is no dead faith, but works by love."[87] The *Confession* presented both the Calvinist doctrine of double predestination and an assertion that man's primordial freewill was restored by conversion:

> All those whom God hath predestinated unto life, and those only, He is pleased, in His appointed time, effectually to call, by His Word and Spirit, out of that state of sin and death, in which they are by nature . . . [88]
>
> Man, in his state of innocency, had freedom, and power to will and to do that which was good and well pleasing to God; but yet, mutably, so that he might fall from it. Man, by his fall into a state of sin, has wholly lost all ability of will to any spiritual good accompanying salvation . . . [However, when] God converts a sinner . . . He frees him from his natural bondage under sin; and, by His grace alone, enables him freely to will and to do

that which is spiritually good; yet so, as that by reason of his remaining corruption, he does not perfectly, or only, will that which is good, but does also will that which is evil.[89]

Scottish Presbyterians were among the first to reintroduce "good works" into Protestant religion. Also, in a move that would have made Ulrich Zwingli turn in his grave, fasting became a common practice.[90] Elsewhere it might have been viewed as an ascetic discipline aimed at spiritual growth, but in pessimistic Scotland fasting attempted to propitiate an angry God who could unleash natural disasters on sinful humanity. Echoes of turbulent 14th-century Europe were clear.

Preaching has always been the central focus of worship services, and many Scottish churches placed the pulpit in the center of the chancel, where the high altar had once been. While the Church of Scotland still has no prescribed prayer book, it does have a hymn book; and guidelines for worship were provided both in the *Book of Common Order*[91] and in a later *Directory for the Publick Worship of God* endorsed by the Scottish parliament. The latter took aim at the Catholic tradition of genuflecting when entering a church: "When the congregation is to meet for publick worship . . . Let all enter the assembly, not irreverently, but in a grave and seemly manner, taking their seats or places without adoration, or bowing themselves towards one place or other."[92]

Two sacraments were recognized: baptism and the Lord's Supper. The *Westminster Confession* condemned the "popish mass" as an "abomination." It rejected the Catholic doctrine of transubstantiation but affirmed the real presence as the product of faith:

> Worthy receivers [of] this sacrament, do then . . . inwardly by faith . . . spiritually, receive and feed upon, Christ crucified, and all benefits of His death: the body and blood of Christ being then, not corporally or carnally, in, with, or under the bread and wine; yet, as really, but spiritually, present to the faith of believers in that ordinance, as the elements themselves are to their outward senses.[93]

That interpretation would not have been endorsed by the Fourth Lateran Council; but it might well have been acceptable to Berengar of Tours and other opponents of Radbertus' ninth-century eucharistic formula. Importantly, there was no suggestion that the Eucharist should be regarded simply as a commemorative ritual, as Zwingli had proposed.

The Church of Scotland is not established and accordingly is free from state control; but it is recognized by law as the "national church." Not all Scottish Presbyterians chose to affiliate with the national church, and at least four other Presbyterian denominations currently operate in Scotland. Scottish emigrants took Presbyterianism to North America and elsewhere and established additional independent denominations.

The Catholic Response

Counter-Reformation

The Church of Rome's initial response to the Reformation was to ignore it. But when it became clear that the Reformation could not be stopped, the church began serious soul-searching, seeking to identify and rectify the problems that had provoked the rift. The process was initiated by the Dutch Pope Adrian VI (r.1522-1523) who ascended to the throne of Peter after a long series of disappointing pontificates. But in his short 13-month reign, Adrian could do little; and his immediate successor, the Medici pope Clement VII, was too involved in Italian and church politics to be an effective reformer. The main work was begun by Paul III (r.1534-1549). Although Paul did not always give papal responsibilities priority over his personal interests, he is still regarded by Catholics and many Protestants as a man of courage.

For some time there was hope that the Protestant-Catholic rift could be healed. Influential people on both sides were interested in rapprochement, among them Philipp Melanchthon and Martin Bucer in the Protestant camp and Cardinals Reginald Pole and Gasparo Constarini on the Catholic side.[94] Unfortunately, their voices were not heard above the din of mutual belligerence. Instead of reaching out in a spirit of compromise, Rome sought to shore up traditional doctrine and practices and launched an aggressive campaign to reconvert Protestant Europe to Catholicism. Thus began the Counter-Reformation, or "Catholic Reformation."

The mood of the Counter-Reformation was grim, contrasting sharply with the exuberance and optimism of the Renaissance. As successive popes imposed new austerity on their courts, support for the arts declined, hastening the end of the Italian Renaissance. In 1586, in an effort to improve standards of popular morality Pope Sixtus V tried to reintroduce the death penalty for adultery. On a more positive note, steps were also taken to promote spiritual renewal. New emphasis was placed on popular devotion and piety; devotions such as the rosary and meditation on the Blessed Sacrament were encouraged. A new breviary and missal were published; and new religious orders were founded.

Significantly, official translations of the Bible into vernacular languages were published in an attempt to compete with those made by the reformers. A German translation drew heavily on Luther's, provoking Luther to complain: "The Papists steal my German of which they knew little before, and they do not thank me for it, but rather use it against me."[95] However, until the late 18th century, Italian translations were banned in the Papal States where Protestant influence could more easily be contained.[96]

In one sense both the Reformation and the Counter-Reformation were responses to the problems that had existed before and during the Renaissance period. But the Counter-Reformation can also be seen as a continuation of the reformist zeal of Catholic Spain, following expulsion of the Moors and unification under Ferdinand and Isabella. It was no accident that the Jesuit Order, founded by Ignatius Loyola who came from northern Spain, would play a major role in the Counter-Reformation.

Council of Trent

Paul III's most important act was to convene the Council of Trent. "Trent" is the English form of Trento, a city in Italy, north of Venice. The council began its deliberations in 1545 and continued through three sessions over a period of 18 years, spanning the reigns of four popes. There were several reasons why it took so long, including poor attendance by bishops from outside Italy, threats of invasion by the Holy Roman Emperor, and hostility to the council's very existence by Pope Paul IV.[97] The council's stated mission sounded like a work of Protestant reformers:

> [T]o restore at length to its native purity and splendour, the doctrine of the Catholic faith, which is in many places defiled and obscured by the conflicting opinions of many who differ from each other; to bring back, to a better method of life, manners, which have divaricated from ancient usage; and to turn the heart of the fathers unto the children, and the heart of the children unto the fathers.[98]

With few exceptions, however, the council adopted the unyielding, confrontational posture that would determine Catholic attitudes for the next 400 years. No attempt was made to undo or even water down the doctrinal developments of the Middle Ages. The council reaffirmed almost all the doctrines that had been rejected by the reformers, including transubstantiation, the seven sacraments, and salvation's dependence on good works. Ironically, the uncompromising restatement of traditional doctrines convinced many borderline Catholics to convert to Protestantism.

A series of decrees refuted, one by one, the doctrinal positions of the reformers. For example, in answer to the basic Protestant claim that the Bible was self-interpreting; the council insisted that only the church could properly interpret scripture:

> [I]n order to restrain petulant spirits, [the Council] decrees, that no one, relying on his own skill, shall . . . wresting the sacred Scripture to his own senses, presume to interpret the said sacred Scripture contrary to

that sense which holy mother Church—whose it is to judge of the true sense and interpretation of the holy Scriptures—hath held and doth hold . . . Contraveners shall be . . . punished with the penalties by law established.[99]

The restraint of "petulant spirits" was to be enforced by requiring the *nihil obstat* and *imprimatur* on all publications containing biblical commentaries.[100] Unfortunately, from the council's standpoint, Protestant authors and publishers lay outside its jurisdiction.

Petulant spirits were also identified in the very celebration of the Mass. The Council of Trent ordered bishops to "banish from churches all those kinds of music, in which, whether by the organ, or in the singing, there is mixed up any thing lascivious or impure; as also all secular actions; vain and therefore profane conversations, all walking about, noise, and clamour, that so the house of God may be seen to be, and may be called, truly a house of prayer."[101] Liturgical music was to be simplified and must avoid the incorporation of secular melodies, a practice that had been popular among composers in the 16th century. An Italian composer whose music not only met the new requirements but set lasting standards of excellence was Giovanni Pierluigi da Palestrina (c.1525-1594). The liturgy was further strengthened by mandate of the Tridentine Mass as the standard Latin format for use throughout the Catholic Church. It remained the standard until the 1960s.

The council sought to tighten internal church discipline and improve pastoral care of the laity. It decreed that all ecclesiastical appointments be made from Rome, ending the tradition of political appointment by secular rulers; bishops were expected to live and work in their jurisdictions, ending tenure of multiple bishoprics and widespread absenteeism. Bishops were given greater power to supervise the religious life of their dioceses but also were to be held responsible for the support of local clergy.

The Council of Trent settled on a format for religious teaching that would become standard for the next 400 years: the catechism. Catechisms in the form of prepared teaching materials had been used by Cyril of Jerusalem in the fourth century.[102] And Martin Luther had developed a catechism in the familiar question-and-answer format in 1530. The advantage of the catechetical format was obvious: an authorized catechism provided the script for teacher-student dialog; even the dullest teacher could ask the right questions, and little children could learn the right answers by rote. Uniformity and orthodoxy of doctrinal teaching could be ensured throughout the church. The first Catholic catechism appeared in 1556.

An interesting outcome of the Council of Trent was the reinstatement of scholasticism as the official approach to doctrinal development. Although the new emphasis on ethical living and piety was entirely in line with Erasmus' teachings, humanism was tainted by his contempt for Rome; that crowning intellectual glory of the Renaissance had also become too closely identified with the Reformation. During the council sessions three books lay on the altar: the Bible, the collected papal pronouncements, and the *Summa Theologiae* of Thomas Aquinas. Pope Pius V (r.1566-1572), who belonged to the Order of Preachers, strongly encouraged the study of his fellow Dominican's work. Soon after the council ended, Pius declared Aquinas, dead for nearly 300 years, to be a Doctor of the Universal Church. An unfortunate consequence of the scholastic revival was that the church was ill-equipped to participate in the great advances in philosophy that would occur in the 17th and 18th centuries.[103]

In parallel with the proceedings of the Council of Trent, two important steps to combat heresy were taken by papal decree. In 1542 Pope Paul III established the Roman Inquisition—the Supreme Sacred Congregation of the Roman and Universal Inquisition—with authority "to maintain and defend the integrity of the faith and to examine and proscribe errors and false doctrines."[104] It was actually the third such tribunal to be created; the Medieval Inquisition had eradicated Catharism in France, and the Spanish Inquisition had eradicated Judaism from Spain. The main goal of the Roman Inquisition was to eliminate Protestantism throughout Italy and to create a strong base from which military action might be taken against the Protestant north. The second step was Paul IV's institution of the Index of Prohibited Books in 1559. Reading a listed book resulted in automatic excommunication. Prominent on the Index were the collected works of Erasmus.[105] However censorship could only be enforced in central Italy and, to a lesser extent, in the rest of Catholic Europe. Elsewhere, for a book to be listed on the Index almost guaranteed wide readership.

Society of Jesus

Most famous of the new religious orders was the Society of Jesus ("Jesuits") founded in 1534 by the Basque nobleman Ignatius Loyola (c.1491-1556) and approved by Pope Paul III six years later. Although the order was founded before the official start of the Counter-Reformation, it became an important reform tool. It also represents one of the ways in which Spanish reform efforts carried over into the Counter-Reformation.[106] Ignatius had been a soldier, and he organized his new order as a rigid hierarchy, reminiscent of the Knights Templar. Indeed, the Jesuits have been called the "foot soldiers" of the Counter-Reformation. They pledged unconditional obedience to the pope; Ignatius is reported to have said: "I will believe that the white that I see is black if the hierarchical Church so defines it." However the Jesuits did not hesitate to point out corruption and spiritual laxity wherever they saw it. For a time they were suppressed by papal order because of disagreements with secular powers.

Ignatius' *Spiritual Exercises* provided a good preparation for the spiritual life, instilling in Jesuits both a spirit of self-abnegation and complete commitment to their work. A major charge of the Jesuits was missionary activity, and they served in the Americas, Asia and elsewhere. But their own rigorous training suited them ideally to preaching and to higher education. The Jesuits founded schools, universities and seminaries throughout Europe, and eventually in many other parts of the world. The hope was that the new seminaries would raise the standard of the secular clergy; but they also attracted some of the greatest minds of the modern era. In recognition of their status, Catholic monarchs often chose Jesuits to be their personal confessors; and the practice gave the Order important influence in the secular arena.

Preaching was obviously important for the education of the laity and reinvigoration of popular devotion. But it was considered even more important to meet the challenge of highly educated Protestant theologians who were winning converts by the power of rhetoric. In the strongly polemical spirit of the Counter-Reformation—and in an ironical tribute to the value humanists attached to *eloquentia*—an intellectual arms-race was developing. In the years that followed, many Jesuit scholars engaged Protestant counterparts in debates. Neither side could expect victory in any definitive sense, but valuable points could be scored.

However, if the rhetoric of humanism was valued, the Jesuits followed the lead of the Council of Trent and lent their own support to the Thomist revival; an appendix to Ignatius' *Spiritual Exercises* included the following rule:

> To praise positive and scholastic learning. Because, as it is more proper to the Positive Doctors, as St. Jerome, St. Augustine and St. Gregory, etc., to move the heart to love and serve God our Lord in everything; so it is more proper to the Scholastics, as St. Thomas, St. Bonaventure . . . to define or explain for our times the things necessary for eternal salvation; and to combat and explain better all errors and all fallacies.[107]

Reflections

In many respects the Reformation was a case study in contradictions. The reformers rejected tradition as a valid source of authority but soon established new authoritative traditions. They challenged Rome's right to interpret scripture, arguing that the Bible provided the exclusive source of divine truth; but then they issued their own interpretations. They criticized religious intolerance in Catholic nations; but the new Protestant churches closely regulated beliefs and practices within their own jurisdictions. The Counter-Reformation sought to reform Catholicism, but the Council of Trent reaffirmed medieval dogma and elevated Thomas Aquinas to a position even higher than he had enjoyed in the 13th century.

The establishment of state churches, coupled with the emergence of powerful nation states, made religious repression even more efficient than it had been before the Reformation. The Church of England frequently used the courts to suppress dissent; for example, John Biddle, one of the fathers of English Unitarianism, was repeatedly imprisoned for his views. Legal discrimination against "Nonconformists"—Baptists, Congregationalists and Quakers—was partially relaxed in 1689, but discrimination against Unitarians and Catholics continued until 1829. As late as the 1880 a number of Anglican clergymen were imprisoned for introducing Roman-style ritual into worship services.[108] Nor was such suppression of dissent confined to England. In 1788 the Prussian state issued the *Edict on Religion* prohibiting pastors from preaching sermons that deviated from approved teachings.[109] Quakers, Baptists and others were persecuted in the theocratic colony of Massachusetts.

Martin Luther's struggle with depression provided an apt metaphor for post-Reformation Christianity. Christianity lost its medieval exuberance and descended into a long period of austerity and pessimism. The reformers emphasized two important precepts: salvation was a matter between the individual and God, and Jesus Christ was the sole intermediary between them. Nobody else—clergy, the church, the saints, or Mary of Nazareth—could intercede with God on behalf of a person, alive or dead.[110] Requiem Masses and indulgences had no value; indeed they were pointless because, without a purgatory, one's fate was completely determined at the point of death. John Calvin believed it was determined even before birth. People had few straws to grasp onto in their suffering and grief. The pilgrimages and holy relics that sustained people in the Middle Ages were no longer permitted. The faithful could not even benefit from "good works;" the only factor of importance was faith. The church's function was to make people aware of Jesus Christ and to offer individuals—at least the elect—the opportunity to believe.

Preaching restored Christianity's teaching role which had been neglected in the Middle Ages, and it affirmed the Path of Knowledge. Sermons were long, but it is not clear how effective they were. Post-Reformation preaching, Catholic as well as Protestant, suffered from preoccupation with hell and personal guilt. Be that as it may, Knowledge was strengthened by the resurgence of theological inquiry by Calvinist and—despite Luther's reservations about human reason—Lutheran theologians. Calvinism/Presbyterianism and Lutheranism both emerged as theologically based religions, in contrast to the Evangelical movements that followed a century later. The Path of Knowledge was also strengthened by popular Bible study.

The reformers justifiably reacted against the abuses of the Church of Rome, but sweeping reform movements always run the risk of throwing out the baby with the bathwater. That is largely what happened in the Protestant Reformation. Martin Luther's rejection of good works and the suppression of monasteries had a lasting, negative impact on the Paths of Service and Renunciation. Although the reformers encouraged popular piety, their disdain for the contemplative life harmed the Path of Devotion. Protestantism acknowledged the role of emotion and intellect in religious expression but paid scant attention to the higher intuition of the mystics. Spiritual healing was conspicuously absent from Protestant and Catholic concerns, as it might have related either to a healing ministry or to healing the religious divisions of the post-Reformation era.

The new Protestant denominations were suspicious of the Path of Ceremony. The Lutheran churches, particularly in Scandinavia, preserved significant elements of pre-Reformation ritual, and the Church of England preserved a strong sense of the sacred through its music. But the liturgy of the Reformed churches has always been impoverished, and the iconoclasts who destroyed sacred art in the 16th and 17th centuries have much to answer for. As Puritanism took hold, anything joyful was immediately suspect; the spiritual path was depicted as harsh and painful. The Protestant churches all sacrificed much that was good in medieval Christianity. With justification we can ask Protestantism: Where are your mysteries? Where are your mystics? And, notwithstanding the portrayal of Queen Elizabeth I as *Gloriana*, where is your goddess?[111]

We have studied the Reformation from a religious standpoint. But in some respects the Reformation was also a rebellion against the social order of the Middle Ages; the church, the nobility, and monarchies all lost positions of privilege and power. The Enlightenment, the emergence of a middle class, and even the rise of socialism in the 20th century have all been traced to the Reformation.

---

1. Although self-flagellation was a common penitential discipline, Luther's use of it may have been influenced by the frequent beatings he received at home and at school. See for example: Erik H. Erikson. *Young Man Luther*. Norton and Co., 1958, pp. 63-67.
2. Luther allegedly suffered from chronic constipation, at least from the Wartburg period onward. However, reports that he composed the 95 Theses in an outhouse are probably apocryphal.
3. Quoted by Peter Kreeft. "Justification by Faith." Catholic Educators' Resource Council, 1988.
4. According to Catholic doctrine, purgatory is a place of temporal suffering where the soul is cleansed of residual guilt, prior to entry into heaven.
5. Clearly abuses were taking place, and eventually the Catholic Church stopped selling indulgences, although it continued to attach them to certain prayers and rites.

6.   Martin Luther. *Address to the Christian Nobility of the German Nation*, 1520. Luther was neither the first nor the last person to call the pope the Antichrist.

7.   Roland H. Bainton. *Here I Stand: a Life of Martin Luther*. Penguin, 1950/1995, pp. 142-144. The "Here I stand . . ." statement is widely believed to have been a later addition to Luther's speech.

8.   Eisenach was the birthplace of Johann Sebastian Bach.

9.   *The Augsburg Confession*, Preface, 1530. (Translated by F. Bente & W. H. T. Dau.)

10.   As it turned out Bible study encouraged by the Reformation helped boost literacy levels.

11.   Philip Schaff. *History of the Christian Church*. Charles Scribner's Sons, 1910.

12.   Martin Luther. *Preface to the Revelation of St. John*. 1522. (Transl: unknown.) His comment was omitted from later editions, and *Revelation* has certainly not been ignored by Protestants since that time.

13.   *Romans* 1:17.

14.   *Romans* 4:5.

15.   *Romans* 5:1.

16.   A passage in the Old Testament was also relevant: "[T]he just [*tsaddiq*] shall live by his faith." *Tsaddiq* (Hebrew: צדיק) can mean "just" or "righteous." See: *Habakkuk* 2:4.

17.   *James* 2:20. That passage may explain why Luther regarded *James* as heretical.

18.   Martin Luther. "The Fruits of Faith—Our Spiritual Service." *Sermons of Martin Luther*, Vol. 7. Baker Books, 2000.

19.   Several misunderstandings over justification by faith were resolved by the Augsburg *Joint Declaration on the Doctrine of Justification*, signed by representatives of the Lutheran World Federation and the Church of Rome on October 31, 1999.

20.   Martin Luther. *Confession Concerning Christ's Supper*, 1528. *Luther's Works*, vol 37. Fortress Press, 1955-1986, pp. 299-300.

21.   *1 Peter* 2:9.

22.   Luther's dislike for the Dominicans no doubt derived in part from his experience with Johann Tetzel.

23.   Foreword to *Symphoniae Iucundae*, published in Wittenberg by Georg Rhau (1488-1548).

24.   Luther composed the hymn at about the time he hid in the Wartburg Castle, but it is unclear whether the castle inspired the theme.

25.   The German Mass was based on the Roman liturgy, but prayers to the saints and to Mary of Nazareth were deleted.

26.   Martin Luther. Sermon: "On the Day of the Conception of the Mother of God." December 1527. Hartmann Grisar. *Luther*. (Transl: E. M. Lamond.) Kegan Paul, Trench, Trubner, 1915, Vol. IV, p. 238. The Catholic Church maintains that the immaculate conception was part of a long tradition; however, the doctrine was not formally defined until 1854.

27.   The system of vowel points currently used was developed by the Masoretes, a group of rabbis in Tiberias.

28.   See the discussion in: Brown, *Heresies*, pp. 346-350.

29.   *Ibid.*, Article 28.

30. Some branches of Lutheranism have now restored an apostolic succession. See Chapter 20.

31. A good example is the present political action to ban same-sex unions to preserve the "sacred nature" of marriage between a man and a woman.

32. See the discussion in: Diarmaid MacCullough. *The Reformation*. Penguin Books, 2003, pp. 150-152.

33. Harold O. J. Brown. *Heresies: Heresy and Orthodoxy in the History of the Church.* Hendrickson, 1984, pp. 591-600.

34. See the discussion in: MacCullough, *The Reformation*, pp. 150-152.

35. Brown, *Heresies*4, p. 314.

36. *Book of Concord.* "Formula of Concord," Preface, 1577. Source: Lutheran Church Missouri Synod. Parentheses in oritinal.

37. *Ibid.*, "Good Works," 7, 1577.

38. *Augsburg Confession*, article 1.

39. Douglas D. Fusselman. "Who Holds the Keys? Luther on the Power of Jurisdiction." *Lutheran Theological Review*, Spring/Summer 1994.

40. *The Augsburg Confession*, article 28.

41. *Ibid.*, articles 16, 28.

42. The extent of Luther's influence on Zwingli is disputed. Zwingli's vigorous denials of influence may have reflected worsening relations between the two men.

43. The famous "ritual meal" was held on March 9, 1522 at the home of Christoph Froschauer, a Zürich printer. Zwingli was there, but reportedly he did not partake.

44. MacCullough, *The Reformation*, p. 147.

45. Philip was the "landgrave" of Hesse. He owed feudal responsibility to the Holy Roman Emperor but exercised sovereign rights within his territory. A landgrave was roughly comparable to a duke.

46. The precise origin of the Anabaptists is disputed. Some authorities claim that Anabaptists emerged independently at several locations, starting around 1525; others see the Anabaptists as a fringe group present much earlier in Christian history.

47. *Schleitheim Confession*, article IV. February 24, 1527. Source: Anabaptist Network.

48. MacCullough, *The Reformation*, pp. 167-168.

49. John of Leiden's style has been played out a number of times by modern cult leaders.

50. *Acts* 2:32-37; 4:32.

51. Those Anabaptist beliefs were expressly condemned in *The Augsburg Confession*, Article XVII, 4.

52. *Institutes*, originally written in Latin, went through several editions, each with significant revisions. French editions appeared in 1545 and 1560.

53. John Calvin. *Institutes of the Christian Religion*, Book IV, ch. 20, §4. (Transl: H. Beveridge.) Hatfield, 1599.

54. His wife, Idelette de Bure, was the widow of a former Anabaptist. She died in 1540, and their only child died in infancy. Calvin never remarried.

55. Quoted in: Marian Hillar. "Sebastian Castellio and the Struggle for Freedom of Conscience." *Essays in the Philosophy of Humanism*, vol. 10, 2002, pp. 31-56.

56. Emphasis added.
57. John Calvin. *Institutes of the Christian Religion*, book IV, ch. 18, §1. (Transl: H. Beveridge.) Hatfield, 1599.
58. See: Hugo Rahner. "The Christian Mystery and the Pagan Mysteries." *The Mysteries*. (Joseph Campbell, ed.) Princeton University Press, 1955, pp. 337-401.
59. Calvin, *Institutes of the Christian Religion*, book I, ch. 16, §8.
60. Augustine of Hippo. *De done perseverantiae*, xxxv, 492 CE. (Transl: J. Mourant.) *Fathers of the Church*. Catholic University Press, 1992.
61. John Calvin. *Treatises on the Eternal Predestination of God*, p. 31. (Transl: H. Cole.) Reformed Free Publishing Association, 1929.
62. MacCullough, *The Reformation*, p. 244.
63. The Arminian view is referred to as *conditional election*, as distinct from the traditional Calvinist unconditional election. It implies that God's will could be frustrated by human resistance to grace.
64. Jansenism, named after the Flemish bishop and theologian Cornelius Otto Jansen (1585-1638), was condemned as heretical.
65. By contrast, Luther was strongly influenced by Paul's Hellenic Christianity.
66. Calvin. *Institutes of the Christian Religion*, book II, ch. 10, §8.
67. See also: *Ibid.*, book IV, ch.16, §14.
68. Darby's work will be discussed in Chapter 17.
69. The Rosicrucian movement began in the Palatinate shortly before the Thirty Years War.
70. This John Sigismund is not to be confused with the king of Transylvania who died the year before the elector was born.
71. Augustine of Canterbury is not to be confused with the more famous Augustine, bishop of Hippo.
72. More and Bishop John Fisher, who was also executed, were revered as Catholic martyrs and canonized.
73. Henry's principal agent in the dissolution of the monasteries was Thomas Cromwell. Even the Catholic Emperor Joseph II (1741-1790) would dissolve monasteries of Austria and seize their property.
74. Act for Uniformity of Service and Administration of the Sacraments throughout the Realm, January 21, 1549. Ironically, Cornwall had earlier been a bastion of Celtic Christianity, bitterly opposed to Roman encroachment.
75. "The Supper of the Lorde and the Holy Communion, Commonly Called the Masse." *Book of Common Prayer*, 1548. The Prayer Book was revised in 1552, 1559 and 1562, each time making it more "Protestant."
76. The Articles had been drafted by Thomas Cranmer ten years ealier.
77. *Thirty-Nine Articles*, XVII. Source: Church of England.
78. The only Catholic monarch after than time was James II.
79. Pius V. *Regnans in execeisis*, Feb 25, 1570; *Damnatio et Ecommunication Elizabetae Reginae Angliae*, 1570.
80. Despite his contribution to religion, James was the subject of court scandals stemming from his relationships with male "favorites."
81. Two prominent Cambridge Platonists were Henry More (1614-1687) and Countess Anne Conway (1630-1679).

82. Upon restoration of the monarchy, Puritanism continued to have broad influence among ordinary people, but a wave of license infused the newly restored royal courts and the courts of the nobility.

83. Numbered among the divines were Jeremy Taylor (1613-1667), Lancelot Andrewes (1555-1626), William Laud (1573-1644), and Henry Vaughan (1622-1695).

84. In 1893 Pope Leo XIII rejected Anglican apostolic succession on the grounds that, during the reign of Edward VI, the mass, "the central priestly function," was no longer regarded as a sacrifice.

85. Mary I of Scotland, "Mary Queen of Scots," is not to be confused with her contemporary and distant relative, Mary I of England.

86. It will be recalled that one of the meanings of the Greek *episkopos* was "guardian."

87. Voltaire. *Letters Concerning the English Nation*, 1733. Isacc Kramnick (ed.). *The Portable Enlightenment Reader*, Penguin Books, 1995, p. 133.

88. *Westminster Confession of Faith*, XI:2, 1648. Center for Reformed Theology and Apologetics.

89. *Ibid.*, X:1.

90. *Ibid.*, IX:2-4.

91. MacCullough, *The Reformation*, p. 557.

92. The *Book of Common Order*, adopted in 1562 upon John Knox's recommendation, was based on the *Genevan Book of Order*.

93. Parilament of the Kingdom of Scotland. *Act of the Parliament Approving and Establishing the Directory for Publick Worship*. Edinburgh, February 6, 1645.

94. *Westminster Confession of Faith*, XXIX:7.

95. MacCullough, *The Reformation*, pp. 226-230, 237. In 1550 the English Cardinal Pole failed by one vote to be elected pope upon Paul III's death. Had he succeeded the subsequent course of the Council of Trent might have been very different.

96. Quoted in: Schaff, *History of the Christian Church*.

97. MacCullough, *The Reformation*, p. 406.

98. The Council did not meet at all during the four years of his reign: 1555-1559.

99. Council of Trent, 18th session, 1562. (Transl: J. Waterworth.) Dolman, 1848, pp. 19-20

100. *Ibid.*, 4th session. 1546, pp. 19-20.

101. These designations—still which apply to all religious pamphlets and books published by Catholics—are issued by a diocesan censor. *Nihil obstat* means "nothing stands in the way;" *Imprimatur* means "let it be printed."

102. Council of Trent, 22nd session, 1557, p. 161.

103. Cyril of Jerusalem is not to be confused with Cyril of Alexandria who lived a century later.

104. Had scholasticism been faithful to Aquinas' real genius, there would have been little conflict with the new ideas of the Renaissance and Enlightenment. However it had long degenerated into a narrow intellectualism and deference to the authority of tradition.

105. The Roman Inquisition was renamed the Sacred Congregation of the Holy Office in 1908, and the Sacred Congregation for the Doctrine of the Faith in 1965.

106. The zealous Pope Sixtus V even wanted a book by Robert Bellamine, Jesuit director of the Index, to be listed; however Sixtus backed down under pressure. See: MacCullough, *The Reformation*, p. 407.

[107.] The Spanish Inquisition kept Aquinas under surveillance on suspicion that his Spiritual Exercises might be heretical.

[108.] Ignatius Loyola. "To Have the True Sentiment which we Ought to Have in the Church Militant," rule 11. *Spiritual Exercises*. (Transl: E. Mullan.) Kennedy, 1914.

[109.] Michael Chandler. *An Introduction to the Oxford Movement*. Church Publishing, 2003, pp. 114-117.

[110.] Brown, *Heresies*, p. 405.

[111.] See the discussion in: MacCullough, *The Reformation*, p. 576.

[112.] Queen Elizabeth I was portrayed as the divine *Gloriana* in Edmund Spenser's epic poem *The Faerie Queen*, 1590-1596.

Part V
Christianity in the Modern World

A certain tendency to insanity has always attended the opening of the religious sense in men, as if they had been "blasted with excess of light." The trances of Socrates, the "union" of Plotinus, the vision of Porphyry, the conversion of Paul, the aurora of Behmen, the convulsions of George Fox and his Quakers, the illumination of Swedenborg, are of this kind. What was in the case of these remarkable persons a ravishment, has, in innumerable instances in common life, been exhibited in less striking manner. Everywhere the history of religion betrays a tendency to enthusiasm. The rapture of the Moravian and Quietist; the opening of the eternal sense of the Word, in the language of the New Jerusalem Church; the *revival* of the Calvinist churches; the *experiences* of the Methodists, are varying forms of that shudder of awe and delight with which the individual soul always mingles with the universal soul.

Ralph Waldo Emerson. The Over-Soul.[1]

Chapter 16
Bridge to the Modern World

Religious Conflict

In the wake of the Reformation sectarian tensions developed not only between Catholics and Protestants but also among the various branches of Protestantism. Those tensions turned Europe into a tinderbox waiting to be ignited. Relatively minor religious wars had already been waged in Switzerland and Germany, but larger conflicts erupted in France and the Netherlands. Spain tried to conquer England. Finally the Thirty Years' War devastated much of Europe. Ostensibly those wars were all religiously motivated, but wars rarely have single causes or clearcut outcomes. Participant nations recognized opportunities to settle old scores and make territorial gains.

On the Catholic side, several secular rulers embraced the ideals of the Counter-Reformation, including King Philip II of Spain, the Emperor Ferdinand II, and the Guise dynastic family of France. Albrecht V of Bavaria purged his duchy, which was part of the Holy Roman Empire, of all Protestant influence and turned it into a staunchly Catholic state. The Jesuits played a major role, serving as guarantors of orthodoxy in churches and schools and as censors of publications within the duchy. Using Bavaria as a base, Counter-Reformation activity spread north and west until the cities of Cologne, Aachen and Strasburg were reconverted to Catholicism. Meanwhile the Roman Inquisition was empowered to root out Protestantism in the parts of Europe under Catholic control.

One of the very few causes that united western Christendom after the Reformation was the suppression of witchcraft. As had been the case with the campaign against heresy, the secular judicial system was used as the enforcement mechanism. Both Catholics and Protestants zealously prosecuted alleged witches, misfits and others thought to be allied with Satan. The papal bull *Summis Desiderantes*, issued by Pope Innocent VIII in 1484, had authorized torture to secure confessions in witch trials. Despite its Roman origin, it was adopted by the major Protestant denominations, and 28 editions were printed over a period of 120 years.[2] From 1500 onward Europe was caught up in a witch-hunt mania in which thousands of people were sentenced to gruesome deaths, often on the flimsiest of evidence. The great majority were women, and, significantly, midwives became favored targets. The mania spread to North America, and in 1692 19 women were executed in Salem, Massachusetts. Judicial executions for witchcraft finally ended in Europe after two Polish women were burned at the stake in 1792.

It took considerable courage to speak out against the witch hunts. However Swiss physician and occultist Theophrastus Philippus Aureolus Bombastus von Hohenheim (1493-1541), better known as Paracelsus, would sneer: "[T]here are more superstitions in the Roman Church than in all these women and witches."[3]

Conflict in Northwestern Europe

Although France was officially Catholic, the monarchy had tolerated some level of penetration by Calvinist Huguenots. However the powerful Guise family took up the Counter-Reformation cause and targeted the then-Huguenot Bourbon family. A bloody civil war erupted in which both sides committed atrocities. In 1562, in a wave of iconoclasm, Huguenot radicals desecrated the tomb of church father Irenaeus in Lyon and the burial site of Marin of Tours.[4] Over time anti-Protestant sentiment increased, the monarchy became involved, and the Huguenot minority suffered terrible persecution.

Persecution of the Huguenots, under King Charles IX and Queen Mother Catherine de Médici, culminated in 1572 with the St. Bartholomew's Day massacre in Paris.[5] Eight thousand people died on that single day, but ten times as many may have been killed over a three-month period. Huguenots who could escape fled to England, the Netherlands and Germany. Their leader, Henry of Bourbon, converted to Catholicism and became King Henry IV, first of the line of Bourbon monarchs who would hold the throne until the French Revolution. The Huguenots won a measure of religious freedom under the Edict of Nantes in 1598; but that freedom was progressively eroded, and further brutal persecution occurred during the reign of Louis XIV. In all, an estimated 250,000 Huguenots were put to death and an equal number left the country. The wholesale extermination of the Huguenots can only be compared to what the Cathars suffered in southern France three centuries earlier.

Europe's most powerful supporter of the Counter-Reformation was King Philip II of Spain (1527-1598). In addition to fighting the Ottoman Turks in the Eastern Mediterranean, he embarked on a campaign to combat the spread of Protestantism in the Netherlands which had long been a Spanish possession. Under his father, the emperor Charles V, the Netherlands had attained a measure of political autonomy and religious toleration. As a result it had become a haven for Anabaptists, Lutherans, and increasing numbers of Calvinists. To remedy the situation Philip moved a large army into the Netherlands, appointed Spanish governors, increased taxation, and gave the Inquisition free rein to deal with Protestants. More Calvinists were burned in the Netherlands than in any other nation. Persecution of Anabaptists was also severe; an estimated 525 women were executed, some of them for preaching.[6]

The repressive measures were bitterly resented by the nobles and middle classes of the Netherlands. Calvinist preachers responded with increased proselytism; and in 1566 a wave of iconoclasm swept the country, resulting in wholesale destruction of religious art. As repression intensified the stage was set for open rebellion. The War of Independence began in 1568 when a number of northern counties proclaimed an independent republic and mobilized an army. Spanish forces made some headway against the north, but Spain's power was broken by the failure of the armada against England. In 1609 Spain was forced to recognize the Dutch Republic, while continuing to hold the Catholic south which eventually became Belgium. The Netherlands finally won international recognition as the sovereign nation at the Treaty of Westphalia in 1648.

Philip II's biggest blunder was a crusade to install a Catholic monarch on the throne of England. His ambitious plan called for a Spanish naval fleet and French ground troops to invade and conquer England. The victorious force would then cross the North Sea to the Netherlands and finally move south into France to bolster its loyalty to Catholicism. As early as 1573, Pope Pius V had urged Philip to take military action against England. Fourteen years later, Sixtus V granted him formal authority to overthrow Queen Elizabeth and turn England into a "feudatory of Rome." Sixtus promised to contribute a million gold crowns to Philip's war chest.

Philip assembled the largest armada that had ever put to sea, far outnumbering the defending English navy. But when it arrived in the English Channel in 1588 the Spanish navy met with one disaster after another. First the French supporting army failed to materialize. Then storms drove the fleet into French and Belgian ports where it was attacked by the English navy under Francis Drake. As the Spanish galleons tried to escape to open water, many were sunk by the smaller, but more maneuverable and heavily armed, English ships. What was left of the Spanish fleet limped home around the north of Scotland to evade English forces. All plans to occupy England, the Netherlands and France were abandoned. Spain's military power was broken, and its political influence greatly curtailed. Angered by the crusade's failure, Pope Sixtus refused to pay Philip the promised million crowns.

Thirty Years' War

The 30 Years' War began in 1618 when the Holy Roman Emperor intervened to prevent Bohemia from becoming a Calvinist nation. Bohemian nobles had rebelled against the emperor and invited the Calvinist Elector Frederick V (1596-1632) of the Palatinate to take the throne. Faced with almost certain war, Frederick appealed unsuccessfully to the Protestant states of Germany for support. Political rivalries and Lutheran-Calvinist tension were so strong that even the Lutheran Elector John George I of neighboring Saxony sided with the emperor rather than with Frederick. When foreign rulers, including his father-in-law James I of England, also refused to help, Frederick's fate was sealed. The imperial Hapsburg army conquered Bohemia and initiated a purge of Protestantism. Meanwhile, a Spanish army occupied the Palatinate, and Frederick fled to the Netherlands.

By 1630 it seemed likely that Protestantism would be eradicated throughout the whole of Germany. The tide was turned only by Sweden's intervention. Alarmed at the encroachment of Catholicism, King Gustavus Adolphus (1594-1632) is reported to have said: "as one wave follows another in the sea, so the papal deluge is approaching our shores." The Swedish army pushed the imperial forces back all the way into the south German heartland. When Gustavus Adolphus died in battle, the army's advance was halted, and the war degenerated into a stalemate. France entered the war, ironically on the Protestant side. But neither the Hapsburgs nor the Protestants could defeat the other.

The war ended in 1648 with the Treaty of Westphalia whose provisions were disappointing for the original protagonists but far-reaching for the future of Europe. Sweden and France annexed German territory. Dutch independence and the sovereignty of Switzerland were both recognized. The emperor was reduced to a figurehead. German princes won almost complete sovereignty in their jurisdictions and selected Catholicism, Lutheranism or Calvinism as their official religion. Religious war essentially came to an end in Europe, and the force of the Counter-Reformation was spent. But not all was lost for the Catholic parties. Six years after the Treaty of Westphalia was signed, Louis XIV was crowned king of France;[7] the richest and most powerful monarch in Europe, he would reign until his death in 1715.

Science, Philosophy and Christianity

Century of Genius

When the Royal Society of London was chartered in 1662, science—or "natural philosophy" as it was still called—hovered between its roots in the Renaissance and its future in the scientific revolution that was already underway. The old Renaissance science, associated with names such as Raymon Lull, Cornelius Agrippa, John Dee, and Robert Fludd, still retained its vitality. The renowned Irish chemist Robert Boyle, nominated president of the Royal Society in 1680,[8] considered himself a "priest of nature," intent on demonstrating the glory of God. Boyle also developed an interest in alchemy that linked him with a tradition stretching from Thomas Aquinas to Isaac Newton. His motivation was not expectations of wealth but the hope of attracting spiritual forces that would confound the atheism of his contemporaries. Support for the Royal Society also came from another direction. The Rosicrucian movement, which will be discussed in Chapter 18, adopted as one of its goals to "lay a new foundation of sciences."[9] It meant Renaissance science, not the empirical sciences of the 17th and 18th centuries.

The Royal Society soon became a bastion of the new empirical science. Although Boyle saw no conflict between science and religion, others did; and science became increasingly secular and hostile to religion. Institutional Christianity, which had largely ignored Renaissance science, could not escape the confident science of the 17th century and found itself on the defensive. By then, western Christianity was represented not just by the Roman church but also by a growing number of Protestant denominations, each forced to work out its own attitudes and response.

The scientific discoveries of the 17th century produced one of the most profound paradigm shifts in human history. Within a period of roughly 100 years, often referred to as the "Century of Genius"[10] or the "Age of Reason," the scientific worldview of Aristotle and Ptolemy gave way to that of Copernicus, Galileo and Newton. The classical medical theories of Claudius Galen (131-201 CE) yielded to the beginnings of modern medicine. The holism of Renaissance science was giving way to the reductionism of insular scientific disciplines—though we shall see that subtle links to the past persisted for some time. From the discoveries of the 17th century a new worldview emerged that envisioned an ordered, predictable—and awesome—universe which exhibited all the characteristics of careful design but which also held out the promise that human beings could understand and even control its workings.

Francis Bacon (1561-1626), statesman, lawyer and writer, was one of the few men since the Gnostics to claim that "knowledge is power."[11] He advocated a cautious, inductive approach to the acquisition of knowledge, in which new generalizations would be made only after earlier theories were firmly grounded. Bacon offered a comprehensive classification of knowledge, dividing "natural science" into physics and metaphysics. Physics and its practical partner, mechanics, dealt with observable phenomena, while "metaphysics" dealt with theoretical interpretations; its partner was magic. Although he recognized mathematics' increasing role in science, Bacon himself steered clear of it, partly because he was unsure how it should be utilized[12] and partly because of suspicion that it was too closely associated with magic.[13] Bacon's nonmathematical empiricism was opposed by René Descartes's (1596-1650) who rejected the dependence on experience in favor of rational deduction. Mind and matter were two distinct realms. The only postulate Descartes was willing to make was his own existence: *Cogito ergo sum* ("I think, therefore I am"). But thought led, among other things, to mathematics and thence to the use of mathematics to describe the physical world. As it turned out, the combination of Descartes' mathematics and Bacons' empiricism provided the firm basis on which the new science would be built.

Polish astronomer Nicholas Copernicus (1473-1543) had already used a combination of observation and mathematics a century earlier. Although he retained the Ptolemaic notion of circular orbits, he proposed that planetary motions could best be explained by a heliocentric model of the solar system.[14] Copernicus sent papers to selected recipients but wisely arranged for his work to be published posthumously. Even then he was condemned by Protestant reformer John Calvin. If Calvin was skeptical of scientific advances, he was equally critical of astrology which enjoyed wide popularity in his time. Calvin strongly attacked the Lutheran scholar Philipp Melanchthon for his astrological pursuits.[15]

Galileo Galilei (1564-1642) was president of the Accademia dei Lincei ("Academy of Lynxes") which had been established in Rome in 1603 with the support of Pope Clement VIII. But the Catholic Church became suspicious when his astronomical observations supported Copernican theory and he boldly asserted that the earth orbited a stationary sun. That was a direct assault on the prevailing doctrine of a geocentric universe—and a moving sun that God could halt in its tracks to help Joshua's army defeat the Amorites.[16] Rome was in no mood for compromise; the Thirty Years' War was in progress, and Catholic forces were embroiled in a life-or-death struggle for the soul of Europe. In 1633 Galileo was forced to retract his findings under threats by the Inquisition.[17]

Johannes Kepler (1571-1630) developed laws of planetary motion that formalized Copernicus' and Galileo's discoveries but also made explicit the notion of elliptical planetary orbits. He too dabbled in Renaissance science, proposing a model of the solar system that involved nested Platonic polyhedra.[18] Kepler managed to avoid persecution for his scientific and metaphysical work but fell out of favor with the Lutheran Church when he rejected the real presence in the Eucharist.[19] He believed that science brought people closer to God. And, echoing the sentiments of Robert Boyle, he went on record with the statement: "[W]e astronomers are priests of the highest God in regard to the book of nature . . . [I]t benefits us to be thoughtful, not of the glory of our minds, but rather, above all else, of the glory of God."

Isaac Newton (1643-1727) was acclaimed as the greatest mathematical scientist of his era. He postulated that events, which he viewed as the motion of rigid bodies like billiard balls, unfolded against a passive backdrop of infinite space and eternal time. He formulated universal, mathematical laws governing the motion of those bodies.[20] Gone was the notion that events reflected the day-to-day whims of a micromanaging Deity. The Deity was still there, very much there; but God now worked through a harmonious order that was accessible to the rational mind.

Newton's model of the universe was restricted to the motion of planets and falling apples; but by extension it soon became the basis of a new intellectual and cultural paradigm. For instance, the magnificent, ordered, harmonious universe was reflected in the ordered harmonies of Baroque music, art and architecture. Human achievement bore eloquent testimony to the divine creation. However it was no longer a living, organic universe in which everything was interconnected. The new universe was inert and unaffected by human consciousness. The combination of Newtonian mechanics and Cartesian dualism meant that the behavior of the billiard balls would be the same whether or not anyone was watching.[21] Even then, Newton could not break free completely from Renaissance holism and magic; he set up an alchemical laboratory on the grounds of Trinity College, Cambridge. He also wrote extensively on theology, though his writings were not well-received by the Church of England. Despite the name of the college where he held the prestigious Lucasian chair, Newton was a Unitarian.

The Enlightenment

The Century of Genius gave way to the Enlightenment, an intellectual revolution that lasted roughly from 1675 to 1800. It evoked, as its name implied, the sense that a light had come on in Europe where previously there had been intellectual darkness. In place of faith, scholars encouraged reliance on human reason, experience and observation. Authority of all kinds: revelation, dogma, tradition, and cultural norms, began to be questioned. Truth was no longer constrained by tradition, ecclesiastical censorship, or the Inquisition; it was to be followed wherever it might lead. In the words of German philosopher Immanuel Kant (1724-1804), the motto of the Enlightenment was "Dare to know."[22]

The Enlightenment began in the relatively liberal nations of England, Scotland and the Netherlands and soon spread to Germany. Not surprisingly, it brought major changes to higher education. In Germany the main thrust was to create new academic freedom in the universities. One specialty that developed there was hermeneutics, the study and interpretation of texts, including religious texts.[23] In the United States the Enlightenment produced the colleges of Yale and Philadelphia[24] and moved Harvard away from its Congregationalist roots. But the most prominent outcome in the Western Hemisphere was the American Revolution and the U.S. Constitution. For much of the 18th century, France—still royalist and staunchly Catholic—continued to maintain tight censorship, but books were smuggled in to feed French intellectuals. When the Enlightenment did erupt in

France, in the latter part of the century, it would surpass in intensity all that had preceded it. Again it stimulated political activism; one of its major products was the French Revolution.

The 17th century had created a new worldview that envisioned an awesome, ordered universe. One outcome was an explosion of cosmological and teleological arguments for the existence of God. But the arguments came under increasing fire. Scotsman David Hume (1711-1776) challenged *a posteriori* arguments for God's existence, pointing out that proponents had focused on the favorable aspects of nature to infer a beneficent god but had overlooked the unfavorable aspects that might imply a wicked or vengeful one. Negative evidence, in Hume's opinion, was more persuasive in rejecting a theory than positive evidence could be in supporting it. The problem of evil clearly posed a threat to any theology that rested on a beneficent but omnipotent deity. In response, some philosophers constructed clever *theodicies*: ways of relieving God from responsibility for what was wrong with the world while still crediting him with what was good. Most famous was Gottfried Wilhelm Leibniz' (1646-1716) suggestion that, despite what we might perceive as flaws in God's work, we lived in the "best of all possible worlds."[25]

A priori arguments for the existence of God came under attack from Immanuel Kant. According to Kant we can only apply reason to objects within space and time, which are not products of experience but forms of "intuition" (German: *Anschausung*).[26] God is an "object" that lies outside space and time; consequently: "we do not have the slightest ground to assume in an absolute manner (to suppose in itself) the object of this idea."[27] Nonetheless, Kant asserted that we have no basis for concluding that there is *not* a God; and he proceeded to argue that we could infer God's existence from morality; from a practical standpoint we should act as though there were a God. Kant never lost his sense of wonder at the magnificence of nature; his tomb in Königsberg (now Kaliningrad) bears the inscription: "Two things fill the mind with ever new and increasing admiration and awe, the more often and steadily we reflect upon them: the starry heavens above me and the moral law within me."[28]

Christian moral law was challenged by the concept of utility: the pursuit of happiness and avoidance of suffering. Such notions date back to classical Greece and can also be found in the teachings of the Buddha; but Hume, Englishman Jeremy Bentham (1748-1832), and others developed them into a secular basis for ethics.[29] Kant offered his own basis for ethics, to which he referred as the *categorical imperative*: "Act only according to a maxim by which you can at the same time will that it will become a general law."[30] To the churches' dismay none of those ethical principles made reference to the Ten Commandments.

Worse, people dared to compare Christians' moral stature—not always favorably—with pagans', or compared Christian achievements with what was possible in secular environments. In a famous passage, the French intellectual and satirist Voltaire noted the atmosphere of harmonious tolerance fostered by commerce:

> Take a view of the Royal Exchange in London, a place more venerable than many courts of justices, where the representatives of all nations meet for the benefit of mankind. There the Jew, the Mahometan, and the Christian transact together as though they all professed the same religion, and give the name of Infidel to none but bankrupts . . . At the breaking up of the pacific and free assembly, some withdraw to the synagogue, and others to take a glass.[31]

Voltaire (1694-1778), whose real name was François Marie Arouet, was one of the most influential but controversial men of his time. Growing up during the reign of Louis XIV, he attended a Jesuit school in Paris where, in his words, he learned nothing but "Latin and the Stupidities." He prayed: "O Lord, make my enemies ridiculous," whereupon, he claimed, his prayer was answered.[32] Imprisoned in France and exiled to England, he was hounded throughout his life by both Catholic and Calvinist authorities. Voltaire is remembered as a crusader against tyranny and bigotry.

Emboldened by new opportunities to question authority, some writers attacked the very roots of Christianity. German theologian Herman Samuel Reimarus (1694-1768) asserted that Jesus was a failed political messiah; after the crucifixion, the disciples stole the body and proclaimed that Jesus had risen from the dead. "Christianity," he claimed, "was a fabrication created out of the conniving minds of Jesus' followers."[33] There was no doubt that Christianity was based on belief in Christ; but that Christ could not be reconciled with the Jesus who lived in Palestine. Charges of fraud and fabrication did not win broad support, but Christians were awakened to the possibility that a meaningful distinction could be made between the Christ of faith and the Jesus of history, a distinction that would be explored further in the 19th and 20th centuries.

The 17th and 18th centuries were times of great optimism for intellectuals, political activists, and the emerging middle classes. There was a sense of progress and empowerment. However progress was anathema to institutions committed to tradition and stasis. Monarchs and the aristocracy clearly felt threatened; the American and French Revolutions showed what could be set in motion. Institutional Christianity was even more worried; for it, the world had been better during medieval times. Faced with the Reformation, the continued fragmentation of western Christianity, and the assaults of science and philosophy, it was hard to view the future with anything but pessimism.

Catholicism, which had built a fortress mentality in the Counter-Reformation, felt gravely threatened by the intellectual developments—more so than by the scientific discoveries. In Rome's view, materialism, secularism and relativism undermined the traditional absolutes of scripture, doctrine, religious observance, and ecclesiastical authority. Church leaders were outraged that scholars were studying philosophy, religion, and theology at secular universities, beyond the reach of episcopal oversight. Worse, influential theologians published works without requesting *imprimaturs*. Rome's goal was to stick to traditional doctrines and to a medieval view of Christianity in the hope that "modernism"—its pejorative term—would either go away or be recognized as a totally evil force and resisted by all Christians. The campaign was finally abandoned in the 1960s, and in 2005 a pope actually *welcomed* the Enlightenment.[34] From the late 19th century onward, the banner of all-out condemnation of intellectual—and many scientific—developments was picked up by the growing body of Evangelical fundamentalists.

Protestant denominations reacted in various ways. Conservative Protestants generally followed the same road as Catholicism in rejecting Enlightenment thinking outright. From their ranks Evangelical fundamentalism would emerge in the late 19th century. In contrast, liberal Protestantism made great efforts to accommodate the new intellectual mindset and build it into mainstream Christianity. Liberal theology and fundamentalism would emerge as polar opposites in the competition for the hearts and minds of modern Christians. We shall see in Chapter 19 how successful they were and what sacrifices each had to make to support its position.

The Eastern Orthodox churches largely ignored the Enlightenment and could do so comfortably because of their isolation from the west. The Enlightenment did reach Russia via French intellectuals in St. Petersburg, but it remained imitative and shallow.[35] The Russian psyche, with its deeply mystical qualities, was more receptive to German idealism and romanticism; it was also receptive to Freemasonry.

Individual Christians in the west also responded to the challenges of the Enlightenment in various ways. Some abandoned religion altogether. This was not entirely a novel departure; the fifth-century BCE Protagoras of Abdera was an agnostic, and the third-century Euhemerus of Messene an atheist.[36] Moreover religious skepticism had smoldered since the 30 Years' War. But out-and-out atheism did not become widespread until the latter part of the 18th century. Most intellectuals continued to believe, sometimes in radical ways, in the reality of God. Deism, Unitarianism and Transcendentalism served their purposes for a while. Other people explored esoteric Christianity or joined Masonic institutions.[37] These responses will be discussed in Chapters 18 and 19.

Voltaire's early idealism came to an end when, appalled by human suffering, he abandoned any notion of the world's perfection.[38] From being one of the Enlightenment's most enthusiastic and colorful exponents, Voltaire recognized its demise. His cynicism nurtured a new secular pragmatism, however, in which people took responsibility for working out their own problems without reliance on divine help. The 19th-century New England Transcendentalists would do the same. Meanwhile, by 1800 the bold optimism of the Enlightenment had evaporated.

A later philosophical movement that stressed personal responsibility was existentialism. Its origins are usually traced to the Danish scholar Søren Aabye Kierkegaard (1813-1855), though the term "existentialism" was only popularized in the mid-20th century by Jean Paul Sartre (1905-1980). In much the same way as *Job* and *Ecclesiastes* did, existentialism viewed the human condition as a state in which individuals strived to make sense of a contingent, unstable, and often absurd world. Existentialism further undermined comfortable trust in the rational universe of the Enlightenment. Meaning, according to the existentialists, is to be sought not in a predictable natural order but in individuals' response to the circumstances in which they find themselves. Choices, including moral choices, cannot be based on rational standards but are purely personal, based on what kind of life one wants to have. At the same time, as Sartre would insist, we must take responsibility for the choices we make and not blame them on circumstances or even on our own emotions. Existentialism did not prescribe a theological position; Kierkegaard retained a strong belief in God, but others like Friedrich Nietzsche and Sartre were atheists.[39]

New Views of Humanity

Christian apologists had always insisted that humankind was a special creation, made in the image of God. But in the spirit of 18th-century rationalism the human entity began to be viewed as a mechanical system. In a book appropriately called *L'Homme Machine*,[40] French physician Julien Offray de la Mettrie (1709-1751) argued that the human "soul" was simply the aggregate of brain and nervous-system activity.[41] La Mettrie refused to place man and animals in separate categories, though he did concede that animals might be morally superior to human beings. Another 18th-century Frenchman, Denis Diderot, speculated that animal species—including man—could evolve through a process of natural selection. He was imprisoned for saying so, but within 100 years his conjecture would become mainstream science.

Despite Diderot's speculations, most early 19th-century naturalists were convinced that living creatures needed a divine designer. They may have recalled John Calvin's praise of the "great Architect" whose perfection was to be recognized in the creation of the world.[42] They would certainly have been aware of the teleological proof for the existence of God offered in 1802 by Anglican priest William Paley (1743-1805). Paley, father of what is now known as "intelligent design," noted how well living species were suited to their environments. Who else than an intelligent creator would so thoughtfully place polar bears in the Arctic, lions in equatorial grasslands, and fish in the sea?[43] And if the lower creatures evidenced divine purpose, how much more convincing was the evidence provided by man? Man, the epitome of design, was created in God's image, placed in a world replete with flowers, butterflies, frolicking lambs and "all things bright and beautiful."

God did not receive credit for his creative excellence for long. In 1858 naturalists Charles Darwin (1809-1882) and his contemporary Alfred Russel Wallace concluded from years of observations that the diversity of biological species could indeed be explained by natural selection.[44] Thirteen years later, Darwin drew the further conclusion that man had evolved from nonhuman ancestors.[45]

Natural selection is based on the argument that random variations invest some members of a species with survival or reproductive advantage, ensuring the propagation of favorable characteristics into the population. Conversely, those carrying unfavorable variations automatically die out. As environments changed, for instance at the end of an ice-age, species adapted to the new conditions or new ones emerged. Darwin did not use the term "survival of the fittest," which was soon connected with natural selection. It was coined by the British economist Herbert Spencer (1820-1903) in the context of what came to be known as "social Darwinism."[46] Be that as it may, natural selection is now known to be even more efficient than Darwin and Wallace envisioned. Random mutation can produce variations, but genetic crossover in sexual reproduction provides a mechanism for much larger variations, quicker response to environmental changes, and greater probability that new species will emerge. Offspring do not necessarily inherit a blend of both parents' genetic characteristics; they can inherit the characteristics of either parent without dilution.

The mutability of species observed by Darwin and Wallace was at variance with traditional beliefs that God placed every known species—that is, every species currently known—in the Garden of Eden. Fortunately, by the time it was recognized that the evolutionary process took millions of years, geologists had already concluded that the earth was older than Archbishop James Ussher (1581-1656) had determined. Ussher, Primate of all Ireland, calculated that God created the world on Sunday, October 23, 4004 BCE.[47] Sir John Lightfoot, Vice-Chancellor of Cambridge University, was even more specific, asserting that creation occurred at 9:00 in the morning,[48] though he did not specify the time zone. Such attempts to estimate the age of the world from scripture resulted from confusion between *mythical* time—in which all earlier religions placed their sacred stories—and the linear, *historical* time of the emerging scientific world-view.[49] To argue the historicity of Jesus Christ is one thing, to try to pin down a creation story is quite another.

Natural selection is considered one of the most successful theories of modern science and is supported by an impressive body of data.[50] Its success raises a number of philosophical questions, the most important being whether it eliminates the need for a creator-god. Darwin never claimed that natural selection was the *sole* mechanism governing biological evolution; nor did he view himself as an atheist.[51] Wallace argued that natural selection could not account for the higher faculties of human beings. Notwithstanding, the debate over Darwin's and Wallace's work soon became entwined in science-religion polemic.

Thomas Huxley (1825-1895) and others enthusiastically proclaimed that, since we are all descended from apes—and, in turn, apes were descended from more primitive animals—there was no need for a creator.[52] Huxley's interpretation became the lens through which Darwin's theory of evolution was generally perceived. Julien de la Mettrie had been right; man was not qualitatively different from lower animals. From being "a little lower than the angels," man was now only a little higher than monkeys. Predictably, conservative Christians reacted with outrage and fought back with every weapon at their disposal. In a famous debate in 1860 Samuel Wilberforce, Anglican bishop of Oxford, asked Huxley whether he was descended from an ape on his grandfather's or grandmother's side of the family. Huxley retorted that he was not ashamed of his ancestry, but "he would be ashamed to be connected with a man who used great gifts to obscure the truth."[53] At that point a woman fainted and was carried from the hall.

Challenges to the theory also came from scientists themselves. American botanist Asa Gray (1810-1888) was sympathetic to Darwin, but he questioned how natural selection could produce complex systems like the eye when incremental stages of evolution conveyed no reproductive advantage. That objection still awaits a satisfactory answer. For a while the origin of life evaded scientific explanation, but laboratory experiments in the late 20th century showed that electric discharges simulating lightning could produce elementary proteins in organic chemical soups. Under favorable conditions life might emerge spontaneously from inanimate matter. Theoretical support for the emergence of life was provided by complexity theory.

Few scientists today doubt the basic premise of natural selection. But paleontology cannot determine conclusively that the process is completely random; because it is difficult to falsify, randomness is a weak scientific hypothesis.[54] Evolutionary processes could possibly be "tweaked" from time to time by a higher power.

"Intelligent design" continues to be a viable theory—albeit a metaphysical, not a scientific, one. Unfortunately it has fed into the political activism of Evangelical fundamentalists, and to speak of intelligent design today either brands one as a fundamentalist or contributes to their cause.

Twentieth Century

Challenges to traditional Christian beliefs continued to pile up in the late 19th and early 20th centuries. In the physical sciences, Albert Einstein's (1879-1955) theories of relativity undermined the reassuringly predictable Newtonian universe and also lent support—albeit just by analogy—to metaphysical and moral relativism. Quantum theory undermined the notion of an inert universe in which events are unaffected by consciousness. It also called into question our understanding of causation and time. Quantum indeterminacy served as a metaphor for the post-modern skepticism toward absolute truth.[55] Truth statements, whether made by religious authorities, politicians, marketers, or anybody else, no longer have the persuasive force they once did.[56] On the other hand modern physics has encouraged belief in the interconnectedness of all things and the relationship between energy and matter. To be sure, Einstein was referring to physical energy, but a relatively small step is required to accept the possibility that spiritual energy can influence the material world. The concept of action at a distance was already well established by Newton's theory of gravity and 19th-century studies of electromagnetic fields.[57]

A tragic outcome of the theory of relativity was the development, actual use, and threatened use on an apocalyptic scale of weapons of mass destruction. Christian apologists had generally supported the notion of just war. But traditional wars had been small compared with the nuclear holocaust that could have occurred during the Cold War. The destruction that a nuclear war would unleash caused many Christians to pause and reconsider whether any nation had the moral right to use those weapons, regardless of circumstances.

Further challenges to Christianity came with the emergence of clinical psychology. Studies of hypnotism raised doubts that the content of human consciousness is entirely under our control; freewill might be illusory. Sigmund Freud (1856-1939) was consistently critical of religion, scornfully rejecting it as everything from mass delusion to attempts to resolve the Oedipus complex.[58] Freud's equation of sexual repression with neurosis stood in stark contrast to Christian teachings of its spiritual benefits. At the same time, his insistence on the irrationality of the *id* was an affront to Enlightenment rationalism. Two generations later, Burrhus Frederic Skinner's (1904-1990) radical behaviorism turned human beings into rats trying to find their way through the maze of life under the control of external conditioning.

Psychology was not uniformly antithetical to religion. Carl Gustav Jung (1842-1896) introduced a spiritual dimension into his work, and transpersonal psychology[59] went farther to consider topics like religious conversion, mysticism, and altered states of consciousness. But those branches of psychology did not attach any special importance to Christianity; rather they tended to express Asian concepts of religion.

The big scientific/technological advances of the late-20th century were the conquest of space; far-reaching discoveries in chemistry and biology, including the structure of DNA, mapping of the human genome, and cellular cloning; and the rapid advances in digital processing and communications. Meanwhile the earth sciences recognized the fragility of the planet and are predicting the dire effects of overpopulation, depletion of natural resources, degradation of water and air quality, and global warming.

Political and Social Upheavals

The centuries following the Reformation were marked by great political and social changes. The Americas had long been served by Spanish missionaries; but most of the settlers there were adventurers and opportunists. Then in 1620, two years into the Thirty Years' War, the Pilgrims arrived in New England.[60] Educated and idealistic, they established the Massachusetts Bay Colony; John Carver (1576-1621), a wealthy merchant from Nottingham, England, became the first governor. In 1636 Harvard College was founded, the first institution of higher education in the Western Hemisphere.[61]

A large-scale immigration of predominantly Protestant Europeans followed, along with the consolidation of eastern North America under British rule. In due course the colonists threw off imperial rule to create that strange blend of Puritan religion and Enlightenment political theory: the United States. One of its founding principles was separation of church and state, based, at least in part, on Martin Luther's doctrine of the "two kingdoms." Religious forms imported from Europe were redefined, and important new forms of Christianity emerged. The new nation would become a great political, industrial and military power, though its history was soiled for nearly 200 years by slavery and then by racial segregation, both of which received significant support from mainstream Christianity. The United States acquired French and Spanish possessions in North America and gradually pushed the once-powerful Mexico back to its present borders. Mexico remained predominantly Catholic; nevertheless anti-clerical political parties long dominated its political scene.

Britain's defeat in the American War of Independence and the United States' increasing influence in both North and South America curtailed European colonial ambitions in the New World. But it did not end the large-scale immigration of Europeans, many of them bringing with them their distinctive religious traditions. Scottish Presbyterians, Irish Catholics, and German Moravians settled in the east; and German and Scandinavian Lutherans in the northwest. Meanwhile European nations began to colonize areas of south Asia, Africa and Australasia. Substantial numbers of Europeans settled in the new colonies of the east, bringing Christianity—mainly Protestant—with them. Missionaries also went into China and Japan.

Convulsions in Europe

The French Revolution, which began in 1789, was a much less successful application of Enlightenment principles. The revolution overthrew the Bourbon monarchy; rejected the claim of divine kingship; and established, for the first time in Europe, the notion that sovereignty could reside in a nation rather than in a ruling dynasty. But it also provoked a ghastly reign of terror that ended only in the creation of a new autocracy. Within a few years Napoleon Bonaparte (1769-1821) seized absolute power, claiming the title of first consul in 1799 and emperor in 1804. However Napoleon initiated important social reforms and partially restored the status of the Catholic Church in France after a period of anticlericalism. In a treaty, or *concordat*, signed in 1801 with the Vatican, Catholicism was recognized, if not as the state religion, at least as "the religion of the great majority of the French people." Sunday, which had been demoted to a working day in the republican calendar, was rehabilitated as a "festival." In return, the church agreed to give up all claims to church property seized during the revolution. The concordat determined that bishops would be appointed, and paid, by the state but confirmed by Rome. The Catholic Church may have hoped to secure a monopoly in France, but freedom of religion was soon guaranteed to both Protestants and Jews.

Napoleon went on to conquer much of Europe. In 1806 the French army defeated the forces of Francis I of Austria, bringing to an end the Holy Roman Empire founded by Charlemagne a thousand years earlier.[62] By 1810 Napoleon controlled most of continental Europe, either through direct rule or by reducing conquered nations to vassal status. His imperial ambitions were finally brought to an end by the retreat from Moscow in 1812 and his defeat in 1815 by a combined British-Prussian army at the Battle of Waterloo. The same year, the Congress of Vienna divided up the spoils and redrew the map of Europe, as the Treaty of Westphalia had done 167 years earlier. It also tried to return to the traditional dynastic structure of Europe as it had been in the late 18th century; but the genii of nationalism, French or otherwise, could not easily be put back into the bottle.

The seeds of unification of both Germany and Italy were sown during the Napoleonic wars, but the process took a further two generations to come to fruition. The Austrian-Hungarian Empire was the main stumbling block, and when the two countries finally achieved unity it was a significant defeat for the Catholic Hapsburgs who had long been central Europe's power brokers. Some decisive battles were fought, but in each case unification was accomplished chiefly through diplomacy rather than by the time-honored methods of revolution and military force.

German unification under Prussian leadership was achieved in 1871. The Prussian King Wilhelm I became the new emperor, or *kaiser*, and Otto von Bismarck-Schönhausen (1815-1898) was appointed chancellor and foreign minister.[63] Although his policies moderated later, Bismarck initially embarked on an antireligious path, targeting both Protestant and Catholic privileges. In an interesting gesture of contempt for Rome he protected Old Catholics, who had defected after the First Vatican Council in 1870, from dismissal from seminary and other academic positions.[64] On the other hand, Bismarck used his considerable diplomatic skills to preserve European peace until Kaiser Wilhelm II (1859-1941), grandson of Wilhelm I, launched Germany onto a path of political and military adventurism.

Italian nationalism grew steadily through the early 19th century; but disagreements ensued over what form a united Italy should take. One proposal in the 1840s would have created a confederation of Italian states under papal leadership. Ultimately the Papal States were overrun, ending the church's temporal rule which began in the eighth century. In 1861 the northwestern states and Sardinia were united into a Kingdom of Italy, with Victor Emanuel II (1820-1878) as king. Full unification was achieved when Italian forces seized Venetia from Austria, in the northeast, and Giuseppe Garibaldi (1807-1882) conquered southern Italy. Rome fell in 1870, whereupon Victor Emanuel became king of the whole of Italy.

Upon the fall of Rome, Pope Pius IX excommunicated the king and sought refuge as a "prisoner" in the Vatican. For several decades the papacy did not recognize the Italian state. The loss of temporal power was a great blow. Nevertheless, Pius IX and subsequent popes negotiated numerous concordats with European governments to secure the rights of Catholics in the respective countries. Most famous, and controversial, of the concordats was the one with Adolf Hitler in 1933. But more important for the papacy was the Lateran Treaty signed four years earlier with Benito Mussolini's fascist government in Italy. The treaty established the 108-acre Vatican City as a sovereign nation, restoring on a very small scale the political independence of earlier times. It also provided monetary compensation for loss of the Papal States and recognition of Catholicism as the official religion of Italy in return for a papal guarantee of neutrality in international conflicts.[65]

World Wars

European nationalism was a major factor leading to the two world wars of the 20th century. World War I pitted Germany, Austria-Hungary, and the Ottoman Empire against France, Russia, Italy and Britain. After untold destruction and human suffering on the battlefield, the war ended in Germany's defeat in 1918. Kaiser Wilhelm II was overthrown by German republicans and went into exile shortly before an armistice brought an end to hostilities. Three other empires with long, influential histories also collapsed. In Russia Tsar Nicholas II (1868-1918) was overthrown in the revolution of 1917 and, along with his family, was executed the following year. Both the Hapsburg Empire and the already weakened Ottoman Empire disintegrated. A new kingdom of Poland was recognized, and new nations like Yugoslavia and Czechoslovakia were created out of the remains of the empires.

The Versailles Treaty of 1919 tried to redraw the map of Europe, as the Treaties of Westphalia and Vienna had done earlier; but it was far less successful. By ignoring Italy, which had fought on the allied side, the treaty fueled the rise of Benito Mussolini (1883-1945). By humiliating Germany and imposing crippling economic sanctions, which would be exacerbated by the Great Depression, it fueled the rise of Adolf Hitler (1889-1945). Europe degenerated into a triangle of conflicting political ideologies: militaristic fascism on the right; revolutionary communism on the left; and weak, unstable democracies in the center. Renewed war became almost inevitable, and institutional Christianity faced the unenviable prospect of having to decide where to place its bets.

Vladimir Ilyich Lenin (1870-1924) sought to lead a revolution in Russia and also to ferment workers' revolutions throughout Europe. That never occurred, but in the Russian homeland the revolution of 1917 was followed by a long period of civil war, power struggles, and finally the purges under Josef Stalin (1878-1953).[66] Vigorous attempts were made to suppress all forms of religion, and dialectical materialism became the centerpiece of Soviet education. Clergy and prominent laypersons were executed or sent to labor camps, church properties were seized, and many churches and monasteries were looted, desecrated, or demolished. The Russian Orthodox Church was allowed a partial recovery during World War II to boost patriotic sentiment, but persecution resumed after the war. Where churches remained open, clergy were often suspected of being government informants.

Transition from the Ottoman Empire into the new Turkish state was marked by national, ethnic and religious conflict. In 1915 a campaign of genocide was launched against Christian Armenians on suspicions that they were collaborating with Russia.[67] After the armistice Greece hoped to regain control over its historic capital of Constantinople and other Greek-speaking areas in Asia Minor. Greek and Turkish forces went to war, leading to a Turkish victory and annexation of the disputed region, including Constantinople. The Treaty of Lausanne provided for a two-way relocation of the respective ethnic groups.[68] The number of Greeks in Constantinople alone declined from 200,000 in the early 1920s to no more than 5,000. Moreover the few remaining Greeks faced ongoing persecution.[69] In the 1950s civil war broke out between Turkish and Greek Cypriots, leading to the partition of Cyprus in 1974. The aftermath of those conflicts is still being played out in mutual hostility between Turkey and Greece. However Turkey is a secular state which so far has resisted the rise of Islamic nationalism within its borders. Its political ambitions lie with Europe rather than with the Islamic states of the Middle East.

The emergence of Italian and Spanish fascism and the rise of National Socialism in Germany were spurred by nationalism and opposition to the threat of communism. In the case of Germany it was also spurred by racist policies.[70] But it should not be forgotten that theories of racial superiority enjoyed support throughout Europe and the United States. Anti-Semitism had particularly deep roots in France. In the 1890s Catholic clergy and influential laypersons were implicated in the notorious persecution of the Jewish soldier Alfred Dreyfus on trumped-up charges of treason.[71] The affair polarized French society and further strengthened anti-clericalism. National Socialism in Germany was supported by the Lutheran establishment[72] and by a number of Catholic bishops. Several Italian bishops were fascist sympathizers.

Much has been written about the Vatican's attitude to the Axis Powers in the 1930s and '40s. In 1937 Pope Pius XI, publicly condemned the Nazi ideology of racism and totalitarianism.[73] But his successor, Pius XII (1939-1958) was criticized—at least retroactively—for alleged failure to confront human-rights abuses by the Nazis and for his continued support of Francisco Franco, the fascist dictator of Spain.[74] If institutional Christianity was reticent in confronting fascism and National Socialism, that policy was motivated by traditional desire to accommodate secular regimes, desire to protect Christians from reprisals, and overwhelming fear of atheistic communism.[75] Given the ideological polarization between right and left, the Vatican and other church authorities saw the right as the lesser of two evils. It must also be remembered that the pope resided in a country that was not only part of the Axis but, after 1943, was under German occupation.

World War II brought about major realignments in world power. The big winners were the United States and the Soviet Union. With the acquisition of nuclear weapons the two superpowers became locked in Cold War until the late 1980s. After 1945 the Soviet Union extended its domination throughout eastern Europe, whereupon Catholicism and Eastern Orthodoxy suffered persecution. The collapse of communism in the late 1980s brought religious persecution to an end both in the satellite nations and the Russian homeland; the Orthodox Church began to restore its churches, rebuild its traditions, and recover—at least to a small degree—the place it enjoyed in pre-revolution Russian society. Communism's militant secularism can obviously be criticized, but it was a stabilizing force. Collapse of the Soviet bloc was followed by sectarian and religious violence in the Balkans and southern Russia. In China, where a communist regime still holds power at the time of writing, all Christian churches are under state control.

European nations on both sides were permanently disempowered after World War II and soon lost their overseas colonies. The few monarchies that remain, including Britain, the Netherlands and Sweden, are constitutional monarchies that function in much the same ways as their republican neighbors. A favorable outcome was the growth of pan-European sentiment, leading to formation of the European Union. Increased focus on economic and cultural cooperation has accompanied the rapid secularization of Europe. Regular church attendance in much of Europe is now less than 10 percent. Nevertheless, Catholic and Protestant traditions remain strong and continue to influence the rest of the world.

Another outcome was permanent disempowerment of the aristocracy and dismantlement of traditional class structures. The rise of western democracy dates back at least to the mid-19th century, but progress has never been uniform. For a considerable time, it was suppressed entirely in the fascist and communist nations of southern and eastern Europe. Moreover, universal suffrage was not achieved until well into the 20th century. Democracy was a founding principle in the United States, though voting rights were not extended to women until 1926 and to African Americans, in any real sense, until the 1960s. More-or-less successful democracies were established in the former European colonies when they won political independence. The rise of democracy and enhanced social consciousness had a significant impact on Christianity. Royal and aristocratic institutions, with which mainstream churches had enjoyed mutually beneficial alliances, lost power. Political and social empowerment not only freed the masses from oppressive overlords, it also freed them from religious exploitation. Increasing educational levels and greater prosperity in much of the world gave people new opportunities and confidence to seek religious paths of their choice, inside or outside Christianity. The rapid spread of Islam has been one result.

By the end of the 20th century the United States survived as the sole remaining superpower. At the time of writing, however, its moral authority is greatly diminished as the result of unwise military adventures, foreign-policy blunders, and insensitivity to foreign cultures. The U.S. has always exhibited great religious strength and diversity; in contrast to the situation in Europe, church attendance approaches 50 percent. But Evangelical fundamentalism has acquired a powerful voice in cultural and political affairs, threatening the traditional separation of church and state.

Social and Other Issues

The last three centuries have witnessed large-scale social changes, and institutional Christianity's involvement in those changes—or resistance to them—has provided an important evaluation of its values. One major change was the abolition of slavery. Slavery, as old as human history, was long regarded as part of a divinely ordained social order. Supporters of slavery could point to scripture and tradition. Although Moses was revered for leading the Hebrew slaves out of Egypt, *Ephesians* offered the admonition: "Servants, be obedient to them that are your masters according to the flesh, with fear and trembling, in singleness of your heart, as unto Christ."[76] Ignatius of Antioch urged masters to not "despise" slaves but warned slaves against becoming "puffed up." "Let them not desire to be set free at the public cost," he wrote, "lest they be found slaves of lust."[77]

The use of African slaves was widespread in North and Central America in the 17th and 18th centuries; and European ships carried the slaves to their destinations, typically under appalling conditions. Attempts to abolish the slave trade met with considerable resistance from mainline Christian factions. In 1791 the bells of St. Mary Radcliffe Anglican Church in Bristol, England, rang out to celebrate defeat of an abolitionist bill before parliament that would have hurt the port city's prosperity. The slave trade was finally outlawed in Britain in 1807;[78] and in 1815 the Congress of Vienna issued a proclamation condemning the slave trade by other European nations. However prohibitions against the slave trade did not bring the economic and social institution of slavery itself to an end. Slavery had been outlawed in Portugal in 1761 and in Scotland in 1776, but it was not abolished throughout the British Empire until 1834 and in the French colonies until 1848. Gypsy slaves were freed in Romania in 1855, and the Russian serfs were freed in 1861—the very year that the American Civil War began. Slavery in the United States finally ended in 1865, upon Union victory over the Confederacy. The last western country to abolish institutional slavery was Brazil, in 1888. Whether slavery persists in other parts of the world today is an open question.[79]

Important social developments of the last 200 years were the rise of the middle class, the labor movement, and the rise of socialism. Beginning in the mid-19th century, the middle classes progressively increased in size and influence. With the gradual introduction of universal male suffrage the middle classes began to exert political power. They brought new cultural norms into western society and significantly influenced the evolution of Christianity. In particular, the emerging middle class would provide an educated laity demanding more participative roles in religious affairs—roles very different from either those of an ignorant peasantry or of the aristocracy in their comfortable power-sharing relationships with ecclesiastical hierarchies. Very significantly, the middle classes would emerge as churches' main financial supporters, not through taxation but through voluntary contributions. No other large group had ever enjoyed the influence that financial power has given them.

The labor movement was a reaction against laissez-faire capitalism and the desperate poverty and exploitation of workers that it produced. The movement began in England in the late 18th century and soon spread to the European mainland; it reached the United States in the late 19th century. The cause was strengthened by initially unrelated developments in political philosophy. In the early 19th century a number of philosophers turned their attention to utopian socialism.[80] Frenchmen Henri de Saint-Simon and François Marie Charles Fourier, and the Welshman Robert Owen, made important contributions to the field.[81] They also became notable for their other interests: Saint-Simon advocated reducing the edifice of Christian doctrine to a few fundamental principles, Owen embraced spiritualist beliefs, and Fourier defended homosexuality.[82]

Socialisms' transition into a political movement is usually traced to the work of Karl Heinrich Marx (1818-1883) whose *Communist Manifesto*, coauthored by Friedrich Engels (1820-1895), was published in 1848—a year when ill-fated revolutions swept Europe. Marx's other famous work, *Capital*, was published nearly 20 years later. The main thrust of his life's work was capitalism's oppression of working people and the inevitability of class warfare. But Marx also charged that religion was both a symptom and a tool of capitalist repression: "Religious suffering is, at one and the same time, the expression of real suffering and a protest against real suffering. Religion is the sign of the oppressed creature, the heart of a heartless world, and the soul of soulless conditions. It is the opium of the people."[83] Marx was a materialist—though he did not coin the term "dialectical materialism" that became a staple of later communist writings.

The growth of socialism as a political force and unrest among the working classes themselves provided major driving forces in the labor movement. The primary objective was to give workers collective bargaining power, via the establishment of labor unions, to guarantee living wages and improve working conditions. But the struggle was long and hard, and conflict was almost universal. Business owners opposed unionization, using the courts, the police, and even the army as tools of repression. Police broke up union meetings, striking workers were arrested, and troops were called in to disperse demonstrations. Many religious leaders supported the factory owners. In 1894 a faculty member at the Presbyterian

Theological Seminary condemned demonstrating Pullman railroad workers in Chicago: "The time has come when forbearence has ceased to be virtue. There must be some shooting, men must be killed, and then there will be an end to this defiance to law and destruction of property. Violence must be met with violence. The soldiers must use their guns. They must shoot to kill."[84] The Pullman strike was crushed by federal troops, and 20 strikers died.

Other religious leaders may have held less extreme views but were still lukewarm to the labor movement and the rise of socialism. Pope Pius IX (r.1846-1878) condemned socialism as an aberration of the secular intellectual climate. His successor, Leo XIII, acknowledged the economic disparities of his age and supported workers' right to a living wage; but he warned against the socialist ideal of a classless society: "[I]t is impossible to reduce civil society to one dead level. Socialists may in that intent do their utmost, but all striving against nature is in vain. There naturally exist among mankind manifold differences of the most important kind; people differ in capacity, skill, health, strength; and unequal fortune is a necessary result of unequal condition."[85]

A strong supporter of the labor movement and socialism was Karl Barth (1886-1968), better known as a Reformed Church theologian. Writing in 1918 he made the bold prediction that a time will come when Marxism "will flare up anew as world truth, when the socialist church will rise from the dead in a world become socialist."[86] While also serving as a pastor, he lectured on union affairs and participated in socialist party activities.

Labor unions did not become effective in time to prevent the abuses of the 19th century; nor could they do much to stem the Great Depression. But by the mid-20th century unionization had succeeded in altering the balance of power in business. Wages, employment conditions, and the dignity of the workers gradually improved in the industrialized nations—ironically not long before the manufacturing sector itself went into decline. Men and women were drawn into white-collar jobs and most recently into the burgeoning service industries. Growth of low-paying service jobs and increasing globalization once again threaten the wellbeing of ordinary people. Sweat shops and child labor remain endemic in much of the Third World. And real poverty persists in major cities in the economically most powerful nations.

Until the 1980s the prevailing view was that governments, big business, and in a few countries the remnants of aristocracy were to blame for the plight of poor and repressed people, including women, racial minorities, and the handicapped. Labor unions, socialist political parties, and anti-segregation and feminist movements played a leading role in addressing the problems, and some systemic evils were corrected. However it became apparent that a top-down approach to alleviating social ills could only be part of the solution. Welfare dependency; single-parent families; inability to take advantage of educational, health-care, or social-service opportunities; and failure to participate in the political process also needed to be addressed. In many countries immigration, legal and illegal, created disadvantaged and exploited subclasses, contributing to existing social problems. Ways had to be found to help the disadvantaged help themselves.

Reflections

I dealism still held sway at the beginning of the 17th century. Luther's and Calvin's followers felt that much had been achieved; and the Counter-Reformation launched Catholicism onto a new path, albeit a defensive, reactionary one. But underlying tensions erupted into war, and by the middle of the century, conflict had taken a terrible toll on Europe. The religious divisions of Europe were obviously permanent, and a period of skepticism and secularism followed. Never again would religion play as large a role in European affairs. Meanwhile dramatic changes were occurring in the political and social environment. The changes continue to play out worldwide.

Some of the early discoveries of the scientific revolution were made in southern Europe; but the Protestant countries of northern Europe, along with Catholic France, provided a more favorable environment for the new science and the intellectual movements to which it gave rise. In due course, scholars in the American colonies and then the United States began to make their own discoveries and to contribute to the intellectual debates. As science became increasingly confident and imperialistic in the 18th and 19th centuries, Christianity was forced onto the defensive. Science claimed that it had supplanted religion as the source of answers to questions of ultimate concern. On the other hand, the emergence and advance of modern science may not have been entirely independent of developments within Christianity. Sociologist Robert Merton (1910-2003) claimed that modern science was largely a product of Protestant pietism.[87]

Potentially, Christianity could have benefited greatly from the Enlightenment. But no attempt was made, for a century or more, to integrate the traditional religious mindset and the evolving rational mindset. Churchmen perceived the Enlightenment as a dangerous threat; and intellectuals dismissed religion—at least in its traditional forms—as anachronistic, irrelevant, and detrimental to human progress. Nowhere was the intellectual-religious divide illustrated more clearly than in the assault on God. Few people had paid attention in the early-14th century when Meister Eckhart said: "We pray God to rid us of God!"[88] But in 1882 Friedrich Nietzsche shocked the world when he announced the death of God. In one of his novels an insane character proclaimed "We have killed him—you and

I. We are his murderers . . . God is dead. God remains dead."[89] "What are these churches now," he added, "if they are not the tombs and monuments of God?"

Ironically the God Nietzsche condemned to death was the product of the Aristotelian revival and scholasticism. The majestic God that commanded awe in the early Middle Ages had been replaced by the First Cause, the Unmoved Mover. Mysticism and sacredness had given way to a mental sterility incapable of comprehending real divinity. An Episcopalian priest put it well:

> As the age of scholasticism advanced and the Church gradually lost the capacity to read its own mystical roadmaps, both its theology and institutional life grew more dogmatic and contentious. The Protestant Revolution, the Renaissance, and finally the Enlightenment are inevitable steps in a domino chain whose cause lies in the gradual loss of the ability to access, and finally even to believe in, the existence of a selfhood deeper than the selfhood of ordinary awareness, or a wisdom way of knowing that relies on subtle perceptiveness invisible to the cataphatic mind. From "blessed are the pure in heart, for they shall see God," the Christian West had become stranded in "I think, therefore I am."[90]

Not surprisingly the Eastern Orthodox churches took pride in their immunity—at least until much later—from scholasticism and their preservation of the vibrant sacredness and mysticism of earlier times. They also managed to preserve sacramental forms that, in the west, fell victim to the Reformation and the Enlightenment.

The Enlightenment left many people questioning whether religion had a future. One group tried to come to terms with the emerging rationalist mindset by exploring new forms of Christianity—or religious forms that were barely recognizable as Christian. Deism emerged in the 18th century, in time to have a major influence on the American Revolution. Another group turned to esotericism which had been growing in strength since the Renaissance and was largely unfazed by scientific and intellectual skepticism. French esotericist Éliphas Lévi dismissed Voltaire as "that marvelous smatterer who thought that he knew so much because he never missed an opportunity for laughter instead of learning."[91] Still other groups felt that no accommodation could be made with the emerging rationalist mindset, and that the only viable response was either the outright rejection of religion or a retreat into fundamentalism. These various responses will be discussed in later chapters.

The political, social and economic changes of the last few centuries have been as dramatic as the scientific and intellectual changes. A beneficial outcome of the Enlightenment—or more precisely from the German Reformation—was the notion of separation of church and state. Enshrined in the constitutions of the

United States and France, it would eventually spread to the Protestant countries in Europe, freeing the churches from destructive entanglement in political affairs. Loss of the Papal States, devastating though that may have seemed at the time, freed Catholicism from a similar burden. "[T]he fusion of faith and political power," to quote Pope Benedict XVI, "has always come at a price: faith becomes the servant of power and must bend to its criteria."[92]

The Enlightenment also fostered a pervasive yearning for freedom.[93] Rebellion against ecclesiastical power; the collapse of monarchies and colonialism; the labor movement; universal suffrage; the civil-rights movement; and expanding opportunities for women, minorities and the handicapped all express that yearning. In recent times, the taste for freedom has led to reluctance to submit to church discipline—presenting authoritarian denominations with difficult challenges. But in many respects freedom remains a dream. Major developments of the 20th century: the rise and fall of world powers, weapons of mass destruction, the threat of terrorism, inequities in wealth and access to basic services, and a looming environmental crisis show that true freedom still eludes us. Pessimism and optimism coexist as people try to make sense of an uncertain world. Whether Christianity can survive and grow in this dynamic environment—and whether it will help or hinder the quest for universal freedom—remain to be seen.

---

1. Ralph Waldo Emerson. *The Over-Soul*. American Book Company, 1934, p.143.
2. Source: *Encyclopedia Britannica*.
3. Paracelsus. *A Book on Nymphs, Gnomes, Giants, Dwarves, Incubi and Succubae, Stars and Signs.*, published sometime after 1541. Henry E. Sigerist (ed.). *Paracelcus: Four Treatises*. Johns Hopkins University Press, 1941, p. 246. The name "Paracelsus" meant "greater than Celsus," the early Roman physician.
4. During the French Revolution the basilica housing Martin's remains was demolished, and two roads were driven through the site to prevent its reconstruction.
5. Novelist Alexandre Dumas wrote a fictionalized account of the massacre: *La Reine Margot*, published in 1845
6. Thieleman J. Van Braght. *Martyrs Mirror of the Defenseless Christians*, 1660.
7. Louis acceded to the throne 1643, when he was five years old, and was crowned in 1654; he assumed full governmental power upon the death of his first minister, Cardinal Jules Mazarin, in 1661.
8. Boyle declined to serve as president of the Royal Society because of scruples about taking oaths.
9. *Confessio Fraternitatis*, ch. IV. (Transl. publ. by Thomas Vaughn, 1652. The Rosicrucian movement will be discussed in a later chapter.
10. The same term is sometimes applied, with justification, to the 18th century.
11. Francis Bacon. "Nam et Ipsa Scientia Potestas Est." *Meditationes Sacræ de Hæresibus*, 1597. Bacon may have been inspired by *Proverbs* 24:5.

12. Source: "Francis Bacon." *Encyclopedia Britannica*, 2003.

13. Francis Bacon may have been suspicious of magic but, like Isaac Newton after him, he dabbled in alchemy.

14. A heliocentric model of the solar system was proposed by Aristarchus of Samos in the third century BCE, but his ideas were not well-received.

15. Diarmaid MacCullough. *The Reformation*. Penguin Books, 2003, pp. 244, 685.

16. *Joshua* 10:12.

17. Upon Galileo's condemnation the Academy of Lynxes was dissolved, but it was re-established by Pope Pius IX in 1847 and eventually became the Pontifical Academy of Sciences.

18. Johannes Kepler. *Mysterium Cosmographicum* ("Sacred Mystery of the Cosmos"), 1596.

19. Kepler identified himself as a Lutheran, but he refused to sign the *Formula of Concord* which affirmed the eucharistic doctrine of the real presence.

20. Newtonian mechanics held sway until the early 20th century, when Einstein's general theory of relativity postulated a combined space-time that interacted with masses within it.

21. Descartes believed that the only contact between mind and matter occurred in human beings, via the pineal gland. Thus the human mind and body could interact. Otherwise the two realms were completely separate.

22. Immanuel Kant. "Answering the Question: What is Enlightenment?" *Berlinische Monatsschrift* (Berlin Monthly), December 1784.

23. The academic freedom and development of this specialty laid the groundwork for pioneering work in liberal theology and modern scriptural criticism.

24. The Academy and College of Philadelphia, founded by Benjamin Franklin in 1749, later became the University of Pennsylvania.

25. Gottfried W. Leibniz. *Theocity: Essays on the Bounty of God, the Liberty of Man, and the Origin of Evil*, 1710.

26. Kant regarded "intuition" and his famous 12 categories as being "hard-wired" (to use a modern term) into the human mind.

27. Immanuel Kant. *Critique of Pure Reason*, book II, ch. 3, p. 559. (Transl: N. Kemp-Smith.) Macmillan, Second edition, 1787.

28. The inscription was taken from the "Conclusion" of his *Critique of Practical Reason*.

29. Utilitarianism is usually traced back to the 5th-century BCE philosopher Parmenides and the 4th-century Epicurus.

30. See the discussion in: Bertrand Russell. *A History of Western Philosophy*. Simon & Schuster, 1945, p. 711.

31. Voltaire. *Letters Concerning the English Nation*, 1733. Quoted in: *The Portable Enlightenment Reader*. Penguin Books, 1995, p. 133. Voltaire tended to idealize England where he was exiled upon release from the Bastille prison in Paris.

32. Voltaire. Letter, May 16, 1767.

33. Herman S. Reimarus. *On the Intention of Jesus and His Teaching*, 1778. Wisely, considering the environment of the time, Reimarus had this work published posthumously. See also: Stanley E. Porter. *The Criteria for Authenticity in Historical-Jesus Research: Previous Discussion and New Proposals*. JSNTSup 191. Sheffield: Sheffield Academic Press, 2000

34. See Chapter 20.

35. Nikolai Berdyaev. *The Russian Idea*. (Transl: R. French.) Lindisfarne Press, 1947/1992, pp. 35-37.

36. Both Greeks, Protagoras argued that one could not determine whether the gods existed or not; and Euhemerus claimed that they were really famous men of the past.

37. Wolfgang Amadeus Mozart was initiated into Masonry and subsequently left the Catholic Church. See: Jacques Henry. *Mozart the Freemason*. (Transl: J. Cain.) Inner Traditions, 1991/2006, p. 12.

38. Voltaire satirized Leibniz' "best of all possible worlds" in his 1759 story *Candide*. A major event that influenced Voltaire's change of outlook was an earthquake in Lisbon that caused widespread loss of life.

39. Nor did existentialism prescribe a political orientation: Sartre was a Marxist while Martin Heidegger belonged to the National Socialist Party in Germany.

40. *L'Homme Machine* was published in 1748.

41. Many neuroscientists hold similar beliefs today.

42. John Calvin. *Institutions of the Christian Religion*, book I, ch. 14, §21. (Transl: H. Beveridge.) Hatfield, 1599.

43. William Paley. *Natural Theology: or Evidences of the Existence and Attributes of the Deity*, 1802.

44. A set of papers, bearing both Darwin's and Wallace's names, was published as a single article: "On the Tendency of Species to Form Varieties; and on the Perpetuation of Varieties and Species by Natural Means of Selection." *Proceedings of the Linnean Society*, 1858. The following year, Darwin published his own book: *The Origin of Species*. Murray, 1859. Neither Darwin nor Wallace seems to have been aware of Denis Diderot's conjecture from the previous century.

45. Charles Darwin. *The Descent of Man*. Murray, 1871.

46. Herbert Spencer. *Principles of Biology*. Williams & Norgate, 1864, vol. 1, p. 444.

47. John Ussher. *The Annals of the World*, iv, 1658. Ussher also calculated that Adam and Eve were driven from Paradise on Monday, 10 November 10, 4004 BCE, and that the ark touched down on Mount Ararat on Wednesday, May 5, 2348 BCE.

48. See for example: Andrew D. White. *A History of the Warfare of Science with Theology in Christendom*. Appleton, 1897, p. 9.

49. See the discussion in: Mircea Eliade. *The Sacred and the Profane*. (Transl: W. Trask.) Harvest Books, 1957, p. 72.

50. The fact that the theory of evolution was deductive offended many scientists of the time who were committed to the principle of induction from observation promoted by Francis Bacon and others.

51. Darwin initially planned to become an Anglican clergyman. But, later in life, he became increasingly concerned about the problem of evil and leaned toward Deism and finally agnosticism.

52. T. H. Huxley. *Man's Place in Nature*, 1863. Huxley coined the term "agnostic."

53. Huxley's retort was taken, inaccurately, to mean that he preferred to be descended from an ape than from a bishop.

54. For example, stock-market data pass statistical tests of randomness, but everybody knows that the market is influenced by major political, economic and other causal factors.

55. Determinism also fails at the macro level in nonlinear systems that exhibit chaotic behavior.
56. An important feature of post-modernism is that truth statements are evaluated with an eye to the power interest of the authorities making them.
57. Both of these refuted the earlier belief that causation demanded body-to-body interaction.
58. Sigmund Freud. *The Psychopathology of Everyday Life*, 1901; Preface to Theodor Reik. *Ritual: Psycho-analytic Studies*, 1919.
59. Transpersonal psychology built on the work of Abraham Maslow (1908-1970) and is noted for the contributions of Roberto Assagioli (1888-1974), Charles Tart and Kenneth Wilbur.
60. More will be said about the Pilgrims and their religious orientation in the next chapter.
61. The college's stated mission was "To advance Learning and perpetuate it to Posterity; dreading to leave an illiterate Ministry to the Churches." Source: Harvard University.
62. As the empire approached its demise, Voltaire would describe it as "neither Holy, nor Roman, nor an Empire."
63. Bismarck's confirmation class in Berlin was taught by renowned Protestant theologian Friedrich Schleiermacher.
64. Paul Johnson. *A History of Christianity*. Atheneum, 1976. p. 463. Old Catholics rejected the doctrine of papal infallibility.
65. A revision to the treaty in 1984 ended Catholicism's status as the state religion.
66. Stalin seized power in 1922 after Lenin suffered the first of several strokes that finally took his life.
67. Estimates of the number of Christian Armenians killed vary from 500,000 to 1,500,000. This was the first of a number of genocidal campaigns in the 20th century.
68. Roughly 500,000 Turks and more than one million Greeks were affected by the treaty. However Greece claimed that Turkey also engaged in a major campaign of ethnic cleansing.
69. The religious repercussions of the war will be discussed in Chapter 20.
70. Italy instituted racial policies in 1938, apparently under German pressure. However Italian troops committed atrocities on a massive scale in Ethiopia in 1936-1937, including the use of chemical weapons against civilians.
71. Dreyfus, an artillery officer in the French army, was sentenced to life imprisonment in 1894 and again when his case was reviewed in 1899. He was finally pardoned in 1906 and eventually earned the Legion of Honor. It is now universally agreed that Dreyfus was innocent.
72. A notable exception was the Lutheran pastor and theologian Dietrich Bonhöffer who was executed by the Nazis for complicity in an assassination attempt against Hitler. Another, who spoke out from the safety of Switzerland, was Karl Barth.
73. Pius XI. Encyclical *Mit Brennender Sorge* ("With burning worry"), March 10, 1937. Copies were smuggled into Germany and read from pulpits throughout Germany.
74. Criticism of Pius XII became organized in the 1960s, partly as a result of Rolf Hochhuth's controversial play *The Deputy: A Christian Tragedy*.
75. Also, the pope was bound to political neutrality by the Lateran Treaty,

76. *Ephesians* 6:5. Although conventionally attributed to Paul, the authorship of this text is disputed.

77. Ignatius of Antioch. Letter to Polycarp, ch. 4, §3. (Transl: J. Lightfoot.) Early Christian Writings, c.105/1891.

78. To mark the 200th anniversary of the Slave Trade Act, Prime Minister Tony Blair expressed deep sorrow and shame for Britain's role.

79. Nazi Germany, the Soviet Union, and other totalitarian regimes subjected ethnic groups and political dissidents to slavery.

80. Thomas More and other 16th-century utopians contributed to a growing awareness of economic and social inequality.

81. Owen was the founder of the cooperative movement.

82. The Spiritualist movement began in 1848 when two sisters, Margaretta and Catherine Fox of Hydesville, New York, claimed the ability to communicate with the dead. By the end of the century séances—at least some of them fraudulent—were being held across North America and Europe.

83. Karl Marx. Preface to: *Contribution to the Critique of Hegel's Philosophy of Right*, 1843. The book was published 40 years later, after Marx' death.

84. Reverend Herrick Johnson. *Washington Post*. July 7, 1894.

85. Leo XIII. Encyclical *Rerum Novarum*. Vatican, 1891, §17.

86. Karl Barth. *Epistle to the Romans*, first edition, 1918. Quoted in: Clifford Green. *Karl Barth: Theologian of Freedom*. Fortress Books, 1989, p. 14.

87. See for example: Bernard I. Cohen (ed.). *Puritanism and the Rise of Modern Science: the Merton Thesis*. Rutgers University Press, 1990. The predominance of Protestants among the founding members of the Royal Society, which he cited as evidence, was not surprising given England's religious sympathies at the time. Merton's thesis can be compared with Max Weber's claim that economic growth in western society resulted from the puritan ethic.

88. Meister Eckhart. Sermon 52: *Beati Pauperes, Matthew* 5:3. See also: Matthew Fox. *Passion for Creation*. Inner Traditions, 1980/2000, p. 15.

89. Friedrich Nietzsche. *The Gay Science*, section 125, 1882. The famous quote also appears in Nietzsche's *Thus Spoke Zarathustra* of 1891.

90. Cynthia Bourgeault. *Centering Prayer and Inner Awakening*. Cowley Publications, 2004, p. 73. "Cataphatic" refers to a belief that God can be known through the intellect.

91. Éliphas Lévi. *The History of Magic*. (Transl: A. Waite.) Samuel Weiser, 1913/1969, p. 30.

92. Benedict XVI. *Jesus of Nazareth*. (Transl: A. Walker.) Doubleday, 2006/2007, p. 40.

93. A leading Protestant theologian who wrote extensively on the theme of freedom was Karl Barth.

Chapter 17
Evangelical and
Charismatic Christianity

A Simple Faith

From very earliest times, certain people sought to escape from mainstream Christianity to practice a faith of greater simplicity and purity; but history has shown that constant vigilance is needed to avoid the remorseless invasion of laxity and complexity. The desert fathers turned away from the materialism of the cities and the increasing laxity of institutional Christianity; they lived lives of solitary asceticism until the church corralled them into monastic institutions. Cistercian monks split off from the Benedictine Order in 1098, seeking to return to its original simplicity. A century later, Francis of Assisi rejected the bourgeois life of the city to live and work among the destitute. But his order of friars eventually became "lax," and the Capuchins split off in the 16th century to form a more ascetic order.

The Cathar *parfaits* reacted against the worldliness and corruption of the medieval church to live simple, austere lives truer to the ideals of Christ. Many Cathar women lived simple communal lives, possibly inspiring the Beguines of the 12th and 13th centuries who flourished until the bishops found their freedom from ecclesiastical oversight intolerable. Also during the 13th century the "Poor Men of Lyons," preached poverty and self-denial until they were targeted by the Inquisition and either fled into the Alps or were executed. A century later the Friends of God rejected central authority, uniform beliefs and practices, and political involvement; they survived only because of a vacuum of authority caused by a church-state dispute.

The Lutheran, Calvinist and Anglican Churches separated from Rome to free themselves from entrenched tradition, complicated dogma, ecclesiastical authority, and clerical excesses. Soon people were criticizing the Protestant churches for similar reasons—"protesting against Protestantism." The prominent, early 18th-century Anglican clergyman William Law confessed that "we live starving in the Coldness and Deadness of a formal, historical, hearsay-Religion."[1] His observation was not an isolated one. Some people responded by abandoning organized religion altogether, while others broke away in yet another attempt to find the elusive religious simplicity.

The present chapter focuses on religious groups that formed in the 17th and 18th centuries. Like so many before them, the dissidents sought to emulate the simplicity of Jesus' life and the purity of the "apostolic church"—on the dubious assumption that there actually was one—or just to recapture "old-fashioned religion." To emphasize a dual emphasis of missionary work and the Bible, they called themselves "Evangelicals;" the Greek word for "gospel" is *evaggelion* (ευαγγελιον), the "good news" of Jesus Christ. Evangelicals sought a simple religion of the heart, a religion of personal experience. Individually and collectively, people testified to their personal encounter with Jesus and encouraged others to do likewise. Another focus was on atonement for sin and salvation. A key biblical passage was "Christ died for our sins according to the scriptures."[2] Scriptural study focused on the "plain sense of the text," laying the groundwork for the literalism of more recent times. Evangelicals in the early church would have felt more at home in Antioch than in Alexandria.

Early Evangelicalism was strongly egalitarian, appealing to people of all socio-economic strata, especially those who felt marginalized by mainstream Christianity. Its portrayal of Lutheranism, Anglicanism and even the Reformed Church as religions of the upper classes was somewhat unfair, and Calvinism would strongly influence major Evangelical movements. Nonetheless, Evangelicalism emerged as a "folk-religion." It made major inroads into rural populations, particularly in the United States where tradition meant little but independence and self-sufficiency were valued. In rural areas it also provided a social function, keeping families together and providing mutual support in times of need. Evangelical Christianity is still expanding today for some of the same reasons.

Despite its common use in the present context, the term "evangelical" is ambiguous. The early Lutherans also considered themselves "evangelical" to emphasize their focus on the gospels; the term contrasted with "reformed" claimed by Calvinists. Many Lutheran denominations still incorporate the term into their names;[3] however they have a different religious outlook from the groups discussed in this chapter. In an attempt to avoid ambiguity some writers have used "pietist" to refer to Evangelicals; but that term applies more specifically to just one of many Evangelical movements.

Evangelical Movements

Congregationalists

After the English Reformation, Protestants were divided between the majority that was satisfied with minimal changes to the Roman church and a minority which favored more radical changes. The latter faction wanted to dismantle the ecclesiastical hierarchy and to adopt simple forms of worship and austere, work-oriented lifestyles. For their dour austerity, which favored strictly patriarchal family life and shunned all forms of entertainment, they came to be known as "Puritans."[4] Many Puritans fled the country to escape persecution during the brief reign of the Catholic Mary I.

Upon Elizabeth's accession to the throne in 1558 the Puritans returned with added reformist zeal but were dismayed to find themselves, once again, outside the mainstream of Protestant Christianity. The restored Church of England still retained many pre-Reformation features, including an episcopal form of governance, and the Act of Uniformity of 1559 made attendance at Anglican worship services a legal obligation. For their insistence on forming congregations independent of ecclesiastical authority, the Puritans acquired a range of additional descriptors: "Congregationalists," "Independents," "Separatists," and "Dissidents." Unable to secure more radical reforms and facing increasing persecution from the established church, many Puritans fled to the Netherlands during the early years of the 17th century; two important groups of those refugees will be discussed shortly,

Puritans who remained in England, under the Congregationalist and other labels, enjoyed temporary relief from persecution during the Commonwealth established after the execution of King Charles I in 1649. Indeed, for a few years, Puritan ideals held sway; for example both the Lord's Supper and the celebration of Christmas were prohibited by law. Oliver Cromwell, Lord Protector of England, not only supported the Puritans but also reached out to aid dissident groups abroad. He threatened to send the English fleet to Rome if attacks on the Waldensians of northern Italy did not cease. When Pope Alexander VII yielded to the threat, giving the Waldensians a brief respite, Cromwell earned the congratulations of the emperor Ferdinand II.[5] After the monarchy and the Anglican episcopacy were restored, discrimination against the Puritans resumed. They and other independent Protestant groups like the Quakers—now lumped together and called "Nonconformists"—were denied participation in many areas of public life until freedom of religion was finally secured in the 19th century. But discrimination against Nonconformists was never as severe as it was against Catholics and Unitarians.

From one of the groups that fled to the Netherlands, 102 Congregationalist "Pilgrims" eventually sailed to Plymouth, Massachusetts, on the *Mayflower* in 1620. The Pilgrims had originally left England in a protest against religious intolerance, but their goal was not to establish a haven of religious pluralism, with church-state separation. They formed a theocracy in which religious and secular authority was combined, and soon they persecuted other Christian dissidents. New England became renowned for its religious zeal, which would affect the American culture for years to come, and more specifically for its preachers. The grandson of one of the early preachers was Jonathan Edwards (1703-1758) whose "hellfire and damnation" sermons found their way into the myth and legend of early American Christianity. He died a few months after becoming the first president of the College of New Jersey, later renamed Princeton University.

Without a denominational infrastructure to promote uniformity, Congregationalists on both sides of the Atlantic exhibited considerable pluralism in beliefs and practices. Calvinist influence was strong in the early days, and in New England some congregations restricted the sacraments to people who made a public "testimony of grace" asserting that they belonged to the elect.[6] However others held antitrinitarian views, and in the early 19th century a group of Boston Congregationalists formed the American Unitarian Church. Over time, many Congregationalists acquired distinctively liberal views; in the 20th century the main body in the United States merged with the Evangelical and Reformed Church to form the United Church of Christ.[7] In the United Kingdom roughly three-fourths of the Congregationalist churches merged with the Presbyterian Church of England in 1972 to form the United Reformed Church. The rest, known as "continuing Congregationalists" preferred to maintain their traditional independence.

Baptists

The second group of Puritans who fled England for the Netherlands rallied around John Smyth (1570-1612), a disaffected Anglican clergyman who had recently been released from prison. In 1609 Smyth founded a church for fellow religious émigrés in Amsterdam. There, he and fellow Englishman Thomas Helwys (1550-1616) came into contact with the Anabaptist Mennonites who practiced adult, or "believer's," baptism. The Amsterdam church adopted the same practice, as did a church Helwys founded in England in 1612.[8] The timing of baptism became the basis of the schism with Congregationalists. Smyth, Helwys, and their followers called themselves "Brethren of the Baptized Way" or simply "Brethren." But by the 1640s "Baptist" had become popular and it would be their permanent name.[9] In the popular imagination, John the Baptist was a "Baptist," and their movement was traced back to him.[10]

Roger Williams and John Clarke brought Baptist beliefs and practices to the American colonies in the 1630s—less than 20 years after the Congregationalists arrived. Williams (1603-1684), a former Anglican priest, preached in New England; but his advocacy of good relations with Native Americans, religious freedom, and the separation of church and state caused problems, and in 1636 he was banished from Massachusetts. Williams and a few followers bought land from Native Americans in what would become Rhode Island. He established the first Baptist church in America at Providence. Clarke (1609-1676) secured the colony's charter from King Charles II and wrote its constitution guaranteeing religious freedom. Attracted by its liberalism, other nonconformist Christians settled in Rhode Island, and a Jewish congregation was established there in 1658. Migrations of Baptist missionaries to other colonies occurred throughout the 17th century.

Smyth and Helwys emphasized God's universal love and—in opposition to the Calvinist doctrine of the elect—insisted that Jesus died for the whole of humanity. People could accept God's grace and enter into an eternal relationship of love and fellowship with him; or they could reject his grace and condemn themselves to eternal separation. In his confession of faith Smyth asserted: "That men, of the grace of God through the redemption of Christ, are able . . . to repent, to believe, to turn to God, and to attain to eternal life; so on the other hand, they are able themselves to resist the Holy Spirit, to depart from God, and to perish for ever."[11] For their belief in a universal redemption Smyth, Helwys, and their supporters became known as "General Baptists."[12]

Others, who subscribed to the Calvinist doctrine of the elect, earned the descriptor "Reformed" or "Particular Baptists." They drew up a series of confessions, the last and best-known being the London Baptist Confession of Faith of 1689. A key statement affirming the doctrine of election was as follows: "All those that are justified . . . by which they are taken into the number, and enjoy the liberties and privileges of the children of God, have his name put upon them, receive the spirit of adoption, have access to the throne of grace with boldness . . . never cast off, but sealed to the day of redemption, and inherit the promises as heirs of everlasting salvation."[13] Reformed Baptists have always been a relatively small group; they resembled Presbyterians except for insistence on adult baptism and the congregational style of governance.[14]

All Baptists emphasized the importance of conversion: the life-changing experience in which an individual repents of sin and accepts Jesus. But disagreements arose in both Europe and America over whether conversion and baptism guaranteed salvation. One faction, that drew upon the Calvinist doctrine of the perseverance of the saints, insisted that after conversion an individual was incapable of sin; the other argued that the person retained freewill and could "backslide;" continued vigilance was needed throughout the person's life.[15] Most General Baptists opposed the idea of guaranteed salvation, but in the 18th century some American congregations found it necessary to emphasize their position by calling themselves "Freewill Baptists."

Notwithstanding Smyth's confession and the 1689 London Confession, Baptists customarily disdained creeds and formal professions of faith. Beliefs were matters of individual conscience. Not until the early 20th century did Baptists once again acquire strong, unifying convictions; and then, with the rise of fundamentalism, scriptural inerrancy and social issues took precedence over the theological concerns of earlier times.

Baptist worship services in the 17th century were long, often lasting most of the day. Several sermons might be preached and numerous biblical passages read. Since there was no singing or music, sitting through those services must have demanded great patience and fortitude. By the 1670s some Baptist churches began to accept the singing of psalms and hymns.[16] In 1691 a London pastor, Benjamin Keach published the first Baptist hymnal: *Spiritual Melody*, containing over three hundred hymns. In due course singing would become a conspicuous feature of Baptist worship.

Pietists

Pietism conventionally is traced to the Alsatian theologian Philipp Jakob Spener (1635-1705). Spener held several positions as tutor or chaplain at noble courts. Later, while serving as pastor of the Lutheran Church at Frankfurt, he recognized his true mission to be church reform. In a book called *Earnest Desires for a Reform of the True Evangelical Church*, Spener proposed six principles that formed the Pietist manifesto:

- Greater emphasis on biblical study
- Recognition of the priesthood of all believers
- The importance of Christian practice over knowledge
- Restraint and charity in religious controversies
- Increased emphasis on piety and devotion in ministerial training
- Preaching of edifying sermons, understandable by the people.

Not unexpectedly, Pietism met with resistance from Lutheran authorities. In 1695 the theological faculty of Wittenberg University charged Spener with 264 doctrinal errors; only his death saved him from formal heresy proceedings. Notwithstanding, the University of Halle was established in 1694 largely in response to Spener's work; unique among universities of its time, it affirmed the rule of academic freedom.[17]

Pietism reacted against the political entanglement of state churches. More importantly, it was a reaction against the perceived intellectualism of the Lutheran Church; what Luther had intended to be a religion of the heart had evolved into a religion of the mind that only spoke to a scholarly elite. Emphasis had shifted from pastoral care of the laity to university theology schools. Pietism was an appeal for emotional commitment and the encouragement of a personal experience of Jesus Christ; what a person believed was considered relatively unimportant.

Moreover, it asserted, everybody could talk to God, without the need for clerical intermediaries. Significantly, Pietism emphasized good works, which Luther had dismissed as of no value. For the Pietists, "good works" meant the adoption of an ascetic, puritan lifestyle that shunned entertainments such as music, dancing, and the theater.

Pietism flourished in the Lutheran strongholds of Germany and Scandinavia but also spread elsewhere in Europe. Pietism never crystallized into a denomination in its own right, but it influenced several Protestant denominations, including Methodism. It also became a major force in the Moravian Brethren. Among Spener's godsons was the German aristocrat Count Nikolaus von Zinzendorf (1700-1760) who studied at Halle as a young man. One of von Zinzendorf's accomplishments was establishment of the village of Herrnhut on his own lands to provide sanctuary for religious refugees. Herrnhut became a haven for people of many persuasions, and despite internal friction, von Zinzendorf managed to build a strong, coherent religious community. Later he became a bishop in the Moravian Church. Among the many visitors to Herrnhut was a young man who would become a leading Protestant theologian of his time: Friedrich Schleiermacher.[18]

Society of Friends

The Society of Friends ("Quakers") was founded by a group of radical Puritans in 1652, during English Commonwealth. The group's leader was George Fox (1624-1691) of Leicestershire, England. Fox distanced himself from complicated doctrines, reminding his followers that the great heroes of the Old Testament, from Abel to David, were simple men, mostly shepherds or cowherds, not scholars. Fox even criticized those who placed scripture above a personal experience of God. He believed that "God was in every man;" that there was an Inner Light through which we can all experience God and determine right conduct. We did not need organized religion, priests, sacraments, or church buildings—which he derided as "steeple houses." Nor for that matter did we need civil government.[19] Fox often preached outdoors, in town squares or the countryside. Fox was imprisoned several times for public disturbances or "blasphemy."

The Society of Friends soon spread to Ireland and America. The Quakers faced cruel persecution from the Congregationalists of New England. Eventually they found a haven in the colony of Pennsylvania established in 1681 by William Penn (1644-1718). During the 18th century Quakers made their way south and west, establishing numerous frontier settlements. The Society did not appoint official leaders or ministers; however detailed membership records were kept by congregations or "meetings."[20] And, despite Fox's contempt for "steeple houses," meeting houses were built for congregations' use.

Quaker worship services were conducted in silence, broken only if one or more participants felt moved by the Spirit to speak. The Quakers earned their popular name from their tendency to tremble and shake during worship. George Fox did not encourage ecstatic experiences, and members who were strongly drawn to that kind of experience eventually left to found the related group known as the "Shakers." The Quakers, joined only by the Salvation Army among significant Protestant denominations, rejected all sacraments, even baptism.

Quakers affirmed the equality—in civil life as well as in religion—of all people, regardless of gender or social status. In 1660 Margaret Fell published a famous pamphlet justifying equal roles for men and women in the Society[21]—a remarkable achievement at a time when women were discouraged from public discourse. Fell was never ordained because Quakers had no formal ministry; and, over time, women's roles declined. Nevertheless, commitment to social activism increased, and that would become a major defining characteristic.

The Society of Friends was one of the first Christian sects to take a public stance on pacifism, and it would play a leading role in the abolitionist movement. George Fox first came into contact with slavery during a trip to the plantations of Barbados, and he studied it further during an extended visit to the American colonies. During the latter part of the 17th century, Quakers on both sides of the Atlantic issued declarations calling for an end to slavery. The Society's efforts to end slavery increased in the 18th century.[22] By the end of the century, John Woolman (1720-1772) claimed that "there was not a slave in the possession of a Friend in good standing, except where slaves were held by trustees, and state laws did not allow them to be set free."[23] The claim may not have been completely true, but the Society's commitment to the emancipation of slaves continued unabated.

Methodists

Methodism began when a group of dedicated students met in Oxford, England for Bible study and devotions. Two of the participants in those meetings, which lasted from 1729 to 1735, were John Wesley (1703-1791), a recently ordained Anglican priest, and his younger brother Charles. Members of the group sought spiritual growth through fasting and abstinence from entertainments and luxury. They attached great importance to service: frequently visiting the poor, the sick, and prison inmates. Methodism was influenced by the Pietism of Philipp Spener. Interestingly, "Pietist" and "Methodist" both began as pejorative terms, only later accepted by the movements themselves. "Methodists" or, in the vernacular of the day, *Methodies*, referred to the methodical nature of their study and devotion.

As time went on, Wesley focused almost exclusively on preaching a religion based on scripture and devotion. Wesley officially remained an Anglican priest for most of his life, and his goal was to reform the Church of England rather than found a new denomination. Nevertheless he emerged as the spiritual leader of an Evangelical revival that swept England in the 1730s. While the Anglican Church was perceived as the religion of the upper classes, Methodism reached out to ordinary people, and much of its support came from industrial and agricultural workers. Like George Fox, Wesley and his followers became outdoor preachers, finding audiences in towns, villages or even open country. Charles Wesley (1707-1788) wrote hymns to express popular devotion. Along with his grandson Samuel Sebastian Wesley, he is numbered among England's greatest hymn writers.

Because the Church of England was the state religion and he was an ordained minister, John Wesley had to secure local bishops' approval to preach in England, and some denied him permission. However no such restrictions applied in North America. Wesley traveled extensively throughout the colonies, winning many converts and recruiting missionaries. Among those whom he appointed to help in this ministry were the famous circuit rider Francis Asbury (1745-1816) and his close contemporary Thomas Coke. True to their distrust of the Anglican ecclesiastical structure, English Methodists never established an episcopacy; but to Wesley's dismay, Coke founded the Methodist Episcopal Church in Baltimore and declared himself a bishop. American Methodism has retained an episcopacy since that time. Methodism gained prominence after the American Revolution when the Anglican Church fell into disfavor because of its Tory associations.

Early in life John Wesley was attracted to the teachings of William Law and even to those of the Swedish mystic Emanuel Swedenborg.[24] For much longer he was influenced by the Dutch anti-Calvinist theologian Jacob Arminius (1560-1609). He also maintained a close friendship with John Fletcher—"Fletcher of Madeley"—a mystically inclined Anglican priest born in Switzerland.

Wesley lived during the heyday of the Enlightenment, but he was never influenced by the academic skepticism of the time; in fact he was not a great intellectual, preferring action and devotion to theological or philosophical speculation. Nevertheless, he embraced traditional notions of the Trinity and the divinity of Christ. He also embraced the Lutheran tenet of justification through faith, and the need for a "new birth" in Christ. Rebirth could be a highly emotional, ecstatic experience; at one of Wesley's gatherings people "trembled, they cried, they prayed, they roared aloud; all of them lying on the ground. I began to sing; yet they could not rise, but sang as they lay along."[25] But an intense experience did not necessarily imply immediate salvation. Rather, Wesley taught, Christians went through a life-long process of sanctification through which the effects of sin are washed away and we "are enabled, through grace, to love God with all our hearts and to walk in his holy commandments blameless.[26]

The goal of sanctification was to attain, before death, a final state of "Christian perfection." That doctrine was based on scriptural passages such as: "Be ye therefore perfect, even as your Father which is in heaven is perfect."[27] Wesley explained perfection as "purity of intention, dedicating all the life to God. It is the giving God all our heart . . . devoting, not a part, but all our soul, body, and substance to God . . . enabling us to walk as Christ walked . . . loving God with all our heart, and our neighbour as ourselves."[28] Perfection extended beyond religion and morality to include the puritan work ethic and a life of "industry and frugality."[29] Like the General Baptists, Wesley firmly rejected Calvinist notions of predestination, insisting that God's grace and the possibility of salvation were offered to everyone. He was even willing to soften emphasis on "Almighty God," if the concept of omnipotence or omniscience interfered with human choice.

Methodism became the point of departure for a number of new religious movements. George Whitefield (1714-1770), one of Wesley's early collaborators, became a major rival for the hearts and minds of the denomination. Convinced of predestination he eventually led a breakaway group holding beliefs similar to Presbyterianism.[30] Whitefield is considered one of the fathers of American Evangelicalism. Brigham Young (1801-1877) converted to Methodism but later succeeded Joseph Smith as leader of the Church of Jesus Christ of Latter-Day Saints, the Mormons. Social conscience led Methodist minister William Booth (1829-1912) to found the Salvation Army. Another offshoot of Methodism was the Holiness movement that will be discussed later.

Like other denominations in the United States, Methodism had to confront issues of slavery and racial segregation. Before the Civil War, northern and southern Methodists found themselves on opposite sides of the slavery issue, leading to a division that was not resolved until the mid 20th century. In the late 18th and early 19th centuries African-Americans were normally confined to the balconies of churches and excluded from full participation in congregational life. To escape such humiliation, in 1816 a group of African-Americans in Philadelphia formed the African Methodist Episcopal Church. It became the principal black denomination in the United States, playing a leading role through the whole period from the Civil War to the civil-rights movement of the 1960s. Black churches of all persuasions served a vital role, providing members with a supportive community and a sense of dignity in a society where they were so often marginalized.

Universalists

The basic premise of universal salvation can be traced back to church father Origen who argued that the eternity of hell was an affront to God's infinite goodness and the perfection of his creation.[31] But Universalism did not become a significant religious movement until the 18th century. Its birth can be traced to ideas expressed, more or less independently, by two individuals in Britain and three in the American colonies. The former were Welshman James Relly (1720-1778) and his close contemporary, Englishman Richard Clarke.[32] The latter were George de Benneville (1703-1793) and, a generation later, John Murray and Judith Sargent Stevens. In 1782 Stevens, a resident of Gloucester, Massachusetts, published *A Universalist Catechism*; her achievement was comparable with Margaret Fell's.

Reacting against Calvinist doctrine of the elect, Universalists taught that all people are children of God. But going beyond General Baptist and Methodist teachings, they preached a doctrine of universal salvation. The Universalists did not believe that God condoned sin, but they refused to accept that a loving God would submit any of his children to everlasting torment. In Stevens' words: "Though [God] is reconciled to the sinner, yet he is not to their sin, he is a determined foe to every vice: but he beholds mankind cloathed in the righteousness of the Redeemer, in which he can see no spot or blemish."[33] Because of their denial of eternal damnation Universalists earned the popular label "No Hellers." Origen conceded that there might be punishment after death for sin but argued that it must necessarily be of limited duration. Similarly, some Universalists were prepared to accept the need for temporal punishment, though they did not explicitly endorse the Catholic doctrine of purgatory.

The Universalist Church in America was officially organized in 1793, and from then on Universalism spread throughout the eastern United States and Canada. Like many Evangelical movements Universalism challenged people to reach out and embrace those whom society marginalized. The Gloucester church included a freed slave among its charter members. And, beginning in 1863 with Olympia Brown (1835-1926), the Universalists became the first denomination to ordain women to the ministry.[34] In 1961 Universalists in the United States merged with Unitarians to form the Unitarian-Universalist Association,[35] but their roots were distinct, and Universalism was always more Evangelical.

From Tent Revivals to the Southern Baptist Convention

Revivals and Awakenings

The term "revival" is used in two ways. It can denote an event or meeting held at a particular location and lasting a few days. Such events have a number of antecedents, notably the "holy fairs" organized in 17th-century Scotland and Northern Ireland.[36] They remain popular in Evangelical churches to this day. Alternatively, "revival" can denote a general process of religious renewal extending over a period of months or years; the Evangelical revival led by John and Charles Wesley in 18th-century England was a case in point. In the United States the larger-scale revivals became known as "awakenings."

The First Great Awakening took place between 1730 and 1780. It was initiated by Jonathan Edwards (1703-1758), the famous Congregationalist preacher from Massachusetts. Although he was a scholar with strong Calvinist leanings, his goal was to recapture the religious fervor and strict lifestyle of the Pilgrim Fathers. In the combination of intellectual and emotional religious traditions he set a tone that would have considerable influence on American Evangelicalism.[37] A powerful speaker, Edwards preached the fear of God and threat of hell-fire; to illustrate:

> There is no want of power in God to cast wicked men into hell at any moment . . . [They] are held in the hand of God, over the pit of hell; they have deserved the fiery pit, and are already sentenced to it; and God is dreadfully provoked, his anger is as great towards them as to those that are actually suffering the executions of the fierceness of his wrath in hell . . . [T]he devil is waiting for them, hell is gaping for them, the flames gather and flash about them.[38]

Edwards' rhetoric drew large crowds, and many participants had conversion experiences. Methodist George Whitefield joined the movement, traveling throughout the American colonies from his home base in the port city of Savannah, Georgia. Presbyterian preachers from Scotland also participated. They brought with them a tradition of audience participation in which people shouted affirmations like "Amen" during sermons; soon the practice became a hallmark of American Evangelicalism.[39]

By the 1750s and '60s white settlers were pressing westward through Virginia and North Carolina, crossing the Appalachian Mountains into areas still inhabited by Native Americans. The new territories created vast opportunities for missionary work and challenges to meet the religious needs of settlers on the frontier. Presbyterians, Quakers and Methodists were the first to respond. Churches and schools were built, but much of the work was handled by itinerant ministers, or "circuit riders." Methodist Francis Asbury covered a vast territory from Ohio to North Carolina; he was one of the few British missionaries to stay in America after the revolution.

The Second Great Awakening occurred in the 1820s and '30s.[40] Led by Charles Grandison Finney (1792-1875) it was motivated in part by the sense that the American Revolution, with its Deist underpinnings, had produced a secular society in which religion was pushed to the sidelines. Although Finney was a Presbyterian minister, he moved beyond strict Calvinism to preach a message of broader appeal.[41] During a lifetime of fiery oratory he claimed to have converted

500,000 people. He was also a strong supporter of the abolitionist movement; from 1830 onward he denied communion to slaveholders in his churches in New York City.

Although the Second Great Awakening began in New England, it attained its most impressive proportions in Kentucky, Tennessee and Ohio, which by then had attained statehood. Full-time Presbyterian and Methodist preachers continued to serve the vast region. But farmers, artisans and others emerged as self-proclaimed Baptist preachers. Their qualifications might consist of nothing more than intense religious fervor, ability—however limited—to read the Bible, and a gift for oratory. By the end of the Second Awakening, Methodists and Baptists had displaced Anglicans, Presbyterians and Quakers as the largest Protestant groups in America.[42] In an attempt to overcome denominational and doctrinal exclusiveness, former Presbyterian ministers Thomas Campbell (1763-1854) and his son Alexander formed the Disciples of Christ. The Disciples disavowed formal creeds and offered membership to all who would confess belief in Jesus Christ and accept baptism by immersion.

Another significant awakening occurred in the 1850s, and Evangelical revivals were common in the camps of both the Union and Confederate armies during the American Civil War. By the time the war ended in 1865, Evangelical Protestantism was fast becoming the "official" religion of the United States.[43] It was common to speak of the United States as a "Christian nation," on the understanding that the term excluded Catholics, Mormons, and other inconvenient members of the Christian family. In 1870 college president W. A. Stearns could affirm: "Never since the crucifixion has the religion of Christ in its purest forms had a stronger hold on the popular hearth than at this day."[44] Evangelicalism fitted in well with democracy, pragmatism, "Common Sense" philosophy,[45] and laissez-faire capitalism to set the tone of American culture well into the 20th century.[46] The sense of wellbeing and optimism supported the notion of *postmillennialism*—the belief in 1,000 years of human progress, at the end of which Jesus Christ will return to earth.[47] Importantly, during the 1,000-year "kingdom," good will triumph over evil and Christianity will spread throughout the world, spearheaded by American evangelists.[48]

Revivals continued to dominate American popular religion, particularly in the south and midwest, throughout the 19th century and into the 20th. In cities revivals could be held in churches or other large buildings, but in rural areas they were held in barns or tents and eventually in permanent campgrounds. Revivals might last more than a week during which successions of preachers would exhort attendees to turn away from sin and "accept Jesus into their lives." The emotional intensity of revivals, stimulated not only by the preaching but also by days of collective fervor, gave rise to frequent charismatic outbursts, swooning and healings. Converts were baptized in nearby rivers or lakes. The environment of the revival tent was a far cry from the cathedrals of Europe. American poet Walt Whitman (1819-1892) commented on "the earnest words of the sweating Methodist preacher . . . impress'd seriously at the camp-meeting."[49]

Families traveled long distances by wagon and camped at the sites. They often brought with them live animals, even cows, to supply meat and milk during their stay.[50] Surplus food could be traded with other attendees. Tent or camp meetings might be the only formal religious activity rural people experienced. At other times the most they could do was to pray, sing with family members, or—if literate—read the Bible or tracts left by itinerant preachers. Revivals also served an important social function, helping to establish cohesion in thinly populated areas of the country. In due course the successful concept of the tent revival was exported to other countries, even back to Europe where Evangelical Christianity had originated.

The revivalist movement was not limited to camps and sweating preachers. Dwight Lyman Moody (1837-1899) ushered in a new style of revival preachers in business suits. In place of the hell-fire, Bible-thumping style of his predecessors, Moody focused heavily on his own testimony and a message of the love of Christ.[51] The 20th century saw the emergence of stadium rallies and crusades where well-known evangelists, from former baseball player Billy Sunday (1862-1935) to Billy Graham (1918-), attracted hundreds of thousands of participants. The broadcast media provided opportunities to reach even larger audiences. Aimee Semple McPherson (1890-1944), founder of the Angelus Temple in Los Angeles, began radio broadcasts in 1924. Kathryn Kuhlman (1907-1976) and Oral Roberts both made successful transitions from tent revivals to radio and television. Robert Schuler, who initially held services in a drive-in movie theater, became famous for his weekly "Hour of Power" broadcast from the Crystal Cathedral in Los Angeles. Television ministries now broadcast 24 hours a day, seven days a week.

Institutionalized Evangelicalism

Evangelical Christianity has always valued freedom from ecclesiastical authority, and to speak of "institutionalized Evangelicalism" sounds like an oxymoron. Congregationalist and Baptist congregations, in particular, have always operated independently: calling their own ministers, choosing forms of worship, and adopting their own doctrinal leanings and social attitudes. However, from an early date, loose affiliations were formed for mutual support, to explore common interests, and to coordinate missionary activity. American Methodists went further to adopt an ecclesiastical structure that resembled the Catholic, Orthodox and Anglican episcopacies.

The National Assembly of General Baptists was founded in England in 1654; and a regional assembly was founded in Philadelphia in 1707. The first national organization in the United States was the Baptist Board of Foreign Missions, or "Triennial Convention," founded in 1814.[52] The Northern Baptist Convention, successor to the Triennial Convention, was founded in 1907, eventually adopting the more inclusive name: American Baptist Churches in the USA. Cooperative activities among African-American Baptists date back to the 1830s. The National Baptist Convention, currently the largest such grouping, was founded in 1895. A very recent addition to the growing number of assemblies is the Association of Reformed Baptist Churches in America, founded in 1997.

Whereas most denominations restrict preaching to properly ordained ministers,[53] many early Baptist preachers were self-trained, responding to what they believed was a "call" from God. The call could be dramatic, even less than welcome: "Sometimes the call comes by means of an audible voice, accompanied by the bright light or a dramatic vision. In many cases, the person fights against the call as the last possible vocation into which he (or occasionally she) should go."[54] Later, regional and national assemblies established Baptist seminaries to provide formal ministerial training. Each seminary's policies were set by assembly leaders, and its position on theological and social issues—conservative or "moderate"—reflected their biases.[55] Most Baptist assemblies have always been somewhat fluid, merging or dividing according to prevailing currents of opinion; today more than 60 distinct sects or denominations identify themselves as Baptist.

Normally, assemblies or conventions can exert moral pressure but have little or no jurisdictional power. The Southern Baptist Convention, by contrast, has gathered very substantial power. The SBC was established in 1845 amid mounting north-south enmity that culminated in the Civil War. Southern Baptists maintained segregationist policies from then on, and African-Americans were not welcome in most congregations until the late 1960s. In the 1980s fundamentalist elements seized control of the SBC and have exercised steadily increasing control over the policies and operations of its seminaries, missions and other programs.[56] As part of its fundamentalist agenda, the SBC currently promotes the subservience of women and erosion of the traditional separation of church and state. Fundamentalism will be discussed in more detail in Chapter 19.

Many Baptists continue to witness to their faith in much the same way as did John Smyth, Thomas Helwys, and Roger Williams. One of them is former president Jimmy Carter, a lifelong Baptist who freely describes himself as a born-again Christian. He and others grieve over the corruption of their denomination by fundamentalist elements. In 2000 the Southern Baptist Convention adopted a statement: "Baptist Faith and Message," which deleted traditional language affirming Jesus Christ as the sole authority for beliefs and practice. The effect of that deletion, in Carter's words was the "substitution of Southern Baptist leaders for Jesus as the interpreters of biblical Scripture." He added:

> [I]t soon became clear that [the statement] would be imposed as a mandatory creed on all convention officers, employees, deans and professors of colleges and seminaries, and even missionaries who were serving in other countries. The strictness of this mandatory compliance has exceeded that in the Roman Catholic Church or within other Protestant denominations.[57]

In short the fundamentalist leaders have transformed the SBC into something resembling an episcopacy. Southern Baptists form the largest Protestant denomination in America today. Fundamentalists often claim to be "conservative," but that descriptor is suspect because the rigidity of beliefs and political activism represent significant departures not only from Evangelical tradition but from core Christian values.

In addition to assemblies and conventions linking congregations of similar persuasions, like Baptists, multi-denominational groupings have also emerged. In 1846 Christians from ten countries met in London to explore the formation of an interfaith Evangelical organization. That initiative planted the seed which eventually produced a number of national and international associations spanning denominational boundaries. The National Association of Evangelicals was formed in 1942 to coordinate the activities of American denominations and congregations with Evangelical leanings. As of the time of writing, the NAE represents 35 million people in the United States and wields considerable political power. The World Evangelical Alliance, formed in 1951 to provide international coordination, describes itself as

> a network of churches in 121 nations that have each formed an Evangelical alliance . . . to give a worldwide identity, voice and platform to more than 335 million Christians. Seeking holiness, justice and renewal at every level of society—individual, family, community and culture, God is glorified and the nations of the earth are forever transformed.[58]

Multi-denominational institutions with specific agendas have also been established. The work of the Evangelical Climate Initiative and Evangelical Environmental Network will be discussed in Chapter 22.

Charismatic Christianity

No clear dividing line can be drawn between the Evangelical and charismatic styles of Christianity; but charismatic Christianity has roots in history at least as deep. People in some of the earliest Christian communities experienced states of ecstasy, had visions, healed the sick, spoke in tongues, and prophesied. By the end of the second century charismatic practices had been condemned by church officials under the blanket label of "Montanism." But they surfaced at points throughout Christian history, particularly in rural environments, and now they have once again become popular, even in mainstream Christianity.

Early Protestant Charismatics

The Cévenol movement, a cousin of German Pietism, emerged in the 17th century. It developed in the Languedoc region in the south of France, a region noted for its religious independence which had produced the Cathars of the Middle Ages. The Cévenols came under Calvinist influence and were caught in the persecution of the Huguenots under Louis XIV. In 1688 a young peasant girl, Isabeau Vincent, went into an ecstatic trance and began prophesying in a perfect northern French she did not know.[59] A wave of religious fervor followed in which large numbers of people had charismatic experiences. Believing they were guided by the Holy Spirit, the Cévenols took up arms against the French army. They scored some early victories in the mountainous terrain where the army was at a disadvantage, but the rebellion was ultimately crushed. Still, remnants of the Cévenol movement survived for some time. Pietism itself produced its own charismatic experiences; in the late 1720s a spiritual renewal, at Nikolaus von Zinzendorf's Herrnhut village witnessed a bout of visions, prophecy and healings.

The "Shakers" earned their name from the uncontrolled convulsions members exhibited at worship services; people whirled and shook—as they did at some of John Wesley's revivals. The Shakers split off from the Society of Friends in the mid-18th century when their ecstatic worship aroused the criticism of Quaker leaders. Significantly, the number of women who left the Society was disproportionately large, and women would play a major role in the new sect. The situation in their original Quaker home may have been comparable with that in Corinth where an exasperated Paul condemned female charismatics to silence.

An early leader of the Shakers was Englishwoman Ann Lee (1736-1784). While in prison during religious persecution in the 1770s, she had a conversion experience convincing her that the millennium was at hand.[60] She also became convinced that she was the Second Coming of Christ, the female representative of God the Father-Mother, complementing Jesus, the male representative. Followers acclaimed her as "Mother Ann." In 1774 Mother Ann Lee had another vision in which she was told to leave England and move with her husband and several followers to Niskeyuna, near Albany in the colony of New York. From there Shaker communities sprang up throughout the northeast United States. Communities were independent, some supporting themselves through creating hand-crafted

furniture.[61] Work was considered inseparable from religious expression; the
Shakers' motto—worthily echoing Benedict of Nursia's *ora et labora*—was
"Hands to work, hearts to God."

The Shakers expressed a yearning for lives of simplicity, purity and joy. As in
the Society of Friends, men and women enjoyed equality; and, at a time when
racial segregation was the norm in American religion, the communities accepted
free blacks and former slaves. There was no formal ministry, but deacons
and deaconesses were appointed with pastoral and worship responsibilities.
Worship services included both singing and dancing. Citing precedents in the
Old Testament, Shakers emphasized the link between ecstatic dance and praise;
however stories that Mother Ann encouraged people to dance naked are probably
apocryphal.[62] Charismatic healing was another element in Shaker worship, and
Ann Lee herself is said to have healed many ailments during her life.

Although Lee was married, she became convinced that celibacy was essential
for establishment of the kingdom of God on earth. Later generations of leaders
sought to strengthen the sect's ascetic lifestyle by requiring men and women to live
in separate buildings in the communities. After Lee's death followers organized
the United Society of Believers in Christ's Second Appearing, also known as the
Millennial Church. At its peak, at the beginning of the American Civil War, the
Shaker movement had thousands of followers. But since the movement could
only grow by conversion and adoption—by then celibacy was mandated—it soon
dwindled; and now only a handful of Shakers survive.

Not all charismatics were Caucasian. The African slaves imported to the
Americas brought with them forms of religious expression that, when overlaid
by the Christianity their masters forced on them, had much in common with
Shaker practices. Determined efforts were made to suppress hand-clapping,
foot-stomping, and ecstatic outbursts in the churches because such practices
were considered pagan and offended white worshippers.[63] But slaves also held
clandestine religious services where they could give free expression to their
religious aspirations; in those services we find one of the roots of Pentecostalism.
The "spirituals" slaves sang more openly represented another form of religious
expression that won favor beyond it humble origins.[64]

The Holiness and Pentecostal Movements

The Holiness movement was an offshoot of Methodism, driven by the sense that
the parent denomination had lost the simple, emotive appeal of its founders and
had become institutionalized and "mainstream." It began in 1836 when Sarah
Worrall Lankford formed a group in New York City known as the Tuesday Meeting
for the Promotion of Holiness. First attended solely by Methodist women, it soon
attracted both men and women and members of other denominations.

Distinguishing characteristics of the Holiness movement were belief in a life-changing conversion experience and emphasis on the gifts of the Holy Spirit as the means for accomplishing perfection. Whereas John Wesley taught that perfection could only be earned over a lifetime, Holiness members claimed that it could be attained in a single experience of the Holy Spirit. Members also stressed the importance of piety and personal morality, emulating the lifestyle of the early Puritans; dancing, drinking and gambling were prohibited, and conservative attire was required. Initially the Holiness movement spread within existing Evangelical churches; but eventually it took more definite form in a number of new denominations, including the Church of the Nazarene, founded in 1908 by Phineas F. Bresee.

Early Pentecostalism overlapped with the Holiness movement and developed from it; but it also drew inspiration from the charismatic Christianity of the slaves in America. Emphasis was less on a puritan lifestyle and more on demonstrating the gifts of the Holy Spirit. In 1867 the National Camp Meeting Association for the Promotion of Christian Holiness issued an invitation to people "irrespective of denominational tie . . . who feel themselves comparatively isolated in their profession of holiness [and] would realize together a Pentecostal baptism of the Holy Ghost." That may have been the first use of the term "Pentecostal;" but as a distinct movement Pentecostalism dates from the beginning of the 20th century. In 1901 Agnes Ozman (1870-1937) experienced glossolalia, or "speaking in tongues," during a prayer meeting at Bethel Bible College in Topeka, Kansas. Charles Fox Parham (1873-1929), the college's president became the leader of a new group that recognized glossolalia as evidence of "baptism of the spirit," a second decisive experience—the first being baptism by water—that demonstrates lasting holiness. The practice of glossolalia will be discussed in more detail later.[65]

In 1906, William James Seymour (1870-1922), a black Holiness preacher from Louisiana, opened a mission in Los Angeles for a multiracial congregation drawn from the city's lowest socio-economic strata. People had ecstatic experiences, testified, prayed over the sick, danced, fell down in trance, and spoke in tongues.[66] The mission became the Apostolic Faith Movement, and news of its experiences spread throughout the United States and to many other countries. Offended by the multiracialism of Seymour's mission, Parham founded the Assembly of God, also based in Los Angeles.[67] Growing racial divisions in the early 20th century also produced the all-white Church of God and the black Church of God in Christ.[68] However segregation was rarely complete, and the inclusiveness of Pentecostal churches contrasted with the racialism of most American churches. In 1953 the Full Gospel Business Men's Fellowship was founded in California, and before long people from many denominations began to attend.

Whereas Evangelical Christianity and the Holiness movement first flourished in rural areas, early Pentecostalism was a religion of the inner cities. However, in recent decades, Pentecostal churches have sprung up in the affluent suburbs around major cities. William Seymour would not recognize the Pentecostal megachurches attended by tens of thousands of middle-class whites. Pentecostalism is now the fastest-growing form of Christianity in the world, spreading not only in the United States, but in South America, Asia, Africa, Russia and elsewhere. In countries subject to racial discrimination it provided opportunities for minorities to participate, even in leadership positions. In traditionally patriarchal countries it provided similar opportunities for women. If fundamentalist religion became narrow and exclusive, Pentecostalism welcomed all who sought the Spirit.

The Pentecostals of the early-20th century believed that Christ's return was imminent. The second coming would usher in "a new heaven and a new earth;"[69] past injustices would be put right, barriers dividing people would be broken down, and new spiritual and material opportunities would open up. That belief has now undergone a subtle change; many modern Pentecostals believe that the kingdom can be attained here and now. The fervor and enthusiasm of Pentecostal services—and particularly the extravagant choreography in larger churches—not only provide a glimpse of what lies ahead but affirm that all who believe can participate in the good things of life. Many Pentecostals have bought into "prosperity gospel," or "positive confession theology," which holds that material prosperity can be attained by faith and affirmation.[70] Two men who put that principle to good use were evangelist Oral Roberts (1918-) and Norman Vincent Peale (1898-1993) whose book *The Power of Positive Thinking* sold nearly 20 million copies.[71] As will be seen in the next chapter, similar principles were promoted by leaders of New Thought.

Charismatic Religious Practices

Pentecostals are Bible-oriented but may or may not insist on strict literalism. In fact little attention is paid to beliefs of any kind, except for redemption through Jesus, the second coming, and the power of the Holy Spirit. Worship services may include the traditional sermon and scriptural readings; but major emphasis is given to spontaneous testimony and praise. Songs of praise, often consisting of just a few phrases or lines, may be repeated over and over again. Typically, singing is accompanied by a band whose musical genre may stand in stark contrast with the sedate organ music of high-church Christianity.

Pentecostal services are characterized by *enthusiasm*, and we are reminded that the Greek word *enthousiasmos* (ενθουσιασμος) captured the sense of "having God within oneself."[72] Charismatic worship draws upon primal religious impulses.[73] In many countries it has tapped into folk religion, spirit possession, shamanism, and other primitive practices long opposed by institutionalized Christianity. William Seymour and other early black leaders introduced African religious forms into multiracial Pentecostalism and made them acceptable in Christianity in much the same way as jazz musicians brought African musical forms to western society. African religious and musical forms had lain dormant—or in some cases not so dormant—in the black American psyche until the turn of the 20th century. In the new environment of today's Pentecostal megachurches, the "spontaneity" of worship is now choreographed, but the effect on the people is much the same.

The whole congregation may enter an altered state of consciousness in which people sway to the music, weep, cry out, clap their hands, wave their arms, and dance.[74] The experience is one of ecstatic union with God. In the worlds of one charismatic minister: "If we have no joy within our hearts, what does that do for the Gospel of Jesus Christ?"[75] The state of ecstasy may be so intense that worshipers lose consciousness and slump to the floor—the phenomenon of swooning, "being slain in the spirit," "resting in the spirit," or "falling under the power." As we have seen, such experiences were not uncommon at the Evangelical gatherings of earlier times. Several of the great mystics, including Teresa of Ávila (1515-1582), had similar experiences.

One of the defining practices of charismatic Christianity has been *glossolalia*. The term comes from two Greek words: *glossa* (γλωσσα, "tongue" or "language")[76] and *laleo* (λαλεω, "speak" or "exclaim"). Alternative terms are ecstatic utterance, "speaking in tongues," "praying in the spirit," and "private prayer language." People, who may have no gift for conventional oratory or confidence to speak in public, spontaneously break into monologues in "unknown tongues." A preacher in the Church of God described his own experience: "And then th'Holy Ghost came in and I was speakin'. I didn't know what. I knowed my tongue was movin' but I didn't know what I was sayin' till that moved on. I guess it lasted fifteen minutes—or maybe not that long."[77] Interpreters are sometimes employed to translate the speeches for other participants in the service, but most often others simply participate vicariously in the speaker's ecstasy. Practitioners describe the experience as enormously empowering, giving them the conviction of being filled with the Holy Spirit. According to charismatics, the ability to speak in tongues can be acquired through prayer, but it can also be conveyed through the laying-on of hands by someone already baptized of the spirit.[78] The laying-on of hands is significant because the occurrence of glossolalia reported in *Acts* 19:6 followed a combined baptism and confirmation by the apostle Paul.

Linguists have detected occasional words from extant foreign languages, but the content of most glossolalic utterances is unrecognizable.[79] In that sense glossolalia must be distinguished from instances where people like Isabeau Vincent spoke in languages they just did not know. It must also be distinguished from the situation at Pentecost, where "every man heard [the apostles] speak in his own language,"[80] and from prophetic preaching, which is believed to be meaningful communication from God. An important tenet of Pentecostal and other charismatic movements is that revelation and prophecy did not end with canonical scripture but are part of the ongoing dialog between God and his people.

From the first or second century onward, mainstream Christianity perceived the spontaneity of charismatic Christianity as dangerous. In more recent times glossolalia became a major target of criticism. Some authorities feared, as Paul did, that glossolalia might encourage spiritual pride and competitiveness.[81] Bishop James Pike of California condemned glossolalia in the 1960s on the grounds that it verged on heresy.[82] Ironically, Pike later attracted colleagues' criticism for publicly discussing paranormal phenomena experienced after his son's death. Recently a dispute erupted within the Southern Baptist Convention over the right of missionaries to use a "private prayer language"—or the right of seminary professors to advocate the practice. The modern charismatic movement is still viewed with suspicion by leaders of mainstream denominations.

Some Holiness and Evangelical churches practice foot-washing in obedience to Jesus' example at the Last Supper and as a demonstration of humility.[83] Snake- and fire-handling are now extremely rare, but a few churches in remote rural areas retain those practices.[84]

Healing

Charismatic Christians believe that healing was not just a temporary dispensation in apostolic times but is available in our own time.[85] Often referred to as "faith healing," it draws its inspiration from the story of the woman healed of "an issue of blood;" Jesus' comment to her was: "thy faith hath made thee whole; go in peace, and be whole."[86]

From early times people have believed that certain individuals had the gift of healing. In rural areas where professional medical services were unavailable,[87] the sick—or people whose animals were sick—turned to "healers" for relief. Midwives and "wise women" often served as faith healers, though men also practiced the art. Although institutional Christianity generally ignored faith healing, during witch hunts many healers were put to death. Nevertheless, their ministry continued into the 20th century.[88] Typical conditions treated by healers were burns, bleeding, warts, and oral herpes.[89] Therapies included the prescription of herbal medications, invocation of scriptural passages, sucking or blowing over a wound, and the laying-on of hands. Choice of scriptural passage was often kept secret, but some healers disclosed that they used verses from *Ezekiel*.[90] "Healer" might imply that practitioners took credit for the work, but almost all attributed the healing to God; for example: "It ain't me that cures it. I just do th' work and put faith in God and God does the work hisself . . . He does the healin'."[91]

Healing became one of the principal ministries of charismatic Christianity; and interest has since spread across the religious spectrum.[92] Charismatic Christians differ from mainstream Protestants, but agree with Catholics, in insisting that "miracles" are still possible. Many Christian saints and modern charismatics are believed to have facilitated healings. While Catholics in increasing numbers of people flock to shrines like Lourdes, even larger numbers—including Catholics—flock to charismatic healing services. "Spiritual healing" encompasses the various charismatic healing practices. It includes faith healing and also "psychic healing" whose most famous practitioners may have been Ambrose and Olga Worrall.[93] Intuitive, or "psychic," diagnosis will be discussed in the next chapter. If spiritual healing was once restricted to particular social groups, practitioners are drawn from all classes and educational levels.

Chrismation, the anointing with oil, may be employed; but the most common techniques are prayer and the laying-on of hands. Healers pray over the person, usually invoking the Holy Spirit, and either touch the forehead or place their hands on the person's head. Kathryn Kuhlman (1907-1976) often prayed thus:

> Today, Jesus stands ready to hear your cry and to answer prayer for you. He is interested in every detail of your life. He knows you better than you know yourself and is touched with the feeling of your infirmities and your needs. It is my prayer that even now Jesus shall make His Person and Presence a reality to you and give you His faith, and complete confidence in His power and love and promise—and the desire of your heart.[94]

Emphasis may be placed either on curing specific maladies or on "healing the whole person," including physical, emotional and mental conditions or even traumatic life situations. Healing may be offered in one-on-one or group counseling sessions; alternatively, it may be offered at regularly scheduled church services, at tent revivals, or at stadium rallies.

Charismatic healing, particularly at large gatherings, has been the target of considerable criticism. Critics point to notorious cases of fraudulent healers, staged healing demonstration, and exploitation of vulnerable people.[95] On the other hand, not all healers are charlatans, and large numbers of people testify that significant healings can occur.[96] Apparent failure can perhaps be attributed to misplaced expectations; for example, Ruth Carter Stapleton wrote: "When we pray for healing of physical symptoms, we often see no change because we are praying for and expecting God to heal the symptom rather than to make us whole. We must realize that it is God's will for us to be whole and understand that our Father really desires to heal our attitudes."[97]

The conduct of some large healing services, in the eyes of critics, is "theatrical." Certainly an atmosphere of heightened emotion may be created to give participants a sense of expectancy that healings will take place. Swooning may be anticipated and provided for: upon the laying-on of hands the recipient falls back into the arms of strategically placed catchers. But people testify that both the heightened emotion and the swooning have profound effects on them, convincing them of the power of the healing energy. Dominican priest Francis MacNutt conceded that the intensity of the swooning experience does not necessarily correlate with the success of the healing; but he also stressed that "it would be a mistake to prevent its taking place, unless there is a serious reason for doing so . . . I have seen every kind of healing take place while people are resting in the Spirit."[98] In a broader sense the technique is indicative of the potentially profound effects of altered states of consciousness.

Not all charismatic healing practitioners favor large healing services and emotional intensity. The Worralls complained that "results obtained under the emotion-charged conditions of crowds may be of a purely temporary psychological nature, and these results disappear when the emotional setting is removed."[99] Moreover, the expectation of "miracles," fostered at large gatherings, may be unrealistic. By definition, faith healing relies on strong belief in its efficacy; but MacNutt urged caution in raising expectation of instantaneous cures and then either placing the burden on patients to "claim their healings" or failing to provide follow-up care. Those whose hopes are dashed feel abandoned and lose faith in the possibility of longer-term improvement. Sustained healing therapies may be more effective than a single attempt to procure a miracle. MacNutt pointed out that even Jesus had to administer two treatments to cure a man's blindness.[100] He noted that dramatic healings can occur, some even correcting skeletal deformations; but they may take hours or even months to accomplish.[101]

Charismatic healing was practiced on a small scale within the Church of England before and after World War II.[102] But a much-larger charismatic "revival" began in the 1950s. Within a decade a charismatic subculture developed within mainline Protestant and Catholic churches. It remains strong, particularly among ethnic minorities. A recent survey indicated that more than half of Hispanic Catholics and Protestants in the United States identify themselves as charismatics.[103]

Reflections

Tension between a desire for simplicity and the inexorable growth of complexity has been present throughout Christianity's 2,000-year history. People have often yearned for an end to the trappings of ecclesiastical structure and rigid orthodoxy and a return to a simple faith; but efforts to achieve it were only partially successful or temporary in their effects. The Reformation was a reaction against the heavy infrastructure of Catholicism; but the new Protestant churches soon built their own structures, traditions and dogma. Evangelicalism, and more recently Pentecostalism, arose in their wake in further attempts to find that elusive simplicity.

Evangelical and charismatic Christianity emerged in their respective time periods as the religious forms of choice for the masses, accessible to people of all social and educational levels. They appealed to people who rejected what was perceived to be the politicism of ecclesiastical hierarchies, the pomposity of high-church ritual, and the impenetrability and irrelevance of theological speculation. Evangelical and charismatic Christianity continue to prosper for the same reasons—and now also because of disillusionment with the rationalism of modern technological society.[104] They are religions of the emotions rather than the mind, providing comforting reassurance in an increasing volatile world.

Evangelical Christianity applauds personal testimony of the experience of Jesus Christ. The movement began in late 16th-century Europe but found its greatest potential a century later in the United States. It spread rapidly through general missionary activity and through the great "awakenings" of the 18th and 19th centuries. In week-by-week preaching, in tent and stadium revivals, and most recently in radio and television ministries, Evangelical Christianity reached out to large numbers of people.

The Evangelical religious experience has always centered on the Path of Devotion. John Wesley's preference for devotion and religious experience over theological speculation became enshrined in Methodism's strong experiential dimension, compared with the stronger intellectual focus of Lutheranism and Calvinism/Presbyterianism. Even though, in many ways, including its episcopacy, Methodism has become a "mainstream" denomination, the connections with its Evangelical cousins remain clear. Congregational hymn-singing became a staple of Evangelical worship services, and Charles and Samuel Sebastian Wesley are renowned for their contributions to western hymnody. The singing schools of 19th- and early 20th-century America, and particularly the shaped-note and Sacred Harp traditions of musical pedagogy, did much to promote congregational singing in rural congregations.[105] Also, we must not forget the heritage of spirituals sung by enslaved people in the United States.

A common link among the Baptists, Methodists, and the many smaller Evangelical denominations was the emphasis on scripture. Emphasis on Bible study affirmed the Path of Knowledge. From the beginning, the goal was for every household, as well as every church, to read its Bible. In turn, regular Bible study stimulated literacy in Protestant Europe and in America.[106]

Evangelical Christianity also made a worthy commitment to the Path of Service. From the work of John Wesley to the worldwide mission of the Salvation Army, from inner-city soup kitchens to Baptist mission in Third-World countries, Evangelicals have engaged in many kinds of service. Certainly, strings may be attached; missionaries see opportunities to proselytize as well as to alleviate hunger, disease and suffering; but the work gets done, and Christians of all other persuasions can look to Evangelicals as role models. Evangelical Christianity has not neglected the Path of Activism. Roger Williams and John Clarke waged an unpopular campaign for religious and racial tolerance in 17th-century New England. Margaret Fell campaigned against gender discrimination. Quakers and other Evangelicals were prominent in the antislavery movement of the 18th and 19th centuries. Individuals like Jimmy Carter took their campaigns for peace and justice onto the world stage.

Charismatic Christianity flourished in apostolic times; later it was relegated to the fringes of Christianity, and even there it aroused suspicion among religious leaders. It blossomed in the Holiness and Pentecostal movements of the 19th and 20th centuries and finally spread to mainstream Christianity in the charismatic revival of the 1960s. The Pentecostalism of the early 20th century reached out to marginalized groups in blighted urban areas, affirming the Paths of Devotion, Healing and Activism. Ministries of praise, prophecy and healing offered hope, empowerment and relief to people who were hurting and neglected. Pentecostalism's inclusiveness contrasted with the social stratifications and racism of many mainstream Christian churches during the same period.

Today the affirmation of those paths is less clear. The Pentecostal churches of the white suburbs appeal to people, particularly young people, who seek a joyful, intoxicating form of Christianity. They use high-powered marketing and the lure of professional entertainment to draw people by the tens of thousands, but whether they offer true spirituality is an open question. Critics charge that today's Pentecostalism is nothing more than mass hysteria, "feel-good" religion, and escape from the realities of everyday life. On the other hand, even if traditional distinctions between religion and entertainment have blurred, should we judge a celebrity-preacher more harshly than the dark and frightening threats of a Jonathan Edwards?

Both Evangelical and charismatic Christianity emphasize the importance of the conversion experience in which people "accept Jesus Christ as their personal lord and savior."[107] From that point onward individuals consider themselves "saved," or "born again." American philosopher William James (1842-1910) described the transformative effects of conversion: "To be converted, to be regenerated, to receive grace," he wrote, "are so many phrases which denote the process . . . by which a self hitherto divided, and consciously wrong, inferior and unhappy, becomes unified and consciously right, superior and happy."[108] Conversion may be more than a spiritual experience. It can also be personally empowering, leading to enhanced effectiveness as a family member, worker, and member of society.[109]

Despite John Wesley's caution, the concept of instant conversion has won wide acceptance inside and outside Evangelical Christianity. Many of the great saints had life-changing spiritual experiences, and countless people are reporting such experiences in our own time. Debate continues over the "once saved, always saved" issue, but unwarranted trust in the lasting effects of conversion can lead to disillusionment. Evangelist and healer Agnes Sanford pointed out: "[W]e are deceived by the words, 'I am saved,' we say when we have had one experience of the love of Christ. But the experience dims, the love fades away, out of the deep mind there arise miasmas of darkness that choke our thinking and bind our souls in chains."[110] Furthermore, being "born again" can imply a return to a state of childlike dependency. It may imply a refusal to take responsibility for one's own actions as they affect other people, the planet and ourselves.[111] Rather than becoming children of God, perhaps we need to become "adults of God."

In recent years Evangelical and Pentecostal Christianity have been sullied by two regrettable developments. One is the failure of some prominent evangelists to live up to the biblical standards they preach with such seductive emotion. When scandals erupt—inevitably attracting wide publicity and charges of hypocrisy—people who placed trust in the evangelists rightly feel betrayed. The other development is the descent of large segments of Evangelical and Pentecostal Christianity into fundamentalism. Fundamentalist beliefs and attitudes are not "conservative;" they fly in the face of traditional Evangelical and early Pentecostal values. The rise of fundamentalism will be discussed in Chapter 19.

---

1. William Law. *The Grounds and Reasons of Human Regeneration*, Reg-91. London, 1739. Georg O. Verlag (ed.). *Works of the Reverend William Law*. Hildesheim, 1974

2. *1 Corinthians* 15:3.

3. The major Lutheran federation in Germany continues to call itself the *Evangelische Kirche in Deutschland*, EKD ("Evangelical Church in Germany").

4. The "Puritan" label was applied by others. Puritans preferred to call themselves "the Godly." Rigid gender roles were observed within the family, and children were raised in an environment of strict discipline.

5. G. F. Young. *The Medici*. Modern Library, 1930, p. 702.

6. Harold O. J. Brown. *Heresies: Heresy and Orthodoxy in the History of the Church*. Hendrickson, 1984, p. 421.

7. The Evangelical and Reformed Church was itself formed by the merger of earlier denominations primarily of German immigrants. It had Presbyterian leanings but offered more congregational autonomy.

8. Initially, baptism by sprinkling or pouring was accepted, but by the 1620s immersion had become almost mandatory.

9. H. Leon McBeth. *Baptist Beginnings.* Baptist History and Heritage Society, 1979.

10. A corollary of that theory was that Jesus, who John baptized, must also have been a Baptist.

11. John Smyth. *Short Confession of Faith*, 9. Mennonite Archives, Amsterdam.

12. Shortly before his death Smyth abandoned the Baptist denomination he and Helwys had founded and became a Mennonite. Helwys died in an English prison during the reign of James I.

13. *Baptist Confession of Faith of 1689*, ch. 12.

14. Reformed Baptist congregations refer to their governing boards as "presbyteries."

15. The "once saved, always saved" doctrine is not identical to perseverance of the saints. John Calvin believed that backsliding proved that the individual was not one of the elect.

16. This innovation proved controversial, and several congregations severed their connections with the "singing" churches.

17. In 1817 the Universities of Halle and Wittenberg merged to form the Martin Luther University Halle-Wittenberg.

18. Keith Clements (ed.). *Friedrich Schleiermacher: Pioneer of Modern Theology.* Fortress Press, 1987, p. 16.

19. Many Quakers, like the Anabaptists, rejected the authority of government and the courts, refused to swear oaths, and refused to serve in the armed forces.

20. Those records provide invaluable evidence of Quaker migrations.

21. Margaret Fell. *Women's Speaking Justified, Proved and Allowed of by the Scriptures, All Such as Speak by the Spirit and Power of the Lord Jesus And How Women Were the First That Preached the Tidings of the Resurrection of Jesus, and Were Sent by Christ's Own Command Before He Ascended to the Father.* Society of Friends, 1669.

22. John Nash. "Elihu Embree and the Antislavery Movement." *History of Washington County, Tennessee*, 2003, pp. 631-640. In 1820 Embree established the first abolitionist newspaper in the United States.

23. Matilda Wildman Evans. "Elihu Embree, Quaker and Abolitionist, and Some of His Co-Workers." *Bulletin of Friends Historical Association*, Vol. 21, No. 1. Spring 1932, pp. 5-17.

24. Désirée Hirst. *Hidden Riches: Traditional Symbolism from the Renaissance to Blake.* Eyre & Spottiswoode, 1964, pp. 181-198, 200-204. Swendenborg's teachings are discussed in Chapter 18.

25. John Wesley. *Journal*, July 20, 1762, Limerick., Ireland.

26. John Wesley. "Of Sanctification." *Articles of Religion.* United Methodist Church.

27. *Matthew* 5:48

28. John Wesley. *A Plain Account of Christian Perfection*, 27. Thomas Jackson (ed.). *The Works of John Wesley*, 1872, vol. 11, pp. 366-446.

29. Quoted in: Tony Campolo. *Revolution and Renewall.* Westminster John Knox Press, 2000, p. 139.

30. Whitefield's Methodists can be compared with the Reformed Baptists.

31. Origen taught that even demons could eventually be reformed and saved.
32. Clarke was an Anglican priest, but he was also a Hebrew scholar and student of the Qabalah. See for example: Désirée Hirst. *Hidden Riches: Traditional Symbolism from the Renaissance to Blake*. Eyre & Spottiswoode, 1964, pp. 246-263.
33. Judith S. Stevens. *A Universalist Catechism*, 1782.
34. Ten years earlier, Antoinette Brown was ordained by the Congregationalist Church, but her ordination was not recognized by the denomination.
35. Unitarianism is discussed in Chapter 19.
36. MacCullough, *The Reformation*, pp. 602ff.
37. See the discussion in: George M. Marsden. *Fundamentalism and American Culture*. Oxford University Press, 1980, pp. 43-48.
38. Jonathan Edwards. *Sinners in the Hands of an Angry God*. International Outreach, Inc.
39. MacCullough, *The Reformation*, p. 586.
40. Some commentators refer to a third Great Awakening, near the end of the 19th century. However, it was characteristically different from the first two: consisting of a reaction to the increasing secularization of society, assaults on the inerrancy of the Bible, and scientific discoveries like Darwin's theory of evolution.
41. Finney, who was influenced by Jonathan Edwards, rejected the doctrine of limited atonement in favor of the belief that everyone could be saved through faith.
42. Three-quarters of the Anglican membership either joined forces with the British forces in the War of Independence or emigrated to England. Suspicion that the Anglican Church—or its direct successor the Episcopal Church—was somehow "un-American" persisted until the early 20th century.
43. See the discussion in: George M. Marsden. *Fundamentalism and American Culture*. Oxford University Press, 1980, pp. 11ff.
44. Quoted in Marsden. *Fundamentalism and American Culture*, p. 17.
45. Common Sense philosophy, largely the work of Scottish scholar Thomas Reid (1710-1796), was a reaction against the idealism of David Hume and George Berkeley who argued that we only experience *ideas* about the physical world, not the world itself.
46. The fact that the industrial revolution introduced gross inequities in wealth and opportunity and degraded millions of factory and mine workers did not seem to disturb the Evangelical conscience. Interestingly, the loss of the Papal States was viewed favorably as a sign that the reign of the "Antichrist" was coming to an end.
47. Postmillennialism contrasts with *premillennialism*, the belief in some kind of Armageddon, after which Christ will establish the 1,000-year Kingdom.
48. A strong sense developed that the United States *was* the kingdom, a nation singled out to play the leading spiritual role in the centuries to come.
49. Walt Whitman. "Song of Myself." *Leaves of Grass*, first published 1900.
50. Bill Leonard & Paul F. Gillespie. "The Camp Meeting." *Foxfire 7*. Anchor Books, 1973, p. 270.
51. Moody's approach to preaching would be echoed decades later by the mature Billy Graham.
52. As its name implied The Triennial Convention met every three years.

53. In the Church of Scotland ordained ministers were presented with a ceremonial key to the pulpit. See: Diarmaid MacCullough. *The Reformation*. Penguin Books, 2003, p. 585.

54. Bill Leonard. "Historical Overview." *Foxfire 7*, p. 24. Parenthesis in original.

55. During the 1980s and '90s, when the Southern Baptist Convention became increasingly fundamentalist, conservative factions gained control of many Baptist seminaries in the United States.

56. Functional groups that once operated under the general umbrella of the SBC now have their trustees appointed by the SBC leadership which is fundamentalist, politically active, and male.

57. Jimmy Carter. *Our Endangered Values*. Simon & Schuster, 2005, pp. 41-42.

58. Source: World Evangelical Alliance.

59. E. Glenn Hinson. "History of Glossalalia." *Glossolalia*, Abingdon Press, 1967, pp. 59-61.

60. "Lee" was actually a shortened form of her birth-name: Lees.

61. Most of the "Shaker" furniture now available simply imitates the styles made famous by the Shaker communities.

62. That misconception may have arisen from the combination of dance as a mode of worship and Shakers' emphasis of Jesus' exhortation that we should clothe the naked.

63. Bearing in mind that slaves were often required to sit in a balcony at the rear of the church, foot-stomping could not only be noisy but could threaten the structure of the building.

64. Spirituals, which lamented the burden of the slaves' condition and sometimes contained coded instructions for escape, also had an activist dimension.

65. The Church of the Nazarene has no connection with the Nazarene sect in early Judaic Christianity.

66. Harvey Cox. *Fire From Heaven*. Da Capo Press, 1995, pp. 45-65.

67. Charles Parham became a member of the Ku Klux Klan.

68. Particularly in the Pentecostal movement the same name may be used by more than one group.

69. *Revelation* 21:1. See also: *Isaiah* 65:17-25.

70. Positive confession theology, or "prosperity programming," is often claimed to be a product of the New Thought movement. But Pentecostalism is now its main stronghold. Interestingly, people who subscribe to the belief do not seem to mind that leaders may lead lavish lifestyles at their expense; they trust that prosperity will also come to them.

71. Published by Simon & Schuster in 1952.

72. The Greeks distinguished *enthousiasmos* from *ecstasis* (ekstasij, "ecstasy") meaning "being beside oneself," as in a trance state.

73. Cox, *Fire from Heaven*, pp. 81ff.

74. One of the Hebrew words for "praise" is *yadah* (ידה), which literally means "to stretch out one's arms in praise or thanksgiving."

75. David Legge. "A Praise Service to Remember." *Building for God*, part 14. Belfast, Northern Ireland, 2004.

76. *Glossa* can refer to a language or dialect or to the physical tongue; it can also be used metaphorically as in "tongues of fire."

77. Elliot Wigginton. "The People who take up Serpents." *Foxfire 7*, pp. 412-414.

78. E. Glenn Hinson. "Glossolalia Today." *Glossolalia*. Abingdon Press, 1967, p. 11.

79. *Ibid.*, p. 15

80. *Acts of the Apostles* 2:6.

81. *1 Corinthians* 14:1-33.

82. Hinson, "Glossolalia Today," p. 18.

83. *John* 13:1-5; *1 Timothy* 5:10. See the discussion in: Keith Head & Wendy Gutaux. "Foot Washing." *Foxfire 7*, pp. 351-369.

84. *Mark* 16:17-18; *Luke* 10:19. See the discussion in: Willington, "The People who take up Serpents," pp. 370-428. At the time of writing, a few churches in the southeastern United States still practice snake-handling.

85. As already noted, healing was practiced in the early church, but an active healing ministry seems to have come to an end by the late Middle Ages.

86. *Mark* 5:34.

87. City dwellers could scarcely be envied by comparison. Until comparatively recently, the track-record of physicians and surgeons was poor and environmental conditions in the cities unhealthy

88. Elliot Wigginton (ed.). "Faith Healing." *The Foxfire Book*. Anchor Books, 1972, pp. 346-368.

89. That last condition was often referred to as "thrash" or "thrush."

90. For example, one healer invoked *Ezekiel* 16:6 to treat bleeding. See: Wigginton, "Faith Healing," p. 368.

91. Wigginton, "Faith Healing," p. 362.

92. See for example: Morton T. Kelsey. *Healing and Christianity*. Harper and Row, 1973.

93. Ambrose A. & Olga N. Worrall. *The Gift of Healing*. Harper & Row, 1965. Psychic healing can be performed remotely, though the authors claim that physical contact is more effective (p. 166). Some psychic healers invoke the help of angels or other unseen entities.

94. Kathryn Kuhlman. "Jesus the Healer." Source: Kathryn Kuhlman Foundation.

95. See for example: James Randi. *The Faith Healers*. Prometheus Books, 1989.

96. In one survey 21 percent of respondents reported "remarkable" physical healings, and 22 percent reported healing of an emotional or psychological condition. See: Margaret M. Poloma & Lynette F. Hoelter. "The 'Toronto Blessing': A Holistic Model of Healing." *Journal for the Scientific Study of Religion*, June 1998, pp. 257-272.

97. Ruth Carter Stapleton. Introduction to *The Gift of Inner Healing*. Guideposts, 1976. Stapleton (1929-1983) was the brother of President Jimmy Carter.

98. Francis MacNutt. *The Power to Heal*. Ave Maria Press, 1977, pp. 222-223.

99. Warrall, *The Gift of Healing*, p. 166.

100. *Matthew* 8:22-26.

101. MacNutt, *The Power to Heal*, pp. 35-87.

102. Bishop John Perry *et al. A Time to Heal*. Church House Publishing, 2000, pp. 4-6.

103. *Changing Faiths: Latinos and the Transformation of American Religion*. Pew Hispanic Center, 2007.

104. See the discussion on Pentecostalism in: Cox, *Fire from Heaven*, pp. 99-110.

105. Edith Card *et al.* "The Tradition of Shaped-Note Music." *Foxfire 7*, pp. 280-346. Shaped-note notation may date batck to medieval times, but it was popularized by William Little and William Smith in an instructional manual published in 1801.

106. MacCullough, *The Reformation*, pp. 588-589.

107. See for example: Billy Graham. *How to be Born Again*. W Publishing Group, 1978.

108. William James. *The Varieties of Religious Experience*. Modern Library, 1902/1994, p. 210.

109. Tony Campolo. *Revolution and Renewal*. Westminster John Knox Press, 2000, pp. 147-160.

110. Agnes Sanford. *The Healing Gifts of the Spirit*. HarperCollins, 1966, p. 13.

111. See the discussion in: John S. Spong. *The Sins of Scripture*. HarperCollins, 2005, p. 63.

Chapter 18
Esoteric Christianity

Modern Esoteric Christianity

An esoteric tradition in Christianity goes back to the Gnostics, perhaps even to the apostles. Although it was overtaken by politically stronger forces, the esoteric tradition survived—albeit dimly—in Celtic Christianity and among the Manicheans, Bogomils, Cathars, and Friends of God. It survived in a modified form in the religious orders, nourished by prominent mystics like Hildegard of Bingen and Meister Eckhart.[1] However esoteric Christianity, as recognized today, dates from the Renaissance when it flourished among the aristocracy and intelligentsia. By then western esoteric traditions from antiquity had been strengthened by a cross-fertilization of ideas from the Qabalah and Middle-Eastern Hermeticism. Esoteric Christianity gained further momentum after the Reformation, notwithstanding the rationalism of the Enlightenment, and now offers religious alternatives that can no longer be ignored in any comprehensive treatment of Christianity.

Esoteric teachings were shared with initiates in the ancient mystery schools after long training and preparation. Jesus may have shared privileged teachings with trusted disciples that eventually passed to the Gnostics. From the Middle Ages onward, esoteric knowledge was taught in occult societies that operated under the constant threat of exposure and persecution by the institutional church. Now, knowledge that once was revealed only under terrible oaths of secrecy is openly available from bookstores and the Internet.[2] As a result, "esoteric" has taken on a new meaning. But in a real sense esoteric teachings are still protected. The majority of people never bother to read esoteric literature; many shun it in the belief that it is evil, superstitious or nonsensical; and few understand it. The Armenian teacher Georges Ivanovitch Gurdjieff (c.1866-1949) commented that esoteric knowledge is not withheld from the masses but is rejected by them; that it is concentrated in a few hands because they are the only ones who value its importance.[3]

Esoteric religion focuses on subtleties in scripture, teachings and ritual, contrasted with the literal meanings and external observances of conventional, *exoteric*, religion. It is partly mystical, partly intellectual, seeking wisdom in a synthesis of the two. Importantly, esoteric Christianity rejects notions of the hopelessness of the human condition in favor of the potential for human perfectibility. *John* asserted: "He that believeth on me, the works that I do shall he do also; and greater works than these shall he do."[4] Fourth-century Cappadocian father Gregory of Nyssa promoted the notion of human perfectibility, and many have done so since his time.

Esoteric Christianity stresses experience over authority, and in that regard it shares common ground with charismatic Christianity. Francis Lee (1661-1719) linked Manichaeism to the early charismatic Montanist movement: "*Manichaeism* spread itself, after it had been midwif'd and nourished by *Montanism*, and fill'd great part of the world."[5] But, whereas Pentecostalism is emotionally based, esoteric Christianity expresses spiritual experience primarily through intellect—or even through intuition that transcends the intellect.[6] Those on an esoteric path may also be willing to depart farther from doctrinal and scriptural orthodoxy. In sharp contrast to increasingly popular Pentecostalism, esoteric Christianity appeals to smaller numbers of people. A few esoteric denominations have emerged; but most esoteric Christians, like the Gnostics of classical times, pursue independent paths or remain on the fringes of conventional denominations.

Even though the esoteric path has never attracted a large following, we can do no more here than study a small sample of individuals and groups whose insights and gifts have shaped this branch of Christianity. Some were mystics, others were intellectuals, many were committed to lives of service, while a few focused on ceremony and ritual. Some had visions or received personal revelations on which their understanding and teachings were based. But many did not, and there is no suggestion that individual revelatory experiences are essential to esoteric Christianity. General comments will be made about the various individuals and groups; then an attempt will be made to construct consensus statements of esoteric Christian beliefs and practices.

Two Mystical Philosophers

Jakob Böhme and Emanuel Swedenborg lived several decades apart, the former in what is now Poland, the latter in Sweden. Their lives were very different. Böhme had little formal education and plied a trade, whereas Swedenborg came from an upper-class family, received a good education, and spent much of his life in a socially respected profession. However their mystical teachings had much in common; and both regarded themselves as good Lutherans, only to be censured by the church establishment.

Jakob Böhme

Jakob Böhme (1575-1624) was born on a farm near Görlitz, Silesia. His name was sometimes spelled Beheme or transliterated as Boehme. The Böhme family was German-speaking but may have had Slavic roots.[7] Jakob made his living as a cobbler and later as a glove maker. On Trinity Sunday 1600 he had a spiritual experience that launched him onto a lifelong quest for *gnosis*.

When Böhme grew up, the idealism of the Reformation had worn off, Protestantism was fragmenting, and the Counter-Reformation was well under way. Silesia, now part of Poland, was a haven for both Protestant and Catholic dissidents, among whom was the radical reformer Kasper Schwenkfeld (1489-1561). Under Schwenkfeld's influence, Böhme soon found himself part of a group devoted to the work of the Swiss-born physician and occultist Paracelsus (1493-1541);[8] business trips brought him into contact with like-minded people. Böhme's formal education may have been limited, but he became interested in medicine, the Qabalah, and the Hermetic arts. He may also have read the works of Meister Eckhart with whom he shared important beliefs.

Böhme had little interest in promoting his ideas, and records of his studies were kept mainly for personal reference. The books we have were compiled and published by his followers, in some cases without his knowledge or consent. However Böhme wrote long letters to friends, and several have survived. He was critical of institutional Christianity and its warring sects, comparing them to "Babel and the Antichrist." The churches, he wrote, "do boast themselves of their ordinances and of the divine orders in the performance of devout duties, in lip-labour and much prating, and in the stone houses . . . , cathedrals, and cloisters of Christendom . . . ; and spend the time with disputing, confuting, and contending about sects and their differences."[9] Böhme always considered himself a devout Lutheran, but his anticlericalism and unconventional theological views drew continual fire from church authorities. Silenced for several years, he began writing again in secrecy. His nemesis, the chief pastor of Görlitz, Gregory Richter, denounced Böhme from the pulpit and inflamed public opinion against him. On his deathbed Böhme is reported to have said "Now I go hence into Paradise."[10] But his grave was desecrated by a mob.

Jakob Böhme was fascinated by the passage in *John*: "[T]he light shineth in darkness; and the darkness comprehended it not,"[11] and he interpreted it to mean that the Godhead is immanent but unknowable. He referred to the undifferentiated oneness of the Godhead as the *Ungrund*, the "Void," equivalent to the Qabalistic *Ain Soph*. Like Meister Eckhart, Böhme preferred the doctrine of emanation to creation *ex nihilo*; but unlike Eckhart, who probably was not acquainted with the Qabalah, he expressed the doctrine in Qabalistic terms. Böhme argued that the Godhead emanates first as the Trinity and then as a Septenary. These ideas will be discussed later in the chapter.

Also reflecting his Qabalistic influence, Böhme explored the human and cosmic aspects of gender: "[T]he masculine principle is predominantly anthropomorphic and creative, whereas the feminine principle is predominantly cosmic and birth-giving."[12] Echoing a theory usually attributed to Plato's Aristophanes, Böhme asserted that Adam initially was androgynous and virginal.[13] That virginity was embodied in Sophia: "not a female, but a chasteness and purity without a blemish."[14] Adam lost his primeval virginity through the fall, and Sophia's place was taken by his earthly companion Eve. Thereafter man remained in an incomplete state, yearning for his primeval wholeness. The solution lay not in withdrawal into ascetic celibacy, as the church urged, but in a spiritual reunion of the masculine and feminine; through woman man could once again find his primeval Sophia.[15] The masculine-feminine tension was just one expression of the fundamental juxtaposition and resolution of pairs of opposites.[16] The tension might be the source of much suffering, but it provided an environment in which our spiritual potential could be realized.

Jakob Böhme has been hailed as one of the truly original thinkers of the western world. He was a self-taught philosopher able to discuss complex concepts about God and a potentially divine humanity. He was also a mystic—a Protestant one, no less—whose insights compared with those of the great Catholic mystics like Teresa of Ávila and John of the Cross. Böhme's importance was not recognized until several decades after his death; then his work inspired the Philadelphian Society, a nonsectarian esoteric group formed in England in 1670.[17] Anglican churchman William Law endorsed the view of the eternal soul promoted by both Eckhart and Böhme: "The essence of our souls can never cease to be, because they never began to be, and nothing can live eternally but that which has lived from all Eternity."[18] For that affirmation of the soul's preexistence and other views, John Wesley severed his connection with Law. Eventually Böhme's work would influence Friedrich Hegel,[19] William Blake, and psychologist Carl Jung. Böhme was held in high regard in 19th-century Russia, where mystics and even ordinary people referred to him as "the holy Jakob Böhme among our fathers."[20]

Emanuel Swedenborg

Emanuel Swedenborg (1688-1772) was born in Stockholm 64 years after Jakob Böhme's death. His father was a Lutheran bishop and dean of the cathedral of Uppsala, traditional home of the Nordic gods. After a career in engineering with many technological innovations to his credit, Swedenborg began to experience visions that convinced him that new divine revelation was afoot.[21] Unlike Böhme, Swedenborg took great pride in disseminating his ideas; he quit his job and devoted the last 27 years of his life to writing. He kept detailed records of the visions and of numerous conversations with angels and even Old Testament prophets. Those records, together with extensive study of scripture, formed the basis of a huge literary output. His theological works, all in Latin, were written in the same clear, rational style used in his technical works. Philosopher Immanuel Kant initially scoffed at his clairvoyant experiences, calling them "fantastic;" yet he could not fault the validity of the experiences, and he held Swedenborg in high regard.[22]

Between 1747 and 1758 Swedenborg wrote the 12-volume work *Arcana Coelestia* ("Heavenly Mysteries") which consisted of a detailed commentary on *Genesis* and *Exodus*.[23] He used the familiar Bible stories to explore human nature, marriage, religion, rebirth, life after death, and the relationship between the spiritual and natural worlds. In his most influential work, the three-volume *Heaven and Hell*, written toward the end of the same period, Swedenborg provided descriptions of the two end-states in considerable detail. His heaven was not the conventional paradise of clouds and harp-playing but a much more solid place in which souls—or in his terminology "angels"—perform acts of loving service. The angels enjoyed a lifestyle much like that of well-to-do people in northwestern Europe; their dwellings, he wrote,

> are precisely like the dwellings on earth . . . but more beautiful. In them are chambers, inner rooms, and bedrooms in great numbers. There are also courts and around them gardens, flower beds, and lawns. Where they live in societies their houses are near each other, one alongside another, arranged in the form of a city, with streets, roads, and public squares exactly like the cities on our earth.[24]

Hell was another solid place where selfish souls found their own sordid fulfillment. Between heaven and hell lay the "world of spirits" where souls went immediately after death to await final disposition; but each individual's fate was already sealed by choices made during earthly life.

Emanuel Swedenborg promoted the view of an infinitely loving God who lies at the very center of our being. We participate in our own creation, and through life we learn and grow. We must be born again—that is, turn away from love of self and the world—in what Swedenborg called "regeneration." But that was not the one-time conversion experience of Evangelical Christianity. Nor was growth monotonic; life is cyclical, with periods of "heat and cold," "winter and summer," "day and night."[25] Even the angels continued to grow spiritually, becoming ever more perfect.[26]

Like Böhme, Swedenborg became disillusioned with organized religion, blaming doctrine for its sectarian divisions: "In the Christian world it is their doctrines that cause churches to be distinct and separate . . . This situation would never exist if they were to make love to the Lord and charity toward the neighbour the chief thing of faith . . . . If this was so all the different churches would become one, and all the disagreements . . . would disappear."[27] Swedenborg's last work, *The True Christian Religion*, was written in London when he was 80 years old. It criticized the doctrine of the Trinity on the grounds that it alienated Jews and Muslims toward Christianity.[28] He was prepared to consider three *aspects* of God, but to speak of three *persons* was equivalent to denying divine unity. Shortly after the book appeared Swedenborg was forced to return to Sweden to face heresy charges. His writings were banned in Sweden, and Lutheran clergy were forbidden to promote his teachings.

Swedenborg spoke of "the Faith of the New Heaven and of the New Church,"[29] but he never intended to found a religious movement; a useful life represented the sincerest form of worship. Nevertheless, after his death, followers in London founded the Swedenborgian Church, or Church of the New Jerusalem, which still functions on a small scale in Europe, the United States and elsewhere. Among the worshippers at the first service in London, in January 1788, was William Blake.[30] Blake, who was influenced more by Swedenborg than by Jakob Böhme, claimed that some of his own art and writing was inspired by angels. But he differed from Swedenborg on important areas of doctrine, and he regarded Swedenborg as snobbish and pompous.[31]

The Rosicrucian Movement

R osicrucianism was the first significant esoteric movement to emerge from Protestant Christianity. Although it had a distinctively German Calvinist character, it was also influenced by Neoplatonism, the Qabalah and Hermeticism. The Rosicrucian movement reflected the broad dissatisfaction with religion in post-Reformation Europe that John Smyth, Philipp Spener, Jakob Böhme, and Emanuel Swedenborg all shared.

The Rosicrucian movement began in the Rhineland Palatinate with the appearance of two documents known as the Rosicrucian Manifestos. The *Fama Fraternitatis, des Loblichen Ordens des Rosenkreutzes* ("Declaration of the Worthy Order of the Rosy Cross") was circulated informally as early as 1610 and published in 1614. The *Confessio Fraternitatis R.C. ad Eruditos Europea* ("Confession of the Fraternity R.C. to the Erudite of Europe") was published a year later. Authorship of the manifestos has not been established, though speculation has linked them to the English mathematician and occultist John Dee, Protestant theologian Johann Valentin Andreae, or even Francis Bacon. The *Confessio* was published together with an alchemical text: "Consideration of the More Secret Philosophy by Philip à Gabella," a paraphrase of a work by Dee.[32] Also associated with the manifestos was a much longer alchemical allegory: "The Chymical Wedding of Christian Rosenkreuz," published by Andreae in 1616.

Christian Rosencreutz and the Fraternity

The *Fama* and *Confessio* described a mysterious and probably mythical character referred to as "Father C.R.C.," who supposedly was born in 1378 and died at the age of 106. The *Chymical Wedding* identified him as "Christian Rosencreutz," where *Rosencreutz* is the German for "Rose Cross." According to the *Fama*, Father C.R.C. traveled to the Middle East and north Africa where he came into the possession of esoteric teachings, including "mathematics, physic and magic."[33] The teachings would not only "lay a new foundation of sciences" but would change the course of history.[34] Some aspects of the teachings could be reduced to writing, but a major part was revealed by the *Librum Naturae*, the Book of Nature.[35] Importantly, we learned, Father C.R.C. had mastered "the transmutation of metals," though the quest for riches was of no concern to him, and he disdained "all vain glory and pomp."[36] The reference to alchemy came as no surprise since alchemical texts were published together with the manifestos. But, if the manifestos discussed key elements of Renaissance science, they also reflected Baconian empiricism.

Upon returning to Germany in 1408 Father C.R.C. founded the Fraternity of the Rose Cross, a secret brotherhood that resembled a mendicant religious order. By the time of his death, there were eight brothers.[37] The manifestos gave the order "to increase and enlarge the number of our Fraternity."[38] Men from throughout Protestant Europe were urged to join, but all efforts to contact the fraternity failed. Perhaps none of the applicants met the necessary standards: "A thousand times the unworthy may clamour, a thousand times present themselves, yet God hath commanded our ears that they should hear none of them."[39] Scholars have long debated whether the fraternity or Rosencreutz ever existed. Among many theories, Paul Foster Case (1884-1954) suggested that "Father C.R.C." was none other than Jesus Christ.[40] Case also asserted that the Fraternity of the Rose Cross was invisible; but "True Rosicrucians know one another . . . Their means of recognition cannot be counterfeited nor betrayed, for these tokens are more subtle than the signs and passwords of ordinary secret societies."[41]

The Rosicrucian Manifestos advocated overthrow of the papacy, initiation of a "general reformation" in Christianity, and return to an Edenic paradise— presumably under the protection of the elector Palatine, Frederick V, who was held in high regard.[42] However their main thrust was to promote ideals of brotherhood and service.[43] The *Fama* emphasized the fraternity's mission of love and compassion. Initially the brothers "did live together above all others in . . . most kindness towards another." They wanted to document the teachings, but "the unspeakable concourse of the sick hindered them." In due course they dispersed to work in different countries. Before departing, the brothers committed themselves to a number of precepts. They were told to "follow the custom of the country" and not wear distinctive clothing; "The Fraternity should remain secret for one hundred years." They were also told to "profess [nothing but] to cure the sick, and that gratis."[44] One "Brother I.O." allegedly went to England and "cured a young Earl of Norfolk of the leprosie."[45] Even though that particular story seems to have been apocryphal,[46] the ideal of ministering to the sick at no charge was a noble one, previously practiced only by monastic orders. The *Fama* expressed the wish that there were "more love and kindness" among German physicians.[47]

Precisely what kinds of therapies the brothers practiced is unclear. During the period when Father C.R.C. is alleged to have lived, medical practice generally followed the second-century work of Galen, though the "physic" C.R.C. learned on his travels may have been more advanced. By the time the manifestos were published the newer methods of Paracelsus were gaining popularity, and indeed the manifestos seemed to support them. Swiss-born Paracelsus (1493-1541) combined the use of mineral medicines, magnetism, alchemy and magic in his medical practice.[48]

Modern Rosicrucianism and Freemasonry

The conquest of the Palatinate ended any hope that the manifestos' political objectives could be achieved; and accomplishment of the spiritual goals was hindered by widespread witch hunts during the Counter-Reformation and Thirty Years' War.[49] Nevertheless, large numbers of people have been inspired by Rosicrucian ideals. Along with Freemasonry, Rosicrucianism provided a balance to Enlightenment rationalism.

Although none can claim unbroken lineage from the early 17th century, numerous Rosicrucian organizations have been established. The Fraternitas Rosae Crucis was formed in the United States in 1858, and the Societas Rosicruciana in Anglia was founded in Britain seven years later. Still in existence, the latter describes itself as "an independent Christian Society."[50] All of its members are stated to be Master Masons, though the Societas emphasized that "It is something beyond and outside Freemasonry." The Rosicrucian Fellowship, founded by Max Heindel in 1908, described itself as an "International Association of Christian Mystics for the Aquarian Age." When he sought to build a center of healing and a sanitarium, Heindel reportedly was warned, in words that echoed the *Fama*: "If ever you make these priceless teachings subservient to mammon, the light will fade and the movement will fail."[51] The Ancient Mystical Order Rosae Crucis (AMORC) was founded in 1915 by Harvey Spencer Lewis. Its mission statement affirmed that Rosicrucian teachings "allow individuals to direct their own lives, experience inner peace, and leave their mark on humanity."[52]

There is little evidence of institutional links between Rosicrucianism and Freemasonry; but Rosicrucian symbols and rituals are preserved in some Masonic organizations, and the discussion of Rosicrucian influence has become more common. The origins of Freemasonry are at least as murky as those of the Rose Cross. Legend links it to Hiram Abiff and construction of Solomon's temple and somewhat more plausibly to the medieval craft guilds. A Masonic lodge is said to have been formed in Kilwinning, Scotland, in 1286.[53] Lodges of modern "speculative" Freemasonry certainly were in operation soon after the Rosicrucian Manifestos were published.

Several branches of Freemasonry evolved, all with at least three grades or degrees: Entered Apprentice, Fellow Craft, and Master Mason. But the Scottish Rite has 33 grades, and branches have existed with as many as 96. Traditionally, Freemasonry requires that members believe in a Supreme Being, often referred to as the Great Architect of the Universe; but belief in the Trinity normally is not a requirement. Relations between Masonic organizations and institutional Christianity have often been strained, though many high churchmen have been members. Masonic organizations are largely self-serving, but they preserve elements of ancient esoteric teachings. They also perform important service functions. The Ancient Arabic Order of the Nobles of the Mystic Shrine ("Shriners") is committed to "Brotherly Love, Relief and Truth" and undertakes major works of philanthropy.

New Approaches to Healing

Traditional sacramental healing practices were reviewed in earlier chapters, charismatic healing was discussed in Chapter 17, and we have just seen that the Fraternity of the Rose Cross allegedly pursued a healing ministry. Innovative approaches to healing were explored during the 18th and 19th centuries, and two Americans who dedicated their lives to the work were Phineas Parkhurst Quimby and Edgar Cayce. Quimby is regarded as the father of the New Thought movement which made further contributions to healing. Several of the individuals who pioneered the new methods had humble upbringings and experienced serious health problems that proved pivotal to their lives and work.

Phineas Parkhurst Quimby

Phineas Parkhurst Quimby (1802-1866) was born in Lebanon, New Hampshire, and in his teens was apprenticed to a clockmaker. Soon he developed tuberculosis. Although conventional medicine proved ineffective, he improved rapidly after taking up outdoor activities. Quimby had little formal schooling; but he read many books, and in his late 30s he began a study of mesmerism.

Quimby discovered that he could easily hypnotize two brothers, Henry and Lucius Burkmar, and he gave public demonstrations in the early 1840s. Lucius was a particularly good subject; and while in trance he exhibited significant clairvoyance, diagnosed diseases, and prescribed simple herbal treatments.[54] That was the first documented example of what has come to be known as "intuitive diagnosis," though certain individuals, including Russian *startsy*, may have had that gift in earlier times. Quimby himself developed more limited powers of clairvoyance and intuitive diagnosis. Of more lasting significance, he developed theories of mental healing; and in 1859 "Dr. Quimby" opened an office in Portland, Maine. From then until his death he treated an estimated 12,000 patients, inspiring many people with quiet dedication to the work. His son, George Albert Quimby, looked back with pride on his legacy: "'Greater love hath no man than this, that a man lay down his life for his friends.' For if ever a man did lay down his life for others, that man was Phineas Parkhurst Quimby."

In addition to his healing work Phineas Quimby wrote short essays on a variety of subjects. He was acutely aware of the tension between religion and science. Scientific discovery was making great progress, while the credibility of institutional religion was declining. Quimby complained that he received evasive answers when he inquired about Jesus' teachings and healing ministry.[55] Disillusioned, he turned away from formal religion to seek God in nature: "It is the higher principle of our nature. Now let this higher principle rise with me above all the opinions of men about another world, and come up hither and sit on the clouds made by the superstition and look and survey one last space where perfect light and harmony exist."[56] Similar concepts were explored by Quimby's contemporaries—and close neighbors in New England—the Transcendentalists.

New Thought

The New Thought movement is usually traced back to Phineas Quimby's work, but the movement also owed much to the ideas of Emanuel Swedenborg, Franz Anton Mesmer, and Ralph Waldo Emerson. It was an American movement, or more precisely a series of related movements that included Christian Science, the Unity Church, and Science of Mind. In their different ways they all sought to integrate metaphysical concepts into healing and/or religion. New Thought placed great emphasis on the spiritual healing of body, emotions and mind.

Christian Science was founded in 1879 by Mary Baker Eddy.[57] Mary Morse Baker (1821-1910), was born on a farm in New Hampshire and raised a devout Christian, reading the Bible daily. Like Quimby, she suffered ill health in childhood and young adulthood. When conventional medical treatments proved ineffective she sought Quimby's help; and under his care she made a dramatic recovery, reminding her of Jesus' words: "Thy faith hath made thee whole."[58] An accident left her once more near death, but after reading of Jesus' healings she made another dramatic recovery.

Eddy came to the conclusion that healing could be systematized into what she termed "Christian Science." For several years she promoted a new system of healing without the use of medication or surgery. Her techniques were not unlike Quimby's.[59] She strove to alleviate patients' fear by explaining the mental causes of their condition, building confidence that healing was possible, and then encouraging the expectation of healing. Eddy conducted classes, taught a few students more advanced techniques, and started writing. In 1875 she published *Science and Health with Key to the Scriptures*, which soon became the "bible" of Christian Science. Four years later she founded the Church of Christ, Scientist; and by the time of her death Christian Science had spread to many nations; May Baker Eddy is one of the few women to have founded a worldwide religious movement. At age 88 she founded *The Christian Science Monitor* a largely secular newspaper that continues to command wide respect for its news and editorials.[60] One of Eddy's students was the well-known mystic and teacher Emma Curtis Hopkins (1853-1925). Hopkins went on to found the Emma Hopkins College of Metaphysical Science that did much to promote women's roles as ministers and teachers.

The Unity School of Christianity was founded in 1890 by Charles and Myrtle Fillmore. Charles Fillmore (1854-1948) was born on an Indian reservation in Minnesota, the son of a Chippewa trader and a seamstress. His mother raised him as an Episcopalian, but he started reading works on eastern religions, metaphysics and spiritualism. Mary Caroline "Myrtle" Page Fillmore (1845-1931) was a schoolteacher, originally from Ohio. After their marriage, the Fillmores moved to Kansas City, Missouri, in 1884. Myrtle Fillmore developed tuberculosis, but she had a spiritual experience during a lecture on Christian Science given by E. B. Weeks, a student of Hopkins. Myrtle found new hope in Weeks' affirmation: "I am a child of God and therefore I do not inherit sickness." She repeated the affirmation over-and-over, and within a year the tuberculosis was completely cured.

Myrtle Fillmore offered metaphysical healing services and soon developed a following. In 1889 the Fillmores founded *Modern Thought*, a journal that combined the principles of Christian Science with the couple's own insights. Their approach to healing made use of affirmations but also included traditional prayer. The following year, they started a healing prayer group: the Society of Silent Help, which in due course evolved into the Unity School of Christianity, one of the few esoteric Christian denominations. The name "Unity," adopted in 1895, emphasized the school's goal to bring spirituality to the whole of humanity and to embrace what is best in all religions. The widely read *Unity Daily Word* was first published in 1924. In 1929 the denomination's headquarters was established at Unity Village, near Kansas City. Unity continued to grow after the founders' deaths. By 2006, 659 Unity churches and other ministries operated in the United States and a further 246 in other countries.[61] Like other branches of

New Thought, Unity emphasizes the approach to perfection, recognizing that it may take more than one lifetime. Unity takes a favorable view of reincarnation: "Many Unity students accept the concept of reincarnation (re-embodiment after a period of soul rest)."[62]

Science of Mind was the creation of Ernest Holmes (1887-1960). Holmes was born on a small farm in Maine, the youngest of nine sons. He was an introspective teenager, spending most of his time outdoors. At 18 years of age he moved to Boston to work in a grocery store. Holmes discovered New Thought writings, particularly the work of Christian D. Larson who later became a collaborator. He was also influenced by Deism. In 1926 Ernest Holmes published *Science of Mind*, which became one of the most widely read metaphysical religious books of the 20th century. It provided clear instructions on how to meditate, heal oneself, build self confidence, and express love. One year later Holmes launched the periodical of the same name which is still in publication. In addition to publishing *Science of Mind* in 1927 Holmes founded the Institute of Religious Science and the School of Philosophy in Los Angeles.

Distancing himself from Quimby, Holmes rejected any use of clairvoyance or hypnosis. He insisted that healing could be achieved solely by correcting negative thinking: "Healing is . . . accomplished . . . by knowing the Truth. This Truth is that the Spiritual Man is already Perfect, no matter what the appearances may be."[63] By taking prescribed steps, we can achieve perfect health. Whereas Christian Science and Unity emphasized the importance of worship, Ernest Holmes attached little importance to either worship or theology, insisting that he was promoting a purely practical discipline. Reflecting his Deistic orientation, Holmes rejected the notion of a deity answering the prayers of some but not others, arguing that "the universe never plays favorites."[64] Instead, he emphasized individual responsibility for our own health and welfare. Through right thought, operating under definite causal laws, harmony could be restored and true spiritual understanding gained. In the emphasis on personal responsibility we see echoes of Transcendentalist teachings.

Holmes was reluctant to call his movement a religion, and it lacked the customary devotional element. He asserted that we all have divine potential and can attain the consciousness of Christ, we can *become* Christs. Holmes was content to think that Religious Science could complement existing religions; but in 1953 the Institute of Religious Science became the Church of Religious Science.[65] Two years before his death, Holmes reflected:

> We have launched a Movement which, in the next 100 years, will be the great new religious impulse of modern times, far exceeding, in its capacity to envelop the world, anything that has happened since Mohammedanism

started. We have to have the same faith in what we teach and practice that the scientist has, or the gardener has, and when that great simplicity shall have plumbed and penetrated this density of ours, this human stolidness and stupidity, this debauchery of the intellect and the soul, something new and wonderful will happen.[66]

Like their Pentecostal brethren, certain New Thought leaders have advocated the use of "positive confession theology." Unity teaches that positive thinking and affirmations can bring not only good health but material success: "The superconscious mind . . . of the Spirit will guide you in perfect ways, even in the minute details of your life, if you will let it do so. But you must will to do its will and trust it in all your ways. It will lead you unfailingly into health, happiness, and prosperity."[67] Likewise, for Ernest Holmes, perfection is not limited to health and spiritual attainment but also includes material abundance: "Limitation and poverty are not things, but are the results of restricted ways of thinking . . . The power within man can free him from all distasteful conditions if the Law governing this power is properly understood."[68] Positive confession theology has become popular, but it raises red flags, and critics claim that its self-absorption reduces spirituality to the level of sorcery.

In addition to their healing work the key individuals in New Thought made useful contributions to the concepts of God, Christ, and the human condition. Their contributions will be discussed later in this chapter.

Edgar Cayce

Edgar Cayce (1877-1945) was born on a farm near Hopkinsville, Kentucky, and grew up to be a small-town photographer. Whereas Quimby and Holmes had little interest in religion, Cayce was a devout Christian and for long periods taught Sunday-school classes. But, like Quimby, he applied his clairvoyant gifts to healing and counseling. From an early age he discovered the ability to learn by sleeping on his school books. In young adulthood Cayce suffered from progressive throat paralysis which threatened the loss of his voice. Conventional medical treatment offered no relief, and in desperation he induced an altered state of consciousness, a kind of hypnotic sleep, in which he identified the cause of his condition and prescribed a cure. Soon he discovered that, given names and locations, he could diagnose and recommend treatments for others; thus began his lifelong healing work. Cayce became the most renowned psychic and intuitive diagnostician of his time.

Cayce never claimed to have any special gifts; but followers said that he was able to read the *akashic records*, a cosmic database of all past events.[69] Over a period of 43 years he gave more than 14,000 readings. In some cases, to pharmacologists' dismay, the prescribed treatment involved large doses of potent drugs;[70] but most treatments involved everyday substances like castor oil. Sometimes the recommended treatment included prayer: "Father, God, let that ministration bring to my body that as will fit same for a greater and a better service to thee in my dealings with my fellow man. Save, Father, thy servant, now, in thine own way, in thine own manner, as thou would have it, Lord—not my will but thine be done in and through me, now."[71]

An issue that has long perplexed healing practitioners is why efforts succeed in some cases but not in others. Several of Cayce' readings offered explanations; for example:

> This is a promise to thee, to each soul; yet each soul must of itself FIND the answer within self. For indeed the body is the temple of the living God. There He has promised to meet thee; there He does. And as thy body, thy mind, thy soul is attuned to that divine as answers within, so may ye indeed be quickened to know His purpose; and ye may fill that purpose for which ye entered this experience.[72]

That reading, like most, used the archaic language normally found only in liturgical prayer. It was as though Cayce was reading from an archaic script, or someone from the past was speaking through him. In fact he often stated that information came from "the Source;" but there was no change of accent that often accompanies trance communications.

Over time the scope of Edgar Cayce's readings expanded to include dream interpretation, spiritual growth, and prophecy. Some readings provided information about prehistoric civilizations unavailable from conventional anthropological or archeological research. Others were concerned with people and events known to history, including Jesus' life, death and resurrection. Cayce's descriptions of those events generally followed the biblical accounts, though the readings claimed that both Mary and Joseph belonged to the Essenes and that Jesus was raised in the sect.[73]

Many of the later readings explored subject's past lives, the reality of which Cayce only slowly accepted.[74] Of the readings that included reincarnational data, approximately 10 percent of the past lives were said to have been on the lost continent of Atlantis and 20 percent in ancient Egypt.[75] Cayce himself allegedly was the reincarnation of one Ra Ta, a high priest of the Egyptian temple and royal court. Ra Ta's job was to "organize religious practices and bring the people to the idea of the one creative principle through the symbology of the sun and the continuance of individual life." Eventually he was banished from the Pharaoh's court.[76] Transcripts of the readings are preserved by the Association for Research and Enlightenment which Cayce founded in Virginia Beach, Virginia.

Confluence of Traditions II

G ermany, England and Ireland were major centers of esoteric studies in the 17th and 18th centuries; but in the 19th century a new movement developed in France. Social reformer and teacher Barthelemy Prosper Enfantin (1796-1864) proclaimed himself a prophet.[77] He established a commune and, anticipating an attitude more representative of the hippie subculture of the 1960s, promoted free love as a substitute for the "tyranny" of marriage. We shall see later that he also had interesting things to say about a new messiah.

A more significant contribution was made by Alphonse Louis Constant (1810-1875) who wrote under the pseudonym Éliphas Lévi. Born in Paris, he attended a Catholic seminary, only to be dismissed before his ordination; subsequently he was initiated into a Masonic order but resigned his membership. Lévi adopted the title of *magus* and wrote a number of books and articles on ceremonial magic, delving into topics previously addressed only in secret occult societies. His lifelong ambition was to see a rapprochement between magic and Christianity. Lévi's work influenced many others, including Gérard Anaclet Encausse (1865-1916) who chose the pseudonym "Papus." A medical doctor and member of a Masonic order, Papus also wrote important books. In 1893 he was consecrated bishop of a Gnostic-revival church, l'Église Gnostique de France. Other Cathar—and Gnostic-revival churches sprang up in Europe and the United States, and some are still in operation.

While Éliphas Lévi and Papus were working in France, the Hermetic Society of the Golden Dawn was founded in England in 1888. Its three founders were all senior members of the Societas Rosicruciana in Anglia. Most ambitious was Samuel Liddel Mathers (1854-1918), who adopted the persona of "MacGregor" Mathers, claimed to be of Scottish noble descent, and became an autocratic leader. The Society's charter called for preservation of "the body of knowledge known as Hermeticism or the Western Esoteric Tradition."[78] It dedicated itself to the philosophical, spiritual and psychic evolution of humanity, along with tolerance for all religious beliefs.[79] An important policy of the Golden Dawn was that women were admitted on the same basis as men. Many influential people of the period joined, including William Butler Yeats, Arthur Waite, the actress Florence Farr, and Irish freedom fighter Maud Gonne.[80] Lodges were formed in France, Ireland, and the United States.

Even before the turn of the 20th century, the Golden Dawn began to fragment under the strain of internal tensions and resistance to Mathers' leadership style. But a number of derivative organizations are still active, including the Builders of the Adytum, founded by Golden-Dawn initiate Paul Foster Case. Violet Mary

Firth (1890-1946) was born into a Christian Science family. Upon inititation into the Golden Dawn she adopted the pseudonym "Dion Fortune." Later she founded the Society for the Inner Light in 1924 whose stated mission was "the expansion of consciousness . . . not regarded as an end in itself, or a means to personal power or knowledge, but as a way of dedicated service to God and all evolving life." Fortune urged the creation, or recreation, of Christian mystery schools, adding: "[I]n any school of Western Mysticism the author and finisher of our faith must be Christ Jesus, the Great Initiator of the West."[81]

In the 1780s followers of Emanuel Swedenborg established an organization called the Theosophical Society.[82] However the organization of that name more familiar today was founded in New York City in 1888—the same year that the Golden Dawn came into existence. The new Theosophical Society was formed by the Russian aristocrat Helena Petrovna Blavatsky (1831-1891) and American war veteran Henry Steel Olcott (1823-1907). It adopted an ambitious threefold mission not unlike the Golden Dawn's: "To form a nucleus of the Universal Brotherhood of Humanity without distinction of race, creed, sex, caste or color. To encourage the comparative study of religion, philosophy and science. To investigate the unexplained laws of nature and the powers latent in Humanity."[83] Some prominent members belonged to both the Golden Dawn and the Theosophical Society, but the two organizations came from different traditions and pursued distinct paths.

The Theosophical Society soon moved its headquarters to Adyar, India, where its leaders studied Asian philosophies under local scholars. Although Blavatsky had been influenced by the 19th-century spiritualist movement,[84] Theosophy soon distanced itself from spiritualism, and its teachings took on a predominantly Hindu-Buddhist character. The controversial Blavatsky was accused of many things before and after her death, including anti-Christian bias.[85] However some later Theosophists adopted a Christian orientation, even though they retained key Asian doctrines like reincarnation and karma.

Political activist and spiritual teacher Annie Wood Besant (1847-1933) and Anglican clergyman Charles Webster Leadbeater (1853-1934) worked to integrate Christianity into Theosophical teachings. Among their numerous books were Besant's *Esoteric Christianity* and Leadbeater's *The Science of the Sacraments*.[86] In 1910 Leadbeater claimed: "There is nothing in the principles of theosophy which is at all in opposition to the true primitive Christianity, though there may be statements which cannot be reconciled with some of the mistakes of modern popular theology."[87] Besant argued for revival of Christianity's esoteric traditions. The churches, in Annie Besant's words, "vulgarised Christianity [and] presented its teachings in a form that . . . repels the heart and alienates the intellect."[88] An important outcome of those sentiments was involvement in the Liberal Catholic Church, which will be discussed in Chapter 20.

The Theosophical Society remains in operation today, with active lodges in many countries. But a number of prominent members left to form their own organizations, retaining key elements of Theosophical doctrine but building on them in their respective ways. Rudolf Steiner (1861-1925) formed the Anthroposophical Society and became an acclaimed esoteric teacher. His main focus was to westernize Theosophy and to establish a link with Rosicrucian and Masonic traditions.[89] He also gave greater emphasis to the role of Christ and his death on the cross.[90] Among his works are published lectures on the four gospels and a major work: *Christianity as Mystical Fact*.[91] Alice Ann Bailey (1880-1949) founded the Arcane School. Her teachings followed the Theosophical tradition but extended it in a number of areas, placing considerable emphasis on the seven rays that will be discussed later in this chapter.

Theosophy was only one of many channels through which Asian religious and philosophical traditions found their way into western culture during the 19th and 20th centuries.[92] The cross-fertilization of ideas is regarded by some as being comparable in significance to the influx of Middle Eastern knowledge into Europe during the Renaissance; hence this section's heading "Confluence of Traditions II." The process has continued. For example, Dion Fortune and her student Gareth Knight (1930-) integrated some Theosophical teachings into their work on the Qabalah.

Highlights of Esoteric Christianity

To expect a definitive esoteric Christian theology to have emerged in an environment of such fertile ideas, but no central authority, would be unrealistic. Each writer or teacher offered some unique insights.[93] Nevertheless many concepts have won broad acceptance, and we shall an attempt to build a coherent synthesis of beliefs.

Jesus the Christ

Broad consensus has emerged in esoteric Christianity that Jesus should be distinguished from the Christ—as Cerinthus suggested in the second century and the more radical Nestorians in the fifth. The writers we have discussed not only insisted on "Jesus *the* Christ," rather than "Jesus Christ," but assigned different roles or identities to them. Phineas Parkhurst Quimby asserted that Jesus "labored to convince the people that the Christ was the truth which he, Jesus, spake . . . Jesus embodied it in an intelligence called Christ, embracing all the attributes of man, and being a revelation of a higher wisdom than had before appeared on the earth."[94] Mary Baker Eddy agreed: "The word Christ is not properly a synonym for Jesus . . . Christ is not a name so much as the divine title of Jesus. Christ expresses God's spiritual, eternal nature. The name is synonymous with Messiah, and alludes to the spirituality which is taught, illustrated, and demonstrated in the life of which Christ Jesus was the embodiment."[95]

Theosophists went farther to insist that "the Christ" was not just a title given to Jesus, or some kind of vague "spirituality," but was the title of a higher being that entered into a relationship with Jesus and spoke through him during the time in Palestine. At a certain point, usually taken to be Jesus' baptism in the Jordan, the Christ descended into incarnation, using Jesus' physical body as a vehicle. Once the mission in Palestine was completed, the Christ withdrew and once again has a distinct existence. Alice Bailey explained that he is

> the great Lord of Love and of Compassion . . . the World Teacher, the Master of the Masters, and the Instructor of the Angels. [T]o Him is committed the guidance of the spiritual destinies of men, and the development of the realisation within each human being that he is a child of God and a son of the Most High.[96]

When we recall that the Gnostics viewed the human predicament as one in which we descended into ignorance and seek salvation through knowledge, the notion of the World Teacher stands out as particularly apt. Even so, the question remains: what do we mean by the statement that Christ is divine? Russian writer Daniel Andreev, who was not a Theosophist, insisted that divinity is not embodied in Christ but is *expressed* in him: "We call Christ the Word. But a speaker does not after all take shape in a word but expresses himself or herself through it."[97]

Annie Besant claimed that Jesus, as distinct from the Christ, was a man, but no ordinary one; he was an initiate in the ancient mysteries.[98] Bailey added that major initiates who included "Shri Sankaracharya, Vyasa, Mahommet, Jesus of Nazareth, and Krishna" were supported by "those lesser initiates, Paul of Tarsus, Luther, and certain of the outstanding lights in European history."[99] Jesus, rather than the Christ, retains primary responsibility for the Christian religion.[100]

It was Jesus who died on the cross. Theosophist Geoffrey Hodson (1886-1983) suggested that, because of his training in the mysteries, Jesus could have avoided crucifixion: "His submission to martyrdom when he possessed the occult power easily to have saved Himself and confounded his enemies, is one of the sublime acts of submission and self-restraint in the history of mankind."[101] According to Dion Fortune the crucifixion and redemption were aspects of a drama that unfolded on multiple levels of reality: "The crucifixion of Our Lord at the hands of Roman authority was but the shadow thrown on the material plane by the struggle that was going on in the spiritual world. It was not the spilling of the blood of Jesus of Nazareth that redeemed mankind, but the outpouring of spiritual power from the mind of Jesus the Christ."[102]

Similarly, Besant saw the events in Palestine as scenes in a cosmic drama depicted in world mythology in which the Sun-God was born of the zodiacal Virgo, only to be sacrificed in an eternal ritual of death and rebirth. "Why," Besant asked, "have these legends mingled with the history of Jesus?" She answered her own question:

> These are really the stories not of a particular individual named Jesus but of the universal Christ: of a Man who symbolized a Divine Being, and who represented a fundamental truth in nature . . . He was, as are all such, the "Son of Man," a peculiar and distinctive title, the title of an office, not of an individual. The Christ of the Solar Myth was the Christ of the Mysteries.[103]

One of Edgar Cayce's readings, given during the darkest days of World War II, saw hope in the Easter message: "In man's experience in the earth there comes those periods of doubt and fear, and of the loss of hope. Then to all such there should be the reminding of that Easter Morn; and as to what it has meant and does mean in the hearts and minds of those who have and do put their trust in Jesus, the Christ."[104]

Cayce affirmed that, through the redemptive efficacy of the resurrection, "hate, injustice, tyranny, desire to enslave or to impel others to submit to the dictates of this or that power" will all pass away. Elsewhere he commented that the significance of the resurrection depended on how each person "applies same . . . in his daily life, experience and conversation with his fellow man."[105] He urged everyone: "Open thine eyes and behold the Glory, even of thy Christ present here, now, in thy midst, even as He appeared to them on that day!"

Like many others, esoteric writers have discussed Christ's second coming, or "reappearance." By Alice Bailey's description, the reappearance of "Christ, the Avatar of Love" will be profoundly significant for humanity:

> Then shall the Coming One appear, His footsteps hastened through the valley of the shadow by the One of awful power Who stands upon the mountain top, breathing out love eternal, light supernal and peaceful, silent Will. Then will the sons of men respond. Then will a newer light shine forth into the dismal, weary vale of earth. Then will new life course through the veins of men . . . So peace will come again on earth, but a peace unlike aught known before.[106]

A recent book explored the reappearance, with special emphasis on the prophecies and their numerological symbolism.[107] Most esoteric Christians are "postmillennialist" rather than "premillennialist," though it is a stretch to use the terms in this context. There is little support for the conventional "end-time" scenario, and many esoteric writers have taken issue with the notion that Christ will reappear to put things right on earth. Rather, they suggest that he will reappear only when humanity has put its own house in order. But if we are charged with establishing the kingdom, the hope is that we shall not have to keep it running for 1,000 years before the reappearance becomes possible.

Christ in the Sacraments

Rudolf Steiner made much of what he called the "Mystery of Golgotha." Christ in his depiction was the spirit of the earth. When Jesus' blood spilled onto the earth during the crucifixion, that spirit flowed into the fabric of the planet. From then on the earth became the body of Christ; and as a result, anything we eat constitutes a kind of eucharist. Steiner's Christ explained to his inner group of disciples: "When you behold the cornfield and then eat the bread that nourishes you, what in reality is this bread you are eating? You are eating My body. And when you drink the plant sap [it is] My blood."[108]

The work of Masonic organizations, the Golden Dawn, and other occult groups does not all relate to Christianity; nor does it always demonstrate the ideals which Jesus Christ embodied. Nevertheless the tradition of ceremonial ritual that they embodied is relevant to our theme and has shed valuable light on the significance of Christian ritual and the sacraments. More importantly, practitioners' knowledge and expertise could help enhance the effectiveness of sacramental ritual. Here we must distinguish carefully between high, or ceremonial, magic, directed to the good of others, from low magic, or sorcery whose purpose is to enhance the magician's power or harm other people.

The sacraments may originally have been viewed as magic rituals; and as we have seen, similarities were noted during the Renaissance between the consecration of the Eucharist and alchemical transmutation. In recent centuries institutional Christianity has been reluctant to admit such associations. Éliphas Lévi found that understandable because of the abuse of magic by unscrupulous practitioners: "sorcerers outraged the children of the Magi."[109] On the other hand, he complained that in failing to see the magical nature of the sacraments, the churches cut themselves off from a rich tradition. Lévi predicted that a more favorable attitude lay ahead: "Religion . . . can no longer reject a doctrine anterior to the Bible and in perfect accord with traditional respect for the past, as well as with our most vital hopes for progress in the future . . . The crook of the priesthood shall become the rod of miracles."[110]

Dion Fortune felt that the sacraments had degenerated into "vain observances in the hands of those who regard them with superstitious awe rather than an understanding of their psychological and esoteric significance."[111] She added: "[T]he Mass of the Church and the ceremonies of the Freemasons are . . . representative types of magic, whatever their exponents may like to say to the contrary. The Mass is a perfect example of a ritual of evocation."[112] A manual of high magic technique, also in the Golden Dawn tradition, specifically discussed the Eucharist:

> Both the priest and the magician have to pass on the force of the invocation. The priest invokes a god to gain power in order to affect a transformation, and "earths" the force in a Sacrament which becomes (in Christianity) the blood and flesh of God. This then is passed on to the congregation who thereby receive the virtue of the invocation . . . The magician does exactly the same thing . . .[113]

The authors added that power invoked by the magician can be applied for purposes of prophecy, benediction, or the laying-on of hands.[114] Charismatic Christians would say the same about the "gifts of the Spirit."

Charles Leadbeater's clairvoyant abilities allowed him to see angelic presences in religious rituals. He spoke of an "Angel of the Eucharist" present during the Mass. With the collaboration of the celebrant(s) and congregation, the angel builds a thoughtform encompassing the whole sanctuary. Its intensity depends on the congregation's level of devotion and the priests' skill in focusing the energy for the angel's use. Viewed with clairvoyant sight, the completed thoughtform has a central dome surrounded by spires, calling to mind the architecture of the basilica of Hagia Sophia in Constantinople.[115] Geoffrey Hodson, whose clairvoyant gifts were at least as profound, shared his own experience while celebrating the Mass as a priest in the Liberal Catholic Church: "I saw the Christ Presence in the Host flashed out as in golden darts or rays of Himself in each one of the people and became linked thereto, awakening, arousing the Christ consciousness and power."[116]

Esoteric teachings have provided new insights into the doctrine of transubstantiation. Material substances are viewed simply as the lowest forms of realities that extend over a multiple levels of being. Accordingly, transubstantiation can be explained as a transformation of the eucharistic elements on higher planes; physical appearances may stay the same, but their higher reality is changed. Leadbeater, who firmly believed in transubstantiation, remarked that the Mass can indeed be regarded as a sacrifice, not because the consecrated bread and wine are separated, but because Christ descends into the physical elements, recalling what must have been his painful descent into incarnation two millennia ago.[117] The physical world may not be evil, as the Gnostics claimed, but it is an unpleasant place for spiritual beings to visit.

Trinity and Septenary

The notion of a supreme Godhead was explored by both Meister Eckhart and Jakob Böhme. Böhme proceeded to argue that the divine essence emanated from the Godhead first as Three and then as Seven. Although Emanuel Swedenborg was suspicious of the Trinity, most esoteric writers have discussed it in terms generally compatible with those of mainstream Christian doctrine. The only significant difference may be a tendency to abandon co-equality of the persons, or "aspects," in favor of a downward progression of the aspects on the lines proposed by the Neoplatonist Plotinus.[118]

Böhme's sevenfold emanation included the Father, the expression of divine will; the Logos, or Christ; and Sophia, the feminine principle through which the universe came into being.[119] The notion of a septenary emanation had no counterpart in mainstream Christian doctrine, but hints may be found in *Revelation* which referred to "seven Spirits which are before [God's] throne," "seven lamps of fire burning before the throne," and "the seven stars."[120] Another passage related that God held a book with seven seals.[121] The combination of triune and septenary emanations can be reconciled with the ten sephiroth in the Qabalistic Tree of Life.

More recent esoteric teachings have explained the septenary emanation as "seven rays." The term was first used by Blavatsky, and important theological groundwork was laid by Leadbeater and other Theosophical writers;[122] but Alice Bailey provided the most complete description of the seven rays. They are: Will or Power, Love-Wisdom, Active Intelligence, Harmony through Conflict, Knowledge or Science, Devotion or Idealism, and Ceremonial Order.[123] The rays are believed to pervade the whole of creation, and each of us is believed to be the expression of a combination of rays. For example, an individual might have a second-ray soul, a fifth-ray personality, and a physical body "colored" by the first ray.[124] On the other hand, as their names imply, the rays also define activities or spiritual paths, and we shall refer to them in Chapter 22. The Christ expresses the second ray of Love-Wisdom,[125] and religion is considered to be a second-ray activity; Christianity is colored primarily by the sixth ray of Devotion.[126]

Sophia

Esoteric Christianity places considerable emphasis on the feminine aspect of divinity and its expressions in the church and the world. Sophia's place in the classical Gnostic pantheon was noted in Chapter 9. The possibility that she might have divine, or semi-divine, status raises many theological questions. For example, could Sophia be equated to other divine feminine manifestations, like the Greek goddesses or the Shekinah of esoteric Judaism? Was she in some sense a new messiah? And what is her relationship with the Trinity?

The Gnostics regarded Sophia as the bride of the Logos. Montanus' companion Priscilla claimed to have had a vision of Christ in feminine form. And Julian of Norwich referred to God as "our Mother."[127] Jane Ward Lead (1624-1704), who was influenced by Jakob Böhme, had several visions. In the first vision, a woman told her: "Behold I am God's Eternal Virgin-Wisdom, whom thou hast been enquiring after; I am to unseal the Treasures of God's deep Wisdom unto thee, and will be as Rebecca was unto Jacob, a true Natural Mother; for out of my Womb thou shalt be brought forth after the manner of a Spirit, Conceived and Born again . . . Now consider of my Saying till I return to thee again."[128] Speculations about a female messiah occupied the Guglielmites of the 13th century[129] as well as the 18th-century Shaker "Mother" Ann Lee. "Père" Barthelemy Enfantin, who was born 12 years after Lee's death, predicted that he would meet a female messiah and mother of a new savior, though it is not recorded whether he did. Mary Baker Eddy had neither visions nor messianic ambitions; but, like Lee she referred to God as "Father-Mother,"[130] a salutation that has now become more familiar in Christian worship.

In her Latin form, *Sapientia*, Sophia became of interest to Thomas Aquinas: "[H]er fruit is more precious than all the riches of this world, and all the things that are desired are not to be compared with her . . . She is the tree of life."[131] Her qualities were: "power, honor, strength, and dominion."[132] Remarkable words for a cleric schooled in the patriarchal tradition; but he had recently had a profound mystical experience, and he died soon thereafter.

Jakob Böhme's work influenced the Russian philosopher and poet Vladimir Sergeyevich Solovyov (1853-1900).[133] Solovyov had three visions of Sophia. The first was during Mass on Ascension Day, when he was nine years old; a poem he wrote many years later recalled the experience:

> Blue all around. Blue within my soul. / Blue pierced with shafts of gold.
> In your hand a flower from other realms. / You stood with radiant smile, /
> Nodded to me and hidden in the mist.[134]

Solovyov's Sophia shared many of the characteristics customarily attributed to Mary of Nazareth. His second encounter was in the British Museum. As before, he saw Sophia in blue and gold. "Her face shone before me. But Her face alone. And that instant was a long happiness."[135] The third was in the Egyptian desert, where he awoke from sleep "To a scent of roses from air and earth . . . I saw all and all was one. One alone in the image of female beauty."[136]

Solovyov's sensitive poetry blended his devotion to Sophia with romantic yearnings of unrequited love. Indeed, his relationship with the Feminine was not unlike that of the troubadours—or of Dante with Beatrice in the *Divine Comedy*. Solovyov leaned toward Gnosticism in regarding Sophia as the feminine complement of the masculine Logos. Together, in his view, they comprised the overshadowing cosmic Christ. Russian Orthodox theologian Pavel Florensky was more cautious. He too saw Sophia as the Bride of the Logos; she represented God's love for his creation, even providing the channel through which creation was accomplished. But that ability was not hers by right: "One in God, she is multiple in creation and is perceived in creation in her concrete appearances *as the ideal person of man, as his Guardian Angel.*"[137]

Various attempts were made to reconcile Sophia with established trinitarian dogma. To Theophilus of Antioch and Paul of Samosata she was the Holy Spirit. Böhme identified Sophia with the entire Trinity; but, like the Gnostics, he saw a special relationship between her and Christ: "[T]he Virgin, the divine Wisdom, has given me her promise not to leave me in any misery; she will come to help me in the Son of Wisdom."[138] In turn, Florensky identified her as a "nonconsubstantial" fourth person of the Trinity:

> Sophia takes part in the life of the Trihypostatic Divinity, enters into the interior of the Trinity, and enters into communion with Divine Love. Since Sophia is a *fourth*, creaturely, and therefore nonconsubstantial Person, she does not "form" a Divine Unity . . . . As the fourth Person, she, by God's condescension (but in no way by her own nature!), introduces a distinction in relation to herself in the providential activity of the Hypostases of the Trinity.[139]

He added: "From the point of view of the Hypostasis of the Father, Sophia is the ideal *substance*, or ground of creation . . . From the point of view of the . . . Word, Sophia is the *reason* of creation . . . From the point of view of the . . . Spirit, Sophia represents the *spirituality* of creation, its holiness, purity, and immaculateness, i.e., its beauty."[140]

Pavel Florensky was harassed and finally executed in a Soviet purge, but he managed to avoid criticism by the Orthodox Church for his doctrine of the fourth hypostasis. Although Russian priest Sergei Nikolaevich Bulgakov (1871-1944) escaped to the west, he was criticized by the church hierarchy on the grounds that his Sophiology undermined trinitarian doctrine. Forced to distance himself from Florensky's views, he retreated to the position that Sophia is the "nonhypostatic essence" of God. Since the divine essence is shared by all three hypostases, Sophia is neither a fourth hypostasis nor an expression of any one of them to the exclusion of the others: "The three persons . . . have one life in common, that is, one Oursia [divine essence], one Sophia."[141] Bulgakov acknowledged distinct manifestations of Sophia through the three trinitarian persons, however. Her expression through the Son and Holy Spirit is "immediate," while the "relation of Sophia to the Father is mediated through his relation to the other hypostases."[142]

Interestingly, Bulgakov saw Sophia, rather than the Logos, as the mediator between God and the world, arguing that "the hypostasis of the Logos cannot provide such a unifying principle."[143]

Bulgakov saw a close association between Sophia and the Glory of God, which traditionally was associated more closely with the Shekinah of Judaic tradition.[144] "Wisdom," he argued, "is the glory of God and either expression could be used indiscriminately of divine revelation within the Godhead, for they both refer to the same divine essence."[145] Commenting on a passage in *Proverbs* claiming that *Chokmah*/Sophia was with God "from the beginning," Bulgakov identified Sophia as the "prototype of creation."[146] Correspondingly, he saw creation—and particularly humanity—as the "creaturely Sophia," the actualization of that prototype.[147]

For the Russian theologians, Sophia was both a feminine divine aspect, who could appear to Solovyov and others in a form reminiscent of Mary of Nazareth, and also a more nebulous essence subsuming the Trinity. In addition, as we shall see in Chapter 21, she serves as a symbol for the overarching Ekklesia. Sophia is both "bride of Christ" and the cosmic Bride of the Logos.

By the latter half of the 20th century Sophia had been co-opted by feminist theologians seeking a goddess. In the process "Sophia" became a catch-phrase—one selling scores of books—for all things feminine and divine. She now absorbs not only Chokmah and the Shekinah but also the Greek Athena and the Buddhist Prajnaparamita and Kuan-Yin. Yet if Sophia has lost her specific identity, humanity has gained insights into its own nature, including the masculine-feminine balance that Jakob Böhme urged that we re-establish within ourselves. To quote the well-known spiritual writer Carol Parrish-Harra:

> Who is this numinous Sophia? She is Mother Wisdom, come to guide us home . . . [Sophia] dances through my life, peeks through the windows of my mind, whispers words of wisdom, laughing and playing . . . To follow Sophia is the opportunity of our time . . . She leads to dynamic adventure requiring that we face our fears, learn to love, and dare to move more fully toward our potential.[148]

Mary, the World Mother

Protestantism generally has rejected any suggestion that Mary of Nazareth was the mother of God. But her divine motherhood received support from an unlikely quarter: the Lutheran theologian Ludwig Feuerbach (1804-1872): "[T]he Virgin Mary fits in perfectly with the relations of the Trinity, since she conceives without man the Son whom the Father begets without woman; so that thus the Holy Virgin is a necessary, inherently requisite antithesis to the Father in the bosom of the Trinity."[149] He digressed, echoing the sentiments of Julian of Norwich, to attribute feminine qualities to God the Son, returning to his theme with: "the Son implicitly urges upon us the need of a real feminine being."[150] In Roman Catholicism, the Marian cult has grown in strength over the last 100 years, with many reported apparitions and a level of devotion that gives her a special status in the divine order. That status was enhanced by the two Marian doctrines of the immaculate conception and the assumption. In Eastern Orthodoxy Mary has long been venerated as *Theotokos*, Mother of God, and at times she seemed to receive more attention than Jesus. Sometimes Mary is termed "Mother of the World."[151]

Strong devotion to Mary also developed among second and later generations of Theosophists, though their perspective was somewhat different. Mary was perceived to be the incarnation of a cosmic feminine entity. Annie Besant referred to her as Virgo, and Rudolf Steiner as the Virgin Sophia.[152] Echoing the Russian tradition, Charles Leadbeater and others, called her the World Mother:

> The World-Mother . . . is a mighty Being . . . She is in truth a mighty Angel, having under Her a vast host of subordinate Angels whom She keeps perpetually employed in the work which is especially committed to Her.[153]

Mary's work included watching over the women of the world, particularly when they are in childbirth. Leadbeater added that another function is "to try to mitigate the suffering of the world, to act as the Consoler, the Comforter, the Helper of all who are in trouble, sorrow, need, sickness or any other adversity."[154] Wittingly or unwittingly he had emerged as a modern champion of the assertion that the Holy Spirit is God the Mother.[155] The very year that Leadbeater published this work, Besant declared March 24, the traditional feast of the Annunciation, to be World Mother Day.[156]

Esoteric writer Richard Smoley asserted that "God is beyond all gender, beyond any personhood. We, on the other hand, live both as persons and as beings with gender."[157] In order to communicate with us God must manifest in such forms, at appropriate times. As the cosmic Mother, Mary expressed the reality of divine love:

> The divine Son, the immaculate Mother—these archetypes have always been known to humanity. As Mary's earthly incarnation recedes from us in the historical distance, her personal presence fades and she becomes ever more the glass through which we see the shimmering and fecund waters of the world and the infinite compassion that gave them birth.[158]

Geoffrey Hodson, who belonged to the generation of Theosophists after Besant and Leadbeater, took the study of the World Mother a stage further. His understanding went through several stages during his long life. Initially he perceived the Mother as an archetype or abstract principle:

> Behind all womanhood exists the Eternal Woman, the one divine manifestation of femininity. At its origin, it is cosmic, being the half of all creation. The other half is the Eternal Man, and mysteriously these are not two but one . . . What are the essential qualities of the archetypal woman? They are sacrifice, tenderness, graciousness, divine radiance, heavenly fragrance, beauty, and grace . . . They are joyous radiant girlhood, graceful womanhood, creative, preserving, and transforming motherhood. Within the Heavenly Woman is an ascetic refinement of utter purity.[159]

The Mother, Hodson explained, has manifested in a variety of forms over the centuries and millennia: "The different visions and differing appearances and positions which people of various religions and countries attribute to the World Mother are all adaptations of visions and teachings chosen as most suitable."[160] As Hodson's ideas developed he began to see the Mother as an office held by a succession of individuals that included Mary. "As far as my understanding and experiences inform me," he wrote, "the Blessed Lady Mary, Mother of Jesus, is the present Holder of that Office."[161] Distancing himself from Erasmus, he approved of titles such as "Queen of the Angels" and "Star of the Sea." Hodson described a personal vision thus: "At this point, the Blessed Lady Mary becomes visible before me in all Her wondrous blue and, as it were, reaches out and touches my head."[162]

Human Potential

A tenet that has gained near-unanimous agreement in esoteric Christianity is humanity's divine potential. As the Gnostics and Neoplatonists insisted, each of us has—or, at the very center of our being, *is*—a divine spark, a fragment of Godhead and the source of life.[163] Meister Eckhart and numerous others expressed that belief. Humanity is not just body and soul but body, soul and *spirit*. Theosophical writers have devoted much attention to the soul's evolutionary journey in response to spirit. Over the course of countless incarnations, the individual progresses from the state of "ordinary humanity" through the paths of aspiration, discipleship and finally initiation.[164] Aspiration corresponds to involvement in conventional religion; discipleship involves a lifetime commitment to service; and the various initiations are major expansions of consciousness leading to a state of relative perfection.[165] Theosophists are careful to distinguish those initiations from the grades in Mithraic, Masonic, or Golden Dawn orders.

Few modern esoteric writers have embraced the Gnostic view that the physical body is corrupt or evil. Instead, physical health is considered normal; the body can and should be healed of conditions that limit the soul's ability to express itself in the physical world. Of central importance to New Thought was the notion that evil has no substantive reality but is simply the absence of good. Mary Baker Eddy insisted that evil is simply "error, without intelligence or reality."[166] To recognize the nonexistence of evil is the basis of healing. Eddy reported an important insight: "Whence came to me this heavenly conviction . . . that human experience shows the falsity of all material things . . . that the only sufferer is the mortal mind, for the divine Mind cannot suffer."[167] Ernest Holmes put the individual human mind in the context of Infinite Mind, an all-embracing principle not unlike Jakob Böhme's *Ungrund*: the source of universal law and harmony.

The belief that health and wholeness are our natural states pervades all branches of esoteric Christianity. Healing is part of the redemptive transformation. Theosophical writers agree that sickness may originate at the mental—or emotional—level, but they do not share the New Thought belief that evil is illusory. Nor do Theosophical writers agree with the Qabalistic view that good and evil are simply a pair of opposites that need to be brought into balance. Rather, Theosophical teachings emphasize that evil is partly of karmic origin—individual and/or racial—and partly a consequence of the current imperfection of planetary life.[168] Moreover, Theosophy conceives of cosmic evil that is capable of penetrating the protective shield surrounding the earth.

There is also disagreement on how healing should be accomplished. Christian Science regards spiritual healing and conventional medicine as mutually incompatible, whereas Theosophical writers emphasize their interrelationship. For example Theosophist Geoffrey Hodson argued: "The physician is one of the most important . . . assistants of the Supreme Will in evolution. His duties bring him face to face with God, close to the divine in man [at a] time of greatest need, the time of suffering."[169]

Reflections

Esoteric Christianity emphasizes inner spiritual experience over external authority, insight over doctrine, personal growth over salvation through the church, transformation over redemption, and humanity's divine potential over Augustinian/Calvinist "depravity." Modern esoteric Christianity's greatest contribution has been to the Path of Knowledge. The far-reaching work of Jakob Böhme, Emanuel Swedenborg, Helena Blavatsky, and Alice Bailey placed them squarely on that path. Éliphas Lévi, Papus, MacGregor Mathers, Annie Besant, Charles Leadbeater, Rudolf Steiner, Dion Fortune, and Geoffrey Hodson combined the Paths of Knowledge, Ceremony, and to a lesser degree Devotion. Phineas Quimby, Mary Baker Eddy, the Fillmores, and Ernest Holmes primarily walked the Path of Healing, though they also made important contributions to Knowledge and Devotion. Swedenborg's "New Heaven" and "New Church" provided glimpses of the Ekklesia.

The esoteric views of God, humanity and the universe resonate with increasing numbers of people in the modern world. Esoteric Christianity has special appeal to people schooled in western systems of symbolism, such as Freemasonry and the Qabalah, as well as to those exposed to the religions of Asia. It offers an important alternative to mainstream western Christianity which is losing its sense of the sacred—and perhaps its sense of direction—in the collision between liberalism and fundamentalism.

Esoteric Christianity strongly embraces the Gnostic-Neoplatonic principle that each of us has a divine spark within us—or more precisely *is* a divine spark. It may lie hidden beneath layers of physical matter and ignorance, but over time the spark will grow brighter. The notion of *enlightenment* precisely expresses the increase in brilliance and the corresponding blossoming of divine potential. Our destiny, which freewill can nurture or impede, is to move toward perfection; and as latent abilities unfold we find new opportunities to serve. Christ encouraged the use of such abilities in areas such as healing.

Modern esoteric Christianity distances itself from the destructive aspects of Gnostic dualism. The Gnostics recognized the importance of pairs of opposites but failed to grasp their creative potential. We now understand that spirit and matter, in particular, are not eternally opposed; they can be brought into harmony so that spirit is grounded and matter redeemed. The *Gospel of Philip* provided a hint: "Light and Darkness, life and death, right and left, are brothers of one another. They are inseparable. Because of this neither are the good good, nor evil evil, nor is life life, nor death death. For this reason each one will dissolve into its earliest origin. But those who are exalted above the world are indissoluble, eternal."[170] Also we are reminded that "matter is spirit at its lowest point and spirit is matter at its highest."[171] Jakob Böhme observed that the masculine and the feminine are to be brought into harmony in the creative act of new birth—on all levels of reality.

New insights have been gained into the nature and role of Mary of Nazareth. The hope now is that feminist theologians, who have shunned Mary because of her associations with dutiful subservience, will pay more attention to her role in redemption and human transformation. The parallel field of Sophiology, to which Russian Orthodox theologians have made major contributions, speaks to many people of our time. Such studies can help restore balance to Christian views of divinity, which have been warped by an exclusive focus on its masculine aspects. Fears that a divine Sophia undermines belief in the Trinity were overstated.

Some of the spiritual healing modalities studied in this chapter must be approached with caution. New Thought's claim that all disease stems from wrong thinking is exaggerated; emotion as well as genetic and environmental physical factors can undermine health.[172] Moreover Christian Science was wrong to discourage people from seeking medical treatment, and courts have been justified in overruling parents' objections to treatment for their children. Nevertheless New Thought's healing ministry was motivated by genuine compassion, and it provides an interesting complement to the faith healing of charismatic Christianity. It can also complement conventional medicine.

Certain individuals appear to have the ability to make intuitive diagnoses of medical conditions and even to propose effective therapies. Their ability is a great gift, to be welcomed in a world that needs all the help it can get to alleviate suffering and promote wholeness.[173] Medical intuitives can and should work in collaboration with licensed medical personnel; Edgar Cayce set important precedents in that regard. Healing is a broad field, in which spiritual modalities, conventional medicine, and other forms of healthcare can all play meaningful roles.

For esoteric Christians the "sacred" is not something entirely ineffable and mysterious but is part of a natural order that both includes and transcends the physical plane. The natural order is believed to be subject to laws which potentially can be understood and utilized by evolving humanity. From that perspective no intrinsic difference exists between healing, the Eucharist, and other sacraments, on the one hand, and "high magic" on the other.[174] They all depend for their effectiveness on words of power, gestures, symbols, and in some cases sacred objects. Magic has come to be regarded in traditional Christian circles as evil and in secular circles as superstitious or fraudulent; ironically, skeptics also regard the sacraments as superstitious or meaningless. Clearly, healthier attitudes need to be established in both areas as well as in the relationship between them. We might take note of Éliphas Lévi's assertion that magic "combines in a single science that which is most certain in philosophy, which is eternal and infallible in religion."[175] Most importantly, we need to recover the awareness that humanity has access to, and can benefit from, a broad category of phenomena that span the seen and unseen. The very welcome renewal of interest in sacramental ritual will be discussed in Chapter 20.

[1.]   Attempts are often made to identify continuity of esoteric traditions from classical Gnosticism to the high Middle Ages. These attempts are at best speculative. However the secrecy under which groups had to operate makes historical research particularly difficult.

2. It is worth noting that, in the ancient mystery schools, what we now know as high-school geometry was an initiatory secret.

3. P. D. Ouspensky. *In Search of the Miraculous.* Harcourt, Brace & World, 1949, pp. 38ff.

4. *John* 14:12.

5. Francis Lee. *An Historical Account of Montanism*, 1709. Emphasis in original. Quoted in: Désirée Hirst. *Hidden Treasures: Traditional Symbolism from the Renaissance to Blake.* Eyre & Spottiswoode, 1964, p. 290. Lee was the son-in-law and secretary of Philadelphian Jane Ward Lead who is mentioned later in the chapter.

6. Esotericists often stress the importance of the heart. But that is not the emotional heart of Evangelical and Pentecostal Christianity but a heart that links the personality and soul.

7. Robin Waterfield. Introduction to: *Jacob Boehme.* North Atlantic Books, 2001, p. 19.

8. Paracelsus' full name was Theophrastus Philippus Aureolus Bombastus von Hohenheim.

9. Quoted in: Waterfield. *Jacob Boehme*, pp. 154-155. Source not provided.

10. John J. Stoudt. *Sunrise to Eternity.* University of Pennsylvania Press, 1957, p. 191.

11. *John* 1:5.

12. Jakob Böhme. *The Threefold Life of Man.* (Transl: S. Janos.) Quoted in: N. Berdyaev. *Studies Concerning Jacob Boehme*, etude II, 1930, pp. 34-62.

13. In Plato's *Symposium* Aristophanes declared that man was originally androgynous but was cut in two by Zeus to curb his pride. Ever since, man has sought his female half, and vice versa.

14. Böhme, *The Threefold Life of Man*, pp. 34-62. See also Böhme's *Mysterium Magnum.* London, 1654, chapter 18.

15. For a discussion of Böhme's teachings on gender and their influence on William Blake see: Hirst, *Hidden Riches*, pp. 92-96.

16. The pairs of opposites also include good and evil. For a discussion of the opposites as they are addressed in the Qabalah see: John Nash. "Duality, Good and Evil, and the Approach to Harmony." *Esoteric Quarterly*, Fall 2004, pp. 15-26.

17. Prominent members of the Philadelphians were Anglican priest John Pordage (1607-1681) and Jane Ward Lead (1624-1704) who had a number of visions involving Sophia.

18. William Law. *An Appeal to all that Doubt or Disbelieve the Truths of the Gospel.* Quoted in: Hirst, *Hidden Treasures*, p. 194.

19. It is easy to see how Böhme's resolution of opposites fed into Hegel's theory of thesis, antithesis and synthesis.

20. Nikolai Berdyaev. *The Russian Idea.* (Transl: R. French.) Lindisfarne Press, 1947/1992, p. 37.

21. Swedenborg also demonstrated clairvoyant abilities, including becoming aware of a fire in Stockholm while he was visiting Gothenburg, some 300 miles away; subsequent news reports confirmed what he had seen.

22. Immanuel Kant. *Dreams of a Ghost-Seer*, 1766.

23. Reportedly, only four copies of the book were sold during Swedenborg's lifetime, one of them to Kant. See: Bertrand Russell. *A History of Western Philosophy*. Simon & Schuster, 1945, p. 705.

24. Emanuel Swedenborg. *Heaven and Earth*, 184. *Swedenborg Essential Readings*. North Atlantic Books, 2003, p. 125.

25. His "nights" recall the Dark Night of the Soul experienced by John of the Cross.

26. Emanuel Swedenborg. *Arcana Caelestia*, §894, 933, 935, 5202, 9278. *Swedenborg Essential Readings*. North Atlantic Books, 1799/2003. The concept of continued growth in heaven is echoed in Eastern Orthodox teachings.

27. *Ibid.*

28. Emanuel Swedenborg. *True Christian Religion*, §183. (Transl: J. Ager.) Swedenborg Foundation, 1771/1997.

29. Ibid, §1.

30. Hirst, *Hidden Treasures:*, p. 201.

31. *Ibid.*, p. 219-221.

32. "Philip à Gabella" seems to have been a fictional character. No one of that name has been identified in the historical record.

33. *Fama Fraternitatis*. (Transl. publ. by Thomas Vaughn, 1652.)

34. *Confessio Fraternitatis*, ch. IV.

35. *Fama Fraternitatis*. Many people had discussed the *Librum Naturae*, including Thomas Aquinas, but the "book" was a major preoccupation of Renaissance thinkers.

36. *Ibid.*

37. Even eight brothers might seem a very small number, considering the importance of their work. However, with only nine members, the Knights Templar took on the enormous responsibility of protecting European pilgrims traveling to the Holy Land. Several commentators have noted similarities between the Templars and the Fraternity of the Rose Cross.

38. *Confessio Fraternitatis*, ch. IV.

39. *Ibid*, ch. V.

40. Paul F. Case. *The True and Invisible Rosicrucian Order.* Weiser, 1985, pp. 37-64.

41. *Ibid.*, p. 5. By implication Case was able to recognize "true Rosicrucians."

42. Frances A. Yates. *The Rosicrucian Enlightenment*. Routledge & Kegan Paul, 1972, pp. 75ff.

43. For a more complete discussion of the Rosicrucian movement and its goals see: John Nash. "Service Ideals in the Rosicrucian Movement." *Esoteric Quarterly*, Winter 2005, pp. 33-42.

44. *Ibid.*

45. *Fama Fraternitatis*.

46. There was an intermittent line of earls of Norfolk from 1075 to 1660. During the period of possible Rose Cross activity, earls held office from 1399 to 1425 and from 1477 to 1660; however there is no historical record that any of them were stricken with leprosy. The last significant outbreak of leprosy among the English nobility occurred in the 13th century.

47. *Fama Fraternitatis*.

48. Paracelsus' pioneering work on magnetic healing preceded the better-known work of Anton Mesmer (1734-1815) by more than 200 years.

49. Yates. *The Rosicrucian Enlightenment*, pp. 139ff.

50. Source: Societas Rosicruciana in Anglia.

51. Max Heindel. *Echoes from Mount Ecclesia*, June & July 1913, pp. 1-2.

52. Source: *Mastery of Life*. Ancient Mystical Order Rosae Crucis.

53. See the discussion in: Christopher Bamford. Introduction to *"Freemasonry" and Ritual Work*. Steinerbooks, 2007, p. xl-xlviii.

54. A similar diagnostic method would be used a century later by Edgar Cayce.

55. Phineas P. Quimby. "The Body of Jesus and the Body of Christ," 1863. Quimby Library.

56. Phineas P. Quimby. "Belief in Another World," 1864. Quimby Library.

57. Mary Baker was married three times: to George Washington Glover who died within a year, to Daniel Patterson whom she divorced, and in her fifties to Asa Gilbert Eddy.

58. *Mark* 5:34.

59. A long controversy erupted concerning the true author of her methods. Critics claimed that Eddy had plagiarized Quimby's work. But Eddy claimed that Quimby was simply a mesmerist, while she alone understood the Christian basis for healing.

60. The *Monitor* is a national secular newspaper which carries a few articles dealing with issues of relevance to Christian Science.

61. Source: Association of Unity Churches International.

62. Source: Unity School of Christianity. Parenthesis in original.

63. Ernest Holmes. *The Science of Mind*. Tarcher-Putnam, 1938, p. 320.

64. *Ibid.*, p. 26.

65. The Church of Religious Science has no organizational or philosophical connection with the controversial Church of Scientology founded in 1953 by American science fiction writer L. Ron Hubbard.

66. Quoted in: Scott Awbrey. *Path of Discovery*. Los Angeles United Church of Religious Science, 1987.

67. Charles Fillmore. *Prosperity*. Unity Classic Library, 1936, p. 174.

68. Holmes, *The Science of Mind*, p. 321.

69. The concept of the akashic records is derived from Hindu thought.

70. In one case a normally lethal dose of belladonna was prescribed—successfully—for a young child. See: Sidney D. Kirkpatrick. *Edgar Cayce*. Riverhead Books, 2000, pp. 5-8.

71. Edgar Cayce. Reading 1507-4, January 3, 1938. Association for Research and Enlightenment.

72. Edgar Cayce. Reading 69-4, February 8, 1941. Emphasis in original.

73. Kirkpatrick, *Edgar Cayce: An American Prophet*, pp. 327-340.

74. It was 20 years before any of the readings addressed the topic of reincarnation.

75. J. Gordon Melton. "Edgar Cayce and Reincarnation: Past Life Readings as Religious Symbology." *Syzygy: Journal of Alternative Religion and Culture*, vol. 3, nos. 1-2, 1994.

76. Kirkpatrick, *Edgar Cayce: An American Prophet*, p. 280.

77. Enfantin was influenced by utopian socialist Henri de Saint-Simon and, for a time, served as head of St.-Simon's religious sect.

78. Israel Regardie. *The Golden Dawn*. Llewellyn Publications, 1940/1971.

79. *Ibid.*

80. Mary K. Greer. *Women of the Golden Dawn*. Park Street Press, 1995. See also: W. Wynn Westcott. "Historic Lecture." Hermetic Order of the Golden Dawn.

81. Dion Fortune. *The Training and Work of an Initiate*. Aquarian Press, 1930, p. 90.

82. Its name was changed in 1785 to the British Society for the Propagation of the Doctrines of the New Church. See: Hirst, *Hidden Treasures*, p. 208. It should be remembered that, prior to the late 19th century, "theosophy" could refer to a broad range of esoteric topics. Here "Theosophy" (capitalized) refers specifically to the Blavatskian Theosophical Society and its offshoots.

83. Source: Theosophical Society International Headquarters, Adyar, India.

84. Blavatsky and Olcott met in 1874 at the Vermont home of two famous mediums: the brothers William and Horatio Eddy.

85. Helena Blavatsky was incautious in her professional behavior, attracting charges of sensationalism and even fraud. The merits of these charges have been debated at great length in the literature. Whatever conclusion is ultimately drawn, the fact remains that she was able to inspire large number of sincere seekers, and the Theosophical Society has made a major contribution to modern spirituality.

86. Both are published by the Theosophical Publishing House.

87. Charles W. Leadbeater. *The Inner Life*. Theosophical Publishing House, 1910, p. 80.

88. Annie W. Besant. *Esoteric Christianity*. Theosophical Publishing House, 1914/1953, foreword. The foreword to the more generally available 1901 edition is shorter and does not include this quote.

89. Christopher Bamford (ed.). *"Freemasonry" and Ritual Work*. SteinerBooks, 2007.

90. Rudolf Steiner. *Spiritualism, Madame Blavatsky, and Theosophy*. Anthroposophic Press, 1912/2001, pp. 126-130.

91. Steiner's books are published by the Anthroposophical Society.

92. See the discussion in: John Nash. *The Soul and Its Destiny*. Authorhouse, 2004, pp. 4-6.

93. In some cases those insights were attributed to higher entities who guided their writings.

94. Quimby, "The Body of Jesus and the Body of Christ."

95. Mary Baker Eddy. *Science and Health with Key to the Scriptures*. First Church of Christ Scientist, 1875, p. 333. See also p. 336.

96. Alice A. Bailey. *Initiation: Human and Solar*. Lucis Publishing Company, 1922, pp. 43-44.

97. Daniel Andreev. *Rose of the World*, 1.3. Daniel Andreev Charity Foundation, 1997.

98. Besant, *Esoteric Christianity*, p. 89.

99. Bailey, *Initiation: Human and Solar*, pp. 37-38.

100. Alice A. Bailey. *The Destiny of the Nations*. Lucis Publishing Company, 1949, p. 59.

101. Sandra Hodson (ed). *Illuminations of the Mystery Tradition*. Theosophical Publishing House, 1992, p. 258.

102. Dion Fortune. *Applied Magic*. Aquarian Press, 1962, pp. 20-21.

103. Besant, *Esoteric Christianity*, p. 115.

104. Edgar Cayce. Reading 5749-13, March 12, 1941.

105. Edgar Cayce. Reading 5749-12, March 24, 1940.

106. Alice A. Bailey. *The Reappearance of the Christ*. Lucis Publishing Company, 1948, pp. 13-14.

107. Barbara Domalske. *Sword of Shamballa*. Authorhouse, 2006.
108. Rudolf Steiner. *The Gospel of St. John*. Anthroposophic Press, 1908/1940, p. 114.
109. Éliphas Lévi. *The History of Magic*. (Transl: A. Waite.) Samuel Weiser, 1913/1969, p. 374.
110. *Ibid.*, p. 374.
111. Fortune, *The Training and Work of an Initiate*, pp. 88-89.
112. *Ibid.*, p. 78.
113. Francis King & Stephen Skinner. *Techniques of High Magic*. Destiny Books, 1976, p. 159.
114. *Ibid.*, pp. 159-160.
115. Charles W. Leadbeater. *The Science of the Sacraments*. Theosophical Publishing House, 1920, especially pp. 23, 119.
116. Sandra Hodson (ed.). *Light of the Sanctuary*. Theosophical Publishers, 1988, p. 162.
117. Leadbeater, *The Science of the Sacraments*, especially pp. 198-199.
118. For example: Charles W. Leadbeater. *The Chakras*. Theosophical Publishing House, 1927, p. 29. See also the discussion of the Trinity in Chapter 7.
119. Jakob Böhme. *Four Tables of Divine Revelation*. London, 1654. Waterfield, *Jacob Boehme*, pp. 214-217. Böhme's placement of Sophia at the end of his septenary recalls the customary association of *Malkuth*, the last of the lower seven sephiroth, with the Shekinah (שכינה), the feminine divine aspect in esoteric Judaism. See: John Nash. "The Shekinah: the Indwelling Glory of God." *Esoteric Quarterly*, Summer 2005, pp. 33-40.
120. *Revelation* 1:4, 3:1, 4:5, 5:6.
121. *Ibid.* 5:1,5.
122. The evolution of the doctrine is discussed in: John Nash. "The Seven Rays: a Case Study in the Dissemination of Esoteric Knowledge." *Esoteric Quarterly*, Winter 2007, pp. 33-50.
123. Alice A. Bailey. *Esoteric Psychology*, I & II. Lucis Publishing Company, 1936, 1942; *The Rays and the Initiations*. Lucis Publishing Company, 1960. Attempts to correlate the rays with colors, as we understand them, have only been partially successful.
124. In addition each of the lower vehicles, or "bodies," considered in Theosophical teachings, is influenced by a ray. To illustrate, the individual in the example might have a third-ray physical body.
125. Alice A. Bailey. *Discipleship in the New Age*, I. Lucis Publishing Company 1944, p. xiii.
126. Bailey, *Esoteric Psychology*, I, p. 167.
127. Julian of Norwich. *Showings* (Long Text), ch. 52. Paulist Press, 1978, p. 279.
128. Jane Lead. *A Fountain of Gardens*. Journal Entries: 1670-1675. Bradford, 1696. Lead was often spelled "Leade." See also: Julie Hirst. "The Divine Ark: Jane Lead's Vision of the Second Noah's Ark." *Esoterica*, vol. VI, pp. 16-25.
129. The Guglielmites were mentioned in Chapter 5.
130. See for example: Eddy, *Science and Health with Key to the Scriptures*, p. 332.
131. Thomas Aquinas (attributed to). *Aurora Consurgens*, I: 20-25. (Transl: Marie-Louise von Franz.) Inner City Books, 2000, p. 35.
132. *Ibid*, V: 13, pp. 53-55.

133. As noted earlier, Solovyov inspired the character Alyosha in Fyodor Dostoevsky's *The Brothers Karamazov*.

134. Vladimir Solovyov. "The Three Meetings." Quoted in: Eugenia Gourvitch. *Vladimir Soloviev: the Man and the Prophet*. Rudolf Steiner Press, 1992, p. 25.

135. *Ibid*, p. 32.

136. *Ibid*, pp. 34, 36.

137. Pavel Florensky. *The Pillar and the Ground of Truth*. (Transl: B. Jakim.) Princeton University Press, 1997, p. 239. Emphasis in original. Florensky's Sophiological doctrines are interesting since he wrote at length about deep male friendships that express both *agape* and *eros*.

138. Jakob Boehme. *Confessions*. (Transl: W. Scott Palmer.) Harper and Bros., 1954, p. 97.

139. *Ibid.*, p. 252. Emphasis and parenthetical comment in original

140. *Ibid.*, pp. 252-253. Emphasis in original

141. Sergei Bulgakov. *Sophia: the Wisdom of God*. (Transl: P. Thompson *et al.*) Lindisfarne Press, 1993, pp. 35-37.

142. *Ibid.*, p. 52.

143. *Ibid.*, p. 74.

144. Nash, "The Shekinah: the Indwelling Glory of God," pp. 33-40.

145. Bulgakov, *Sophia*, p. 50.

146. *Ibid.*, p. 65. *Chokmah* is the Hebrew word for "Wisdom," as *Sophia* is the Greek, and *Sapientia* the Latin.

147. *Ibid.*, p. 72.

148. Carol Parrish-Harra. Sophia Sutras: *Introducing Mother Wisdom*. Sparrow Hawk Press, 2006, p. 271. Parrish-Harra is founder and spiritual leader of the Sancta Sophia seminary in Oklahoma.

149. Ludwig Feuerbach. *The Essence of Christianity*. (Transl: G. Eliot) 1843, part 1, ch. 4. Feuerbach is mostly remembered for his thesis that God is the creation of man, and divine attributes human attributes.

150. *Ibid*.

151. Maria Skobtsova. *Veneration of the Mother of God*. (Transl: S. Janos.) YMCA Press, Paris, 1992/2001, p. 109-126.

152. Rudolf Steiner. *The Gospel of St. John*. Anthroposophic Press, 1908/1940, p. 191.

153. Charles W. Leadbeater. *The World-Mother as Symbol and Fact*. Theosophical Publishing House, 1928, p. 4.

154. *Ibid.*, pp. 5-6.

155. That assertion was made by second-century Gnostic Valentinus. See Chapter 7.

156. Robert Ellwood. "The Church, the World Mother and the New Age." *The Liberal Catholic*, Easter 1998. Annie Besant was president of the Theosophical Society from 1907 to 1933.

157. Richard Smoley. *Inner Christianity: a Guide to the Esoteric Tradition*. Lindisfarne Books, 2002, p. 151.

158. *Ibid.*, pp. 151-152.

159. S. Hodson. *Light of the Sanctuary*, pp. 81-82.

160. *Ibid.*, p. 284.

161. *Ibid.*, p. 355.

162. *Ibid.*, p. 418.

163. See for example: S. Hodson, *Light of the Sanctuary*, p. xiv. In the doctrine of the divine spark, or monad, we also see a strong connection with the Hindu *atman* which is of one substance with the Brahman.

164. For an exploration of Theosophical perspectives on the soul's progression see: John Nash. *The Soul and Its Destiny.* Authorhouse, 2004.

165. The fifth initiation is regarded as the level of relative perfection possible in the present phase of human spiritual development. Those who attain that initiation are referred to as adepts or masters.

166. Eddy, *Science and Health with Key to the Scriptures*, p. 333. See also p. 469.

167. *Ibid.*, p. 108.

168. The Gnostic Valentinus held a similar view of the earth's imperfection.

169. S. Hodson, *Illuminations of the Mystery Tradition*, p. 179.

170. *Gospel of Philip*, 10. (Transl: W. Isenberg.) Gnostic Society Library.

171. Helena P. Blavatsky. *The Secret Doctrine*, I. Theosophical University Press, 1877, p. 179. Also: Alice A. Bailey. *Esoteric Astrology.* Lucis Publishing Company, 1951, p. 340. Spirit-matter convergence stands in sharp contrast with the view of Mircea Eliade where the sacred is of a "wholly different order." See for example: *The Sacred and the Profane.* (Transl: W. R. Trask.) Harvest Books, 1959, p. 10.

172. Carl Jung criticized Christian Science for that reason. See: Morton T. Kelsey. *Healing and Christianity.* Harper & Row, 1973, p. 292.

173. Intuitive diagnosis can be regarded as a gift of the Spirit, perhaps a subcategory of prophecy.

174. Leadbeater, *The Science of the Sacraments*. See also: Alice A. Bailey. *A Treatise on White Magic.* Lucis Publishing Company, 1934.

175. Lévi, *The History of Magic*, p. 29.

Chapter 19
Liberalism and Fundamentalism

Definition of Terms

Terms like liberal, conservative, progressive, traditional, radical, fundamentalist, "left" and "right" are used in the attempt to classify individuals and groups based on attitudes to change. In some cases the descriptors are claimed with pride, while in others they are pejorative. In all cases the terms can be misleading because of their multidimensionality. Nevertheless "liberalism" and "fundamentalism," the subjects of this chapter, have reasonably precise meanings in relation to modern Christianity, and they capture a polarity which is important to our theme.

The word *liberal* means "free" and generally refers to the rejection of intrusive authority, burdensome traditions, and outworn values. Liberal Christianity is characterized by a willingness to explore theological issues from fresh perspectives and to base moral standards on circumstances rather than scriptural or tradition. It promotes the view that key religious decisions should be made by informed, sincere individuals, not by ecclesiastical authorities. Pockets of liberalism probably existed in early Christianity, and we have already identified some in the Middle Ages.[1] The Reformation created an environment in which liberalism could expand; and the Enlightenment launched it on the vigorous path it has followed since then.

Today's liberal Christians are typically middle-class; they are suspicious of emotional religion, reject Biblical literalism, lean toward moral relativism, and support progressive social and political initiatives. They are not opposed to theological complexity so long as it is of their own making. Some of the greatest academic theologians of the 19th and 20th centuries were attracted to liberal Protestantism. Whether or not it was wise to do so, one of their major causes was to purge Christianity of "mythology" and "superstition."

To fundamentalists, the "freedom" that defined liberal Christianity, implied a rejection of everything that Christianity ever stood for. Their response was to launch an all-out war to defend core principles—though, as we shall see, some of those principles came from fictional literature rather than the Bible. Fundamentalism emerged separately in the Roman church and in Evangelical circles. Catholic fundamentalism became a recognizable force in the mid-19th century and lasted roughly 100 years. Evangelical fundamentalism, primarily an American movement, began in the late-19th century and has gained in strength since then.

"Fundamentalist" should be distinguished from "conservative" and "traditional," which have broader and more positive meanings. Fundamentalism, a relatively new phenomenon, is rigid, narrow, activist and militant—defined more by what it opposes than by what it supports. Fundamentalists may be socially conservative, but they have deviated in important ways from traditional Christian principles such as the primacy of compassion over moral legalism.

Religions of the Enlightenment

One response to the Enlightenment was experimentation with new religious forms, free from the trappings of traditional western Christianity. No mass movements emerged. Those involved in the experiments were a relatively few intellectuals and social activists; it was their standing in society that gave them disproportionate influence. To what extent the new religious forms could be considered "Christian" was debated at the time and is still debated today.

Deism

The religion of choice among Enlightenment intellectuals was Deism. It became popular in 18th-century England, France, Germany, and the United States. Deism offered a major challenge to all world religions, except perhaps Buddhism; or maybe it was intended to supersede the religions of its time and create a new synthesis. An early writer who influenced Deism's emergence was the English aristocrat Edward Herbert of Cherbury (1583-1648). In his book *De Veritate* ("On Truth") he listed five articles to which he believed people of all religions could subscribe:

- Belief in the existence of a single supreme God
- Humanity's duty to revere God
- Linkage of worship with practical morality
- God will forgive us if we repent and abandon our sins
- Good works will be rewarded [and evil punished] both in life and after death.[2]

More directly, Deism expressed the new worldview created by the scientific revolution. Newton's discovery of universal laws governing terrestrial and celestial mechanics undermined prevailing belief in a micromanaging deity. Rather, God had wound up the cosmic clock, set the universe in motion, and then sat back to watch it unfold. To be sure, God "saw that it was good;" in fact it was so good that he no longer needed to rewind the clock, adjust the time, or make repairs. The universe was a closed system, eternal and perfect in its operations. Newton's work applied to the physical world, but Deist philosophers saw in it the larger message that God no longer needed, or wanted, to intervene in human affairs.[3] Deists dismissed the possibility of divine revelation and totally rejected any notion of miracles. However—and this was a principle of far-reaching importance—if the universe was perfect, then humankind, which was part of the universe, had the potential to become perfect.

Deism acknowledged the existence of a Supreme Being that merited worship; but we should not project human qualities onto it. Prominent English Deist Matthew Tindal (1657-1733) criticized typical images presented by scripture and popular piety: "Do not we bring God down to ourselves, when we suppose he acts like us poor indigent Creatures, in seeking worship and honour for his own sake? Nay, do we not cloathe him, who has neither parts not portions, with the worst of our infirmities, if we represent him as an ambitious, suspicious, wrathful & vengeful Being?"[4] "Being" might suggest some degree of anthropomorphism, but in Deism we come closest, among all the religious movements discussed in this book, to the notion of a pure, unknowable Godhead, free from anthropomorphic manifestations, including the persons of the Trinity.

Deists rejected organized religion as a needless, harmful, and self-serving institution that hindered instinctive worship of the Supreme Being. Churchmen and theologians, Tindal claimed, purported to tell people what to believe, but they could not agree among themselves. What was fundamental in one church was "damnable error in another." As a result we find "Popes against Popes, Councils against Councils, some Fathers against others . . . the Church of one Age against the Church of another Age."[5] The problem stemmed from trying to capture truth in complicated doctrinal formulas:

> How can we suppose some of the most necessary duties of Religion, are only to be found in voluminous books, which the greatest part of mankind have, perhaps, never heard of, & that those who have, not one in a thousand understands a tittle of the language they are writ in, or is capable of examining into those records, from which the authority of these books are to be deriv'd?[6]

Thomas Paine (1737-1809), idealist and founding father of the United States, was equally scathing in his condemnation of organized religion, particularly state churches: "All national institutions of churches—whether Jewish, Christian, or [Muslim]—appear to me no other than human inventions set up to terrify and enslave mankind and monopolize power and profit."[7] Much of the pressure to build separation of church and state into the U.S. constitution came from the anticlerical, Deist sentiment of the founding fathers.

Deism promoted an idealistic universal morality based on the nobility of humankind, desire for happiness, and revulsion for pain. Therein it shared important features with the Stoicism of classical Greece but also reflected the ethical theories of David Hume and Jeremy Bentham. People generally behave properly not because they are coerced by rewards and punishments but because they recognize the effects on society and themselves. Interestingly, similar notions of natural morality were proposed by Bishop Joseph Butler (1692-1752), a leading moral theologian of the Anglican Church.[8] In a series of published sermons Butler argued that humankind was endowed by God with reason and conscience; and those qualities motivate people to seek happiness, which is our birthright.[9] He contended that we have a duty to love ourselves, because only then could we love our neighbor.[10] Foreshadowing the economic theory of Adam Smith (1723-1790), Butler also insisted that universal benefit flowed from the aggregate effect of enlightened self-interest. His views, and those of the Deists, were in striking contrast to the pessimism of John Calvin.

Many Deists believed in an afterlife, if only to ensure that moral behavior received its just reward. For example, American soldier and statesman Ethan Allen (1738-1789) argued that divine justice was attainable at least in the hereafter: "God is ultimately Just . . . and Justice in all events does not take place in this World. Therefore there must be an existence beyond this life, wherein the ultimate Justice of God will take place."[11] Although the Supreme Being remained aloof from the universe, it still served as the ultimate moral arbiter.

Deism reached the peak of its influence toward the end of the 18th century. But then it went into rapid decline. One outcome was a descent into materialistic rationalism, modern secular philosophy, or "modernism."[12] Scientific discoveries progressively pushed back the need for an explanatory deity. The "god of the gaps" was shrinking by the day and, in many people's minds, shrank to the point of nonexistence in the 19th and 20th centuries. Atheism became the standard metaphysic for most scientists and intellectuals; conventional religion was nothing but superstition, and "the spiritual" another name for ignorance. However new religious options for a few intellectuals opened up in the forms of Unitarianism and Transcendentalism.

Unitarianism

Unitarianism's roots go back far in history. Its direct antecedent, antitrinitarianism—denial of the Trinity—extended back to early Christianity, perhaps even to the apostle Paul; but more meaningfully it began with the Evangelical Rationalists of the 16th-century. The term "Unitarian" emerged when the antitrinitarian movement acquired organizational coherence. In the late 18th and early 19th centuries, Unitarianism offered an important alternative for people disillusioned with Deism. In the process it took on distinctive characteristics which related it firmly to the mindset and social concerns of the Enlightenment.

Early heroes of the antitrinitarian movement included Martin Cellarius (1499-1564), a friend of Luther, and the Italian Lelio Francesco Sozini (1525-1562) and his nephew Fausto Sozini, whose Latinized name, Socinus, provided the alternative term "Socinianism." During the reign of John Sigismund (1540-1571), and for some time thereafter, religious freedom was preserved in Transylvania, and dissidents of many stripes found safe haven there.[13] But few other countries offered religious tolerance, and Antitrinitarians were frequent targets of persecution; in Cracow, Poland, the 80 year-old Catherine Vogel was burned for apostasy in 1539. The 16th-century Michael Servetus' book *On the Errors of the Trinity* so angered John Calvin that he lured Servetus to Geneva and sent him to the stake. English schoolmaster and biblical scholar John Biddle (1615-1662) was imprisoned four times for his antitrinitarian views. He narrowly avoided the death penalty, only to die in his forties from the effects of incarceration. During his short life, Biddle wrote numerous pamphlets and published his *Twofold Catechism* in 1654.[14] One response to his teachings was the issuance in 1648 of the Ordinance for Punishing Heresies and Blasphemies. After Biddle's death the antitrinitarian movement began to evolve into a recognizable denomination with the "Unitarian" label.

Despite the treatment it received from the mainstream, Unitarianism still considered itself Christian and was scripturally oriented. But its rejection of key doctrines and disdain for ecclesiastical authority appealed to some prominent scientists of the period. One was the great Isaac Newton, though modern Unitarians are loath to claim him because of his interests in mysticism and alchemy. Another, with more acceptable credentials, was the British chemist Joseph Frederick Priestley (1733-1804).[15] Although he was an ordained Presbyterian minister; growing doubts about the virgin birth and other doctrines persuaded Priestley to join the Unitarian movement. After his laboratory in Birmingham was burned by a Christian mob, he emigrated to the United States and founded a Unitarian society in Philadelphia in 1799.

The emergence of American Unitarianism as a distinct denomination can be traced to Massachusetts Congregationalist minister William Ellery Channing (1780-1842). At that time the religious scene in New England was dominated by Congregationalists, descendents of the Pilgrim Fathers. While beliefs varied from one congregation to another, most were strongly Calvinist. However Channing and a few others embraced Unitarian sentiments, whereupon a conservative newspaper claimed that Channing had forfeited any right to be called a Christian. To refute that claim and similar ones, he preached a sermon in 1819 entitled "Unitarian Christianity."[16] Channing identified the Unitarian movement as a "rational and amiable system," based on the primacy of reason together with a strong social conscience. He retained a belief in the divinity of Christ but, following Unitarian tradition, rejected the Trinity. In 1825 Channing helped form the American Unitarian Association. Boston, Massachusetts, remains its spiritual center.

Although Unitarianism rejected institutional religion and its dogmas, it valued communal worship. Sunday services had an intellectual flavor; otherwise they followed traditional Congregationalist patterns. Over time, worship patterns changed; and social causes, including opposition to slavery and concern for the urban poor, attracted growing attention. But a number of prominent Unitarian ministers felt that their church had not moved far enough, or fast enough, from its Congregationalist roots. Social reformer Theodore Parker (1810-1860) was ostracized by Unitarian congregations and started preaching in concert halls and other secular establishments. Ralph Waldo Emerson left the ministry altogether. Both men allied themselves with the new Transcendentalist movement.

One prominent minister who remained loyal to his Unitarian roots was James Freeman Clarke (1810-1888). A Harvard professor of comparative religion, he promoted contacts with other world religions but insisted that Christianity was the most "progressive and universal." He is remembered, among much else, for affirming "the fatherhood of God, the brotherhood of man, the leadership of Jesus, salvation by character, and the progress of mankind, onward and upward forever"[17]—a confession that became popular in liberal Christian churches.

Unitarianism continued to evolve during the 19th century and beyond. The "biblical Unitarianism" of Michael Servetus and John Biddle gave way to modern "rational Unitarianism." A leading Unitarian of a later period was the philosopher Henry Nelson Wieman (1884-1975). Originally ordained a Presbyterian minister, he became a Unitarian five years before his death. A lifelong proponent of "natural religion," he asked: "How can we interpret what operates in human existence to create, sustain, save and transform toward the greatest good, so that scientific research and scientific technology can be applied to searching out and providing the conditions—physical, biological, psychological and social—which must be present for its most effective operation?"[18] His conclusion was that the operative presence in human existence was what we call God. Wieman's work would influence civil-rights leader Martin Luther King Jr. (1929-1968).

In the 20th century Unitarianism took strong social-activist positions, supporting the causes of racial and gender equality and protection of the environment. But modern Unitarianism's connections to Christianity are tenuous, and frequent appeal is made to the teachings and scriptures of other world religions.

Transcendentalism

The Transcendentalists of New England were a group of intellectuals that included political activist Henry David Thoreau and feminist Margaret Fuller. Its chief spokesperson was former Unitarian minister Ralph Waldo Emerson (1803-1882). Transcendentalism was a uniquely American religious movement, and Emerson pressed Americans to distance themselves from European religious traditions and authorities. Rejecting much of Christian orthodoxy, he promoted a spiritual path that emphasized self-reliance, individualism, and—highly offensive to mainstream Christianity—moral relativism. He studied Greek philosophy, and his work represented one of the many revivals of Platonic thought. Emerson also was one of the first western scholars to be influenced by the newly discovered eastern religions. He was also influenced by Immanuel Kant, and Kant's use of the word "transcendental" gave the new movement its name.

Emerson's first major work: *Nature*, published in 1836, claimed that nature is a divine entity. But, distancing himself from the Deists, Emerson asserted that we apprehend this divinity through native innocence rather than through any kind of rational process. "The lover of nature," he wrote, "is he whose inward and outward senses are still truly adjusted to each other; who has retained the spirit of infancy even into the era of manhood."[19] And in divine nature we find not only beauty and harmony but also a natural morality unrelated to the dicta of moral theologians. If *Nature* was an affront to Enlightenment rationalism, it paid tribute to the romanticism of English poets like Samuel Taylor Coleridge and Thomas Carlisle. It also expressed some of the same sentiments promoted by Phineas Parkhurst Quimby.

Ralph Waldo Emerson contributed an important understanding of the soul and its relationship with God in his doctrine of the *oversoul*. Following the Neoplatonists he spoke of the oneness of all creation and an all-pervading spirit of the universe:

> Unity, that Over-Soul, within which every man's particular being is contained and made one with all other; that common heart of which all sincere conversation is the worship . . . the universal beauty, to which every part and particle is equally related; the eternal One . . . We see the world piece by piece, as the sun, the moon, the animal, the tree; but the whole, of which these are the shining parts, is the soul.[20]

Emerson stressed the importance of personal experience and affirmed our ability to transcend the materialistic world. By turning inward toward our own souls, we could become aware of the all-pervading spirit of the universe. Here we find one of the few links between any of the religious forms discussed in this chapter and esoteric Christianity. Indeed, Emerson is sometimes portrayed as an esotericist. On the other hand, despite his rejection of both early Boston Unitarianism and Enlightenment rationalism, Emerson's ideas greatly influenced modern rational Unitarianism.

Henry David Thoreau (1817-1862), Emerson's foremost disciple and friend, made important contributions as a naturalist, both during his two-year stay at Walden Pond and on trips around the northeastern United States. Thoreau is sometimes regarded as the father of the environmental movement. But he is best remembered for his political and social theories. His *Resistance to Civil Government*, published in 1849, became the bible of civil disobedience, influencing Mahatma Gandhi, Martin Luther King, Jr., and human-rights activist and president of Poland Lech Wałęsa (1943-). Thoreau's work was held in high regard by the Russian writer Leo Tolstoy, and in turn Tolstoy's views on nonviolence also influenced Gandhi.[21]

Scriptural Criticism

The critical analysis of scripture has a long history—and an equally long history of making ecclesiastical officials uneasy. John Scotus Erigena's pioneering work in the ninth century and Dutch humanist Erasmus's work in the 16th were cases in point. The normally broadminded people of the Netherlands strongly resisted efforts by Benedict Spinoza (1632-1677) to conduct scriptural research.[22] Yet by 1800 the Enlightenment had ushered in a new atmosphere of free inquiry, and academic scholars were studying the Bible in ways that were even more exciting and threatening.

Scriptural criticism did not imply that scholars set out to "criticize" the Bible. Rather their purpose was to analyze and evaluate scriptural texts using the same methods they would apply to the works of Ovid or Shakespeare. Several specialty areas emerged. "Lower criticism" was a quest for textual purity: seeking to strip away later interpolations and other changes to discover a text's original content.[23] Lower criticism rarely provoked controversy; even Biblical literalists applaud its objectives.

"Higher criticism," by contrast, raised conservative ire from the beginning. Its goal was to identify the sources, authorship, date, place and circumstances of a text's composition; it also sought external confirmation of the events described. Higher criticism began in Germany, in the early 19th century, with the work of Friedrich Schleiermacher, at the Universities of Halle and Berlin, and David Strauss and Ludwig Feuerbach at the University of Tübingen. German universities offered academic freedom at a time when religious authorities still controlled higher education in most other countries.²⁴ Scholars were drawn from around the world. In the late-19th century, Baptist Crawford Toy and Presbyterian Charles Briggs studied in Berlin and then returned to promote scriptural criticism in the United States. Briggs served as a professor of Hebrew and biblical theology at Union Theological Seminary in New York City. In 1892 the presbytery of New York charged him with heresy, whereupon Union severed its connections with the Presbyterian Church.²⁵ Briggs was eventually acquitted and became an Episcopal priest.

In the 20th century higher criticism expanded into further subspecialties. "Form criticism" analyzed texts by genre, such as lamentations, wisdom sayings, and prophetic or apocalyptic statements. "Redactive criticism" focused on authors' intentions, including the "spin" put on events. "Narrative criticism" examined the events, characters and settings from a literary standpoint.

Several new approaches to textual analysis also appeared. German historian Wilhelm Dilthey (1833-1911), who was influenced by Schleiermacher, argued that textual interpretation is subjective; readers can only derive meaning from a text by way of their own experiences.²⁶ Subjectivism was taken a stage further by French philosopher Jacques Derrida (1930-2004) who asserted that textual meaning reflects underlying assumptions, ideas, and conceptual frameworks which may be unapparent to both authors and readers.²⁷ As a result, one reader's interpretation may be quite different from another's—or from what the original author intended. That kind of deconstruction was precisely what the school of Antioch feared in the third century concerning the allegorical interpretation of scripture. Extreme deconstruction may be absurd and nihilistic. But a broad consensus has developed that meaning is both subjective and contextual; and the way we read biblical texts may be quite different from how they were read, or written, 2,000 years ago.

Modern scriptural analysis has reached a number of important conclusions, some of which were noted in Chapter 2:

- The gospels were written several decades after the crucifixion by individuals or groups who were not eyewitnesses to the events in Jesus' life.
- The New Testament was assembled over a 300-year period from a large number of competing texts, and the selection process was at least partly political.
- Numerous changes, interpolations, and difficulties in translation make it hard to determine the content of the original manuscripts, all of which have been lost.
- Key events reported in the New Testament might not have been recorded accurately—or might not have happened at all. Jesus may not have made statements attributed to him.

- Other gospels, epistles and commentaries, which date from the same period as the New Testament, depict Jesus and the early church in ways other than what has traditionally been believed.
- All scriptural texts must be read with an eye to the social, cultural, intellectual and linguistic context in which they were written.

Higher scriptural criticism called into question many time-honored Christian beliefs. A typical complaint was: "Scriptural studies have lapsed into a state of confusion in our time, for students applaud nothing but novelties and the masters . . . draw up new and modern little summaries and supporting commentaries on theology, and with these they lull, hold, and deceive their listeners."[28] That particular complaint actually came from a French bishop in the 12th century; but it could easily have been made by church authorities in the 19th or early 20th century. Pope Pius X (r.1903-1914) attacked all scholars involved in higher criticism.[29] Most contemporary Catholics agreed with him, and Pius was canonized. Scriptural criticism posed an even greater challenge to Protestants who regarded the Bible as the sole source of religious authority. It came under particularly intense fire from Evangelicals. Charles Hodge (1797-1878), president of Princeton Theological Seminary, acknowledged that the Bible was written by human authors but insisted that it was the inspired word of God and therefore infallible.[30]

Until recently, the mass of the faithful was protected from the results of scriptural criticism. What was known to the scholars was treated as occult knowledge, too dangerous to be revealed to the uninitiated. Ordinary people continued to believe, and were encouraged by their clergy to believe, that the Bible was a unique body of revelation, divinely inspired, and protected from error. However popular books and articles began to appear, and a few brave pastors shared the new knowledge with their congregations. The response was mixed. Some Christians welcomed the new openness, but a great many felt that the foundation on which they had built their whole faith in Jesus and the church had crumbled. The comforting, solid bedrock of scripture had given way to a shifting, unreliable body of literature, perhaps no more believable than Greek mythology or fairy stories. Another response was to condemn higher criticism as the work of Satan. The 19th-century Russian author Vladimir Solovyov, whose work was discussed in Chapter 18, wrote a satire in which the Antichrist received an honorary doctorate from the University of Tübingen.[31]

Higher criticism has now won support from the highest level of the Catholic Church. Pope Benedict XVI (r. 2005-) distanced himself from his sainted predecessor to give it a ringing endorsement: "I write with profound gratitude for all that [higher criticism] has given and continues to give us. It has opened up to us a wealth of material and an abundance of findings that enable the figure of Jesus to become present to us with a vitality and depth that we could not have imagined just a few decades ago."[32] On the other hand Benedict quoted Solovyov to warn against its abuse to reconstruct Jesus according to modern materialistic assumptions.[33]

Modern Protestant Theology

Many Lutheran, Reformed and Anglican theologians of the 19th and 20th centuries sought to come to terms with the mindset of the Enlightenment and to embrace rather than dismiss the conclusions of higher scriptural criticism. German scholars—some of whom had been involved in higher criticism—played a leading role, and their work is often regarded as comparable in impact to that of Martin Luther, Ulrich Zwingli, and John Calvin. The fact that so many of them are titled "father of . . . ." attests to the influence they have had on more recent theological and philosophical studies.

Friedrich Daniel Schleiermacher (1768-1834) is often regarded as the father of modern Protestant theology. He was born in Breslau, Silesia, the son of a Reformed Church chaplain in the Prussian army.[34] Aware of the skepticism of his time, he believed that Christianity could be made invulnerable to philosophical attack by emphasizing its experiential aspects. Experience was primary. Metaphysical constructs could be built upon experience, but they were derivative and non-unique: alternative, even contradictory, constructs could be built on the same experience. In his most radical book, *On Religion: Speeches to Its Cultured Despisers*, published in 1799, Schleiermacher argued that religion should be based on a mixture of insight and "feeling."[35] In *The Christian Faith* of 1821 he described religion as a "feeling of absolute dependence" (German: *Gefuhl schlechthinniger Abhängigkeit*) on God.[36] "Dependence" was to be understood as immersion in a relationship with God rather than as groveling subservience.[37] The goal of religious experience—indeed the expression of absolute dependence—was the realization of God-consciousness. Christ's act of redemption was to make his profoundly higher level of God-consciousness available to us.[38] One traditional doctrine that Schleiermacher rejected was eternal damnation.[39]

Søren Kierkegaard (1813-1855),[40] considered the father of existentialism, also stressed the importance of personal experience. Like Martin Luther, he suffered from chronic depression, and that may have influenced him to turn to religion for solace. Initially he planned to become a Lutheran priest, but it became clear that he was ill-suited to the ministry. Kierkegaard reacted against the rational idealism of Georg Hegel.[41] He became convinced that to become a Christian—and he argued that this was easier than discarding the baggage of a Christian upbringing—was not a rational choice. It required a leap of faith, a commitment of passion; and it must be entirely personal, unconstrained by the beliefs, practices or attitudes of others. By contrast, institutional Christianity was based on standardized beliefs, collective observance, and peer pressure, all of which stifled individual experience. Kierkegaard remained a devout Christian; but in his latter years he became convinced that the Church of Denmark was crippling true Christianity, and he advised people to leave it.[42]

Neo-Orthodoxy and Liberal Theology

From those early beginnings, two major theological movements emerged in the 20th century. Each movement embraces a fair range of positions, and most of today's mainstream Protestant theologians can identify with one or the other.

One movement, often referred to as "neo-orthodoxy," is traced to the Swiss-German professor and Reformed Church pastor Karl Barth (1886-1968). As a young man, Barth was influenced by Schleiermacher; but later he became increasingly critical of the notion that religion can only be experiential. Barth insisted that God transcends creation, and certainly transcends human experience. God speaks to humanity through Jesus Christ—and through scripture; but, since the Bible is written in human language, it can never capture the totality of divine revelation.[43] Neo-orthodoxy gained considerable support among religious conservatives in the United States, though fundamentalists remained ambivalent. Despite its label, neo-orthodoxy is significantly more "liberal" than traditional orthodoxy that affirms the inerrancy of scripture and such doctrines as the virgin birth, atonement through the cross, and Jesus' corporeal resurrection.

More liberal than Barth, but still considered to belong to the neo-orthodox camp, was the scriptural form-critic Rudolf Bultmann (1884-1976). His goal was to strip away layers of "mythology" in the New Testament which he felt hindered modern Christians' faith. Scripture, in his view, reflected "the contemporary mythology of Jewish apocalypticism and of the Gnostic myth of redemption. Insofar as it is mythological talk it is incredible to men and women today because for them the mythological world is a thing of the past"[44]—though he conceded, somewhat patronizingly, that mythology played a useful role in religious aspiration. Like the Deists, Bultmann insisted that supernatural power could not interrupt the laws of cause and effect; biblical references to miracles "mistakenly objectified the transcendent into the immanent."[45] However scripture did contain underlying revelation, the *kerygma* (Greek: κερυγμα), or "message of God's decisive act in Christ."[46] The kerygma was to be found in the post-resurrection Christ of faith. Who the pre-crucifixion historical Jesus was, or whatever he might have done, was of little concern.

To deny the objectivity of Jesus' miracles was not new. David Strauss (1808-1874), one of the early Tübingen scholars, had already done that. In his book *The Life of*

Jesus Critically Examined, Strauss contended that Jesus' miracles and healings were myths created to bolster claims that he was the messiah; the gospels told us more about what a messiah was supposed to do than what Jesus actually did. Predictably, Strauss' book outraged conservative Christians.[47] It recalled the skepticism of Herman Reimarus and also the cynicism of the English Romantic poet Percy Bysshe Shelley (1792-1822) who dismissed miracles as the supposed works of an "irrational god . . . invented to prove the divine mission."[48] Perhaps the miracles seem improbable to the rational mind. However it is hard to prove that they did not happen; at best the evidence is indirect. Strauss and Bultmann claimed that Jesus never walked on water or cured a man of leprosy,[49] whereas the gospel writers claimed that he did. Which claim was more persuasive? Many people sided with Strauss and Bultmann, but some of the latter's neo-orthodox colleagues strongly disagreed. To de-mythologize scripture, in their view, was to strip away anything that the materialistic mindset found disagreeable. To deny Jesus' ability to perform miracles was to deny his divinity.[50]

The other major theological movement of the 20th century was farther to the left even than Bultmann. "Liberal theology," as it came to be known, was not only skeptical of Jesus' miracles but distanced itself from all notions of a Christ of faith and divine revelation through scripture. Liberal theology is usually traced to the work of Lutheran minister Paul Tillich (1886-1965). Tillich was born in Germany but emigrated to the United States in the 1930s, after criticism of the Nazis cost him his university tenure. He was influenced both by Existentialism and by Schleiermacher, but his work took a different direction from Bultmann's. Tillich rejected traditional notions of a theistic God described in terms such as "father," "lord," or "he" in favor of a pantheistic one.[51] God is not separate from creation but is expressed *through* creation. He drew upon Jakob Böhme's concept of the *Ungrund*, to speak of the "Ground of Being," "Being Itself."[52] Tillich viewed the fall as man's estrangement from the infinity of his own being. However, Jesus Christ was the "New Being." "In Christ, the conflict between the essential unity of God and humanity and human beings' existential estrangement is overcome."[53]

Anglican Bishop John A. T. Robinson (1919-1983) built upon Tillich's work to promote a kind of Christian naturalism. In his best-selling book *Honest to God* (1953) he argued that we must replace the notion of a transcendent God "up there" or "out there" by an immanent one "down here." "What place," he asked, "does God have in my life or in society today?" Furthermore, Christians should focus not on the promise of eternal reward in heaven but on acting in an ethical, loving compassionate way in this world; we should do what is right because it is right. Along with Harvard theologian Harvey Cox, Robinson developed the new field of "secular theology." Liberal Protestantism had moved a long way in the direction of 18th-century Deism.[54]

Martin Luther King, Jr., approved of the emphasis Tillich and Unitarian Henry Nelson Wieman placed on the immanence of God but questioned whether such a God merited worship: "Both Tillich and Wieman reject the conception of a personal God, and with this goes a rejection of the rationality, goodness and love of God in the full sense of the words."[55]

The Historical Jesus

Many Protestant theologians have sought to distinguish—as Herman Reimarus did—the historical Jesus from the Christ of faith. Protestantism traditionally emphasized the divinity rather than the humanity of Jesus Christ. Did not Charles Wesley refer to "Christ . . . *veiled in flesh*, the Godhead see, hail the incarnate Deity?"[56] The Docetists of the early church would have agreed with him. However liberal theologians of the early 19th century began to emphasize Jesus' humanity. Friedrich Schleiermacher never denied the divinity of Christ, but he leaned toward an adoptionist position, in which Christ became the Son of God as the result of his exemplary life. Jesus was a "hero"—not only in the Greek sense of someone with a divine parent, but in the modern sense of a worthy role model—who raised religion to its highest possible level. But who precisely was Jesus?

Rudolf Bultmann, for whom the Christ of Faith remained a core belief, regarded the historical Jesus as both unknowable and irrelevant.[57] Albert Schweitzer (1875-1965), better known as a missionary and musician, tended to agree. In an influential book: *Quest of the Historical Jesus*, Schweitzer concluded that the historical Jesus could not be found in scripture: "The Jesus of Nazareth who came forward publicly as the Messiah, who preached the ethic of the Kingdom of God, who founded the Kingdom of Heaven upon earth, and died to give His work its final consecration, never had any existence."[58] But others felt that discovering the historical Jesus was both feasible and necessary. John Dominic Crossan (1934-), Bible scholar and former monk, sought to place Jesus in the cultural, religious, economic and political context of first-century Palestine: Jesus was a "Jewish peasant."[59] But despite his humble status Crossan's Jesus was a courageous man of great wisdom who taught a message of inclusiveness, tolerance and freedom.

Crossan and Robert W. Funk (1926-2005) founded the Jesus Seminar in 1985. It brought together an impressive group of biblical scholars to try to determine the probability that Jesus actually made the statements attributed to him in the gospels. After detailed examination of the texts—extra-canonical as well as canonical—the scholars voted on the authenticity of each statement, using the now-famous red, pink, grey and black scores. The results were published in 1993.[60] Significantly, no "red" statements were identified in *John*; but several were identified in *Thomas*. Certainly the results were controversial, but the

Jesus Seminar served an important purpose in disseminating the conclusions of academic research to an informed public.

Episcopal Bishop John Shelby Spong (1931-) emerged as an influential writer and speaker promoting new perspectives on Jesus. He agreed with Bultmann that many of the gospel stories about Jesus were myths and legends inspired by Jewish prophecy or pagan beliefs. But Spong considered himself primarily a follower of Tillich and became a vocal critic of traditional theistic religion. He argued that we must separate "the experience of Jesus from the theological interpretation of that experience found in the New Testament as well as in the doctrinal development of the church."[61] The humanity of Jesus, for Spong, was more important than traditional notions of the incarnation: "I believe that Jesus was a God presence, a powerful experience of the reality of the Ground of Being undergirding us all at the very depths of life."[62] Despite the insistence on this "God presence," Spong's Jesus was more human—a teacher and compassionate social reformer—than divine.

Many modern Christians feel that the historical Jesus is more accessible than the Christ of faith. But why should people identify with an individual, however inspiring he may have been, who lived 2,000 years ago in an environment very different from our own? Rudolf Bultmann had a point that only the Christ of faith has timeless relevance.

Changing Face of the Church

Nearly 200 years ago Søren Kierkegaard expressed concerns that the church had become a dispenser of dogma rather than a facilitator of spirituality; he complained that priests were required to preach "official" interpretations of scriptural passages. Instead he proposed a stronger liturgical emphasis in worship services, including time for private reflection: "The congregation assembles; a prayer is said at the church door; a hymn is sung; then the priest goes up to the speaker's seat, takes out the New Testament, pronounces the name of God, and thereupon reads from it before the congregation that definite passage, loudly and distinctly, whereupon he has to be silent for five minutes in the pulpit, and then he can go."[63]

Reaction to the burden of traditional dogma increased in the 20th century. Lutheran minister Dietrich Bonhöffer (1906-1945) asserted that organized religion impeded genuine faith and argued for a new "religionless Christianity," free from the trappings of belief in the abstract deity of philosophical and theological speculation. Writing from his jail cell in 1944, awaiting execution by the Nazis, he explained:

> What is bothering me incessantly is the question what Christianity really is . . . The time when people could be told everything by means of words,

whether theological or pious, is over, and so is the time of inwardness and conscience—and that means the time of religion in general. We are moving towards a completely religionless time.[64]

God, in Bonhöffer's view, could only be known through his operations and interaction with humanity in daily life. John Robinson affirmed similar principles.

Kierkegaard's emphasis on liturgy rather than dogma has been endorsed by numerous writers; but the sense is that the liturgy needs also needs work. Charles Leadbeater, bishop in the Liberal Catholic Church, reacted against psalms "which complain, grovel or curse."[65] Other people have reacted against aspects of the liturgy that assume an untenable scientific mindset or present attitudes to human dignity—female or even male—that are no longer morally acceptable. Finally, there has been reaction against traditional roles of the clergy.

Bishop Spong agreed with Kierkegaard that clergy should serve as liturgical facilitators rather than intermediaries between God and humanity. But, with more daring than could have been expected in the mid-19th century, he recommended that lay people as well as priests celebrate the Eucharist—honoring the "food of life" rather than the body and blood of Christ.[66] Spong asserted that the liturgy should still celebrate the major events in Jesus' life—the birth, baptism, death and resurrection—as well as rights of passage in the lives of the faithful. But, echoing Paul Tillich's views, he urged that such rites be stripped of their theistic trappings and presented in terms of participants' own divine potential. Alienated from traditional Christianity, Spong considered himself to be in "exile," like the Jews in Babylon, cut off from traditional religious support and forced to confront core truths and values.[67]

Progressive Christianity

A movement that has emerged in the last few decades to change the face of the church is "progressive Christianity." Religious commentator Hal Taussig defined the new branch of Christianity as "An unorganized but broad-ranging kind of Christian response to felt needs for vital spirituality, intellectual integrity, new ways of expressing gender, an alternative to Christian sense of superiority, and a desire to act more justly in relationship to the marginalized."[68] A conspicuous characteristic of progressive Christian congregations is a refusal to view their own religious beliefs and practices as competing with others', Christian or non-Christian; the value of a religious system lies not in any inherent superiority but in the power with which it speaks to its own adherents. Another characteristic, according to Taussig, is a yearning for experiential, expressive forms of worship, contrasting with what he viewed as the "stodginess" of more traditional church services. Interestingly, that same yearning propelled the Pentecostal movement forward a century ago. Yet another characteristic, which will be discussed later, is inclusiveness.

Tausig showed that progressive Christianity cuts across traditional denominational boundaries. Notably it could be found within or alongside Catholicism, even among women's religious orders.[69] Progressive Christianity is a grassroots movement, not a denomination. Nevertheless a number of organizations have emerged to support it. For example the Center for Progressive Christianity defined its mission as:

- To reach out to those for whom organized religion has proved ineffectual, irrelevant, or repressive, as well as to those who have given up on or are unacquainted with it.
- To uphold evangelism as an agent of justice and peace.
- To give a strong voice both in the churches and the public arena to the advocates of progressive Christianity.
- To support those who embrace the search, not certainty.

Progressive Christianity should not be viewed simply as an extension of liberal Protestantism. Its adherents do not necessarily subscribe to liberal Protestant theology, and many progressive Christians are not Protestant. Its defining qualities are social rather than doctrinal, and Progressive Christianity has affirmed social values that the older liberal movements have been reluctant to embrace.

Unifying and Divisive Causes

The great unifying social cause of the 17th and 18th centuries was the abolition of slavery. Support from Christians was far from unanimous, but it brought together activists of diverse backgrounds, including Quakers George Fox (1624-1691) and Elihu Embree (1782-1820), Frenchman Jacques Pierre Brissot (1754-1793),[70] Anglican bishop Beilby Porteus (1731-1809), and British politician William Wilberforce (1759-1833).[71] Unitarian minister Theodore Parker defied the Fugitive Slave Act to welcome runaway slaves into his home and church; fearing attack by slave-catchers he preached with a gun on his pulpit.[72]

The social causes that received attention after slavery was abolished rarely commanded so broad a response from across the religious spectrum. Factions embraced—or were branded by others as—"conservative" or "liberal;" but such descriptors often fail to capture the range or specificity of the causes involved.[73] During the late 19th and early 20th centuries "temperance," which meant banning the sale and consumption of alcohol, won broad support from Evangelicals. Later in the 20th century social causes opposing abortion and same-sex marriage gained prominence among fundamentalists. Meanwhile, dismantling structures of racial and gender discrimination became a major liberal cause. Washington Gladden (1836-1918), president of the American Missionary Association was shocked at the condition of Southern blacks and started speaking out against racial segregation early in the 20th century. Other important causes included pacifism, social justice, and protection of the environment.

Attitudes to war have long been divisive. Mainstream Christianity embraced the "just war" theory of Aristotle, Cicero and Augustine, and deemed the crusades against Muslims, Cathars, Hussites and others to be "just." The great majority of Christians have been willing to fight in the armed forces of their respective countries—even, as in the two World Wars, when their countries were pitted against one another. Some Christians have supported controversial wars, including the Spanish Civil War in which they sided with the fascists. In 2002 Richard D. Land, president of the Ethics and Religious Liberty Commission of the Southern Baptist Convention, sent a letter to President George W. Bush providing theological justification for the invasion of Iraq.[74]

Other Christians went on record, warning against wars that lacked clear moral justification or opposing war altogether. Quakers have always taken pacifist stance, citing for support Jesus' Sermon on the Mount.[75] In the mid-19th century Theodore Parker spoke out against the Mexican War which he described as "an utter violation of Christianity." "If war be right," he continued, "then Christianity is wrong, false and a lie. Every man who understands Christianity knows that war is wrong. War is treason to the people, to mankind, to God."[76] Pope Benedict XV made strenuous efforts to end World War I by peaceful negotiation, only to be criticized for his pacifist views and accused of pro-German bias. Theologian Karl Barth was greatly saddened when 93 German intellectuals, including a former teacher, signed a manifesto in 1914 supporting their country's war effort.[77] He opposed both world wars and spoke out against the Vietnam War.

Social Justice

Concern for the poor and the sick began with the apostles and has continued among people of almost every religious affiliation—and people of no religion at all. Evangelicals were heavily involved, and the important work of the Salvation Army will be discussed in the next chapter. But Evangelicals were less ready to engage in social activism targeting the systemic inequities that produced and perpetuated poverty.[78] Addressing those problems became a distinctively "liberal" cause. The labor movement, discussed in Chapter 16, never received broad-based support from organized Christianity.

Two major initiatives motivated by social-justice concerns were the Social Gospel movement and Liberation Theology. The loose-knit movement known as Social

Gospel began in the United States toward the end of the 19th century. It was a response to the plight of the poor and society's indifference toward them. Social Gospel was supported by people from various backgrounds, including New England Transcendentalists; also a few Evangelicals distanced themselves from the majority of their brethren and played leading roles. Baptist preacher Walter Rauschenbusch (1861-1918) became convinced that too much emphasis was placed on a future kingdom of God and not enough on improving conditions in this world. In 1892 he organized the Brotherhood of the Kingdom in New York City.[79] Four years later Congregationalist minister Charles Sheldon (1857-1946) published *In His Steps* which became the movement's bible. To guide social attitudes he asked a question that caught the popular imagination: "What would Jesus do?" Two other participants were Washington Gladden, whose campaign against racial segregation has already been mentioned, and Josiah Strong. Strong (1847-1916) formed the League for Social Service and edited its magazine *The Gospel of the Kingdom*. Social Gospel was influenced by socialist ideals, but it rejected class warfare in favor of negotiated agreements between management and labor. Initially Protestant, Social Gospel later gained considerable support from rank-and-file Catholics; but it never received enthusiastic support from leaders of any major denomination.

Liberation Theology, a movement with similar goals, acquired prominence within Catholicism after the Second Vatican Council. It is usually traced to the work of Peruvian theologian and priest Gustavo Gutiérrez Merino. It focused on the suffering of the poor, their struggles, and their perspectives on society and Christianity. Liberation Theology has often been referred to as Christian socialism; indeed some of its proponents embraced such Marxist concepts as perpetual class struggle. Moreover it portrayed Jesus as a political revolutionary.[80] Liberation Theology gained wide support from the laity and pastoral clergy in South and Central America; but in 1979 Pope John Paul II—whose view of communism had been molded by experiences in his native Poland—formally condemned its Marxist associations. One year later, Archbishop Óscar Romero San Salvador, a vocal critic of what he considered the church's indifference to the poor, was assassinated during Mass by a right-wing death squad. Although he was hailed as a martyr, his death did not change hardening ecclesiastical attitudes. The preaching of Liberation Theology was suppressed by Vatican edicts in the 1980s.

Closely related to the Liberation Theology movement was the formation of "base communities" in Latin America. Each community consisted of a few dozen people. They were formed in the 1960s, mostly in poor areas, to foster religious awareness, encourage service, and engage in political activism. They soon became targets of both right-wing governments and Rome. They are still in operation in the region, but numerous community leaders have been murdered, and tensions with the church have been exacerbated by the appointment of increasingly conservative bishops.[81] In concept, if not in precise form, base communities can be viewed as the precursors of the small Christian communities that emerged elsewhere in the world from the 1980s onward.[82]

Environmental problems have gained public attention in recent years, and congregations and even whole denominations have stepped forward to promote action. Increasing population levels; depletion of natural resources; pollution of soil, water and air; global warming, and erosion of the ozone layer are just some of the problems facing humanity. Many scientists predict catastrophic consequences for the planet if the problems are not addressed in a timely manner. International response has been encouraging. The Kyoto Protocol, negotiated under United Nations auspices, was a major step forward; but the United States and some other large nations failed to ratify it.[83] Big businesses have actively campaigned against prompt action, and powerful political and religious factions in the U.S. continue to deny that any significant environmental threat exists. Although world population is increasing, the populations of Europe and Japan are declining, and far-reaching changes are taking place in humanity's racial balance.

Inclusiveness in the Churches

The apostle Paul affirmed: "There is neither Jew nor Greek, there is neither bond nor free, there is neither male nor female: for ye are all one in Christ Jesus."[84] But intolerance and prejudice against ethnic groups, women, and social and other minorities have a long history. Sadly, rather than taking a lead in promoting acceptance of all "God's children," the churches have often perpetrated serious forms of internal discrimination as well as supporting discrimination in society.

Before the American Civil War several Christian denominations split on racial lines or over attitudes to race. And re-integration was a slow process thereafter. Augustine Tolton (1854-1897), a former slave, was ordained in 1886, the first African American to be accepted into the Catholic priesthood; but when he died he was denied his own burial plot.[85] In the 1960s Martin Luther King, Jr., lamented that many churches continued to be segregated, either by policy or by preference. Certainly, racial discrimination is not a thing of the past. On the other hand, immigration from Latin America, Asia, and the Middle East has resulted in far greater racial diversity in most western countries, helping diffuse remaining black-white polarities. Furthermore, integration in the workplace and elsewhere, and the increasing number of interracial families, have done much to improve understanding and acceptance. Few instances remain of systemic racial discrimination in Christian churches.

Women's roles in the churches have mirrored or, more commonly, lagged behind those in society as a whole. Women have served in the ministry since the 1850s, but acceptance has often been grudging. In 1853 Antoinette Brown became the first woman minister in the United States; but she was dismissed the following year by her Congregationalist superiors. Olympia Brown was ordained a Universalist minister in 1863. But it was another 80 years before the Anglican Communion ordained its first female priest; Florence Li Tim Oi of Hong Kong was ordained in 1942 "on an emergency basis." The Episcopal Church voted to admit women to the episcopacy in 1976,[86] and the United Methodist Church followed suit in 1980. The Evangelical Lutheran Church in Germany has appointed female bishops since 1992, and the Czech Hussite Church since 1999. By that same year the Unitarian Universalist Association had a majority of female clergy. The Society of Friends and the Salvation Army have always rejected clerical sexism, though they do not ordain ministers in the conventional sense.

The Southern Baptist Convention refuses to license women preachers. And the Roman and Eastern Orthodox churches, the Lutheran Church-Missouri Synod, and the Church of Jesus Christ of Latter-day Saints all oppose the ordination of women. Rome's refusal to accept women into the priesthood has contributed to an acute shortage of priests, forcing the consolidation of many parishes and reliance on visiting clergy to serve others.[87]

Aside from the Roman church, most denominations now welcome divorced people into their congregations, to the sacraments, and occasionally into the clergy. But fewer denominations have expressed openness to homosexuality. The United Church of Christ permitted the ordination of openly gay ministers in the 1970s, and in 2005 it formally endorsed the blessing of gay and lesbian couples. The Church of Sweden agreed to welcome partnered gay and lesbian clergy in 2006. The Episcopal Church in the United States has consecrated an openly gay bishop but is under intense pressure from the Anglican Communion to tighten eligibility policies. A defining characteristic of Progressive Christianity has been an "open and affirming" attitude—including eligibility for ordination—to homosexual, bisexual and transgendered persons.[88]

Sexual orientation remains a "hot-button" issue in many denominations, despite growing awareness—even now among some fundamentalists—that sexual orientation is not a sinful choice but is genetically determined. This is not the place for an extensive debate of the issues. However it is worth noting that Jesus never discussed homosexuality. Biblical proscriptions of homosexual acts are found in the *Pentateuch*, along with laws permitting fathers to execute rebellious sons but prohibiting them from wearing clothes made from two types of cloth.[89] The only reference to homosexuality in the New Testament is found in *Romans*, where

Paul condemned "vile affections."[90] Given the culture that Paul was addressing, he may well have been referring to prostitution or pederasty. Clearly, committed same-sex relationships must be judged differently from promiscuity, rape, incest, child molestation, and prostitution; the same would be said of heterosexual relationships.

Christian Fundamentalism

Fundamentalism is the very antithesis of the liberal, progressive forms of Christianity we have been discussing. Fundamentalism is the dogged adherence to traditional beliefs, practices and attitudes in defiance of developments in philosophy, science, biblical scholarship, and human consciousness. Until the 19th century most Christian denominations were conservative. But the Church of Rome emerged as the first major denomination to take an overtly fundamentalist position, and it maintained that position for roughly a century. By then Evangelical fundamentalism was well-established, driven by a combination of simplistic religious convictions and reactionary social attitudes.

Catholic Fundamentalism

The Counter-Reformation and Council of Trent of the 16th century launched Catholicism onto a path of extreme conservatism and defensiveness. One of the threats that the church felt obliged to counter in the mid-19th century was "modernism," a catch-all term for the intellectual and social movements that developed from the Enlightenment.[91]

Pope Pius IX (r.1846-1878) was not the most conservative pope of his era, but in 1864 he issued the *Syllabus of Errors* which condemned 80 symptoms of the prevailing intellectual climate. In sweeping statements it condemned "socialism, communism, secret societies, biblical societies, and clerico-liberal societies," along with freedom of religion and the separation of church and state.[92] The *Syllabus* also condemned pantheism, naturalism, rationalism, "indifferentism" and "latitudinarianism."[93] *Indifferentism* was defined as the assertion that all religions can provide valid paths to God. *Latitudinarianism*, a term first applied to some 17th-century English theologians, claimed that the doctrinal differences among Christian groups were of secondary importance. The *Syllabus* did not condemn the many scientific developments of the age; and we shall see in the next chapter that Catholicism has shown surprising openness in that area.

Infused with the same fundamentalist spirit, the First Vatican Council (1869-1870) confirmed most of the condemnations listed in Pius IX's *Syllabus*. Its proceedings were also rich in anti-Protestant polemic. The council mocked Protestantism for having "collapsed into a multiplicity of sects," adding that "by this means a good many people have had all faith in Christ destroyed."[94] It went on to reaffirm Rome's exclusive claim to represent Christianity: "it has always been necessary for every church—that is to say the faithful throughout the world—to be in agreement with the Roman church."[95]

Pius X (r.1903-1914) was the archenemy of modernism, which he regarded as "the summation of all heresies."[96] One of his most infamous steps, taken in 1910, was to require all Catholic clergy to take the "Oath Against Modernism." All "clergy, pastors, confessors, preachers, religious superiors, and professors in philosophical-theological seminaries" were required to swear to uphold a number of traditional church teachings and to reject the precepts of modern academic scholarship, including scriptural criticism, which threatened those teachings. The oath ended with: "I promise that I shall keep all these articles faithfully, entirely, and sincerely, and guard them inviolate, in no way deviating from them in teaching or in any way in word or in writing. Thus I promise, this I swear, so help me God."[97] The oath was rarely enforced in later decades, but it was not formally rescinded until 1967.

During its fundamentalist phase Catholicism exhibited the characteristic tribalism of exclusive religions and ideologies.[98] The sense was that Catholics had to band together against foes on all sides. Every opportunity was taken to attack rivals, while misdeeds by fellow Catholics were condoned. Given that mindset it is not surprising that the fascists of Italy and Spain received such strong Catholic support.

The long period of official Catholic fundamentalism came to an end with the election of Pope John XXIII in 1958. His pivotal achievement was to convene the Second Vatican Council in the early 1960s. In his address announcing the council John affirmed "I want to throw open the windows of the Church so that we can see out and the people can see in."[99] The council's attitudes stood in sharp contrast to those of its 19th-century predecessor. Unfortunately John died before he could see the results of his vision. Since then, defensiveness has crept back into ecclesiastical thinking and policy. Individual bishops, priests and prominent laypersons continue to hold fundamentalist views and—in one of the strangest ironies of modern Christianity—have joined forces with Evangelical fundamentalists to pursue their cause.[100]

Evangelical Fundamentalism

Primarily an American religious phenomenon, Evangelical fundamentalism can be dated to the latter years of the 19th century. It grew out of Evangelical Christianity but betrayed some of its most important values. The Evangelicalism of John Smyth, Margaret Fell, Philipp Spener, and John Wesley was motivated by yearnings for religious freedom similar to those expressed by liberals. Moreover, early Evangelicals, especially the Quakers and Universalists, were the gentlest of people, regarding Christianity as broadly inclusive. By sharp contrast, the new fundamentalism became a religion of exclusiveness and absolutes. All-important distinctions were made between the saved and the damned, among members of different congregations, among those who favor different translations of the Bible, and among those who vote for different political parties.

Why did segments of Evangelical Christianity embrace ideals so different from those of its founders? Religious historian George Marsden traced its development to the Great Awakenings that promoted stark contrasts between God and Satan, heaven and hell, good and evil.[101] American people had scant regard for the mediating influence of tradition. No gray areas were recognized, and no compromises tolerated; Christianity demanded life-or-death choices and total commitment. Scriptural literalism, strict moral imperatives, and narrow social attitudes took hold.

No love was ever lost between Catholicism and Evangelicalism—at least until the late 20th century. Nevertheless, Evangelical fundamentalism shared a fear of modernism with its Roman counterpart. In a statement that would have earned Pius X's congratulations, American divine James Marion Gray (1851-1935) declared: "Modernism is a revolt against the God of Christianity, a revolt against the Bible of Christianity, and a revolt against the Christ of Christianity."[102] But Evangelical fundamentalism was a distinct movement, and Catholic fundamentalism was already in decline by the time of its most rapid growth. The two major threats that defined and galvanized Evangelical fundamentalism were Darwin's theory of evolution and higher scriptural criticism. American Evangelicals were quick to point out that both—along with modernist philosophy, Unitarianism and socialism—were European abominations, threatening the purity and innocence of New World Christianity.[103]

Just three years after Darwin published *The Descent of Man*, American Presbyterian theologian Charles Hodge (1797-1878) asked: "What is Darwinism?" Answering his own question, he exclaimed: "It is Atheism."[104] Evangelical seminaries and colleges continued to teach from William Paley's *Natural Theology* which provided a teleological argument for the existence of God. Common Sense philosophy was invoked to support both Paley and the plain-text creationism of *Genesis*.[105] Nevertheless, as Darwin's theory gained acceptance, in America as well as in Europe, Evangelical fundamentalists tried by every available means to protect people from it. A key battle was the Scopes "monkey trial" in 1925 in Dayton, Tennessee. In what became a media circus, high school biology teacher John Scopes was convicted of teaching evolution in violation of state law.[106] A year later the Tennessee Supreme Court reversed the decision on a technicality. By that time the issue had become moot, and the court commented: "Nothing is to be gained by prolonging the life of this bizarre case." Despite the setback attacks on "Darwinism" continues unabated.

Higher criticism's challenge to Biblical inerrancy was viewed as even more destructive. To understand the importance of inerrancy it is necessary to examine the changing view of the Bible since the Reformation. Soon after Martin Luther established the principle of *sola scriptura*, Protestants started referring to the Bible as "the Word of God," or simply "the Word." However the same term appeared in the King James Bible to translate *Logos* which referred to Christ. What ensued was an unconscious—or conscious—affirmation that scripture was not only divine revelation but was itself divine; in that regard, Protestantism can, with justification, be accused of *bibliolatry*.[107] To make matters worse, the German scholar Gottfried Menken (1768-1831) referred to the Bible as the "Light of Light," a term which the Nicene Creed applied to Christ.[108] In such an environment higher criticism was perceived as an assault on God as well as on scripture. The response was to affirm inerrancy ever more strongly and to demonize the whole field of academic scriptural research.

An early stand against higher criticism was taken by Baptist minister William Bell Riley (1861-1947) who, for more than 40 years, served as editor of *The Christian Fundamentalist*. At a conference held in 1895 at Niagara Falls, New York, attended by Episcopalian, Methodist, Presbyterian and Lutheran conservatives, Riley and his supporters prepared a formal statement that came to be known as the "Fundamentals of the Faith." It listed five principles to which every true Christian was expected to subscribe:

- The inerrancy of Scripture
- The deity and the virgin birth of Jesus Christ
- Substitutionary atonement (Christ died for our sins)
- The bodily resurrection of Jesus
- The personal return of Christ in the second coming.

Over the next decade the declaration, which lent its name to fundamentalism, became a confession of faith. In 1902 Riley founded the Northwestern Bible Training School.[109] Riley and a few others began meeting in 1918 to discuss responses to liberalism. A year later, the group formed the World's Christian Fundamentalist Association with Riley as president. Among Riley's publications was the 40-volume *The Bible of the Expositor and the Evangelist*.

In 1978, 300 Evangelical leaders reaffirmed belief in the inerrancy of the Bible by signing the so-called *Chicago Statement*:

- God, who is Himself Truth and speaks truth only, has inspired Holy Scripture in order thereby to reveal Himself to lost mankind through Jesus Christ as Creator and Lord, Redeemer and Judge. Holy Scripture is God's witness to Himself.

- Holy Scripture, being God's own Word, written by men prepared and superintended by His Spirit, is of infallible divine authority in all matters upon which it touches: it is to be believed, as God's instruction, in all that it affirms, obeyed, as God's command, in all that it requires; embraced, as God's pledge, in all that it promises.

- The Holy Spirit, Scripture's divine Author, both authenticates it to us by His inward witness and opens our minds to understand its meaning.

- Being wholly and verbally God-given, Scripture is without error or fault in all its teaching, no less in what it states about God's acts in creation, about the events of world history, and about its own literary origins under God, than in its witness to God's saving grace in individual lives.

- The authority of Scripture is inescapably impaired if this total divine inerrancy is in any way limited or disregarded, or made relative to a view of truth contrary to the Bible's own; and such lapses bring serious loss to both the individual and the Church.[110]

Scriptural inerrancy—and its stronger derivative, literalism—have emerged as central articles of faith uniting Evangelical fundamentalists and even some others. For example, Jehovah's Witnesses also affirm the inerrancy of scripture and the second coming, though they reject the Trinity.[111]

Fundamentalist leaders shunned mainstream institutions of higher education, instead relying for the education of their supporters on Bible conferences or new Bible colleges that would be isolated from secular academia.[112] Early 20th-century fundamentalists were not interested in forming a new Christian denomination. Instead, they planned to infiltrate existing denominations and lure members away from traditional beliefs. In the 1920s J. Frank Norris, a Texan leader, harshly criticized the Southern Baptist Convention.[113] But the strategy worked so well that by the 1980s the SBC was firmly under fundamentalist control.

Emotion plays a conspicuous role in fundamentalist worship and perhaps an even greater role in its activism. But to accuse fundamentalism of being totally anti-intellectual or anti-scientific may be unfair;[114] its basic premises and sources of data are simply different from those of the modern world. Fundamentalists regard themselves as empiricists and view the Bible as a valid source of knowledge—more trustworthy than scientific observations. Scriptural empiricism is not new; Archbishop James Ussher invoked it to make his estimate of the age of the earth. But it has been raised to new heights in *presuppositional theology* which argues that Christians must accept the Bible because there is no comparable basis for knowing God or making sense of the human experience.[115] Inconsistencies and the many other problems of scriptural reliability discussed in Chapter 2 are resolved in a comprehensive act of faith. To quote presuppositionist Gordon Haddon Clark (1902-1985), "an all-inclusive axiom that swallows everything at one gulp is most desirable." [116] Rigor, according to proponents, is preserved in the ability to test deductions for consistency and comprehensiveness. In a strong defense of fundamentalist Christianity's intellectual basis, Clark went on to assert: "Those who make religion an emotion and discount intellect deny or at least dilute the terrible Biblical words of condemnation."[117]

Evangelical fundamentalism has steadily increased in strength, particularly in the United States, acquiring a reputation for polarizing attitudes and aggressive social and political activism. Given Evangelicals' voting strength in the United States it is not surprising that their causes would become politicized. The unholy alliance with fundamentalist Catholics has created an even more formidable political force to influence legislation and the appointment of judges. The deadly impact of fundamentalism in other world religions has become all too familiar. So far its Christian form has remained less extreme, but violence is regarded in some fundamentalist circles as acceptable when key issues are at stake.

Fundamentalist Attitudes

Evangelical fundamentalism affirms faith in Jesus Christ and the Bible. Naturally fundamentalists insist that their beliefs and attitudes have firm scriptural support. Former president Jimmy Carter, a self-styled "born-again Christian" but sharp critic of fundamentalism, explained: "We Christians can buttress our arguments on almost any subject by careful selection of certain Scripture verses, and then claim that they should be applied universally."[118] Typically, supporting scriptural passages are drawn from the Old Testament rather than the New. The God of Love and Jesus' Sermon on the Mount take a back seat to the pre-Axial Age Yahweh. The fundamentalists' vengeful, vindictive God could be appeased only by the blood sacrifice of God's own son; in turn, Jesus will return to destroy the greater part of humanity.[119] Those depictions go hand-in-hand with confrontational, combative attitudes. Fundamentalists appropriate to themselves God's pledge to Abraham: "I will bless them that bless thee, and curse him that curseth thee." It is not good to be their enemy.

Fundamentalist rigidity contrasts with the liberal attitudes of early Evangelicals. It contrasts with—indeed is an intentional reaction against—the permissiveness of modern society. And where beliefs are concerned it contrasts with a strong American tradition of intellectual pragmatism.[120] Trust in absolutes is curiously out of context in an age when society in general has become well adjusted to the uncertain, the questionable, the transient, and the unknowable. Religious fundamentalists of all persuasions view the secular as a terrible threat. In particular they view "liberal secular humanism" as a savage attack on Christianity by Satan and his human allies. Carter described the process thus:

> Fundamentalists are militant in fighting against any challenge to their beliefs. They . . . resort to verbal or even physical abuse against those who interfere with the implementation of their agenda. [They] tend to make their self-definition increasingly narrow and restricted, to isolate themselves, to demagogue emotional issues, and to view change, cooperation, negotiation, and other efforts to resolve differences as signs of weakness.[121]

The battle lines are drawn and Evangelical fundamentalists have gone to war on behalf of God, the Bible, and every traditional value they hold dear. They view themselves as God's shock-troops, much as the Society of Jesus did in the Counter-Reformation. But there is one important difference: the Jesuits far surpassed the average fundamentalist in intellect, education and discipline.

Carter noted that Evangelical fundamentalist movements invariably are led by authoritarian males who consider themselves superior to others.[122] That craving for superiority, turned even against their own wives, sisters and daughters, betrays deep-rooted insecurity and paranoia. The real world clearly is a deadly threat to the beliefs and values of Evangelical fundamentalism, but fundamentalists have to live in the world. To function, they are forced to separate the religious and secular assumptions on which their lives are based, inevitably causing emotional and mental stress. A psychologist explains fundamentalism as "a primitive defense of the collective, tribal, group self—an infectious narcissistic rage, an emotional flooding that inflates the ego with holy vengeance and wrath."[123] Evangelical fundamentalists have adopted a characteristic tribal mentality that harks back to the defensiveness of the Israelites.

Like Calvinists, Evangelical fundamentalists see themselves as participants in a new covenant.[124] But, unlike the Jews of the first covenant, fundamentalists make strenuous efforts to impose their values on the general population. Certain types of behavior must be eradicated from society as a whole, and certain types of knowledge suppressed. Evangelical fundamentalists continue to oppose the teaching of evolution in American schools. One approach is to force local school systems to include a statement in biology textbooks claiming that Darwinian evolution is "only a theory." Another has been to force schools to teach "creation science" or "intelligent design" in biology courses. Creationism, based on a literal reading of *Genesis*, was struck down by the courts as nothing but religious belief. Intelligent design has merit as a topic of philosophical interest; but critics assert that it is being used as a Trojan horse to get creationism back into science education. Anti-evolution activism reveals an important principle; since the Bible is true, it must be imposed on the science curriculum, whether or not it belongs there and whether or not the students are fundamentalist or even Christian. To acknowledge religious diversity would be to admit the relativism of Christianity, and to allow scientific truth to challenge religious truth would be an intolerable affront to God's word.

Opposition to the teaching of biological evolution is just one aspect of the "culture wars" currently being fought in western nations, particularly the United States. Great efforts are being made to reintroduce organized school prayer, despite court rulings curtailing the practice. Schools are described as "godless, bastions of liberal humanism," and where they cannot be controlled through the political process, parents are urged to withdraw their children and either enroll them in religious schools or "home-school" them.

Evangelical fundamentalists have become heavily involved in a number of other social issues, including include women's rights, abortion, stem-cell research, the right to die, sex education, and same-sex marriage. Fundamentalists insist on secular endorsement of religious notions of marriage as "a union between a man and a woman."[125] Same-sex unions threaten the "sanctity of the family;" the fact that it is already sullied by a 50-percent divorce rate, marital infidelity, and domestic abuse at all levels of society is discounted. Abortion and even "morning-after" contraception are portrayed as child-murder, and violence against family-planning personnel may be justified in the name of protecting "defenseless children."

It must be stressed that not all Evangelicals subscribe to the aggressiveness and polarization associated with fundamentalism. Jimmy Carter expressed the pain he and many others feel:

> As an Evangelical Christian, I am deeply concerned about the many divisive arguments that have driven . . . deep wedges between us. The most highly publicized differences involve social issues . . . Almost invariably, the divisions among Christians are based on the preeminence of one group over others. [That attitude] can lead to ignoring, condemning, or even persecuting those who are different.[126]

Carter was not alone in speaking out against fundamentalism. Joel Hunter, pastor of an Evangelical megachurch in Orlando, Florida, has emerged as another prominent critic of the religious right. And there are signs of a growing backlash, particularly among younger Evangelicals who want to promote a "compassionate agenda" that includes such issues as the environment.

Armageddon and the Rapture

Many Christians look forward to the second coming of Christ and the establishment of his kingdom, but there is disagreement over the order in which the events will occur. We have already seen that *postmillennialism*, the belief that the kingdom will be established first—or already has been established—and that Christ will come later, was popular among 19th-century Evangelicals and 20th-century Pentecostals. *Premillennialism* takes the alternative view, asserting that Christ will come first and then establish his kingdom. The latter belief was popular in the early church and the Middle Ages. Many dates were set for the second coming, and when they passed the prophets were discredited. Nevertheless, premillennialism secured a limited following in the late 19th century; and it has now become the consensus fundamentalist belief. The second coming is considered imminent and the terrible Armageddon scenario described in *Revelation* at hand.[127] A great battle will be fought between Jesus Christ and the Antichrist, and humanity—except for the "saved"—will face unprecedented suffering and turmoil.[128]

Premillennialism fits into the theory of *dispensationalism*: that human history can be divided into distinct phases. The basic premise of dispensationalism is not new. Joachim of Fiore (1130-1201) divided history into three ages corresponding to the Trinity and predicted that the third age, associated with the Holy Spirit, would begin no later than 1260. Calvinist covenant theology identified three "covenants" between God and the elect, the third of which was initiated when Jesus died on the cross. Modern dispensationalism can be traced to the work of John Nelson Darby (1800-1882), a disaffected priest in the Church of Ireland and founder of the Plymouth Brethren. Darby identified a sequence of seven "dispensations;" currently we are in the sixth dispensation, and the seventh will be the millennial kingdom.

In contrast to the postmillennialists' optimistic sense of human progress, premillennialism assumes that humanity can make no positive impact on unfolding history. The major turning points, all of them catastrophes like the flood, resulted from divine intervention.[129] Civilizations always declined ahead of divine interventions. We have no hope of improving conditions in the world or any responsibility to try to do so.[130] The most "optimistic" assessment of the present world situation is that things are getting so bad that the end times must be imminent. Preliminary skirmishes between angels and demons, both acting through human agents, are believed to be in progress now. That view is inspired by the scriptural passage: "[W]e wrestle not against flesh and blood, but against principalities, against powers, against the rulers of the darkness of this world, against spiritual wickedness in high places. Wherefore take unto you the whole armour of God, that ye may be able to withstand in the evil day."[131]

Frank Peretti's best-selling novel *This Present Darkness*, published in 1986,[132] stimulated great paranoia—and a flurry of similar books—about the end times and the impending cosmic battle. Peretti's original demon was the New Age movement, but imitators have identified their own religious, political, philosophical, or life-style enemies as demonic agents. Televangelist, and one-time candidate for president of the United States, Pat Robertson (1930-) did not coin the term "New World Order," but he promoted it to depict an insidious conspiracy by evil forces to take over the world.[133] The United Nations has often been associated with that new order. Robertson and others responded to the supposed conspiracy by initiating one of their own: to seize control of all governmental, judicial, educational, and cultural institutions and make them instruments of the fundamentalist agenda.

In addition to his theory of dispensation, John Darby proposed the notion of the rapture, based on a literal reading of a passage in *1 Thessalonians*:

> For the Lord himself shall descend from heaven with a shout, with the voice of the archangel, and with the trump of God: and the dead in Christ shall rise first: Then we which are alive and remain shall be *caught up* together with them in the clouds, to meet the Lord in the air: and so shall we ever be with the Lord.[134]

The Latin for "caught up" is *rapere*, from which Darby coined the word "rapture." When the tribulations described in *Revelation* are about to begin, he asserted, the elect will be taken up bodily into heaven, leaving the rest of humankind to face their terrible fate. Darby's rapture met with little response in Britain, but it attracted a large, and still growing, following in the United States. In the popular *Scofield Reference Bible*, Cyrus Ingerson Scofield (1843-1921) incorporated a discussion of the rapture into his commentary, leading many people to believe that the concept had scriptural support. Institutions like the Moody Bible Institute and Dallas Theological Seminary were founded largely to promote dispensation and rapture teachings.[135]

Frank Peretti's work demonstrated the extent to which Christian fundamentalism has been molded by fiction.[135] Apocalyptic literature has fed deep-rooted anxieties and paranoia to the point that many people regard it as divine revelation. The best-selling novel *Left Behind*, published in 1996 by Tim LaHaye and Jerry Jenkins,[137] created the popular image that people will be plucked from airplanes, cars, and their homes, leaving frantic relatives and friends to search for them—and to realize that they themselves are not among the elect. Made into a motion picture, *Left Behind* stimulated a flurry of books, including eleven sequels to the original novel.[138]

The combination of end-times beliefs and political activism has had serious political consequences, including disregard for the environment. Global warming, environmental pollution, and depletion of natural resources are dismissed because the rapture will occur before their impact will be felt. Another consequence—a very curious one—is emergence of the Christian Zionist movement. After centuries of spiteful anti-Semitism, fundamentalist Christians are now among Israel's strongest supporters, providing both money and lobbying muscle in the

Unites States Congress.[139] The consensus belief of Christian Zionists is that foundation of the State of Israel in 1947 fulfilled biblical prophecy and threats of a major war in the region signal the imminence of Armageddon. One version of the story is that, as a final gesture in God's covenant with the Jews, Jesus will intervene to prevent the destruction of Israel. Another is that, when Jesus returns, 144,000 Jews will repent for rejecting Jesus and convert to Christianity.[140] That latter belief worries some Israelis who sense that, rather than being helped, they are being used to further the fundamentalist religio-political agenda.

Among the victims of the Christian Zionist movement are Christians in the West Bank and Gaza, whose traditions go back to the time of Christ. Their rights are being trampled on and their very existence threatened by fundamentalists' uncritical support for Israeli subjugation of the Palestinians and the expansion of Jewish settlements in the occupied territories in defiance of international law. A more positive outcome from Christian Zionism is a willingness on the part of Evangelicals to examine the Judaic roots of Christianity. Perhaps we are seeing a revival of the early Nazarene and Ebionite movements that were left behind in the mass trend toward Pauline Christianity in the late first century CE.

"Why," asked one writer, "have narratives of world destruction played such a large part in religious consciousness?"[141] Satisfactory answers may be hard to find; but the whole notion of the Armageddon raises further troublesome questions about those who are obsessed with it—and about the God they worship. Even if we were to concede that the fundamentalists are right and the rest of us wrong, biblical scholar John Dominic Crossan questioned the justice of a deity who would set in motion "apocalyptic consummation, divine ethnic cleansing, and terminal annihilation of the evil and the unjust."[142] Fundamentalists' belief that they will look down—with a sense of vindication—on the destruction of the "wicked" during Armageddon is, to say the least, unhealthy.

Reflections

The Enlightenment was a most significant development in western civilization; but its impact on Christianity—summarized by Friedrich Nietzsche's "death of God"—was mixed. A positive outcome was experimentation with new forms of religion, free from the trappings of institutional Christianity. Although Deism, modern Unitarianism, and Transcendentalism attracted relatively few followers, they had a significant influence on Protestant theology and, more generally, on American culture. We also note that Freemasonry's theological foundations are compatible with Deism and rational Unitarianism. A negative outcome of the Enlightenment was the coupled emergence of liberal and fundamentalist Christianity, polar opposites locked in mortal combat of their own making.

Liberal Protestantism was less radical than Deism, but it responded to some of the same challenges to traditional Christianity. In the attempt to make Christianity acceptable to a skeptical age it embraced higher scriptural criticism, and some of its leading theologians were involved in both. Liberal theology let in a breath of fresh air, offering new interpretations of God, Christ, and the church. Neo-Orthodoxy preserved a transcendental God and a "Christ of faith." But emphasis shifted increasingly to an immanent God and the historical Jesus. The work of the liberal theologians was well-received by people who found themselves at odds with outworn teachings and practices.

Liberal Protestantism, Deism, and esoteric Christianity all shared visions of human perfectibility, and at least the two latter shared belief in a universe governed by potentially comprehensible laws. Moreover the Deists' infinitely remote God had much in common with the Godhead of Gnosticism and modern esoteric Christianity—though esotericism populates the space between the Godhead and ourselves with lower divine emanations. In almost all other respects, the esoteric view of the cosmos and humanity and the view taken by Deism and liberal Protestantism are diametrically opposite. Liberal theology would reject any belief in sacramental magic or the Divine Feminine as strongly as it rejects the mysticism of Catholicism and Eastern Orthodoxy. Fundamentalism would reject all of those things.

Liberal theology sought to distance itself from the "myths" of scripture and traditional religion. Combined with higher scriptural criticism, it dissected Jesus almost to the point of nonexistence. We are reminded of the modern physicists who dissected the atom to find mostly empty space, and then dissected the nucleus to find that protons and neutrons are not solid either. Repeated dissection inevitability leads to nothingness. Liberal Protestantism's "logical conclusion" is precisely what Friedrich Schleiermacher sought to avoid. Those who destroy tradition bear the responsibility to build something in its place; and liberals have been slow to do so. They have left us with little more than secular religion. Mircea Eliade might well have been speaking of the liberal theologian when he said: "The sacred is the prime obstacle to his freedom. He will become himself only when he is totally demystified. He will not be truly free until he has killed the last god."[143] Emphasis on a "god down here" neglects the transcendent God that embraces the whole of life.

Until the mid-19th century the Christian ministry was dominated by white males. Since then, almost all denominations have accepted racial minorities—though many congregations serve single ethnic groups, particularly those new to a host country. Most Protestant denominations have also welcomed women into the ministry, and a few accept openly gay clergy. Nevertheless, gender issues remain deeply divisive, with social conservative and liberal factions pressing their respective agendas. The "progressive Christianity" movement, which emerged in the 1980s, adopted inclusiveness as a defining characteristic. Progressive Christianity can be viewed both as an offshoot of liberal Protestantism and as a reaction to it. Time will tell whether the reaction will become real and permanent. Meanwhile progressive Christianity is found as a subdenomination in both Protestant and Catholic churches.

Evangelical fundamentalism refused to acknowledge the death of the Nietzsche's God. It presented itself as taking God's side against modern scientific "theories," the prevailing climate of secularism and materialism, and the "betrayal of Christian values" by liberals and progressives. Fundamentalists are still bent on preserving a style of religion that was already in decline in the first century CE. They have recaptured the legalism, narrowness and vindictiveness of Old Testament Judaism that Jesus expressly sought to lay to rest. Fundamentalism's exclusiveness, fear and suspicion are far removed from the love, inclusiveness and hope that Jesus taught. Moreover, its absolutism is based on a primitive understanding of truth and on the curious notion of scriptural empiricism. Fundamentalism preys on people's deep insecurity, its yearning for religious certainty, and a desire to stand aside from an increasingly complex, fast-moving world. The "left-behind" novels provide an apt metaphor for Evangelical fundamentalists' own story.

Like its counterparts in other world religions, Christian fundamentalism is reactionary, polarizing, combative and dangerous. Intimidation has allowed fundamentalists to secure major political influence, particularly in the United States.[144] The hope is that fundamentalism will fail as people eventually see through its thin façade of legitimacy and recognize its sacrifice of core Christian values. Programs to indoctrinate children and teenagers meet with a high attrition rate when target groups reach college age. Our best hope may lie in young people's innate good sense.

An interesting insight into both liberal and fundamentalist Christianity is gained by reflecting on the activities of prominent people on both sides in the light of the seven spiritual paths. Much has been done to strengthen the Path of Knowledge. The religions of the Enlightenment explored important alternatives to traditional Christian teachings. And great advances were made in theological development, names like Schleiermacher, Kierkegaard, Barth, Bultmann and Tillich will long be remembered; even individuals like Gordon Clark shared evocative ideas. Worthy contributions have also been made to the Path of Activism. Large numbers of people devoted their lives to the abolition of slavery, the elimination of segregation and prejudice, and the alleviation of poverty. John Biddle and Joseph Priestley campaigned against religious intolerance. Fundamentalists have devoted great energy to activism, whether or not their efforts are wise. But what about the other five paths? What have liberals and fundamentalists contributed to Devotion, Ceremony, Service, Healing, and Renunciation?

We are forced to conclude that the spiritual life of liberal Protestants—with the possible exception of the Transcendentalists—and Evangelical fundamentalists is shallow and impoverished. Each, even more than Protestantism in general, has destroyed within its respective constituency the sacred, the mysterious, the mystical, the unseen dimensions of Christianity.

---

1.   Some of the groups discussed in Chapter 13 merit the "liberal" label.

2.   Edward Herbert. *On Truth*. Paris, 1624; London 1633.

3.   That divine indifference recalled the attitude of the Greek gods, although the Deist divinity was much more abstract.

4.   Matthew Tindal. *Christianity as Old as the Creation or the Gospel a Republication on the Religion of Nature*, 1731, p. 33.

5.   Tindal, *Christianity as Old as the Creation*, pp. 265-266.

6.   *Ibid.*, p. 266.

7.   Thomas Paine. *The Age of Reason*, Part 1, section 1. As was customary in the period, Paine consistently used "Turk" to mean Muslim.

8.   We should not conclude from this that Butler leaned toward Deism; indeed he became an outspoken critic of many of its tenets. He also opposed the spread of Methodism and forbade John Wesley from preaching in the Durham diocese.

9.   Joseph Butler. *Fifteen Sermons on Human Nature*, 1726.

10. *Matthew* 19:19; *Mark* 12:31; *Luke* 10:27.

11. Ethan Allen, *Reason, the Only Oracle of Man*. New York: Scholars' Facsimiles & Reprints, 1940.

12. Philosophical "modernism" is not to be confused with the modernist movement in art and esthetics. The term "modernity" is often preferred.

13. David Parke. *The Epic of Unitarianism: Original Writings from the History of Liberal Religion*. Skinner House Books, 1820/1985. Decrees of religious toleration were issued in 1557 and 1563. In 1568, at the king's urging, the Transylvanian Diet approved the Act of Religious Tolerance and Freedom of Conscience which was unique for its time.

14. All but two copies of the Catechism were seized and burned by the public hangman. See: Allon Maxwell. "The Development of Biblical Unitarianism in Europe England and America." *Bible Digest*, no. 49.

15. Priestley's greatest scientific feat was the discovery of oxygen.

16. William E. Channing. "Unitarian Christianity. Sermon delivered at the Ordination of Rev. Jared Sparks in the First Independent Church of Baltimore, May 5, 1819.

17. James F. Clarke. *Vexed Questions in Theology*, 1886.

18. Henry N. Wieman. Preface to 1971 edition of *Religious Experience and Scientific Method*. Macmillan, 1926.

19. Ralph W. Emerson. *Nature*. Penguin Classics, 1836/2003, ch. 1.

20. Ralph W. Emerson. "The Over-Soul." *Emerson*. American Book Company, 1934, p. 135.

21. Reportedly Tolstoy was puzzled why Americans pain less attention to Thoreau's work than they did to the barons of industry.

22. Benedict Spinoza. *Tractatus Theologico-Politicus*, 1670. Spinoza was of Portuguese Jewish extraction, but lived in Amsterdam. Even in that most liberal of cities, publication of the *Tractatus* was banned because it was considered too inflammatory.

23. This was problematic since the earliest scriptural manuscripts with any significant content date from about 200 CE.

24. University College London was founded in 1826 when Oxford and Cambridge still restricted admission to members of the Church of England. Secular universities, modeled on German precedents, were created in the United States from 1850 onward.

25. Robert T. Handy. *A History of Union Theological Seminary in New York*. Columbia University Press, 1987.

26. See the discussion in: Keith Clements (ed.). *Friedrich Schleiermacher: Pioneer of Modern Theology*. Fortress Press, 1987, pp. 49-50.

27. See for example: Richard Rorty. "From Formalism to Poststructuralism." *The Cambridge History of Literary Criticism*, vol. 8. Cambridge University Press, 1995.

28. Stephen of Tournai (1192-1203). Quoted in: Matthew Fox. *Sheer Joy*. Tarcher/Putnam, 1992, p. 20.

29. Paul Johnson. *A History of Christianity*. Atheneum, 1976, pp. 472-473.

30. See for example: John A. Battle. "Charles Hodge, Inspiration, Textual Criticism, and The Princeton Doctrine of Scripture." *Journal of the Western Reformed Seminary*, August 1997, pp. 28-41.

31. Vladimir Solovyov. *The Antichrist*. 1900.

32. Benedict XVI. *Jesus of Nazareth*. (Transl: A. Walker.) Doubleday, 2006/2007, p. xxiii. Benedict stressed that he was expressing his personal opinion.

33. *Ibid.*, p. 35.

34. King Friedrich II of Prussia annexed Silesia in 1742.

35. Robert M. Adams. "Faith and Religious Knowledge." *Cambridge Companion to Friedrich Schleiermacher*. Cambridge University Press, 2005, pp. 35-51.

36. Schleiermacher's *The Christian Faith* has been compared, in its scope, to John Calvin's *Institutes of the Christian Religion*.

37. Keith Clements comments that the concept was influenced by the intimate friendships Schleiermacher enjoyed with his many friends. See: *Friedrich Schleiermacher: Pioneer of Modern Theology*, p. 20.

38. *Ibid.*, pp. 56-57. See also p. 105.

39. Adams, "Faith and Religious Knowledge," p. 46.

40. Kierkegaard's name meant "Church Garden."

41. In his influential dialectic theory of history, Georg W. F. Hegel (1770-1831) gave an idealistic account of human progress, emphasizing the collective consciousness which, in his view, was infused with a universal spirit, or *geist*.

42. Source: "Søren Kierkegaard." William McDonald. *Stanford Encyclopedia of Philosophy*, 2005.

43. Clifford Green. *Karl Barth: Theologian of Freedom*. Fortress Books, 1989, pp. 23-24.

44. Rudolf Bultmann. *New Testament and Mythology*, 1941. (Transl: S. M. Ogden.) Fortress Press, 1984, pp. 2-3.
45. *Ibid.*, p. 99.
46. *Ibid.*, p. 12.
47. According to Slovenian scholar Anton Strle, Friedrich Nietzsche lost his faith while reading Strauss' book.
48. Percy B. Shelley. *The Necessity of Atheism*, 1813. H. Buxton Forman (ed.). *The Works of Percy Bysshe Shelley in Verse and Prose*, 1880. For his views Shelley was dismissed from Oxford University.
49. Higher critics customarily assert that Jesus' miracles were "improbable," given what we know of the laws of nature and human capabilities. But "probability," as the term is used in that sense, is simply a statement of belief; we are not talking about throwing dice.
50. See the discussion in: Morton T. Kelsey. *Healing and Christianity*. Harper & Row, 1973, pp. 236-237.
51. Whether Tillich's God could be described as *panentheistic* is debatable.
52. Paul Tillich. *Systematic Theology*. Vol. 1. University of Chicago Press, 1951, p. 240.
53. *Ibid*, Vol. 2, 1957, p. 125. See also pp. 118-120.
54. We may also see parallels between liberal theology and Reconstructionist Judaism.
55. Martin L. King, Jr. "A Comparison of the Conceptions of God in the Thinking of Paul Tillich and Harry Nelson Wieman." Ph.D. Dissertation, Boston University, 1955.
56. Charles Wesley. *Hark the Herald Angels Sing*, verse 2. Emphasis added.
57. Bultmann concluded that the evangelists were more interested in promoting doctrine than in recording history, with the result that the real Jesus was submerged under the mythology of Pauline Christianity.
58. Albert Schweitzer. *The Quest of the Historical Jesus*, ch. 20, 1906. English edition: A. & C. Black, 1910.
59. John D. Crossan. *The Historical Jesus*. HarperCollins, 1991.
60. Robert W. Funk *et al. The Five Gospels*. Harper Collins, 1993. A "red" score indicated consensus that Jesus probably made the statement; a "black" score indicated that he most likely did not make the statement. "Pink" and "grey" scores indicated intermediate probabilities.
61. John S. Spong. *Why Christianity Must Change or Die*. Harper-Collins, 1998, p. 73.
62. *Ibid*, p. 221.
63. Søren A. Kierkegaard. *What Christ Judges of Official Christianity*. (Transl: D. A. Storm.) 1855/2005, pp. 132ff.
64. Dietrich Bonhoeffer. *Letters and Papers from Prison*. MacMillan, 1981.
65. Charles W. Leadbeater. *The Science of the Sacraments*. Apocryphile Press, 1920/2000, pp. 61, 75-86. Leadbeater's work was discussed in Chapter 18.
66. Spong, *Why Christianity Must Change or Die*, especially pp. 178-199.
67. *Ibid*, pp. 22ff.
68. Hal Taussig. *A New Spiritual Home*. Poleridge Press, 2006, pp. 2-3. Taussig's research was carried out in the United States, but it may apply to other countries too.
69. *Ibid.*, pp. 91ff. In some cases progressive Christian groups have had to move out of ecclesiastical facilities because of hostility from higher authorities.

70. Brissot, who lived at the time of the French Revolution, assumed the name of de Warville.

71. Wilberforce had a conversion experience in 1785 that launched him on the path of abolitionist activism.

72. The Fugitive Slave Act, passed by the United States Congress in 1850, made it a federal offense for any person to provide food or shelter to a runaway slave. The penalty was six months' imprisonment and a $1,000 fine. There is no evidence that Parker ever used the gun.

73. The notion that liberalism and conservatism can apply separately to doctrinal, social, and other issues will be explored in more detail later.

74. "The Land Letter," dated October 3, 2002, was cosigned by four other Evangelical leaders. The signatories noted: "while we cannot speak for all of our constituents, we are supremely confident that we are voicing the convictions and concerns of the great preponderance of those we are privileged to serve."

75. Particularly *Matthew* 5:9, 39.

76. Theodore Parker. Sermon, 1847. Quoted in: Henry Steele Commager. *Theodore Parker: Yankee Crusader*, 1936. Evidently Parker was not opposed to gun ownership.

77. World War I Document Archive.

78. See the discussion in: George M. Marsden. *Fundamentalism and American Culture*. Oxford University Press, 1980, pp. 11-14.

79. As noted later in this chapter, "Kingdom" has special significance for Evangelical Christians.

80. In the mid-19th century Frenchman Alphonse Esquiros was imprisoned for depicting Jesus as a social reformer

81. Barbara Fraser & Paul Jeffrey. "Base Communities, Once Hope of Church, Now in Disarray." *National Catholic Reporter*, November 12, 2004.

82. Bernard J. Lee *et al. The Catholic Experience of Small Christian Communities*. Paulist Press, 2000, pp. 7-8.

83. The Kyoto Treaty was negotiated in 1997 and took effect in 2005. As of the time of writing, 165 nations have ratified the agreement. However the United States and Australia have not; and, under present rules, signatories India and China are not required to reduce carbon emissions despite their relatively large populations.

84. *Galatians* 3:28.

85. Caroline Hemesath. *From Slave to Priest*. Ignatius Press, 2006.

86. At the time of writing the presiding bishop of the Episcopal Church is female.

87. In the United States many priests have been brought in from Third-World countries in an interesting reverse missionary effort.

88. *Romans* 1:26-27.

89. *Deuteronomy* 21:18-21; 22:11. Later chapters describe relationships between notable biblical characters that could be construed as homosexual. Frequently cited are the relationships between David and Jonathan and between Ruth and Naomi.

90. *Romans* 1:24-27. See the discussion in: John S. Spong. *Sins of Scripture*. HarperCollins, 2005, pp. 111ff.

91. Elsewhere "modernism" is usually applied to developments in the arts. What religious leaders called modernism is more commonly referred to as "modernity."

It is interesting to note that by the mid-19th century Enlightenment rationalism was also attracting opposition from philosophy and the arts.

92. Pius IX. "Syllabus of Errors." Appendix to encyclical: *Quanta Cura*. Vatican, December 8, 1864, §§ IV, VI. Initially Pius IX earned a reputation for his liberalism; for example he announced a general amnesty for political prisoners. But he grew steadiy more conservative during his long reign.

93. *Ibid.*, §X.

94. Decrees of the First Vatican Council, session IIII, 5. Vatican, 1870.

95. *Ibid.*, session IV, 2:4. 1870.

96. Canonization by Pius XII was widely interpreted as an endorsement of Pius X's conservative views.

97. Pius X. Oath *Sacrorum Antistitum*. Vatican, 1910. See also: Encyclical *Pascendi Dominici Gregis*, 1907.

98. See the discussion in: John S. Spong. *Jesus for the Non-Religious*. HarperCollins, 2007, pp. 239-248.

99. John XXIII. Address, 1959. Vatican.

100. See for example: Charles W. Colson *et al. Evangelicals and Catholics Together: Toward a Common Mission*. Nelson, 1995. However, not all Evangelicals welcome the alliance.

101. Marsden, *Fundamentalism and American Culture*, pp. 223-225.

102. Gray served as president of the Moody Bible Institute from 1904 to 1934.

103. Marsden, *Fundamentalism and American Culture*, pp. 16-18.

104. Charles Hodge. *What is Darwinism?* Scribner, 1874, pp. 168-177.

105. Marsden, *Fundamentalism and American Culture*, pp. 16-17.

106. The chief prosecuting attorney, William Jennings Bryan, won a conviction, but he was turned into a laughing stock by the press. He died a few days after the trial.

107. One individual who made this charge was Aldous Huxley (1894-1963).

108. Harold O. J. Brown. *Heresies: Heresy and Orthodoxy in the History of the Church*. Hendrickson, 1984, pp. 425-426.

109. The school eventually was expanded into a seminary headed by Billy Graham.

110. *Chicago Statement*. International Council on Biblical Inerrancy, 1978.

111. Jehovah's Witnesses regard the second coming of Christ as a central doctrine but reject the notions of hell and the immortality of the soul.

112. Bible colleges do not offer academic freedom. Nor are they recognized by the accreditation bodies that assess the quality of other institutions of higher education.

113. Marsden, *Fundamentalism and American Culture*, pp. 16-190.

114. *Ibid.*, pp. 225-228. Fundamentalism represented a significant break with traditional Evangelicalism and Pentecostalism where emotion rather than intellect was the principal driving-force.

115. Presuppositional apologetics emerged in the 1920s with the work of Dutch theologian Cornelius Van Til and became popular in the Calvinist tradition.

116. John W. Robbins (ed.). *The Works of Gordon Haddon Clark*, vol. 4. Trinity Foundation, 2004, p. 301.

117. *Ibid.*, p. 179.

118. Jimmy Carter. *Our Endangered Values*. Simon & Schuster, 2005, pp. 34-35.

119. For a discussion of the "theology of violence," with particular reference to fundamentalist beliefs, see: John D. Crossan. *God and Empire*. HarperCollins, 2007, especially pp. 191-235.

120. American philosopher John Dewey (1859-1952) is usually considered to be the father of modern pragmatism, but he was influenced by William James and others.

121. Carter, *Our Endangered Values*, pp. 34-35.

122. *Ibid.*

123. William J. Ventimiglia. "Where is God Gone?" *Parabola*, Winter 2005, pp. 64-71.

124. Calvinists were exclusive in drawing the distinction between the elect and those predestined for damnation.

125. This definition might be tenable except that a significant number people have some form of physical, psychological or other sexual ambiguity. Estimates vary, but one study concludes that one percent of the population has a body that differs from the standard male or female. See: Melanie Blackless *et al.* "How Sexually Dimorphic are We? Review and synthesis." *American Journal of Human Biology*, 12, 2000, pp. 151-166.

126. Carter, *Our Endangered Values*, pp. 37-38.

127. The scenario also received support from *Mark* 13. Since *Mark* was written shortly after the destruction of Jerusalem by the Romans, many scholars believe that the doomsday speech was put into Jesus' mouth to provide a prophecy of the events that had transpired. Its relevance to any future event is doubtful.

128. Armageddon, judgment by a cosmic redeemer, separation of the righteous from the sinners, and the establishment of a new kingdom are all Zoroastrian concepts that found their way into late Judaism from Persian contacts.

129. Marsden, *Fundamentalism and American Culture*, pp. 62-68.

130. Interestingly, Marsden shows that the rise of fundamentalism was culturally conditioned. *Ibid.*, pp. 223ff.

131. *Ephesians* 6:12-13.

132. Published by Crossway Books, 1986.

133. Pat Robertson. *New World Order*. Word Publishing, 1991. Marion "Pat" Robertson is a Southern Baptist but holds pentecostal views. He is also part of the religious right that supports the Republican Party.

134. *1 Thessalonians* 4:16-17. Emphasis added.

135. In 1895 Schofield became head of Dwight Moody's Bible Training School in Northfield, Massachusetts.

136. Perhaps it would be kinder to say that fundamentalists have been influenced in their beliefs by *mythology*. From that perspective they are not very different from other Christians.

137. Tyndale House Publishers, 1996.

138. The *Left Behind* books have sold more than 65 million copies, together with 10 million related items, such as computer screensavers, postcards, calendars, board games, music, apparel, and collectibles.

139. Given the combined strength of Evangelical fundamentalist and Jewish lobbyists the course of American foreign policy since 1980 is not hard to explain.

140. That claim is based on *Revelation* 7:1-14. Another interpretation of the 144,000 is that it is the number of people who will be rescued in the rapture.

141. Rosemary R. Ruether. *Gaia and God: An Ecofeminist Theology of Earth Healing*. HarperCollins, 1992, p. 61.

142. John D. Crossan. *A Long Way from Tipperary*. HarperCollins, 2000, p. 184.

143. Mircea Eliade. *The Sacred and the Profane*. Harvest Books, 1957, p. 203. Actually he was discussing "modern nonreligious man." But the quote leaves us wondering what kind of "freedom" liberal theologians are seeking.

144. Religious intimidation of secular authorities is certainly not new. Fundamentalists have simply adapted Christianity's long record of intimidation to the modern democratic environment.

Chapter 20
Developments in
Mainstream Christianity

M ainstream Christianity was not immune to the political, social and intellectual turmoil that rocked the west from the 18th century onward. The Church of Rome was forced to make painful adjustments to the realities of the modern world, but it also moved forward on several fronts, assuring a continued role in the 21st century. The Eastern Orthodox churches were seriously impacted by the expulsion of Greeks from the modern Turkish state and by the Russian Revolution. However, in the resulting diaspora, the rich traditions of Eastern Orthodoxy have become more accessible to people in the west.

Protestant denominations had to make their own difficult adjustments, including the exportation of national and ethnic churches from comfortable European homelands to new political and social environments. The blurring of denominational distinctions and easing of traditional enmities have facilitated ecumenical outreach; and in a few cases Protestant denominations have merged or entered into mutually supportive relationships. But consolidation has rarely escaped controversy. The fragmentation of Christianity continues, and all mainstream denominations are experiencing worrisome declines in membership.

In addition to reviewing these developments, the present chapter studies a number of significant trends in worship, pastoral work, and religious lifestyles that cut across denominational boundaries. The trends—many of them conservative in nature—stand in contrast to the liberal theology and progressive social attitudes also gaining momentum.

Developments in Catholicism

T he Reformation and the failure of the Thirty Years' War to reunite Europe under Catholicism were terrible blows to the Church of Rome; loss of the Papal States in 1870 was a further blow. But dire as the political events seemed, they helped focus leaders' attention more closely on religious affairs. Most modern popes have taken their responsibilities very seriously. In contrast to the situation a few centuries earlier, there have been few examples of moral failure; and only two recent popes: Pius VIII and John Paul I, died under suspicious circumstances.[1] Significant papal interference in European politics had ended by the late 19th century, but secular interference in papal affairs continued. In the conclave of 1903 the emperor Franz Joseph I of Austria-Hungary vetoed the frontrunner's election, whereupon a minority candidate became pope; he took the name Pius X.

A popular but controversial pope, Pius X (r.1903-1914) reorganized Vatican administration, advocated frequent communion, reformed the liturgy, encouraged the revival of Gregorian chant, and promoted popular Bible study—not insignificant since Catholicism had always been ambivalent about lay scriptural study. For 200 years Italian translations of the Bible were listed on the Index of Prohibited Books;[2] and Pius IX had condemned "biblical societies" in which people studied scripture without clerical oversight.[3] Two of the best-loved popes: John XXIII and John Paul II, lived in our own times. They both emerged as worthy role models for people outside the church as well as for Catholics. Pius X was declared a saint in 1954, and steps have already been initiated to canonize John XXIII and John Paul II. Benedict XVI (r.2005-) has emerged as one the preeminent scholar-popes of recent times.

Criticism of modern popes, when it arose, has focused on their political and social attitudes. Leo XII (r.1823-1829), one of two popes elected by the ultraconservative *Zelanti* faction among the cardinals, turned the Papal States into a police state and persecuted Jews, Freemasons, and supporters of the Italian nationalist movement;[4] people openly celebrated when he died. Several popes of the late-19th and early 20th centuries were criticized for their unyielding opposition to religious freedom and democracy. Despite his canonization, Pius X has been criticized for his fundamentalism. Benedict XV (r.1914-1922) was criticized for his pacifist stance during World War I, and Pius XII (r.1939-1958) for reticence in confronting the Holocaust.

Papal Infallibility and New Doctrine

The Catholic Church was considerably smaller after the Reformation, but the relative power of the papacy was enhanced. Tension between Rome and the bishops, which produced the 15th-century conciliar crisis, may continue indefinitely; but the Council of Trent affirmed papal power over the bishops, and the First Vatican Council proclaimed papal infallibility.

Papal primacy, as it was envisioned in the fifth century, did not mean infallibility. Only general councils of bishops were believed to be guided by the Holy Spirit to make binding pronouncements on matters of faith and morals. But increasing papal autocracy encouraged suggestions that the pope himself might be able to formulate doctrine without episcopal concurrence. Pope Pius IX asserted such authority in 1854 when he unilaterally defined the doctrine of Mary's immaculate conception. Sixteen years later Vatican I affirmed his authority. As a thunderstorm broke over the city, the assembled bishops approved a resolution that "The Roman Pontiff cannot err in defining matters of faith and morals." More specifically, the council declared that when the pope

> defines a doctrine regarding faith or morals to be held by the universal Church, by the Divine assistance promised to him in Blessed Peter, [he] is possessed of that infallibility with which the Divine Redeemer willed that his Church should be endowed in defining doctrine regarding faith or morals, and that therefore such definitions of the Roman pontiff are of themselves . . . irreformable.[5]

The case for papal infallibility rested on the "binding and loosing" passage in *Matthew*.[6] But the bishops attending the Vatican Council were by no means unanimous, and some pointed to the condemnation of Honorius I for heresy, some 1,300 years earlier. When the resolution affirming infallibility was passed a number of bishops seceded from the church. Not surprisingly, the doctrine was also rejected by both the Protestant and the Eastern Orthodox churches, and many people felt that it further alienated Rome from its Christian neighbors.

Infallibility refers to intentional statements of doctrine made *ex cathedra*, that is "from the chair [of Peter]." Several conditions were imposed. For example the pope must act "in his public and official capacity as spiritual head of the church universal, not merely in his private capacity as a theologian." And the declaration must define a doctrine of faith or morals intended to be binding on the whole church. If the conditions are met, the declaration carries the same weight as the pronouncement of a general council. Both are considered to be part of the *magisterium extraordinarium*, contrasting with the *magisterium ordinarium* of routine religious teaching. Exercise of papal infallibility was intended to be rare. Since Vatican I it has been used only once: in 1950, to define the doctrine of Mary's bodily assumption into heaven. The Second Vatican Council (1962-1965) confirmed the proclamation, asserting that "the Immaculate Virgin, preserved free from all stain of original sin, was taken up body and soul into heavenly glory, when her earthly life was over, and exalted by the Lord as Queen over all things."[7] Whether "infallible" pronouncements will ever be made again and whether they will have any credibility outside, or even inside, the Catholic Church remain to be seen.

The formulation of new doctrine rarely begins with the pope. More frequently, factions within the church make their case, and if enough support develops the issue may be offered for formal definition. Not all such initiatives are successful. In the 1960s the Belgian theologian Edward Schillebeeckx and others tried to reopen the ninth-century debate on the doctrine of transubstantiation. Their goal was to focus on the meaning and purpose of the Eucharist rather than on the change of substance of the elements. Schillebeeckx proposed two new categories: "transsignification," which described the significance of the consecrated elements in the minds of participants, and "transfinalization," the purpose for which the elements were to be used.[8] He presented the proposal to Vatican II, but Pope Paul VI rejected it.[9]

A successful initiative concerned the long-standing, but frequently criticized, doctrine of limbo. In April 2007 Benedict XVI endorsed the recommendation of a theological commission that the doctrine be abandoned.[10] The notion that infants who died before being baptized would be denied entry to heaven was offensive to modern understanding of divine justice and compassion. But the change could open the door to a reexamination of related doctrines; for example, if being born in original sin is not an impediment to salvation, what force does it have?

Doctrine has always been of central importance to Catholicism. Dominican priest Matthew Fox (1940-), who described himself as a "spiritual theologian," agreed that doctrine plays a useful role: "Much as a painter needs a frame within which to paint the best picture she can, so doctrine allows persons to concentrate on in-depth play."[11] But he warned: "When doctrine becomes a starting point for faith, I fear faith is already dead." In 1988 Fox was silenced by his superiors and, five year later, was dismissed from the Dominican Order. He left the church and was ordained an Episcopal priest. Fox is best known for spearheading the Creation Spirituality movement.

Attitudes to Science and Social Issues

On occasion the Roman church has been suspicious of scientific discovery or technological advances. The Inquisition condemned Galileo. And Pope Gregory XVI (r.1831-1846) opposed the construction of railroads and the use of gas lighting in the Papal States.[12]

More often it has been remarkably tolerant of scientific discoveries. That most Catholic king, Louis XIV, founded the French Academy of Sciences in 1666, four years after the Royal Society was chartered in London. Pope Pius IX embraced the new technologies resisted by Gregory and even re-established Galileo's Academy of the New Lynxes which had been dissolved two centuries earlier. In 1976 its name was changed to the Pontifical Academy of Science, and a new charter charged it with promoting "the progress of the mathematical, physical and natural sciences, and the study of related epistemological questions and issues."[13]

Over the years the academy has earned an impressive reputation for supporting scientific research.

John Paul II (r.1978-2005) took the bold step of formally rehabilitating Galileo. He accepted a report from the Pontifical Academy conceding that theologians "failed to grasp the profound non-literal meaning of the Scriptures when they describe the physical structure of the universe. This led them unduly to transpose a question of factual observation into the realm of faith [and] to a disciplinary measure from which Galileo 'had much to suffer'."[14] Admitting that the Bible might have "non-literal meanings" was a bold step with broader implications.

Catholic scientists have made numerous contributions to modern science. For example, in 1927, the Belgian priest Georges-Henri Lemaître proposed the Big Bang theory of the origin of the universe. Despite a mixed reception by Albert Einstein, who insisted on a static universe, the theory remains the dominant cosmological model. Catholic theologians were among the first to acknowledge that there is no essential conflict between the theory of evolution and Christian faith. Jesuit priest and paleontologist Pierre Teilhard de Chardin (1881-1955) rejoiced at the moment when man "discovers that he is not an isolated unit lost in the cosmic solitudes, and realizes that a universal will to live converges and is hominized in him."[15]

Three years after Teilhard's book was published, Pius XII outlined Rome's position: "[T]he Teaching Authority of the Church does not forbid that, in conformity with the present state of human sciences and sacred theology, research and discussions, on the part of men experienced in both fields, take place with regard to the doctrine of evolution, in as far as it inquires into the origin of the human body as coming from pre-existent and living matter."[16] John Paul II, writing in 1996, acknowledged that evolution is "more than a hypothesis." "It is indeed remarkable," he commented, "that this theory has been progressively accepted by researchers following a series of discoveries in various fields of knowledge."[17]

Although the *Syllabus of Errors* had condemned "modern rationalism," Pope Benedict XVI stressed the primacy of reason. Also, borrowing a position long held by liberal Protestants, he claimed the Enlightenment for Christianity:

> From the beginning, Christianity has understood itself as the religion of the "Logos," as the religion according to reason. [T]he Enlightenment is of Christian origin and it is no accident that it was born precisely and exclusively in the realm of the Christian faith . . . . It was and is the merit of the Enlightenment to have again proposed these original values of Christianity and of having given back to reason its own voice . . . Today, this should be precisely [Christianity's] philosophical strength.[18]

On the other hand, there was a limit to how far, or fast, the church would move. When Teilhard de Chardin questioned the *Genesis* story of the fall of man, he was banished to China. Much of his work was only published after his death.

From the mid-20th century onward the Catholic Church has come under increasing fire for its conservative attitudes to contraception, abortion, euthanasia, homosexuality, clerical celibacy, and the ordination of women. To cite just one issue: John XXIII (r.1958-1963) appointed a commission to discuss the issue of artificial contraception, one with wide-ranging consequences for health, family stability, poverty, and world population. The commission's report favored relaxing the tradition ban—as virtually all other Christian denominations had done. But, determined to rein in the new radicalism, John's successor, Paul VI, rejected its recommendations and reaffirmed the position that artificial contraception was sinful, even for married couples.[19] The bishops of both the United States and Canada opposed the ruling and issued statements arguing that such a private matter should be decided by individual conscience. The pope's ruling has been ignored by a majority of Catholics throughout the world, creating a major challenge to church discipline. Meanwhile, the church is trying to recover from allegations that high officials covered up incidents of clerical child abuse.

Schisms and Grassroots Movements

A number of bishops who voted against infallibility at Vatican I withdrew from the Roman communion. They rallied around the diocese of Utrecht, in the Netherlands, which, since the 12th century, had enjoyed a papal dispensation to elect its own bishops. The dissenters formed the Old Catholic Church, whose name emphasized the view that Rome had deviated from tradition. It is still in existence, though some component groups no longer recognize the primacy of Utrecht. In 2000 Rome acknowledged that churches which preserved the apostolic succession and "a valid Eucharist" are "true particular Churches."[20] Observers assumed that this statement referred, among other bodies, to the Old Catholic Church.

Vatican II triggered further defections in the 1960s. The council's work covered a broad field, and most Catholics applauded the new openness and ecumenical spirit. But in the area of liturgical reform, a sizeable minority felt that Rome had violated sacred heritage.[21] The decree *Norvus Ordo Missae* ("New Order of the Mass") became a lightning rod for protest.[22] Ostensibly it gave bishops discretion to use vernacular languages in the Mass; but the result was that Latin virtually disappeared worldwide, and with it Gregorian chant. There was considerable opposition, even among Catholics who did not otherwise hold conservative views. A seminary professor expressed the depth of feeling: "the ancient rite of Mass is actually the product of the hand of God Who used saints throughout history to develop it according to His holy intention."[23] Efforts to revive the use of Latin will be discussed later in this chapter.

Several bishops and priests opposed ecumenism and use of the vernacular so strongly that they left the church to form the loose-knit Traditional Catholic movement. The prominent Archbishop Marcel LeFevre (1905-1991) emerged as its *de-facto* leader. He founded the seminary of St. Pius X in Ecône, Switzerland, which has supplied priests to the small number of Traditional parishes around the world. Announcing his decision to consecrate four new bishops LeFevre proclaimed: "No authority can force us to diminish our Catholic Faith."[24] More extreme elements in the movement refused even to recognize the election of popes since Pius XII and have elected antipopes. For example, in 1998 the True Catholic Church elected a former Capuchin monk Lucian Pulvermacher as the antipope Pius XIII. Not since the English Prayer Book rebellion of 1548 had the Latin Mass found such determined supporters.[25]

Nor was Pius XIII alone. In 1978 Clemente Domínguez y Gómez was crowned Pope Gregory XVII by the schismatic Palmarian Catholic Church of Seville, Spain. Domínguez, a former insurance broker, claimed to have had a vision in which Mary of Nazareth told him to form the new church, since Rome had fallen under heretical and communist control.[26] In 1983 the Palmarian Church affirmed as dogma the presence of Mary in the Eucharist.[27] Among Domínguez' official actions were to excommunicate John Paul II and canonize the former dictator Francisco Franco, Christopher Columbus, and Paul VI. Needless to say, the canonizations were not recognized by the Vatican. Upon his death in 2005 Gregory was succeeded by the antipope Peter II.

The return to traditional conservatism in the church's official policies since Vatican II has, to some extent, undermined the schisms we have mentioned, though the Latin Mass remains a sensitive issue. At lower levels in the church the situation is very different. John XXIII's determination to "throw open the windows of the Church" did not fall on deaf ears. Many initiatives have been taken by laypeople, members of religious orders, and even bishops to change the face of Catholicism. A development of potentially far-reaching importance has been the emergence of small communities within, or in some cases outside, the traditional parish structure. A recent survey identified 37,000 such groups in the continental United States alone, with a membership approaching one million.[28] Although it is too early to say than an "underground church" is emerging, those groups operate for the most part beyond the reach of episcopal oversight. The survey found that members were more committed to traditional religious observance than the Catholic population as a whole; but they also exhibited attitudes of independence. A large proportion wanted more participation in church decisions and was willing to follow individual conscience rather than papal edicts.[29] Religious commentator Hal Taussig felt confident in announcing: "American Roman Catholics as a denomination have the most liberal social beliefs of any denomination."[30]

Developments in Eastern Orthodoxy

Eastern Orthodoxy has continued to evolve, driven largely by political developments and demographic movements. Over the centuries national churches emerged, and many of them won independence from the traditional patriarchates. Currently there are 15 fully independent, *autocephelous*, orthodox churches, including the Greek, Russian, Bulgarian, Serbian, Romanian, Georgian, and Syrian (Antiochian) churches. Missionary activity, followed by large-scale emigration to the west, extended the reach of Orthodox Christianity. Russian Orthodox monks established churches in Alaska in the early 18th century and sent missionaries into the western United States.[31] A Greek Orthodox church was established in Galveston, Texas, in 1862, and the first Greek Orthodox diocese in America was founded in 1921 under the jurisdiction of the ecumenical patriarch of Constantinople.

Greece secured its independence from the Ottoman Empire in 1829. Four years later the Church of Greece became the established church, operating under the presidency of the archbishop of Athens but acknowledging fealty to the patriarch of Constantinople. After World War I, hopes were raised that Constantinople might once again be the capital of an expanded Greek nation.[32] Had that happened, Greek Orthodoxy would have been greatly strengthened; but the new Turkish regime seized Constantinople and the Greek-speaking region of Asia Minor. Most ethnic Greeks were forced to leave the country; the few remaining Greeks in Istanbul were subjected to repeated pogroms, and religious sites were vandalized.[33] The activities of the patriarch of Constantinople are still severely restricted within Turkey. But he retains his official status as ecumenical patriarch and "first among equals" and continues to exert considerable influence abroad. He has direct jurisdiction over the Greek Orthodox Church in Crete and oversight of all churches in western Europe and North America that are not part of other autocephalous patriarchates. A number of organizations have been formed to support the patriarchate of Constantinople, including the Archons of the Ecumenical Patriarchate and the Order of St. Andrew. Meanwhile international efforts continue to secure religious tolerance in Turkey.

Mainland Greece, the Greek Aegean islands, Cyprus and Crete remain the stronghold of Greek Orthodoxy. Even in that region, political instability and the civil war in Cyprus have done much harm, nationally and religiously. In Greece the overwhelming majority of the population still belongs to the national church, but the general indifference sweeping Europe has taken its toll, and religious observance has declined. The notable exception is Mount Athos which, under the jurisdiction of the patriarchate of Constantinople, remains a strong center of Orthodox monasticism and a favorite pilgrimage destination.[34]

The Russian Orthodox Church came under severe persecution after the Bolshevik Revolution of 1917. Religious teaching was forbidden, and education systems were reoriented toward "scientific materialism." Nikolai Berdyaev, Vladimir Lossky, Sergei Bulgakov, and other scholars were expelled or fled to the west. Pavel Florensky (1882-1937) gained considerable recognition for his contributions to science, but he faced continual harassment by Soviet authorities because of his theological writings and eventually was executed.[35] Intellectual and poet Daniel Andreev (1906-1959) was arrested in 1947 and his writings destroyed. Amazingly, during the ten years he spent in a labor camp, he managed to write much of *Rose of the World*, which expressed his vision of a unified Christianity.[36]

The emigration of Orthodox clergy and laity from traditional Byzantine areas, and particularly the flight of Russian theologians during the Soviet era, brought the riches of Orthodox Christianity to the west on the scale even greater than occurred in the 15th century. Émigré theologians continued to develop their religious ideas, though it is not yet clear whether their work will be integrated into mainstream Orthodox teachings. Important texts were translated into western languages. Seminaries, colleges and patriarchates sprang up in many countries, and influential writers and teachers were able to reach a new audience. The Fellowship of St. Alban and St. Sergius, founded in Britain in 1928, was just one organization founded to encourage east-west religious contacts.[37] Its stated goal was "to pray and work for Christian unity, and provide opportunities for Orthodox Christians and Christians of Western traditions to meet and get to know one another, and so to deepen their understanding of each other's spirituality, theology and worship."[38] One of the Fellowship's members was Timothy Ware (1934-). A former Anglican, he converted to Orthodoxy and in 1982 became Bishop Kallistos of Diokleia, serving the Ecumenical Patriarchate in Great Britain.[39]

Twenty-three separate Orthodox jurisdictions now operate in the United States, most of them serving specific ethnic groups; Greek, Russian and other Orthodox churches may coexist in the same city. "Pan-Orthodoxy" has yet to take root. Sadly, the strong ethnic identities have hindered the dream of making eastern Christian traditions accessible to the west; few Orthodox churches offer themselves as potential spiritual homes for western Christians.[40]

Despite the persecution of the Soviet era, the Russian Orthodox Church is regaining strength in the homeland; more than 90 percent of ethnic Russians still identify themselves as Orthodox. The church fiercely defends its monopoly on Christianity. Russian Orthodox authorities have strongly opposed efforts by western denominations, particularly Pentecostals and Roman Catholics, to proselytize in its jurisdiction—a policy that has caused considerable friction with other branches of Christianity. Although Pope John Paul II visited more than 100 countries during his reign, he was never invited to Russia.

Eastern Orthodoxy is known for its conservatism. Emphasis is placed on tradition in relation to doctrine, liturgy and discipline. The liturgy has remained unchanged for centuries—something that many westerners applaud—and few concessions have been made in observances like fasting to appease modern resistance to religious discipline. We shall see in the next chapter that the Eastern Orthodox churches also remain uncompromising on matters of doctrine and have been reluctant to engage in ecumenical dialog.[41] Doctrine is still based firmly on the teachings of the church fathers, uncontaminated either by scholasticism or the Enlightenment; there is no counterpart in the east to liberal theology. On the other hand, just over the last two centuries, Eastern Orthodox theologians have made major contributions in fields ignored by western mainstream denominations. Their work on the Divine Feminine has already been mentioned. In Chapters 21 we shall consider Russian scholars contribution to the concept of the Ekklesia and the unity of Christianity.

Developments in Major Protestant Denominations

Lutheranism

The Protestant Reformation officially began in 1517, producing in its first phase the proliferation of Lutheran state churches in the principalities of northern Germany. Germany can be proud of the many notable Lutheran theologians it has produced, including Philipp Melanchthon, Dietrich Bonhöffer, Rudolf Bultmann, and Paul Tillich. And, despite a general decline in European religious consciousness, Germany remains the spiritual center of Lutheranism.

Lutheranism did not long remain a purely German phenomenon; within ten years of its inception, it spread north of the Baltic. In 1530 the Mass was celebrated in the vernacular in Sweden. The following year, with the support of King Gustav I, Archbishop Laurentius Petri of Uppsala embraced Lutheranism. The archdiocese of Uppsala had served as the preeminent bishpric since 1164, and it continued to do so as the center of Swedish Lutheranism. The Church of Sweden became the state religion and for two centuries was the only one allowed to conduct worship.[42] In 1726 attempts to introduce the Swedenborgian Church were suppressed. Not until 1784 was it lawful once more to celebrate the Roman Mass in Sweden.[43] Finland seceded from Sweden in 1809 to join the Russian Empire, and the Evangelical Lutheran Church of Finland was established as its state religion, imposing similar restrictions.[44]

Lutheranism also spread to Denmark and to Iceland which was then a Danish colony. In 1536 Catholic bishops in Denmark were imprisoned and church lands seized. Jón Arason, the last Catholic bishop of Hólar, Iceland, was executed in 1550, along with his two sons. The Evangelical Lutheran Church, which owed allegiance to the crown, became the state religion of Denmark and its foreign possessions. As in other Scandinavian countries, no other religion was permitted until the 18th century. Prominent existentialist and critic of institutional religion, Søren Kierkegaard, was a Dane; but liberalism did not take root in Denmark until the mid-20th century. Since 1947 women have been admitted to the priesthood, and based on present trends they may soon make up a majority of the clergy;[45] the first female bishop was elected in 1995.

The exportation of Lutheranism to North America provided a case study in the introduction of a conservative European religious tradition, used to monopolistic state protection, into an environment of religious pluralism and church-state separation. Like Eastern Orthodoxy, Lutheranism's identity in the New World was for a long time linked to the ethnicity of its members. German-speaking immigrants brought Lutheranism to the American colonies, and a further influx from the mid-19th century onward swelled its ranks. The German Evangelical Lutheran Synod of Missouri, Ohio, and Other States, founded in 1847, conducted worship services in German until the early 20th century. Only in 1947 did it change its name to the Lutheran Church-Missouri Synod.[46] Large numbers of immigrants also came from Scandinavia and the Baltic region, bringing with them their respective cultural heritages. The Norwegian-Danish Evangelical Lutheran Church of America and the Estonian Evangelical Lutheran Church had clear ethnic associations.[47]

Lutheranism is still widely viewed as a denomination for white Protestants of German or Scandinavian origin, and that perception has hindered efforts to reach out to African-Americans, Asian-Americans, Hispanics, and other minority groups.[48] Lutheranism's ethnic roots are less strong today, however, as successive generations have become assimilated into American society. Following successive mergers, the number of Lutheran synods—ethnic, geographical and confessional—in the United States has dropped from more than 100 in the mid-19th century to a mere handful today. The Evangelical Lutheran Church in America (ELCA), established in 1987, is the largest with about 10,000 churches and 5 million members. The Missouri Synod, the second largest, is roughly half that size. The Missouri Synod values its conservatism and insularity, while the ELCA is more liberal and ecumenically active.

Since the 1970s American Lutheranism has moved toward greater centralization of authority. Synod and district presidents in the ELCA are now called bishops. Among other things, that step facilitated the establishment of full communion with the Episcopal Church and, in turn, mutual recognition of clergy, liturgy and sacraments. Affirmation of the historic episcopacy and ordination of priests by bishops were also required, and some groups seceded from the ELCA in protest.[49] Greater authority of the bishops and curtailment of lay participation in doctrinal decision-making have caused some commentators to speak of a new Lutheran *magisterium*.

Reformed Churches

The Reformed churches flourished in Switzerland, Germany, the Netherlands, and Scotland. In several countries Calvinism or Presbyterianism became the official religion, and that status provided a strong basis for stability. Among the most enduring denominations has been the Church of Scotland. The Dutch Reformed Church, which also had a long record of stability, merged in 2004 with the Reformed Churches in the Netherlands and the Evangelical Lutheran Church in the Kingdom of the Netherlands to form the Protestant Church in the Netherlands (*Protestantse Kerk in Nederland*, or PKN). The merger was not achieved without opposition, and critics claimed that it destroyed the purity of the Reformed tradition.

Dutch settlers brought Reformed Christianity to the New World in the 1640s and Scottish immigrants brought Presbyterianism soon thereafter. In 1729 the Synod of Philadelphia adopted the Westminster Confession as its doctrinal standard. But candidates for the ministry were permitted to "scruple articles" with which they disagreed; the local presbytery would then judge whether a particular article was "essential and necessary" to the Christian faith. That loophole would cause endless debate among American Presbyterians, and it opened the door to revision of the Westminster Confession—and further controversy.

Away from the stabilizing influence of state establishment, the Reformed churches, like other Protestant denominations, experienced a pattern of mergers and schisms. A major controversy arose in the 1920s and '30s within the Presbyterian Church in the U.S.A. It divided fundamentalists, who subscribed to the 1895 Niagara Falls declaration of "Fundamentals of the Faith" from "modernists." The controversy resulted in a schism and the formation of the Orthodox Presbyterian Church; it also strengthened the Westminster Theological Seminary, which became an important center of fundamentalist teachings. By contrast, Princeton Theological Seminary, which had a conservative reputation, began to hire a more liberal faculty.

Mergers have taken place not only with other churches of the Reformed tradition but with churches of other traditions. The United Church of Canada was formed in 1925 from a merger of the Presbyterian Church in Canada, the Methodist Church of Canada, and two smaller groups. It leans toward Presbyterianism but can no longer be considered purely Reformed; in fact inclusion of the Methodists led some conservative Calvinists to secede to form the "continuing" Presbyterian Church in Canada. The Presbyterian Church of England and the Congregational Church in England and Wales merged in 1972 to form the United Reformed Church (URC). Subsequently the Reformed Association of Churches of Christ and the Congregational Union of Scotland joined the URC. The Presbyterian Church of Australia and the Congregational Union of Australia merged in 1977 to produce the Uniting Church.

The Presbyterian Church in America (PCA), currently the second-largest Reformed denomination in the United States, remains loyal to traditional Calvinism and is considered conservative is its attitudes to scriptural interpretation and social issues. Core beliefs, such as predestination, are rarely discussed, but they remain "on the books." The largest Presbyterian denomination, the Presbyterian Church USA {PC(USA)}, has about 3.5 million members.[50] Rather than affirming the Westminster Confession as its sole authority, it adopted the *Book of Confessions*, offering multiple sources of authoritative tradition. The PC(USA) has taken a liberal stance on a number of social issues, but it continues to wrestle with gender issues. While it makes no restrictions against the ordination of women, at the time of writing the PC(USA) has taken a deliberately ambiguous position with respect to gays and lesbians in committed relationships. The blessing of same-sex marriages and the ordination gays and lesbians also proved divisive in the United Church of Canada. Nevertheless, in 2003 its General Council affirmed that "human sexual orientations, whether heterosexual or homosexual, are a gift from God and part of the marvelous diversity of creation."[51]

Influential theologians from the Reformed churches span the whole range of doctrinal positions. Among early writers who helped define Calvinist tradition were Martin Bucer, Heinrich Bullinger, and Théodore de Bèze. More modern conservative theologians included Jonathan Edwards, John Gresham Machen, Charles Hodge, and the neo-orthodox Karl Barth. Liberals included Friedrich Schleiermacher, Harry Emerson Fosdick and Charles Briggs.

Anglican Communion

From its very beginnings, the Church of England sought to be a broadly inclusive denomination, and it has remained so. "Low church" Evangelicals, "broad-church" mainstream Anglicans, and "high-church" Anglo-Catholics can all find a common spiritual home. Low-church Anglicanism is a remnant of Puritan infiltration in the

16th century and continued Nonconformist influence. High-church Anglicanism dates back to those who sought to preserve some pre-Reformation ceremony and protect the episcopacy; one of its strongest supporters was William Laud (1573-1645), archbishop of Canterbury, who was beheaded during the English Civil War.[52] Anglo-Catholicism, an extension of high-church Anglicanism resulting from the 19th century Oxford Movement, will be discussed later. "Broad-church" is a modern term adopted by the Anglican mainstream to distinguish itself from the two extremes. The substantial diversity reflects long debate—often heated and occasionally leading to criminal charges by one faction against another—over the core principles of the Church of England.

The Anglican Communion, the totality of churches of the Anglican tradition, recognizes Canterbury as its spiritual center; but the archbishop of Canterbury has limited power. Similarly, the Lambeth Conference, a periodic gathering of Anglican bishops, seeks consensus, but it can exercise little coercive authority. While the *Thirty-Nine Articles* are still regarded as the standard of Anglican orthodoxy, since 1865 clergy have had to declare only that the *Articles* are "agreeable to the Word of God." Of the four jurisdictions—England, Wales, Scotland, and Northern Ireland—that comprise the United Kingdom, England is the only one that still has an established church.[53] The British monarch legally is Head of the Church of England and "Defender of the Faith;"[54] as a result, bishops are appointed by the prime minister, the monarch's chief "adviser." Few monarchs in recent times have expressed opinions on doctrine or religious practice, but some have had scruples; George IV feared that he had violated his coronation oath when he signed the Roman Catholic Emancipation Act in 1829.[55]

British colonial excursions of the 17th-19th centuries exported Anglicanism to many countries, including North America. It was the dominant denomination in the southern colonies until the American Revolution, after which Evangelical Christianity gained the ascendancy. The Episcopal Church, an autonomous branch of the Anglican Communion, officially dates from 1789. The name "Episcopal" helped distance the American church from its then-unpopular English associations; it also reflected the consecration of its first bishop, Samuel Seabury by the Scottish Episcopal Church.[56]

The Episcopal Church preserves traditional Anglican inclusiveness, but in recent years it has come under fire for being *too* inclusive with regard to eligibility for ordination and episcopal appointment. At the time of writing conservative Episcopalians are rallying around an African bishop to form a separate denomination in the United States. The archbishop of Canterbury is trying to preserve the integrity of the communion amid continual threats of schism. But large-scale secessions may be limited more by court decisions upholding the Episcopal Church's ownership of church property than by the persuasive force of Canterbury or the Lambeth Conference. Meanwhile, Africa has emerged not only as the bastion of Anglican conservatism but also as the only region of significant growth.

Since the beginning of the 20th century theological issues have proved less divisive. The Anglican Communion has produced some prominent liberal theologians, including Bishops John Robinson and John Shelby Spong, and Jesus scholar Marcus Borg.[57] Not everyone agrees with them, but their views have not created rifts comparable with those resulting from disciplinary controversies.

Trends in Religious Practice

As noted in Chapter 19, labels like "conservative" and "liberal" can be misleading. Conservatism and liberalism are multidimensional, referring variously to doctrine, liturgy, organizational structure, ministry, or social attitudes; significant correlation among the various dimensions cannot be taken for granted. Individual Christians, congregations, and in some cases larger groups may hold conservative positions on some issues but liberal positions on others.[58] Despite the momentum for reform and "progress" in mainstream churches, some long-established Christian traditions are being recognized for their continued value. In this section we explore a number of them that span denominational boundaries. They are of potentially far-reaching significance

Worship and the Arts

Worship acknowledges the gulf in consciousness between ourselves and God; but in the process it raises human consciousness and ennobles humanity. In 1981 Joseph Ratzinger—distinguished theologian, cardinal, and future Pope Benedict XVI—wrote: "Only as man, every man, stands before the face of God and is answerable to him, can man be secure in his dignity as a human being."[59] In Chapter 8 we examined the ways in which music, art and architecture contributed to Christian worship. They reached heights of excellence during the Renaissance and Baroque periods; but art forms continue to evolve, and who can say that the best lies in the past?

For centuries sacred music has graced the liturgy. Musical settings of the Mass provided the ultimate challenge for Protestant as well as Catholic composers. The Protestant reformers were not unanimous in their support for sacred music; but Martin Luther, who as a young man had been a chorister, placed "music next to theology" and gave it his highest praise. David Tame, a 20-century musicologist, agreed but insisted that music and theology were distinct paths: "To listen to [George Frideric] Handel's *Messiah* is not to debate intellectually about religion; it is to feel and become one with that surging inner flame of devotion."[60] One of

Johann Sebastian Bach's (1685-1750) most famous works was his *Mass in B-Minor*.
Bach, a Lutheran, asserted that music was intended for the glory of God and the
betterment of mankind; and few composers expressed that intent more successfully
than he did. Not that Bach was the only worthy composer of sacred music, however;
Karl Barth conceded that the angels probably played Bach when they "go about
their task of praising God," but he asserted that "when they are together *en famille*,
they play Mozart—and [then] our dear Lord listens with special pleasure."[61]

By the 18th century Masses on the largest scales were being written for concert
rather than liturgical use; but they continued to offer opportunities for spiritual
expression as well as for musical composition and performance. Motets, anthems,
and settings of the psalms offered equally great opportunities to composers from
Josquin des Prez (c.1453-1521) to Charles Villiers Stanford (1852-1924). In our
own time John Rutter urged us to sing: "Eternal God, we give you thanks for
music, Blest gift from heaven."[62] Cardinal Ratzinger encouraged the use of sacred
music of the highest order to make the church a "place of glory;" perhaps we
could extend that to "the world."

Congregational hymn singing came into its own in Protestant churches and
continues to play a major role across the religious spectrum. A favorite theme in
Evangelical hymns has been the attainment of a personal relationship with Jesus;
examples are the 17th-century "Fairest Lord Jesus" and Joseph Scriven's "What
a Friend We Have in Jesus." Another popular topic, reflecting the pessimism
of the Reformed tradition, has been humankind's corruption. John Newton's
(1725-1807) "Amazing Grace"—more popular in the United States than in its
native England—emphasized the need for grace to save "a wretch like me." Yet
another topic is the pre-Axial Age notion of blood-atonement that appeals so
strongly to Evangelical Christians. Elisha Hoffman (1839-1929) had us sing: "Are
you washed in the blood, / In the soul cleansing blood of the Lamb? / Are your
garments spotless? Are they white as snow? / Are you washed in the blood of the
Lamb?"[63] Many traditional hymns captured the spirit of the church militant. Martin
Luther's "A Mighty Fortress is Our God," harmonized by Johann Sebastian Bach;
John Monsell's "Fight the Good Fight;" and Sabine Baring-Gould's "Onward
Christian Soldiers" are cases in point. Commenting on the popularity of his
hymn, Baring-Gould (1834-1924) confessed: "It was written in great haste, and
I am afraid some of the rhymes are faulty. Certainly nothing has surprised me
more than its popularity."

Despite its broad popularity, congregational singing was banned for a time in
Protestant Zurich, and instrumental music was prohibited in John Calvin's Geneva
for more than a century. Although singing and organ music were eventually
reintroduced, the musical heritage of the Reformed tradition remains impoverished

compared to that of Lutheranism, Catholicism and Eastern Orthodoxy. But support for sacred music has not been uniform even within the latter denominations. In the mid-16th century, Chiara Cozzolani and her nuns were criticized by the archbishop of Milan for the "worldliness" of their music and other "irregularities." During the same period the Vatican banned women from church choirs, an action that propelled boys' choirs to greater popularity and launched the great era of castrati. Men who could combine a soprano range with the strength of the adult male voice featured prominently in the choral liturgy of the Roman church until "the great sacrifice" was banned in 1903.[64]

Byzantine and Anglican chants are sacred musical forms of the highest order; capturing a sense of timeless mystery, they continue to play major roles in their respective liturgies. Gregorian chant survived in Catholicism until Vatican II. By contrast, in recent years many Christian congregations have moved to "contemporary music," which is claimed to draw young people who might not otherwise attend religious services. In many churches percussion instruments and high-powered audio equipment are now considered as essential to the liturgy as incense and candles were in Roman and Orthodox churches. The music ministry in a modern Pentecostal church may be hard to distinguish from a secular rock band.

The arts find their highest expression in religion; and perhaps religion rises to its highest form through the arts.[65] Art, in the words of a church historian, is "an embodiment of devotion in beautiful forms, which afford a pure pleasure, and at the same time excite and promote devotional feeling." He continued: "Poetry and music, the most free and spiritual arts, which present their ideals in word and tone . . . lead immediately from the outward form to the spiritual substance."[66] Even in a secular age, artists and architects are still moved to express spiritual aspirations through their work. Works of artistic creation are investments of spiritual energy. In Eastern Orthodoxy the painting of icons is held to be more than the production of sacred art; it is a form of prayer.

In statements that would have been applauded by their Renaissance predecessors, recent popes have lent strong support to the arts. The future Benedict XVI noted the relationship between beauty and love, commenting that they "form the true consolation in this world, bringing it at near as possible to the world of the resurrection."[67] John Paul II affirmed the importance of the decorative arts:

> Sacred art is true and beautiful when its form corresponds to its particular vocation: evoking and glorifying, in faith and adoration, the transcendent mystery of God—the surpassing invisible beauty of truth and love visible in Christ, who "reflects the glory of God and bears the very stamp of his nature" . . . This spiritual beauty of God is reflected in the most holy Virgin Mother of God, the angels, and saints. Genuine sacred art draws man to

adoration, to prayer, and to the love of God, Creator and Savior, the Holy One and Sanctifier.[68]

The resources invested in cathedrals, basilicas, and other large, impressive houses of worship could obviously have been directed elsewhere. But it is hard to make a convincing case that the priorities were totally wrong in terms of the ultimate benefit to humanity. Critics might want to consider whether large houses of worship represent less worthy investments of resources than entertainment facilities, sports stadiums, or military bases.

Pope Julius II laid the foundation stone of St. Peter's basilica, Rome, in 1506. The completed Renaissance-style basilica, designed by a series of architects including Michelangelo, was dedicated by Urban VIII 120 years later. Its claim to be the largest church building in the world is now challenged by the Basilica of Our Lady of Peace at Yamoussoukro, Ivory Coast, and the nondenominational Lakewood Church in Houston, Texas.[69] Of course, bigger is not necessarily better, and countless small churches throughout the world express, in their architecture and decoration, and in the spirituality of the people who worship there, the exquisite spiritual vision of their creators.

Liturgy and Sacraments

Anglicanism, Lutheranism and, to a far greater degree, Calvinism emerged from the Reformation with stripped-down theologies and little of the rich liturgical and sacramental traditions of earlier Christianity. The Evangelical churches inherited still less. The last 200 years have witnessed signs of dissatisfaction, however; and a number of initiatives, extending over multiple branches of Christianity, have sought to recover forms of worship and even some doctrines from the medieval church.

In the 1830s a group of Anglican clergy at Oxford University looked back with nostalgia at what they considered the golden age of English Christianity and expressed dissatisfaction with the spiritual laxity of their time. Edward Bouverie Pusey (1800-1882), a leading spokesperson for the group, insisted that the Anglican church was not "a new Church of the Reformation" but a "purified" form of the unified Christianity that had existed from the time of the apostles.[70] Whether that was a legitimate view, or the revivalists were trying to rewrite history, continues to be debated. But Pusey and others pointed out that Henry VIII had preserved medieval beliefs and practices and that both Elizabeth I and the Caroline Divines had initiated restoration movements.[71]

Over time the group's deliberations, speeches and publications came to be known as the Oxford Movement.[72] Initially the movement took a doctrinal focus, seeking to recover belief in the real presence in the Eucharist and Mary's status as the Mother of God. Twenty years later the focus shifted to reviving the liturgical traditions of the medieval English church. The outcome of the movement was self-identification by clergy and parishes within the Anglican Communion as "high-church" or "Anglo-Catholic." Resistance from mainline Anglicans resulted in the prosecution and incarceration of several Anglo-Catholic priests.[73] Persecution continued until 1890 when charges against Edward King (1829-1910), bishop of Lincoln, resulted in an inconclusive ruling.[74] Anglo-Catholics recognize the validity of all seven traditional sacraments and celebrate the Mass with Roman-style vestments, incense, candles and gestures—including genuflection and the sign of the cross. Their churches typically are decorated in traditionally elaborate styles. Anglo-Catholics remain a minority within the Anglican Communion, but their influence has been substantial both in Britain and abroad. An Anglo-Catholic church was established in Asheville, North Carolina, in 1849.[75]

A similar movement within European Lutheranism is referred to variously as high-church Lutheranism or Neo-Lutheranism. As already noted, the Church of Sweden and other Scandinavian Lutheran churches preserved pre-Reformation liturgical forms more faithfully than did their counterparts in Germany and elsewhere. Neo-Lutherans have restored the seven sacraments and celebrate the Mass with most of the pomp of Roman Catholicism. With the cooperation of bishops in the Old Catholic Church, Swedish Neo-Lutherans restored the apostolic succession to their episcopacy.

In 1851 Episcopal priest William Augustus Muhlenberg published a periodical called *The Evangelical Catholic* in New York City. This title gave rise to a movement in North America known as "Evangelical Catholicism" (not always capitalized). Participants were Protestant groups that consider themselves in communion with the "catholic" church of the Nicene Creed. Evangelical Catholics emphasize continuity with the medieval church of both west and east and encourage efforts to bring about the reunification of Christianity. They promote recognition of the seven sacraments and a return to traditional liturgical practices, including celebration of the Mass and frequent receipt of the Eucharist. Priests and congregations that identify themselves as Evangelical Catholic Lutherans are represented in both the Missouri Synod and the ELCA, though the latter's growing social liberalism has discouraged their participation.[76]

The symbolism and power of sacramental rituals in Roman Catholicism, Eastern Orthodoxy, Anglo-Catholicism, Neo-Lutheranism, and Evangelical Catholicism certainly is not ignored; but they are described in traditional Christian terms. The Liberal Catholic Church took the further step of interpreting the sacraments as rituals of ceremonial magic. The Liberal Catholic Church was founded in 1916 by James Ingall Wedgewood (1883-1951), a former ministerial student who was influenced both by Anglo-Catholicism and by Theosophy. Wedgewood was consecrated a bishop in the Old Catholic Church, thereby securing the apostolic succession. The LCC developed close ties to the Theosophical Society, and through it the Society expanded its embrace of Christianity. Theosophist Charles Leadbeater (1853-1934), who had also been influenced by Anglo-Catholicism, became the church's second presiding bishop. The "liberal" label, which contrasts with the LCC's strong liturgical conservatism, stemmed from a desire to avoid the doctrinal constraints of the Roman Catholic and Anglican Churches: "a man's belief upon any point is exclusively his own affair, . . . we are concerned only with his actions."[77]

The Liberal Catholic Church's stated mission was to combine "Christian sacramentalism of which the Roman Catholic, Orthodox and Anglican Churches have long been the principal custodians" with "the esoteric Wisdom Tradition."[78] Wedgewood, Leadbeater and others drew upon the age-old lore of ceremonial magic, helping fulfill Éliphas Lévi's hopes for a rapprochement with religion. Whether or not the sacraments were originally viewed as magical rituals, the objective was to provide a more systematic understanding of the sacraments and thereby enhance their efficacy. The LCC's liturgy was modeled after that of the Roman church.[79] But Leadbeater explained that his church selected for its psalms "only verses which bear some intelligible meaning, [and avoided] all those which complain, grovel or curse."[80] "Groveling" referred to the confession of sins in the Roman and Anglican liturgies; for example, in preparation for the Eucharist, Anglicans "acknowledge and bewail our manifold sins and wickedness" that provoke "most justly thy wrath and indignation against us . . . The burden on them is intolerable."[81] The Liberal Catholic Church continues in operation, though schisms have arisen over issues like the ordination of women and disagreements over whether clergy must embrace Theosophical teachings and asceticism.[82] It views itself as being part of a wider Catholic communion; but it is not recognized by either Rome or Canterbury.

While various Christian groups have sought to recover forms of ceremonial worship that had fallen into disuse, the Church of Rome abandoned the traditions of Latin and Gregorian chant in the 1960s. As noted, this led to outright schism on the part of some dissenting bishops. A number of groups, including the Adoremus Society and the Priestly Fraternity of St. Peter, are working within mainstream Catholicism to restore the use Latin at least on a small scale. Their efforts have been rewarded by the relaxation of restrictions on celebration of the Latin Mass. It remains to be seen whether restoration would simply appease the dwindling ranks of pre-Vatican II Catholics and facilitate reconciliation with schismatic groups, or whether younger generations will see beauty and timeless relevance in western Christianity's sacred language. Gregorian chant continues to be performed by secular choirs interested in ancient music, but it is doubtful whether it will ever again play a significant role in the Roman liturgy.

Healing Ministries

While sacramental healing has been practiced in an unbroken tradition in Eastern Orthodox Christianity, it was allowed to lapse in the Roman Church. The Protestant reformers rejected sacramental healing altogether; as part of their broad-based assault on the Roman sacraments, Martin Luther and John Calvin discounted any role for the church in healing. Calvin claimed that "the gift of healing disappeared with the other miraculous powers which the Lord was pleased to give for a time . . . [I]t pertains not to us, to whom no such powers have been committed."[83] The reformers scorned any reliance on saints' relics and pilgrimages to sacred sites to seek cures; in consequence people were condemned to hopelessness in the face of ever-present sickness.[84] With the rejection of the doctrine of purgatory, people were even denied the consolation of praying for their dead loved ones.

Healing became even more unpopular during the Enlightenment. The consensus developed that God did not intervene to benefit individuals,[85] and biblical reports of healings were dismissed as figments of primitive "mythology" or "superstition."[86] Little attention was paid in any major western denomination to the possibility that healing might be a natural, but undeveloped, human capability or even that it might be a legitimate gift of the Holy Spirit.

The first signs of renewed interest in spiritual healing in the west came from the fringes of Christianity. Eighteenth-century charismatics, like Mother Ann Lee, practiced healing; and, as we have seen, their ministry evolved into the spiritual healing of our own time. Separately, the New Thought movement and the work of intuitives like Phineas Parkhurst Quimby and Edgar Cayce opened up new approaches to healing.

The revival of a healing ministry in mainstream western Christianity dates from the early 20th century. In 1905 an Australian layman, James Moore Hickson (1868-1932), founded the Society of Emanuel, later renamed the Divine Healing Mission. In the 1920s he received the archbishop of Canterbury's blessing to introduce charismatic healing in Anglican churches. The Lambeth Conference appointed a commission in 1920 to study spiritual healing in the Church of England. Its report, presented four years later, acknowledged that healing was "part of the redemptive work of our Lord."[87]

In 1932 John Gayner Banks, an Episcopal priest, and his wife Ethel Tulloch Banks, founded the Fellowship of St. Luke. By the 1950s it had evolved into the International Order of St. Luke the Physician, an interdenominational Christian fellowship of clergy and lay people interested in the healing ministry.[88] Prayer, anointing, and the laying-on of hands were all included in its repertory. The Order proclaimed: "The revival of Christian healing in the church today may be a means of the greatest advance of Christianity in this century. God's healing power operates within the church which is the body of Christ on earth."[89] Further studies of the healing ministry were conducted, including one commissioned by the archbishops of Canterbury and York in 1953 "to consider the theological, medical, psychological and pastoral aspects of Divine Healing."[90] It recommended an expansion of the healing ministry and "increasing understanding and cooperation between [clergy] and the medical profession."

By the 1950s Methodist churches were incorporating healing ministries.[91] The first official initiative within the Church of Rome came from Vatican II in the 1960s. The council recommended that extreme unction, long viewed as a "sacrament of the dying," be restored to its original form as a sacrament of the anointing of the sick. The action brought the Roman church into line with traditional practice in Eastern Orthodox churches. Vatican II also defined penance as the "sacrament of reconciliation," and Pope John Paul II later emphasized that it was to be regarded as a healing sacrament.[92]

Coincident with Vatican II, the charismatic revival was sweeping mainstream Protestant and Catholic churches. Local congregations began to experiment with charismatic healing practices, with or without ecclesiastical approval. Expressing satisfaction with the progress made, Morton Kelsey reported: "This new emphasis on healing in the Christian churches is anything but an isolated phenomenon. It is worldwide . . . Clearly, a new spirit is moving among men, which speaks of their need for healing."[93] Francis MacNutt, a Dominican priest, published several books reporting his studies of charismatic practices and their relevance to the church's healing ministry. But high-ranking Catholic officials became nervous about the charismatic revival. MacNutt left the Dominican order to found an ecumenical healing center in Florida. In 2000 the Vatican issued a directive warning against insertion of unauthorized healing prayers or rituals into the Mass,[94] and the directive has been interpreted by some as an attempt to dampen the growth of the healing ministry.

Notwithstanding occasional setbacks, the healing ministry continued to expand, and by the end of the 20th century a great deal had been done to integrate healing into the ongoing liturgical, counseling, and other work of mainstream Christianity. An Anglican report published in 2000 proclaimed: "Prayer for healing is offered to individuals during or after the usual Sunday liturgy. The laying on of hands is widely used, sometimes with anointing. Counseling of various kinds is available in many parishes. The ministry of deliverance [i.e. exorcism] is practised in some. And, most notable of all, increasing numbers of laity are involved."[95] Finally, we must not forget the continuing popularity of sacred sites like Lourdes and Fatima that draw millions of ordinary people seeking cures. The Roman Church established procedures to examine claims of healings and established criteria for what could be considered "miracles." A substantial number of such events have been recorded; many more people may have experienced less dramatic healings.

Religious Orders and Asceticism in the Modern World

T he great monastic and mendicant religious orders of the Middle Ages continue to play major roles in Catholicism. Fortunately the mendicant orders are sufficiently well-endowed that their members no longer have to beg. As noted in Chapter 15, the Society of Jesus grew to become one of the most powerful orders; and many new religious orders have been established in recent centuries. The Dominicans and Jesuits are renowned for their teaching and scholarly pursuits. In 1639 the women's order, known as the Ursulines, founded a school in Quebec, Canada, for the education of Native American women; and within a century a second school was founded in New Orleans. From those bases schools spread throughout the continent, including important centers in the Rocky Mountains and Alaska.

Many of the newer religious orders have embraced service missions. For example, the Sisters of Charity, which had been co-founded by Vincent de Paul, established a convent in Maryland in 1809, the order's first community in the United States. Also inspired by Vincent's example, eight men founded the Society of St. Vincent de Paul which works among the poor in many countries. However both men and women continue to be attracted to traditional contemplative monasticism. In 1664, with a vision of monasticism similar to that of John of the Cross, Armand de Rancé, a Cistercian abbot, reformed his abbey of La Trappe in France to place emphasis on penance, austerity, and expiation for sin. His monks became known as Trappists, and monasteries following the same rule were founded in many countries. In 1892 the Trappist Observance was constituted as an order separate from the Cistercians of the Common Observance.[96] A notable Trappist discipline is complete silence for most of the day, except for the recitation of the daily offices. The Carthusian Order places even greater emphasis on silence.[97] Benedictine monks, whose emphasis on silence is less strict, engage in pastoral work and teachings and offer retreats for laypeople.

Thérèse of Lisieux (1873-1897) has become a greatly revered saint of modern times. Named in honor of Teresa of Ávila, Francoise-Marie Thérèse had a profound spiritual experience on her 14th birthday. The following year she entered the Carmelite convent at Lisieux in northwestern France. Thérèse, also known as Thérèse of the Child Jesus and or "the Little Flower," impressed everyone with her devotion and simplicity of spirit. Although she died of tuberculosis at the early age of 24, she contributed much to western spirituality and was canonized in 1925.

The Padre Pio (1887-1968), the famous Capuchin monk of San Giovanni Rotondo, Italy, was ordained in 1910. Eight years later he received the stigmata, the marks of Jesus' crucifixion on his body, and bore the wounds for 50 years.[98] He was said to be capable of levitation and bilocation, and many miraculous healings were attributed to him. One of the best-known contemplatives of modern times was the Trappist monk Thomas Merton (1915-1968). Upon taking his vows at the Abbey of Gethsemani in Kentucky in 1941, he imagined God explaining to him: "[Y]ou shall taste the true solitude of my anguish and my poverty and I shall lead you into the high places of my joy and you shall die in Me and find all things in My mercy which has created you for this end and brought you . . . to the Cistercian Abbey of poor men who labor in Gethsemani."[99] Merton became an admirer of Asian religions and died a few months after a famous meeting with the Dalai Lama.

Although Catholic religious orders continue to flourish, the concept of the religious life has become more flexible, particularly among women's orders. The traditional veil and habit have all but been abandoned, and women religious who work in the world may be indistinguishable from their secular sisters. The Leadership Conference of Women Religious, which represents more than 60,000 nuns, has promoted women's roles in society and in the church. It also supports environmental consciousness, peacemaking and reconciliation, and initiatives to help disadvantaged women and children.[100] Several of the LCWR's members are involved in various types of activism. The Carmelites of Indianapolis are a contemplative order, but they maintain an Internet website that includes prayerful commentary on the day's news.[101]

The Protestant reformers strongly opposed the monastic orders. But notions of communal life and withdrawal from the world were preserved by Mennonites, Amish and Shakers. More recently, as part of the broader movement to recover pre-Reformation practices, interest has arisen in the formation of Anglican communities and religious orders resembling those of Catholicism and Eastern Orthodoxy. The International Order of St. Luke the Physician, dedicated to the healing ministry, has already mentioned.

Anglican monastic or semi-monastic orders date from mid-19th century. Under the impetus of the Oxford Movement, Englishwoman Marion Rebecca Hughes took vows of poverty, chastity and obedience in 1841 and later became superior of the Convent of the Holy Trinity at Oxford.[102] Another Englishwoman Anne Ayres emigrated to the United States and aspired to become a nun. Finding no Protestant religious orders, in 1850 she founded the Sisterhood of the Church of the Holy Communion, the first order of deaconesses in the Episcopal Church.[103] A nursing sisterhood, the Society of St. Margaret, was established in England in 1854, and an American branch was founded 19 years later. The first Anglican religious order for men, the Society of St. John the Evangelist, was formed in 1865. The Community of the Resurrection is modeled on the Catholic Dominican Order; it was founded in 1892 and maintains monastic houses in Britain and South Africa. Residential religious communities—not all of which require members to take formal vows—continue to gain in popularity. In 2000, 40 communities reportedly operated in the Church of England, and more in the larger Anglican Communion.[104]

In Methodism, the Order of St. Luke, not to be confused with the Order of St. Luke the Physician, was established in 1946 as a lay order for men and women. It is committed to "the worship and sacramental practice which has sustained the Church since its formation in Apostolic times. At the same time we seek to help the Church rediscover the spiritual disciplines of the Wesleys as a means of perceiving and fulfilling the mission for which the Church was formed."[105]

Traditionally, a religious order was affiliated with a single denomination. But a few modern orders welcome people from multiple denominations. One is the Ecumenical Order of Franciscans whose focus is devotion to Francis and Clare of Assisi. The order emphasizes its inclusiveness:

> We are a diverse group in many ways: theological, denominational affiliation, gender orientation, and vocationally . . . No matter the background, we find ourselves drawn together by the Eucharist and by a commitment to the gospel of liberation and justice for all God's creatures. As a community, we commit ourselves to a common Rule, a structure of intentional spiritual formation and accountability both within the Order and with a local spiritual director. Ours is a community of faith and life, sharing a love for all of Creation and those who have been marginalized by a society fraught with greed and despair.

Special mention must be made of the initiative taken in 1865 by Methodist minister William Booth (1829-1912) and his wife Catherine. They formed an Evangelical group to alleviate the appalling poverty in London's East End. The work was based on the interdependence of material, emotional and spiritual needs. In addition to preaching, the Booths and their followers fed the hungry, provided shelter for the homeless, and helped rehabilitate alcoholics. Originally known as the Christian Mission, the ministry was reorganized in 1878 into a quasi-military organization and renamed the Salvation Army. The founder became "General Booth," and his immediate subordinates were given officers' ranks. The Army never imposed the traditional vow of celibacy; but soldiers and higher ranks took covenant vows called the "Articles of War," which relate to doctrine and evangelism and also to matters of loyalty, generosity, and abstinence from liquor and tobacco. The Army has always ordained both men and women, but in the early days a woman was prohibited from marrying a man of lower rank. Consistent with its Evangelical Christian roots, the Army's attitudes to sexual orientation and the family are conservative. The Salvation Army and the Quakers are the only Christian denominations that reject all sacraments, including baptism.

The Salvation Army is of considerable interest to our theme. While retaining its Evangelical character, it is also a military religious order in the tradition of the Knights Templar and Knights Hospitalers. The Army currently has about 3,600 officers—the equivalent of clergy—more than 100,000 soldiers, 400,000 "adherents," and 3.5 million volunteers; it operates in more than 100 countries.[106] While its ranks are declining in the United States and Europe, growth continues elsewhere.

Many religious or semi-religious fraternal organizations have emerged in recent centuries, and in some cases it is hard to distinguish them from military religious orders. Falling into a gray area are the Knights of St. Columbus and the various Masonic Orders. Separately, patterns of communal living continue to gain favor in reaction to the stresses, complexity, and social isolation of modern city life. Intentional communities, with or without a religious focus, are gaining in popularity.[107] Although some religious communities are authoritarian and cult-like, the great majority are run democratically.[108] Interestingly, many intentional communities place new members in a probationary category, reminiscent of the practice adopted by the Essenes.

Asceticism has always met a deep-rooted need among Christians to emulate the sufferings of Jesus or simply to introduce discipline into the quest for spiritual growth. Ascetic practices did not end with the Middle Ages; and we have already seen that regular fasting is still expected of all members of the Eastern Orthodox churches. In the west Puritanism introduced its own forms of asceticism.[109] The Roman church has largely abandoned traditional requirements of fasting and abstinence, and most people immediately took advantage of the new laxity.[110] However religious orders and a small minority of laypeople have adopted levels of asceticism beyond what their persuasions require. The relaxation of church-mandated ascetic discipline has created new opportunities for self-discipline. People of all religions—or no religious affiliation—often fast for health or other reasons.

Self-mortification, to "subdue the flesh," is not entirely a thing of the past. The 20th-century mystic Padre Pio emphasized that the goal of self-mortification is to "make sure that it hurts."[111] Pope Paul VI was obviously inspired by his New Testament namesake when he wrote: "The necessity of the mortification of the flesh . . . stands clearly revealed if we consider the fragility of our nature, in which, since Adam's sin, flesh and spirit have contrasting desires."[112] He added that self-mortification "does not imply a condemnation of the flesh" but is aimed at the liberation from "concupiscence." Most modern proponents of self-mortification agree that the objective is to strengthen the will. Public flagellism persists in Guardia Sanframondi, Italy; the Philippines; and various parts of South America. Members of some religious orders, and even lay members of the Catholic prelature *Opus Dei*, are encouraged to use a scourge, often referred to as "the discipline," or the *cilice*, a spiked metal chain worn around the upper thigh.[113] To what extent such practices overlap with sadomasochism or with the behavioral condition known as self-injury is unclear.

A persuasive argument against extreme asceticism may be that it does nothing to alleviate the needs and suffering of humanity. Another argument is that it places the religious focus on a low physical level, far from where the Divine is likely to be encountered. In 1989 then-Cardinal Joseph Ratzinger warned that hatha yoga can lead to a "cult of the body."[114] He should have applied that characterization to self-mortification.

Reflections

After the disasters of the late-medieval and Renaissance periods, the papacy regained much of its moral standing. The most recent popes have been effective spiritual leaders, exercising a major influence on modern Christianity. They have sought to right a number of past wrongs involving the suppression of scientific advances and violence against other Christians and non-Christians. They have reached out to people of other persuasions to improve mutual understanding and promote dialog. On the other hand, the papacy remains more conservative than many people would prefer, and Vatican II's promise to usher in new openness has not been fulfilled. Perhaps the greatest potential lies at grassroots levels. Popular movements are displaying commendable independence and are leading the way to new expressions of Catholicism.

The Eastern Orthodox churches' destructive political entanglements are largely at an end. Although greater openness would be welcome, the insularity of the eastern churches has been lessened by the emigration of large numbers of people, including prominent scholars, to the west. Treasures of Orthodox Christianity, including rich liturgical and sacramental traditions, are now being shared with a new audience. Eastern Orthodoxy has the potential to play a major, worldwide role in the Christianity of the future. Meanwhile, major Protestant denominations have also broken free from political entanglements and are trying to adapt to modern environments. A major thrust has been toward denominational mergers, some of which have eroded traditional boundaries between Lutheran, Calvinist, and Reformed traditions.

Membership in the Catholic and mainstream Protestant denominations continues to decline, and it is not hard to see why. Religion depends for its success on a careful balance of conservatism and liberalism. A denomination's attractiveness is based not only on its overall position on the right-left spectrum but on where it stands on major issues. For example, people may react against outworn dogma and a repressive moral code but cherish a denomination's liturgy. Or they may be attracted to progressive social attitudes but are appalled at the abandonment of key Christian beliefs.

Facing mounting pressure to adapt to modern society, Catholic and Protestant churches have frequently made counterproductive choices. The Roman church preserved regressive gender and social policies and a doctrinal emphasis on sin, judgment and hell; but it abandoned rich liturgical traditions. Traditionalists complain, with some justification, that abandoning the Latin Mass did nothing to encourage popular devotion; instead it ushered in a period of decline in church attendance and a precipitous decline in seminary enrollment. Former monk John Dominic Crossan wryly observed that Vatican II "should have halved the dogma and doubled the chant."[115] Mainstream Lutheranism, Calvinism and Anglicanism, whose liturgy was already impoverished, embraced liberal theology and scriptural criticism to the point of abandoning a transcendent God, a divine Christ, and any sense of mystery. Esoteric, earth-centered, and Asian spiritual practices have found broad resonance in the general population and might be welcomed into Christianity; but suspicion of such practices remains high.

Traditionalist movements represent a broad-based reaction against those counterproductive choices. For example, liturgical restoration movements span multiple denominations. Elaborate ritual will never again be the sole format of Christian worship; nor should it. One of the reasons it went into decline was resistance, indifference, carelessness and embarrassment on the part of clergy and laity who were not drawn to the Path of Ceremony but were forced to participate. However Christianity can accommodate ceremony along with all other forms of worship within a legitimate framework of diversity. Where ceremony is revered, and where the necessary resources are available to perform it with the excellence it deserves, it can make a admirable contribution to the richness of Christianity. To many of us the magnificence of the Gothic cathedrals, the great works of sacred music—from Gregorian chant to John Rutter—and the centuries-old liturgy of east and west provide an essential pillar of Christianity and a true path to the Divine.

Another traditionalist response has been the new interest in religious orders. Many people are attracted to the religious life because of the service opportunities it provides. But the more ascetic, contemplative monastic orders continue to command attention.

Their ability to compete in the modern world is a tribute to the timeless appeal of the contemplative life. Growing understanding of the power of contemplation can insulate monasticism from cynical charges of narcissism and escapism. Anyone who questions the propriety of withdrawal from the world should refer to the Carthusian rule of Bruno of Cologne: "Separated from all, we are united to all."[116]

Perhaps the most significant conclusion from this chapter is the vitality of the various spiritual paths in mainstream Christianity. Marion Rebecca Hughes, Anne Ayres, Thérèse of Lisieux, the Padre Pio, and Thomas Merton all chose the Path of Renunciation; and that path has been strengthened further by the emergence of new religious orders and lay religious communities. The Path of Devotion is well-represented by the music, art and other forms of creative expression we have discussed. The Path of Ceremony has been strengthened greatly by the liturgical revival movements. The Path of Knowledge has been strengthened by the educational programs of the religious orders, by the émigré Russian Orthodox scholars, and by individuals like Teilhard de Chardin and Pope Benedict XVI. The Path of Service is well-represented by the millions of "soldiers" and volunteers in the Salvation Army as well as by volunteers in virtually every denomination. Popes Benedict XV and John XXIII, Patriarch Bartholomew of Constantinople, and Anglican archbishop of Cape Town Desmond Tutu[117] made notable contributions on the Path of Activism.

Revival of an active healing ministry in western Christianity confirms that the Path of Healing is "alive and well." Stimulus has come from several quarters, including the charismatic movement, esoteric Christianity, and the eastern churches. The two-millennium-long tradition of sacramental healing and centuries-old practices of pastoral counseling in Eastern Orthodoxy may prove to be the most important in the years to come. But further expansion of the healing ministry in mainstream western Christianity may be limited by liberal theology's reluctance to admit the reality of Jesus' "miracles." To deny the possibility of healing, whether by Jesus or anybody else, is to claim that we fully understand the laws of nature. Natural laws may well allow unusual events to occur under favorable circumstances, and our concern should be to try to discover how they work. From a larger perspective, instead of dismissing Christ's divinity, we should affirm and encourage the unfolding divinity of humanity.

[1.] Numerous conspiracy theories have emerged concerning the death of John Paul I. His death in 1978, according to the Vatican, was "possibly associated to a myocardial infarction;" however no autopsy was performed and his remains were embalmed the next day.

[2.] Diarmaid MacCullough. *The Reformation*. Penguin Books, 2003, p. 406.

3. Pius IX. "Syllabus of Errors." Appendix to encyclical: *Quanta Cura*. Vatican, December 8, 1864.

4. The other *Zelanti* pope was Gregory XVI (r.1831-1846).

5. First Vatican Council, Session IV, *Const. de Ecclesia Christi*, c. iv.

6. *Matthew* 16:19; 18:18.

7. Source: *Catholic Encyclopedia*. Robert Appleton, 1917/2005. Neither Marian doctrine had scriptural support.

8. See for example: John Macquarrie. *A Guide to the Sacraments*. Continuum, 1998, ch. 12.

9. Paul VI. Encyclical: *Mysterium Fidei*, §11. Vatican, September 1965.

10. Limbo had never been defined as dogma by an ecumenical council or papal pronouncement.

11. Matthew Fox. *Original Blessing*. Bear & Co., 1983

12. The other *Zelanti* pope was Leo XII (r.1823-1829).

13. Source: Pontifical Academy of Science, Rome.

14. Cardinal Paul Poupard. *Galileo: Report on Papal Commission Findings*. Pontifical Academy of Science. Vatican, 1992. See also: John Paul II. "Lessons of the Galileo Case." Address to the Pontifical Academy, October 31, 1992.

15. Pierre Teilhard de Chardin. *The Phenomenon of Man*. Book 1, Foreword. Harper, 1947, p. 36. Teilhard also proposed a new model of the evolution of human consciousness, anticipating by many years the Gaia theory, complexity theory, and perhaps even the Internet.

16. Pius XII. Encyclical: *Humani Generis*, 36. Vatican, 1950.

17. John Paul II. Address to the Pontifical Academy of Sciences. Vatican, October 22, 1996.

18. Benedict XVI. Address: "The Religion According to Reason." Vatican, April 1, 2005. The address was given the day before his predecessor John Paul II died.

19. Paul VI, *Humanae Vitae*.

20. John Paul II. Declaration: *Dominus Iesus*, IV:17. Vatican, August 2000.

21. See for example: Martin Mosebach. *The Heresy of Formlessness*. Ignatius Press, 2006.

22. Paul VI. Constitution on the Sacred Liturgy: *Sacrosanctum Concilium*, XXXVI:2. Vatican, December 1963.

23. Chad Ripperger. "The Spirituality of the Ancient Liturgy," Part 1. *Latin Mass*, Summer 2001.

24. Marcel LeFevre. Declaration, November 21, 1974.

25. In reaction to a 1548 royal decree prohibiting the Latin Mass, a rebellion began in Cornwall and spread throughout the southwest of England. The rebellion was crushed the following year.

26. In 1976, Domínguez was blinded in a car accident. Supporters claimed that he had received the stigmata; but in 1997 reportedly he confessed to sexual improprieties with priests and nuns.

27. Interestingly Domínguez' contemporary and rival, Pope John Paul II, also affirmed strong devotion to Mary.

28. Bernard J. Lee *et al*. *The Catholic Experience of Small Christian Communities*. Paulist Press, 2000.

29. *Ibid.*, pp. 10-11, 63-69, 74.

30. Hal Taussig. *A New Spiritual Home.* Poleridge Press, 2006, p. 91.

31. Russia had colonized Alaska but sold it to the United States in 1867. The sale was motivated in part by determination to halt British westward expansion from Canada.

32. See the discussion in Chapter 16.

33. A notorious pogrom in 1955, allegedly orchestrated by the Turkish government, resulted in numerous atrocities and the destruction of 90 percent of church property in Istanbul.

34. Only male pilgrims are permitted to visit Mount Athos. The church in Crete is also under the direct jurisdiction of Constantinople.

35. Florensky was executed by the NKVD. The date of his execution is disputed. Soviet authorities originally listed it as 1943, but more recent research indicates that he was shot in 1937.

36. Daniel Andreev. *Rose of the World.* Daniel Andreev Charity Foundation, 1997. Andreev was finally released after suffering a heart attack and died two years later. Remarkably he was able to conceal the manuscript of *Rose* from prison guards who would have confiscated and destroyed it.

37. The fellowship's work is endorsed by local Orthodox hierarchs and representatives of the Anglican and Catholic Churches.

38. Source: Fellowship of St Alban and St. Sergius.

39. Before his ordination, when he received the name Kallistos, Ware studied at the Monastery of St. John the Theologian in Patmos and also at Mount Athos. In 2007 he was given the status of titular metropolitan.

40. Timothy Ware relates that when he contacted a Greek Orthodox church the clergy was puzzled by his interest.

41. Conservative elements within Eastern Orthodoxy refer to ecumenism as the "heresy of heresies." They term other Christian denominations "heterodox."

42. The Church of Sweden remained the official state religion until 2000.

43. Source: Church of Sweden.

44. It should be noted that the term "Evangelical" incorporated into the names of Lutheran churches has a meaning distinct from that of "Evangelical Christianity" as it has been discussed in this book.

45. Source: Royal Danish Ministry of Foreign Affairs.

46. Mary Todd. "The Curious Case of the Missouri Synod." Richard Cimino (ed.). *Lutherans Today.* William Eerdmans, 2003, pp. 26-44.

47. The Norwegian-Danish Evangelical Lutheran Church of America became part of the United Norwegian Lutheran Church of America in 1890.

48. Newer immigrants, from Asia, South America and elsewhere, have been encouraged to form congregations that worship in their own languages. All mainstream denominations are doing likewise. However efforts to appeal to non-European ethnic groups have often involved the sacrifice of traditional Lutheran forms of worship in favor of alternative formats; one wonders, for example, what is achieved by imitating Pentecostal worship services.

49. Mark Granquist. "Word Alone and the Future of Lutheran Denominationalism." Cimino, *Lutherans Today*, pp. 62-80.

50. Despite mergers and schisms, the present PC(USA) is a direct descended of the earlier Presbyterian Church in the USA. The taxonomy of Presbyterian churches, often with closely similar names, is extremely complex.

51. United Church of Canada, 37th General Council, 2003.

52. Laud was condemned by the parliamentary faction not only for his rigid ecclesiastical policies but also for his support of Charles I, who was also beheaded.

53. The Anglican Church was disestablished in Ireland in 1871 and in Wales in 1914. The Church of Scotland was disestablished in 1921 but is recognized as the "national church."

54. The latter title was bestowed by Pope Leo X on Henry VIII; but it was retained even after the English church seceded from communion with Rome.

55. Michael Chandler. *An Introduction to the Oxford Movement*. Church Publishing, 2003, p. 3. Emancipation pressure built up because of the substantial increase in Catholic citizens following the union of England and Ireland in 1801.

56. Seabury (1729-1796) could not obtain consecration in the Church of England because the Oath of Supremacy prohibited the consecration of a non-citizen. The Scottish Episcopal Church, part of the Anglican Communion, seceded from the Church of Scotland in 1582, when the letter rejected the episcopal style of governance.

57. Borg was raised a Lutheran but later became active in the Episcopal Church and is married to an Episcopal priest.

58. The Liberal Catholic Church is case in point. It adopted the "liberal" title because of the doctrinal freedom it espoused, but it takes a strongly conservative position on liturgical issues.

59. Joseph Ratzinger. *Feast of Faith*. (Transl: G. Harrison.) Ignatius Press, 1981, p. 7.

60. David Tame. *The Secret Power of Music*. Destiny Books, 1984, p. 111.

61. Karl Barth. *Wolfgang Amadeus Mozart*. (Transl: C. Pott.) Eerdman's, 1956, p. 23.

62. John Rutter. *Eternal God*. Hinshaw Music.

63. Elisha A. Hoffman. "Are You Washed in the Blood?" *Spiritual Songs for Gospel Meetings and the Sunday School*. Barker & Smellie, 1878.

64. Castration as an ascetic practice was prohibited from 1870 onward.

65. See the discussion in: David E. Klemm. "Culture, Arts and Religion." *Cambridge Companion to Friedrich Schleiermacher*. Cambridge University Press, 2005, pp. 251-268.

66. Philip Schaff. *History of the Christian Church*, Revised Edition. Charles Scribner, 1910, vol. II, ch. 6, §76.

67. Ratzinger, *Feast of Faith*, pp. 124-125.

68. Apostolic Constitution. *Catechism of the Catholic Church*, Part III, 2502-2503, 1995.

69. The basilica, completed in 1989, is claimed to seat 18,000 people. The Lakewood Church, a converted basketball stadium, can seat 16,000 people and has parking for 8,000 vehicles.

70. Letter to Bishop Bagot. Quoted in: Chandler, *An Introduction to the Oxford Movement*, p. 48. Pusey contrasted the Church of England with churches that had been founded by Martin Luther, Ulrich Zwingli, and John Calvin.

71. From the reign of Charles I to the restoration under Charles II the Caroline Divines, a group of Anglican churchmen, worked to preserve traditional English religious

practices in the face of Puritan assault. Among other things they affirmed the real presence, the sacrament of penance, and the observance of fasts and religious festivals.

72. Great significance lay in the movement's emergence in Oxford, the bastion of mainstream Anglicanism.

73. Even before prosecution became a real threat, resistance from the Anglican establishment persuaded several members of the Oxford Movement, including Frederick Oakeley and Henry Newman, to defect to Rome. Oakely preached at St. Margaret's chapel in London and is best-known for translating the carol *Adeste Fideles* into English. Newman, one of the Movement's leaders, was later named a cardinal.

74. Chandler, *An Introduction to the Oxford Movement*, pp. 117-118.

75. St. Mary's Church was founded by Bishop Levi Silliman Ives.

76. Richard Cimino. "The Evangelical Catholics." *Lutherans Today*, pp. 81-101. This is an example of correlation between liturgical and social conservatism.

77. Charles W. Leadbeater. *The Science of the Sacraments.* Apocryphile Press, 1920/2000, p. 171. In liturgical matters the LCC is a very conservative denomination.

78. Source: The Liberal Catholic Church Worldwide.

79. Grape juice is typically preferred over wine because of Theosophy's insistence on abstinence

80. Leadbeater, *The Science of the Sacraments*, pp. 61, 75-86.

81. *Book of Common Prayer*. General Confession in the rite of Holy Communion, 1945.

82. For example, some branches of the LCC require clergy to be vegetarian and abstinent; belief in reincarnation may also be encouraged.

83. John Calvin. *Institutes of the Christian Religion*, book 4, ch. 19:18. (Transl: H. Beveridge.) Arnold Hatfield, 1599.

84. We might argue that it was better for people to face the facts of their hopeless conditions. On the other hand, positive attitudes have been shown to contribute to survival and recovery.

85. That viewpoint reflected the influence of 18th-century Deism.

86. "Demythologizing" the Bible was the special mission of Rudolf Bultmann.

87. *The Ministry of Healing*. Lambeth Conference of the Anglican Communion, 1924.

88. This order is not to be confused with the Methodist Order of St. Luke,

89. Source: International Order of St. Luke the Physician.

90. *The Church's Ministry in Healing*. Archbishops Council, 1958.

91. One of these was the New Life Healing Clinic founded in Baltimore, Maryland, in 1950 by Methodist minister Albert Day and spiritual healer Olga Worrall.

92. John Paul II. *Reconciliation and Penance*. Post-Synodal Apostolic Exhortation, Vatican, 1984.

93. Morton T. Kelsey. *Healing and Christianity*. Harper & Row, 1973, p. 242.

94. Congregation for the Doctrine of the Faith. "Instruction on Prayers for Healing." Vatican, September 2000.

95. *Ibid.*, p. 11.

96. In 1902 the Trappists took the name of the Order of Cistercians of the Strict Observance (OCSO).

97. Christopher Jamison. *Finding Sanctuary: Monastic Steps for Everyday Life*. Liturgical Press, 2006, p. 40.

98. Numerous doctors examined Padre Pio's stigmata, finding no physical cause. However the wounds completely healed on his deathbed, leaving no scars.

99. Thomas Merton. *The Seven Storey Mountain: an Autobiography of Faith*. Harcourt Brace, 1948, p. 462. Merton's master's thesis was concerned with the art of William Blake.

100. Source: Leadership Conference of Women Religious.

101. Currently their Internet address is www.praythenews.com.

102. Chandler, *An Introduction to the Oxford Movement*, p. 96.

103. George William Douglas. "Anne Ayres." *Project Canterbury: Essays in Appreciation*. Longmans Green, 1913. The sisterhood was formed with the support of Episcopal priest and philanthropist William Augustus Muhlenberg.

104. Bishop John Perry. *A Tine to Heal*. Church House Publishing, 2000, p. 70.

105. Source: Order of St. Luke.

106. Source: Salvation Army, 2005.

107. Although not ostensibly religious, some communities have an environmental focus and seek to develop sustainable patterns of living. They are sometimes referred to as *ecovillages*.

108. See for example: C. McLaughlin & G. Davidson. *Builders of the Dawn: Community Lifestyles in a Changing World*. Book Publishing Company, 1990.

109. The Puritans viewed any kind of pleasure or self-indulgence with suspicion; and many of their tenets have passed into modern culture, for example: "No pain, no gain."

110. Members of denominations, like Catholicism, that demand a high level of obedience usually comply with mandated ascetic practices. But they feel no personal obligation to maintain the practices once rules are relaxed. Official rules create both a minimum and a maximum level of asceticism.

111. Padre Pio. *Correspondence with Raffaelina Cerase, Noblewoman*. Letter 291914. (Transl: G. Di Flumeri.) San Giovanni Rotondo, Italy.

112. Paul VI. *Apostolic Constitution on Penance*, ch. 2, 47-50. Vatican, 1966.

113. Source: Information Office, Opus Dei USA. This influential lay organization was founded in 1928 by a 26-year-old Spanish priest named Josemaría Escrivá. Dan Brown's *The Da Vinci Code* no doubt exaggerated the solidarity's ascetic practices; but it did not invent them.

114. Joseph Ratzinger. "Letter to the Bishops of the Catholic Church on Some Aspects of Christian Meditation." Congregation for the Doctrine of the Faith, December 14, 1989. The letter was approved by Pope John Paul II.

115. John D. Crossan. *A Long Way from Tipperary*. HarperCollins, 2000, p. 58.

116. Carthusian Rule, Statute 34.2.

117. Archbishop Tutu of the Anglican Church of South Africa not only worked to end apartheid and bring about racial reconciliation, he is also engaged in the global campaign against AIDS. He received the Nobel Peace Prize in 1984, the Albert Schweitzer Prize for Humanitarianism, and the Gandhi Peace Prize.

Part VI
The Future of Christianity

The Christian: we must be agreed that we do not mean *the Christians*, not the multitude of the baptized . . . nor even the cream of the noblest and most devoted Christians we might think on: the Christian is *the Christ*. The Christian is that within us which is not ourselves but Christ in us . . . And "Christ in us" understood in its whole Pauline breadth is a warning that we shall do well not to build again the fence which separated the chosen from the rest—Jews from Gentiles and so-called Christians from so-called non-Christians. The community of Christ is a building open on every side . . . There is, in us, over us, behind us, and beyond us a consciousness of the meaning of life, a memory of our own origin, a turning to the Lord of the universe, a critical No and a creative Yes in regard to all the content of our thought, a facing away from the old and toward the new age—whose sign and fulfillment is the cross.

Karl Barth. "The Christian's Place in Society."
Address to the Conference on Religion and Social Relations,
Tambach, Germany, September 1919.[1]

Chapter 21
The Ekklesia

What is Christianity?

In the Introduction to Volume 1 we posed the questions *What is Christianity?* and *Who is a Christian?* By now it should be clear that there are no easy answers. Christianity is a complex web of interacting traditions, each expressing the message of Jesus Christ according to its own doctrinal, liturgical and cultural assumptions. Similarly, Christians exhibit a broad spectrum of beliefs, religious practices and attitudes and perhaps as much variation in outward behavior. Our goal has been to find the *real* Christianity and the *real* Christian; and now we must pull together what has been learned.

Jesus Christ, to the extent that we know anything about him, never presented himself as anything but a Jew; and, although he may have inspired many people, he never founded a religion. The ecclesiastical structures, clergy, ordinances, liturgies, cultic symbols and images that we call Christianity were human creations. They emerged from people's experiences of Jesus; the awe they felt in his presence: physical or otherwise; the conviction that he was divine; the urge to emulate his life and testify to his message. Different forms of Christianity arose because people had different experiences. Christianity became pluralistic and remained so throughout its 2,000-year history. Pluralism will be explored more fully in the next chapter in the context of the seven spiritual paths. This chapter acknowledges diversity but emphasis is placed on its accommodation within a unified Christianity.

The present chapter explores the vision of the archetypal unity, the Ekklesia, that transcends all experiences, religious forms, and paths. We shall try to reconcile this archetype with what we know of Christianity, as it has manifested in history, and reflect on how it could manifest in more perfect form in the future. The discussion is not entirely theoretical; we shall address some very practical issues relating to the expression of the Ekklesia in the world.

The Mystical Church

Jesus Christ served as the channel through which a great surge of light, love and life flowed into the world. That impulse created the archetype that we have termed the *Ekklesia* (Greek: Εκκλησια). In classical Greece "ekklesia" referred to an assembly of citizens or soldiers, summoned for civic purpose by a herald or crier.[2] Its Hebrew equivalent: *qahal* (קָהָל) had greater religious significance, denoting "congregation," as in the "assembly of the congregation of Israel" which Moses led from bondage in Egypt.[3] The concept of the Ekklesia, as we use the term in this book, gained strength in Christian writings. It is the "Kingdom of God," which Jesus proclaimed 90 times in the synoptic gospels alone.[4] Jesus was surely referring to the unity of the Ekklesia when he said of the apostles: [T]hey all may be one; as thou, Father, art in me, and I in thee."[5] Paul surely referred to the Ekklesia when he affirmed: "There is one body, and one Spirit . . . One Lord, one faith, one baptism, One God and Father of all, who is above all, and through all, and in you all.[6] Ignatius of Antioch surely had the Ekklesia in mind when he spoke of the "universal catholic church,"[7] a church that was not restricted to a particular ethnic or social group, or to a particular region of the world, but was to reach out to all nations.

The archetypal Ekklesia lies beyond space and time. The *Shepherd of Hermas* referred to "The Church . . . created before all things."[8] The *Second Epistle of Clement* described "the first Church, which is spiritual, which was created before the sun and the moon;"[9] it also provided an early reference to the Ekklesia as both the Body and the Bride of Christ: "[T]he living Church is the body of Christ: for the scripture saith, God made man, male and female. The male is Christ and the female is the Church . . . Now the Church, being spiritual was manifested in the flesh of Christ."[10] *Eugnostos the Blessed* described the "Assembly of the Holy Ones, the Shadowless Lights," adding: "when these [Holy Ones] greet each other, their embraces become angels like themselves."[11]

Eastern Orthodox theologians identified the Ekklesia with Sophia, eternal bride of the Logos, present "from everlasting, from the beginning, or ever the earth was."[12] The Gnostics and other regarded the Ekklesia/Sophia and the Logos as complementary feminine and masculine aspects of a higher divine reality.[13] This Ekklesia is not the Christianity we know, the imperfect church struggling through history, but the *Church*: a perfect Platonic Form. Russian theologian and scientist Pavel Florensky (1882-1937) contrasted the Mystical Church, "the unifying, preexistent, heavenly, mystical form," with the "historical church." He recognized that the latter has never measured up to the heavenly form but could come closer if sectarian divisions were healed. Florensky urged the disparate denominations to come together to be "deified and eternalized in the unifying form."[14] Here we see not only his ecumenical ideals but, more importantly, the notion of deification, or *theosis*, which in Orthodox teaching is the goal of human spiritual development.

Russian Orthodox priest Sergei Bulgakov (1871-1944) also invoked the notion of theosis, but he stressed the Sophianic role: "The Church in the world is Sophia in process of becoming, according to the double impulse of creation and deification." He added: "The Church is . . . not only the body of Christ, but also the temple of the Holy Ghost . . . [T]he conjoint revelation of the Son and the Spirit in the Church . . . is effected by the twofold mission of the two divine persons from the Father to the world. This is what makes the Church the revelation, in terms of created Wisdom, of the divine."[15] A near-contemporary of Bulgakov, the Russian poet and visionary Daniel Andreev (1906-1959), preserved the ecumenical dream. The world's religions, he wrote, "will be transformed from a collage of separate petals into one single, whole spiritual flower the Rose of the World."[16]

"Ecumenism" is derived from the Greek *oikoumene* (οικουμενη) which originally referred to the inhabited world; a related word was *oikema* (οικημα) which meant a house. Accordingly we could view the ecumenical movement as the attempt to bring all Christians under the same roof. But Russian Orthodox writers offer a more beautiful image of the mystical unity or catholicity of the church. The term *sobornost* (Russian: соборность) was coined by writers of the slavophil school, notably Ivan Kireevsky (1806-1856) and his contemporary Aleksey Khomyakov.[17] Its original intent was to emphasize that Russian Christians worshiped in unison rather than as individuals. *Sobornost* is often translated as "unity," "togetherness" or "brotherhood." But its root is *sobor* (собор, "gathering" or "cathedral"), and a better sense of sobornost is gained by visualizing the faithful gathered together under the soaring dome of a vast sacred space.[18] Esoteric students will immediately recognize sobornost as an expression of group consciousness. The Ekklesia is the invisible "House" or "Cathedral" where all Christians can share a sacred experience.

Where can we find the Ekklesia? Certainly not in a corporate entity, a denomination, or any kind of human creation. The Ekklesia transcends all religious institutions. Russian theologian Vladimir Lossky asserted that it "is not of this world, though . . . it exists in the world and for the world."[19] The Mystical Church descended into manifestation when the Logos was made flesh and will remain in manifestation for as long as the Logos remains in mystical union with humanity. Christ entrusted his mission not to the separative Christian churches but to the Ekklesia. He sustains the Ekklesia through the ages. The Holy Spirit descended on the Ekklesia at Pentecost; the Ekklesia received and serves as custodian of the ageless wisdom. It is the soul—or perhaps we should say, with Ralph Waldo Emerson, the *oversoul*—that lies above and beyond all things aligned with the Christ. In everything Christian, the Ekklesia is the origin of life, the source of distinctive identity, and the driving force behind spiritual growth and the expansion of consciousness.[20]

The Ekklesia manifests, albeit partially, in all who open themselves up to *theosis*: all who allow the life, love and light of Christ to flow through them—and contribute thereby to the deification of humanity. We witness the Ekklesia in the lives of the great saints, martyrs, mystics, teachers and healers. Its power flowed through Hildegard of Bingen, Francis of Assisi, Julian of Norwich, Thomas Aquinas, Meister Eckhart, Sergius of Radonezh, Nilus of Sora, John and Charles Wesley, William and Catherine Booth, the Abbé Pierre, and Mother Theresa. The power flowed through Michelangelo, Giovanni da Palestrina, Chiara Margarita Cozzolani, Johann Sebastian Bach, Wolfgang Amadeus Mozart, William Shakespeare, William Wordsworth, Blaise Pascal, and Isaac Newton. Perhaps it flowed through Jakob Böhme, Pavel Florensky, Edgar Cayce, Albert Schweitzer, Geoffrey Hodson, Martin Luther King, Jr., John Rutter, John Lennon, and Billy Graham. We all have our heroes and heroines, our own criteria for canonization.

The Ekklesia can manifest individually and collectively in all who reach out selflessly to others. We affirm that it can also manifest in "people who have other names for the way to God's realm."[21] If the Ekklesia extends back to "the beginning," then presumably it manifested in the great figures of the Axial Age: Isaiah, Jeremiah, Plato, Confucius, Lao Tzu, and the Buddha. Mahayana Buddhism—which came into existence around the time of Christ—expressed "Christian" virtues to a particularly high degree. Moving to our own time, who would disagree that the Mahatma Gandhi and the Dalai Lama have expressed the values of Christ? The Ekklesia manifested in the countless millions whose names were never recorded but who overcame self-interest, served humanity, raised the vibration of their environments, and praised God. Did not Jesus Christ come to earth for them as much as for bishops, reformers and evangelists?

The Ekklesia is the communion of the faithful, infused by the love of the Christ and unified by the authentic response to his message. It is the communion united in love of neighbor, seeking the best for humanity and the planet, demonstrating the progression of all life toward its glorious destiny. The Ekklesia is the communion into which spiritual energy has been invested through the ages by ordinary people as well as by the Christ and the great saints. The real future of Christianity lies in this mystical communion; through this communion Christ's mission will not only continue but will be taken to a new level.

As a perfect archetype the Ekklesia is forever unified; only its imperfect manifestations in history have been divided and set against one another. As Florensky noted, the archetype could be brought into more complete manifestation by the reunification of Christianity; and the modern ecumenical movement has done much to accomplish that goal. But ecumenism must never be confused with the creation of homogeneous sameness, like the medieval church. Separateness must be overcome, walls must come down; but standardization according, to the narrow visions of bishops, synods, or heads of state churches is an affront to the richness of the Ekklesia.

The Ekklesia's manifestations in the world will always exhibit natural variations. Diversity among Christians, and differences between Christianity and other world traditions which may have been touched by the same divine impulse, should be accepted, honored, and rejoiced over. All sincere seekers who express love and compassion must be accepted into the Christian communion. Christ spoke and continues to speak to them. Episcopal bishop John Shelby Spong asserted that Christ can no longer be considered the exclusive property of a particular tradition or even of Christianity as a whole; rather, Christ will say "Come unto me and discover the infinite dimensions of transcendent wonder" within each human being.[22]

The Historical Church

Much of this book has been devoted to what Florensky called the "historical church." The historical church is the shadow of the Ekklesia on the cave wall of human affairs. Like any manifestation of a higher archetype it is imperfect; but important lessons have been learned, and it has grown in perfection. We have not glossed over the church's failures in our survey, but neither have we ignored its achievements. Christianity has been a remarkable endeavor, surpassing in its accomplishments and durability any comparable human endeavor.

Institutional Christianity saw Jesus Christ as the redeemer, the sacrificial lamb willingly accepting the cross to save humanity from spiritual death. It set out to create a new religion, not pertaining to an ethnic group or seeking a "homeland," but one of global relevance. The institutional church created an environment in which countless people worshipped, received the sacraments, were encouraged to lead moral lives and promised eternal reward in heaven. The church offered the ministry for men—and in a very few cases women—to serve the faithful in the world. It offered the monastic system to women and men who aspired to higher levels of spiritually in isolation from the world. The monasteries of east and west gave us many great saints and most of the greatest Christian mystics.

Institutional Christianity created a heritage of great architecture, art and music. It stimulated learning through works of the church fathers, the Carolinian schools, the great universities of medieval Europe; scholasticism, the Renaissance, and humanism. Liberal Protestants and most recently Benedict XVI acknowledged that it gave us the Enlightenment. Long before secular welfare systems were established the church cared for the sick, fed the hungry, "clothed the naked," and sheltered the homeless. The institutional church provided outstanding leaders whose authority and spiritual stature are recognized even beyond Christianity. At the same time the church demanded obedience and loyalty from its members, much as Yahweh did from the Israelites; church doctrine was absolute and its moral law disobeyed only at terrible cost.

Eastern Orthodoxy, Catholicism and Protestantism, all the many churches, denominations and sects, brought their understanding of Christ's message to the people. They exhibited strengths and weaknesses according to their inherent soundness and their leaders' wisdom, sincerity and responsiveness. At the same time the humanness of the historical church was revealed in its paradoxes; while teaching unity, universal values, peace and holiness, Christianity too often descended into sectarianism, conflict and corruption.[23] The major fragmentation that occurred between the 11th and the 17th centuries led to endless bickering, competitive claims, and in a few instances outright war. Now, faced with a myriad of modern challenges and lacking the secular support of earlier times, mainstream Christianity is declining in power; Chapter 20 examined some of the reasons why.

On the other hand, we must be cautious in equating "Christianity" to the institutional church of the Middle Ages or collectively to the denominations of modern times.[24] Whatever church leaders might prefer to think, institutional Christianity's rise to power was not predestined, and the forms it took were largely fortuitous; at many pivotal points in history the dice could have rolled a different way. How might Christianity have developed if

- the early church had chosen James the brother of Jesus or Mary Magdalene, "apostle to the apostles," to be its leader instead of Peter
- the Gnostic Valentinus had become pope
- John Nestorius—or later, his nemesis Cyril of Alexandria—had won their respective theological arguments
- Pope Leo IX and Patriarch Michael Cerularius had settled their differences
- Martin Luther had died on the way to class at the University of Erfut
- the Spanish Armada had succeeded, or King James I of England had supported the Elector Palatine Frederick V at the outbreak of the Thirty Years' War
- Boston preacher Jonathan Edwards had become the spiritual father of the American Revolution, rather than the Deists Thomas Paine and Thomas Jefferson?

Would Christ's essential teachings have been communicated more or less successfully if one or more of those contingencies had actualized? What indeed are the criteria of success? Must a religion or a denomination have mass appeal in order to claim legitimacy? Is a form of Christianity that appeals to a handful of people and wields no political power necessarily less valid than one with millions of members, capable of intimidating emperors or voters? In every era small groups—even individuals—left indelible imprints on Christianity and contributed to its richness; perhaps that is even truer today. The Ekklesia lives on, expressed through large and small groups and individuals of extraordinary ability. Christianity's greatest days may lie ahead.

Ecumenical Movement

Pavel Florensky observed that healing the sectarian divisions in Christianity could create a more perfect manifestation of the archetypal Ekklesia. A number of ecumenical initiatives had already been taken when he made that observation, and the process has accelerated since then. In earlier chapters we mentioned the meeting in Florence in the late 1430s to try to heal the Great Schism. We discussed the famous meeting in 1529 between Martin Luther and Ulrich Zwingli, and the efforts of moderate Protestants and Catholics to bridge the Reformation divide. A century later the Czech scholar Jan Comenius (1592-1670) and the Hussite *Unitas Fratrum* also promoted Christian unity.[25] King Friedrich Wilhelm III of Prussia (r.1797-1840) pressed for union of the Lutheran and Reformed branches of German Protestantism, and Friedrich Schleiermacher's *The Christian Faith* (1822) offered a theological basis for a united Prussian church.[26]

Interest in reuniting the Catholic and Eastern Orthodox churches grew in the 19th century, but the First Vatican Council's proclamation of papal infallibility stiffened Orthodox resistance. Undeterred, the Russian mystic Vladimir Solovyov continued to pursue rapprochement; with a letter of introduction from the Catholic bishop from Croatia, he sought to meet with Pope Leo XIII in 1888. Even though the meeting never took place, Solovyov was accused of converting to Roman Catholicism. In his last poem he reflected that "blissful dreams of all too short duration suddenly dissolve."[27] Daniel Andreev looked forward to an "Eighth Ecumenical Council" which could reexamine "the entire mass of old doctrines and [embrace] a number of beliefs based on the spiritual experience of the last one thousand years."[28] Karl Barth, critical as he was of Schleiermacher on other issues, continually urged the reunion of Christianity, which he said must begin separately within the Protestant churches before there could be hope for a larger synthesis.

The ecumenical dream long remained unfulfilled because the will was not there to act on it. The 16th-century Lord Burghley's comment still summed up prevailing attitudes: "[T]hat state could never be in safety, where there was toleration of two religions."[29] When James Gibbons, archbishop of Baltimore, led the 1893 Parliament of World Religions in Chicago in the Lord's Prayer, he and other Catholic leaders were reprimanded by Leo XIII for participating in a "promiscuous" assembly.[30] Leo followed up with censure of "Americanism," which included religious tolerance.[31] The identification of religious tolerance with America may have had some merit; even before 1800, Lutheran leaders were concerned about the impact of American attitudes on the purity of the religion they had brought from Europe.[32] The Anglican archbishop of Canterbury turned down an invitation to participate in the Chicago parliament.

Defensiveness among the major branches of Christianity remained the norm until early in the 20th century. Each denomination claimed to be the only legitimate representative of Jesus Christ. Finally a few Protestant denominations began to reach out to one another. The Edinburgh Missionary Conference was convened in June 1910 to explore the potential for joint missionary activity; almost as an afterthought it also provided opportunities for ongoing dialog. Subsequent contacts led in 1948 to formation of the World Council of Churches where Christian denominations could discuss common concerns and affirm common aspirations.[33] By 2005 the WCC had 347 member churches in 120 countries.[34] Although the Church of Rome never joined[35] and some other denominations have been less-than-full participants, the WCC has become an important corporate voice for Christianity in the world. Numerous organizations have been created in attempts to improve relations between specific denominations or denominational groups. The Fellowship of St. Alban and St. Sergius, committed to improving understanding between Eastern Orthodox and western Christians, has already been mentioned.[36]

In some cases ecumenical contacts have led to denominational mergers, and notable examples were discussed in Chapter 20. Mergers normally require substantial unanimity on beliefs and practices; but the United Church of Christ, founded in 1957, was an important exception. It was formed from the union of the Evangelical and Reformed Church and the Congregational Christian Churches, each of which had resulted from previous successful mergers. The UCC affirmed that diversity among and within member congregations could be accommodated within an overall framework of loyalty to core Protestant principles; it invited all Christians to testify to their faith but imposed no creed as a criterion of membership. The UCC's diversity was possible because of its characteristic doctrinal, liturgical and social liberalism; more conservative denominations might not tolerate a comparable level of internal pluralism. Potential mergers can cause dissent within denominations. Hardliners may oppose dialog or derail possible mergers. Influential members or congregations may develop strong links with other denominations, only to be denounced by their own leaders. On the other hand, what passes for ecumenical contact sometimes has a hidden agenda;

Evangelical and Catholic fundamentalists have built political alliances, though they have little interest in exploring commonality of faith.

A less ambitious, but possibly more successful, alternative has been the establishment of "full communion" with denominational neighbors. Full communion acknowledges distinctions but affirms agreement on major doctrines and recognition of each other's sacraments; it also opens the door to the exchange of clergy. One of the earliest accords of this nature was the 1931 Bonn Agreement between the Anglican Communion and the Old Catholic Church. More recently the Anglican Communion has established full communion with the Mar Thomas Syrian Church of India and the Philippine Independent Church. Ecumenical contacts have also been made with Lutheran, Orthodox, Catholic, and other denominations. In 1999-2000 the Evangelical Lutheran Church in America and the American Episcopal Church agreed on full communion; and since then communion has been extended to the Presbyterian Church USA, the United Church of Christ, the Reformed Church in America, and the Moravian Church in America. The United Methodist Church has established full communion with the African Methodist Episcopal Church, the African Methodist Episcopal Zion Church, and the Christian Methodist Episcopal Church. Further accords are expected within the next few years.

From a position of rigidity, the Church of Rome has taken its own steps toward ecumenism; the Second Vatican Council was an important turning-point. In 1965 the council agreed that "the heritage handed down by the apostles was received with differences of form and manner, so that from the earliest times of the Church it was explained variously in different places, owing to diversities of genius and conditions of life."[37] In place of the defensive attitudes of the Counter-Reformation, the council urged Catholics: "to avoid expressions, judgments and actions which do not represent the condition of our separated brethren with truth and fairness."[38] It went on to urge dialog among "different Churches and Communities," which could prepare the way "for cooperation between them in the duties for the common good of humanity which are demanded by every Christian conscience; and, wherever this is allowed, there is prayer in common. [Furthermore], all are led to examine their own faithfulness to Christ's will for the Church and accordingly to undertake with vigor the task of renewal and reform."[39]

The Church of Rome has full communion with eastern-rite churches, including the Coptic Catholic Church, the Maronite Church, and the Syro-Malankara Catholic Church of India. Rome considers itself in "partial communion" with the Oriental Orthodox and Eastern Orthodox churches. In 2004, the 800th anniversary of the Fourth Crusade, Pope John Paul II apologized to the patriarch of Constantinople for the atrocities committed by western armies. Rome has also negotiated agreements on specific issues. For example, in 1999 representatives of the Catholic Church and the Lutheran World Federation signed the *Joint Declaration on the Doctrine of Justification*, resolving misunderstandings over the doctrine of justification by faith.[40] In 2006 members of the World Methodist Council endorsed the same declaration.

The Eastern Orthodox churches are in full communion with one another; but generally they have been reluctant to engage in ecumenical dialog with other denominations on any terms other than acceptance of the "fullness of truth." Writing in the 1960s Timothy Ware, the future Metropolitan Kallistos, explained the implications of this condition: "Orthodoxy insists upon unity in matters of faith. Before there can be reunion among Christians there must be first be full agreement in faith . . . Orthodox are not willing to take part in a 'minimal' reunion scheme, which secures agreement on a few points and leaves everything else up to private judgement."[41] The Russian Orthodox Church was lukewarm toward possible union with the Anglican Communion, citing the latter's "pluralism" of beliefs and ordination of women.[42] Several Eastern Orthodox churches have withdrawn from the World Council of Churches despite efforts to increase Orthodoxy's voice and recognize its unique heritage.[43]

Dismantling Barriers

Organizational mergers and agreements on full or partial communion are commendable, but they represent just one step toward a more perfect manifestation of the Ekklesia on earth. Other necessary steps are improving attitudes to diversity, building a pervasive sense of acceptance of people of other persuasions, and encouraging a sense of belonging to a larger Christian corpus that spans denominational boundaries. Commitment is needed not just by denominational leaders but by rank-and-file Christians. The unification of Christianity requires active engagement, love of people because they too are made in the image and likeness of God, acceptance of some measure of diversity, and a willingness to compromise on inessentials in order to achieve larger goals.

The early 21st century offers a unique opportunity to further the cause of religious tolerance and to end the sectarian hostility, persecution and violence that have disgraced the historical church for 2,000 years. Inter-denominational relations and mutual understanding are better than they have ever been; Christians are learning not just to tolerate but to accept one another. Distinctions among mainstream Protestant denominations have progressively eroded. A century ago, being a Methodist rather than a Presbyterian or an Anglican was perceived as critically important. Denominations were distinguished not only by beliefs and practices but by ethnicity, family loyalty, or social class. Today those distinctions have largely disappeared; for example, Methodists have become more intellectual and Presbyterians more experiential in religious expression. A casual visitor to a worship service might be hard-put to identify the church's denominational affiliation. Mainstream Protestantism has arrived at an unexpected—and perhaps unintended—uniformity.

In increasingly pluralistic societies and a shrinking world, Christians are being forced to confront attitudes not only to one another but toward Judaism, Islam, Hinduism, Buddhism, and other religions. Official attitudes vary widely among Protestant denominations, but there have been some encouraging signs of greater understanding. The Evangelical Lutheran Church in America issued a declaration in 1993 repudiating Martin Luther's anti-Semitism and acknowledging that: "In the long history of Christianity there exists no more tragic development than the treatment accorded the Jewish people on the part of Christian believers." It added: "Grieving the complicity of our own tradition within this history of hatred, moreover, we express our urgent desire to live out our faith in Jesus Christ with love and respect for the Jewish people."[44] The Catholic Church has also reached out to other world religions. In 2000 John Paul II apologized to the Jewish people for atrocities committed against them in the name of Christianity;[45] he also made determined efforts to reach out to Muslims. United Religions Initiative, founded in 2000, actively encourages dialog among world religions. Its charter urged "respect [for] the sacred wisdom of each religion, spiritual expression and indigenous tradition" and commits members "to promote enduring, daily interfaith cooperation, to end religiously motivated violence and to create cultures of peace, justice and healing for the Earth and all living beings."[46] Understanding, mutual respect, and overcoming attitudes of superiority can do much to bridge age-old divisions and hostilities.

Christianity has long faced the question of reconciling faith with tolerance. The conviction that one's own beliefs are right seems automatically to imply that contrasting beliefs must be wrong. To concede that another's beliefs might possibly be true—even "for that person"—is tantamount to denying one's own faith; any suggestion of relative truth is a dangerous form of "modernism." The result has been contempt, condemnation, and resolve to stop others from promulgating "false" teachings; the mortal fear of every religious zealot is that competitors will win converts. The paradox of faith and tolerance cannot be resolved by intellect, still less by emotion. The paradox is actually spurious. The equation of faith with belief in doctrinal formulations was a late perversion of its meaning; "faith" (Greek: *pistis*, πιστις), as it appeared in the New Testament, meant *trust*. Christian faith should be trust in the redemptive power of Christ and the infinite potential of redeemed humanity. Its most important products are love and wisdom.

We are reminded of the words of the 15th-century French theologian Sebastian Castellio: "Let us who are Christians not condemn one another, but, if we are wiser than they are, let us also be better and more merciful."[47]

Debating issues of doctrine is unlikely to encourage a sense of Christian unity; its very nature is to draw attention to differences. Attention must be focused on what we all share. Joint worship offers considerable potential, but certain forms of worship work better than others. For example, interdenominational prayer has been proposed as a way to bring people together, but the results have often been disappointing. A commission of the World Council of Churches had to admit: "Praying together has also revealed many of the challenges along the way towards unity. This is in part because of confessional and cultural backgrounds leading churches to worship in different ways . . . Indeed, it is in common prayer that the pain of Christian division is most acutely experienced."[48] The creation of a meaningful prayer liturgy, free from a separative doctrinal substrate, still eludes us. Nonverbal forms of worship should be explored. Collective silent meditation would offer obvious advantages, and the unifying power of sacred music and the arts was discussed in Chapter 8. The greatest potential for encouraging a sense of Christian unity lies in interdenominational service projects; to focus on the needs of others affirms our collective humanity and distracts attention from what may divide us.

A valuable object lesson was provided by the famous meetings in 1968 between the Dalai Lama and Trappist monk Thomas Merton. They met in a spirit of mutual respect, focusing not on doctrine but on the mystical insights each had gained during decades of meditation. In the inner knowingness that came from the contemplative life they found an unexpected degree of commonality and understanding of each other's faith. The Dalai Lama praised Merton as having a more profound understanding of Buddhism than any other Christian he had known.

Where love and wisdom prevail, people of strong faith can come together in a spirit of joyful sharing instead of confrontation. We begin to appreciate what others believe, why they believe it, and what it means to them. Doctrinal and other differences can either be set aside to explore what is held in common; or they can become springboards to new insights and to a larger synthesis of ideas. Tolerance ceases even to be an issue when we affirm our place and theirs in the family of humanity, accepting their limitations as they accept ours. We find ourselves worshipping together in the cathedral of the Ekklesia.

The New Face of Christianity

The Ekklesia is envisioned as an eternal reality embracing people in every nation and on every continent; but its expressions on the plane of human affairs have changed from place to place and from one era to the next. Important changes were set in motion by the Great Schism, the Reformation, and the emergence of Evangelical Christianity. Further changes are taking place now, putting a new face on Christianity. While we are mindful of the Mystical Church's timeless perfection, we need to explore the implications of those changes in the historical church.

Religious Options

In the past, religion was tightly regulated, and denominations often held monopolies in the countries in which they operated. At best, a few powerful denominations divided up the religious "market" in an oligopoly.[49] Now the situation is very different. In an age of "deregulation" and a shrinking market for formal religion, denominations and congregations are forced to compete against one another, promoting themselves like business enterprises; even Catholicism has resorted to newspaper advertising. Some churches have offered monetary or other incentives to first-time visitors in hope of boosting pledging membership. Similarly, Christianity is forced to compete against other world religions, even in traditionally Christian countries. The religious marketplace is now approaching what economists call perfect competition. We enjoy religious options that would have been unimaginable a few generations ago. We can choose a traditional form of Christianity, an innovative form, some other religion, or no religion at all with a freedom that Søren Kierkegaard would have envied. Religious choices can be made almost as freely as we choose a telephone company.

Loyalty to traditional religious practices is declining. The United States has one of the highest rates of church attendance in the world: nearly one-half of the population attends church at least once per month.[50] In many parts of Europe, by contrast, baptisms, marriages and funerals may be the only time people go to church.[51] Europe's religious indifference is often blamed on long-standing resentment against powerful established churches. But that may not be the only factor; church attendance in Mexico is relatively high despite a history of anticlericalism. Even in countries where church attendance remains high, not all is well for organized religion. Large segments of the population feel that Christianity has failed in its mission or has become irrelevant to modern life. Institutional Christianity has lost its power to coerce and in some instances even to inspire.

A tradition that is fast disappearing is the notion of the "parish church" serving a local geographical area. Even in moderate-sized cities, people have access to churches of various persuasions or offering different types of experience. People may drive considerable distances to attend a church of their choice rather than patronizing one, even in the same denomination, closer to home. They are drawn to a preacher, a music program, a religious culture, or a community of shared values. Alternatively, people can "participate" in religious services carried by the broadcast media without ever leaving home. Lifelong allegiance to a denomination is becoming a thing of the past. People leave their childhood denomination for a wide variety of reasons; some are even forced to leave.[52] Growing numbers of people identify themselves as Christian but do not belong to specific denominations. For creedal or other reasons, they may resist formal membership but actively participate in the life of a congregation and support it financially; or they may distance themselves from organized religion altogether.

Christians may participate in the lives of more than one denomination or congregation. The practice is common in multi-faith families, but it also occurs more generally. People belong to a congregation "while selectively adopting spiritual practices from other traditions."[53] They may attend midnight Liturgy at a Russian Orthodox church one week and then participate the following week in a praise service or a new-age gathering. Attendance at a worship service should never be treated like a night at the movies; visitors must exercise sensitivity to customs and respect applicable restrictions; for example, liturgically conservative churches may restrict access to their sacraments. Visitors must also behave responsibly; churches cannot be expected to provide drop-ins with free entertainment; they need resources, and not just financial ones, to function. But to experience a variety of religious formats can nourish spiritual growth. Thankfully "participating in the services of false religions"—meaning other Christian denominations—is no longer considered idolatrous.

Decentralization

Christianity's earliest organizational forms were very simple. The communities of the first century were forced to operate unobtrusively, often in secrecy. They were local and autonomous; and although members shared an evolving faith, there may have been little sense of belonging to a larger religious entity. By the fourth century the situation was very different. A cohesive organizational structure had emerged, modeled on the Roman Empire and emulating its centralized authority. By the Middle Ages that structure had evolved into a tall hierarchy in which vast spiritual and temporal power was concentrated in popes, patriarchs, and bishops. Ecclesiastical power has eroded significantly since the Reformation, but the Catholic, Orthodox, Lutheran, Anglican and Methodist churches retain traditional hierarchical forms.

Large Christian denominations have always wielded considerable influence, and with millions of members they also have substantial resources at their disposal. Where power is concentrated in few hands, decisions on how to use those resources can be made very efficiently. Smaller, or more democratic, institutions could not have molded western civilization as did the medieval church, or even the major post-Reformation churches. They could not have built the Gothic cathedrals or provided the environment in which Johann Sebastian Bach composed his *B Minor Mass* or Michelangelo painted the ceiling of the Sistine Chapel. Certainly there have been similar concentrations of wealth in the royal courts of Europe, in government cultural agencies, and in the hands of successful industrialists. But it is questionable whether any of them could have funded, still less inspired, the large-scale works of Christian artistic heritage. Not even the largest denominations today have the resources of the medieval or Renaissance church; but size is still a significant factor, and it is too early to write off major denominations as a thing of the past or underestimate what they can offer modern Christianity.

The political and social power of large denominations is still apparent today. But moral authority is coming to depend more on the spiritual stature and leadership qualities of prominent office-holders. A John XXIII can sway more people than an Alexander VI or even a Boniface VIII. The same is true outside Christianity. The Dalai Lama's influence has steadily increased since he left Tibet, notwithstanding the tragedy in his homeland. In a world no longer impressed by monarchical systems, leaders are expected to earn the right to speak with authority. Fortunately the medieval environment that enabled most unsuitable men to assume positions of ecclesiastical leadership has been swept away. In recent times, the major denominations have generally been careful to choose men of outstanding distinction; some of them are beginning to choose women.

Although autocratic denominations still exist, the Reformation set in motion a shift in emphasis from ecclesiastical autocracy toward more democratic forms of governance. John Calvin introduced notions of representative democracy: governance by the "communion of believers." But the Reformed churches retain a measure of centralized authority. Other Protestant denominations have moved toward much greater decentralization; Unitarian, Baptist and Pentecostal congregations, and congregations in the United Church of Christ base their identities on larger groupings but operate with almost complete autonomy.[54] They establish their own expectations of membership, select styles of worship, decide on appropriate avenues of outreach, and specify who may speak and act on their behalf. Independent congregations raise funds; acquire, own, and manage their own property; and hire personnel, free from ecclesiastical oversight.

Infrastructures, where they exist at all in decentralized denominations, may consist of little more than the permanent staffs associated with conferences or assemblies. They function in support roles and provide a voice for their religious persuasions. They may offer ministerial training, placement services, and healthcare and retirement benefits that would be more expensive and less transportable if provided at the congregational level. Denominational organizations may publish religious materials, coordinate programs, offer seminars, and explore opportunities to express collective ideals. They can coordinate large-scale service or missionary endeavors. A British Baptist group described its work thus:

> Our aim is to be the churches' best friend in mission. By mission we mean reaching out to people in the name of Jesus. This may involve evangelism, community projects, church planting, regeneration and social inclusion, youth and children's work and much more. We exist to enable churches to be better placed to engage in their God-given work. We often arrange conferences, seminars and training events to spread the message about the work we do and the services we can offer.[55]

Denominations can provide essential assistance—financial and otherwise—to congregations that are too small to be self-supporting. Rural or inner-city congregations with only a handful of members, all of whom may be poor, may depend for their very survival on a visiting minister and donated worship and study materials.[56] By contrast, large nondenominational congregations, including most big-city megachurches, have dispensed altogether with affiliational identity and support; they are not necessarily isolated from one another, but they are self-reliant.

The democratization of Christian denominations may have gone a long way, but religious institutions at all levels still exert considerable power over clergy and laity. Synods or even congregations can be as dogmatic in matters of faith and morals as bishops or popes. Certainly, in most parts of the world, the churches have lost the political and military power to coerce, but they have not altogether set aside the use of fear as an instrument of persuasion. That situation needs to change. Institutional Christianity should view its mission less in terms of authority and coercion and more in terms of inspiration and spiritual leadership. As noted in Chapter 16, the yearning for freedom has come to characterize western—and more recently eastern—society. On the other hand, as always, new freedom conveys new responsibilities; if the laity is not to be told what to believe and do, it must take greater responsibility for its own spiritual development. The religious self-reliance preached by the Transcendentalists is now becoming a necessity.

Even within traditional denominations, congregations have re-emerged as the basic units of Christianity; people often are drawn to a particular congregation more than to the denomination with which it is affiliated. "Baptist," "Christian Science," or "Greek Orthodox" may provide important determinants of a congregation's outlook, priorities and activities; but individual congregations can differentiate themselves by offering programs tailored to specific religious needs and aspirations. By targeting people of a particular ethnicity, age, educational level, or attitudes to doctrinal, liturgical or social issues they can create strong cohesion and sense of family. Whether it is appropriate for them to do so will depend on the availability of resources and the choices available to people of other persuasions in the locale; issues of insularity and self-absorption also need to be addressed. Where feasible and appropriate, such targeting can increase the likelihood that people will find a spiritual home. However many people are looking for groups even smaller than the typical congregation—or groups that function in ways other than traditional congregations.

In his evaluation of the modern religious scene Wade Clark Roof noted the traditional pattern of religious expression: "For many Americans experience of the sacred happens through regular and committed involvement in religious organizations. In religious community, in the shared context of worship, ritual, and affirmation of faith, the spiritual is kept alive." But he also noted that others are seeking new ways to express their Christianity. Their quest, he explained, "can lead to the evolution of new structures, to small groups, to extended networks, to informal gatherings and celebrations."[57] Roof distinguished between "believers" and "seekers." Even when they coexist within the same congregation, in his observation, the former preferred conventional worship services, while the latter gravitated to small groups that met at other times.[58] However the two types of activity are not always viewed as alternatives; another study suggested that the small-group experience may actually encourage participation in traditional worship at the congregational level.[59]

Since the 1980s "small Christian communities," or "innovative Christian communities," have emerged across the religious spectrum. In some cases they are organized by congregations, meet in church buildings, and function within a larger framework of congregational programs. In other cases, communities intentionally distance themselves from existing congregations as well as from the traditions they represent. They may prefer to meet in private homes, offices, rented meeting rooms, warehouses, or outdoors. Such environments lack the familiar characteristics of the "sacred space;" but they seem to provide a sense of freedom, avoiding negative associations with traditional Christianity.

In their structure and modes of operation, small Christian communities have several important precedents. Obvious ones are traditional adult Sunday-school classes and the "base communities" of Latin America;[60] we can also point to the lay communities organized by *Raskolniki*, or "Old Believers," in 17th-century Russia. But more important precedents can be found in the Christian communities of the first and second centuries.[61] To be sure, there are important internal and environmental differences; members of today's communities are responding less to an external Jesus and more to the values he embodied and to an inner spiritual awareness. Over the last 2,000 years those values have penetrated human consciousness through institutional Christianity's efforts but also, in an interesting sense, in spite of its efforts. In any event, the freedom from ecclesiastical authority is a common factor; in the early centuries it had not yet developed, and now it is in decline.

Although the focus of today's small Christian communities varies enormously, the common feature is sharing. The fourth-century Pachomius of Thebes used the Greek term *koinonia* (κοινωνια) to capture the notion of communion and sharing—not unlike the Russian *sobornost*, but operating on a smaller scale. Members of small communities come together to express common spiritual visions, aspirations, ideals and challenges and to achieve common religious goals.[62] Free from ecclesiastical oversight, participants—who may or may not include ordained clergy—can choose their own forms of worship, study, discussion, healing or ritual; also they can invite people who might not be welcome in traditional congregations.[63] Some communities experiment with new forms of worship, incorporating art forms of various genres, including sacred dance; still others take an esoteric, new-age, feminist or ecological focus. Participants can pray, share spiritual experiences, study scripture, seek fellowship and support, seek healing, or engage in outreach and service. To quote Ruth Carter Stapleton: "Perhaps no atmosphere is more conducive to creative service than that of a small group where there is an element of personal commitment to the welfare of the other members. And when we add the dimension of Christ's Spirit, we find the ultimate source of service. The spiritual service group is what the New Testament calls the Body of Christ."[64]

Some communities have adopted patterns of communal living. A wide range of possibilities has opened up. At one end of the spectrum are communities that emphasize the contemplative life and take vows of celibacy; at the other end are families living separately but sharing facilities and participating in group activities.[65] Communes of the type that became popular in the 1960s occupy a middle ground. Residential communities resemble the monastic communities of the Celtic church; medieval communities of the Beguines, Friends of God, and Brethren of the Common Life; and post-Reformation communities of Waldensians, Mennonites and Amish. Those various models all emerged at times when people were forced to turn to one another by a sense that institutional Christianity was not meeting their needs. Some people would say that similar conditions exist today.

Some communities incorporate *play* into their repertories. When a modern "Mary Magdalene" was asked how God should be worshipped, she replied: "With tears and with laughter, and in all that you do, and with song and dance, and in every way the Spirit inspires."[66] Carol Parrish-Harra expressed the value of playfulness well: "Dare we not play? Our disciplined self has been made to feel we must conceal our creative urges somewhere deep like an illegitimate child, too often excluded from the delight of daily life. Could we be rushing headlong into distress if we do not laugh, dance, sing, make love, or act [with] spontaneity?"[67] Certainly there are times when we must face harsh challenges, and maturity will dictate when levity is inappropriate. But Christianity must avoid the dour, kill-joy puritanism with which it has so often been associated. It must move away, in the words of two others, from "the long drawn countenance—or even the long-drawn multisyllabic words—as the essential aura in which all things spiritual must be surrounded."[68]

As increasing numbers of Christians invest their religious identity in small communities rather than in congregations or denominations, the structure of Christianity will change. In one sense such a development represents a further fragmentation of Christianity—not just into thousands of denominations or millions of congregations but possibly into tens of millions of small communities. The potential threat to Christian unity needs to be considered, and mechanisms may be needed to provide support and encourage interaction. On the other hand, the unity of the Ekklesia does not necessarily depend on organizational coherence; it can be expressed through a new spiritual awareness. Each unit of Christianity—denomination, congregation or community, or even individual person—can be seen, and can see itself, as a member of a worldwide family united in the love of Christ. Each can find its place, like a musician in an orchestra, contributing a note, a chord, a melody, or a drumbeat to the magnificent symphony of the Ekklesia. Each can share in the challenges and the rewards of a sacred communion that transcends not only our differences but also the conventional limitations of earthly existence.

Stratification

The emergence within organized Christianity of differentiated congregations or small communities represents "horizontal" segmentation of the Ekklesia. Here we explore the need for "vertical" segmentation. It becomes obvious, when we study the history of Christianity, that people's ability to understand, practice and express their religion varies tremendously. The great saints demonstrated in their lives a level of commitment that the average Christian may be unable to make;[69] perhaps we are all created equal in potential, but we are very *unequal* in our ability to actualize that potential. All of us can be Christians, however. As the English hymnodist William Walsham How (1823-1897) urged us to sing: "We feebly struggle, they [the saints] in glory shine. Yet all are one in thee, for all are thine."[70]

Institutional Christianity wisely sought to serve the masses rather than a spiritual elite. To the few who were capable and willing to make a greater commitment it offered the ministry, the religious orders, and organized lay service under ecclesiastical supervision. But in many respects the churches never knew what to do with exceptional mystics, outstanding theologians, even the greatest saints. Ecclesiastical authorities, with their pastoral instincts, have always found it easier to herd sheep than goats. In the future, greater opportunities need to be provided for people at every level of ability to express their highest aspirations and be challenged to grow spiritually at a corresponding pace. Christianity must not fail its greatest success stories.

Theosophist Annie Besant commented that people at all levels need religion, but "Religion must be as graduated . . . else it fails in its object."[71] Some form of stratification is needed, and the two-tier system adopted by the Manichaeans and Cathars provided an elementary model. Or perhaps Christianity should establish initiatory grades, comparable to those in ancient mystery schools or Masonic organizations. We note that the frequently maligned goats, in the biblical animal metaphor, symbolize "initiated disciples and . . . those who have climbed the mountain of initiation."[72] As people progress they should be offered more advanced teachings, encouraged to greater asceticism, invited to participate in more powerful rituals, and/or urged to take on more challenging works of service. A graduated moral code may also be appropriate to challenge more advanced Christians to meet higher standards; moral imperatives at every level should be presented in terms of the quest for perfection. Greater diversity of expression could be expected at the higher levels: "When people have reached the step where they begin to independently seek their way to knowledge, life branches out into variety of options . . . another level of potency."[73]

The purpose of a stratified Christianity would not be to create a patronage system, still less a system of political dominance. No special status should be attached to particular levels, and attitudes of inferiority and superiority must be avoided. Valentinus' scorn for *choics*, or "mud people"—even his patronizing attitude to *psychics*—can have no place in a future Christianity. Every soul is valuable, and Christ came to serve the whole of humanity. Opportunities should be provided for people to grow spiritually and to move up through the ranks at their own pace; a person who "fails" to move up may be living at a level which is appropriate to his or her abilities.[74] The ideal should be for everyone to find a level at which he or she feels comfortable and is challenged to achieve self-set goals, guided where appropriate by a spiritual adviser.

Clergy at all levels of a stratified Christianity would need to be insightful, wise, and sensitive to the needs of the people they served. But the responsibilities of clergy and laity would vary from one level to another, and in some cases the distinctions might become blurred. At the lower levels, clerical and lay roles could remain essentially as they are now. At the higher levels, some clergy would resemble the *gerontes* or *startsy* of Eastern Orthodox tradition or the spiritual directors in the major western religious orders. Other clergy might serve as liturgists, hierophants, or healing practitioners. Lecturers and leaders of service projects would likely be laypeople. At the very highest ranks, the "laity" might function independently, with little or no need or desire for support—but with great opportunities to serve. Service at all but the lowest levels would include assistance to congregations or communities at other levels.

Spirituality

The fear expressed a century, or even 50 years, ago that secular materialism would become the cultural norm of modern society turned out to be unjustified. Certainly we enjoy and are dependent on technological advances; but the post-modern era has produced widespread disillusionment with the worldview that science, technology, and academic philosophy offers us. Most importantly, scientific atheism's imperialistic claim to represent the only defensible metaphysic is dismissed.[75] The sense that there is "something more" to human life is growing in strength, leading to a large-scale search for "the spiritual."

The suggestion that "spirituality," rather than organized religion, should be the inspirational, ethical force in people's lives is not new; precisely that suggestion was made by the Transcendentalists in the early 19th century. However it still meets with scorn; critics dismiss "spirituality" as a hackneyed marketing slogan to promote fad cults and sell new-age products. Certainly the marketplace is flooded with offers of "instant enlightenment;" but discriminating people are searching for something of more lasting value and are ready to make the necessary investment of time and effort.

We are witnessing a transition from traditional religious forms—and here our focus is specifically on Christianity—toward what lies behind or beyond them. Increasing numbers of people are no longer content to make a profession of faith, accept baptism, pay their tithes, and await entry to heaven. Dependence on, or obedience to, religious authority is giving way to the authority of personal conscience and inner guidance.[76] Notions of vicarious redemption are giving way to less well-defined but more satisfying notions of personal transformation. Here we see the profound influence that esotericism has had on the popular consciousness, even though many seekers might distance themselves from major aspects of esoteric teachings. Importantly, the spiritual quest is valued more than any particular destination. Even regular churchgoers may now regard the local church as a catalyst for spiritual development rather than a one-stop supplier meeting all their spiritual needs.

Seekers trade the security of a familiar community, the certainty of faith, and the support of authority for uncertainty, aloneness, and possible disillusionment; but the quest also offers excitement, challenge, a sense of autonomy, and spiritual awakening that might otherwise have been unattainable. In the *Gospel of Thomas*,

Jesus warned of the challenges but promised great rewards: "Those who seek should not stop seeking until they find. When they find, they will be disturbed. When they are disturbed, they will marvel, and will reign over all."[77] Taking responsibility for one's own spiritual growth can be enormously empowering. "Most of us," wrote Elaine Pagels, "sooner or later, find that, at critical points in our lives, we must strike out on our own to make a path where none exists."[78]

What begins as a solitary quest may bring the seeker into new alliances. Seekers may find companionship and share experiences with fellow-travelers and groups on similar—or even contrasting—journeys. Those who have traveled farther can acquaint their slower brothers and sisters about what lies ahead and can offer encouragement. Meanwhile, participation in service projects can bring together people at different stages or on different journeys. A new sense of connectedness may help anchor the seeker, nurture commitments—not necessarily permanent but at least enduring—and overcome the pitfalls of eclectic spiritual tourism.

Some who set out on individual spiritual journeys eventually return to more traditional Christian forms—stripped, perhaps, of outworn trappings but capturing the spiritual energy of their heroes and heroines. They may seek to recapture the spirituality of the Celtic Church, the mysticism of the early and high Middle Ages, the communalism of the Beguines, or the spontaneity of the early Pentecostals. Prodigals rarely limp back empty handed—or penitent; they stride back with confidence, bringing with them the treasures and stories of their adventures. For them, and for those who welcome them back, the "traditional" forms take on new life and meaning. The prodigals may see tradition as something to be cared for, something entrusted to collective stewardship. Christianity will be expressed in a number of ways in the modern world, and the Ekklesia is big enough to accommodate all of them. Some will be completely new, free from traditions that people have rejected. Others are likely to grow organically out of traditional ones, allowed to evolve in the light of modern understanding and needs. Evolution, rather than revolution, allows centuries of invested spiritual energy to be preserved.

Tradition must never be allowed to become a straightjacket. But it can preserve the collective experiences of centuries and of millions of believers. Perhaps the accumulated wisdom has value; perhaps the past and present leaders of conventional Christianity have something worthwhile to say. Tradition can provide something larger than the individual's own aspirations: a framework of continuity as well as a foundation for whatever may lie ahead. Having said that, we must acknowledge that some seekers will never find a place in traditional, or even nontraditional, forms of "social Christianity" but will remain on their solitary journeys. Or they may live lives of compassion and service but disdain anything to do with "religion." They can be part of the Ekklesia too. Here we confront an important truth: the Ekklesia has both an immanent and a transcendent dimension. Not only does it transcend all authentic religious forms, it also resides in the hearts and souls of all authentic Christians. With Jesus we affirm: "The kingdom of God is within you."[79]

Membership in the Ekklesia, or Who is a Christian?

S ince the time of the apostles, individuals and groups have made judgments about who should or should not be recognized as a Christian. Such judgments must be approached with great caution; none of us can see into the hearts of others, and even if we could it is unlikely that we could evaluate what we saw. Other people's beliefs, attitudes and observances may be significantly different from ours, yet they may claim to be committed Christians and demonstrate ample sincerity. The thesis that anyone who claims to be a Christian should be accepted as one may be too radical.[80] Yet we should remind ourselves that Jesus demonstrated a remarkable degree of inclusiveness. He went out of his way to embrace people marginalized by society—lepers, Samaritans, publicans, tax-collectors, and women taken in adultery. He demonstrated a willingness to step aside from religious tradition when circumstances demanded prompt action and compassion. Inclusiveness should be our watchword too.

One of the most famous biblical passages is: "God so loved the world, that he gave his only begotten Son, that whosoever believeth in him should not perish, but have everlasting life."[81] Christianity asserts that the Son of God came to earth, taught principles of compassion, and then willingly sacrificed his life for humanity. In imitation of him, we should likewise be moved by compassion and willingness to sacrifice ourselves for others. The primary criterion for membership in the Ekklesia should be whether an individual lives according to the ideal of love expressed by Jesus Christ.

In assessing the role of beliefs, perhaps we should follow Charles Sheldon's example and ask "What would Jesus do?"[82] Would Christ have excluded someone from the Ekklesia for believing that he (Christ) became the son of God at the annunciation rather than "in the beginning"? Would he have exluded someone who believed that Christ was two persons and natures rather than one person with two natures; that the Holy Spirit proceeded from the Father alone rather than from the Father and himself; or that Mary was only the mother of his human nature? Would Christ have condemned someone who believed that there are 365 levels of reality between our world and the pleroma; that through woman man will eventually find the primeval Sophia; or that the Sun-God is born of the zodiacal Virgo and sacrificed in an eternal ritual of death and rebirth? He may even have preferred some of those ideas to an orthodoxy supported by the rack and the stake.

Beliefs should take a relatively low priority in determining who belongs in the Ekklesia. Despite what ecclesiastical dogmatists may have said for the last 2,000 years, beliefs pale in importance compared with what those beliefs motivate us to do. Enlightenment will flow not from believing one doctrine or another but from putting Christ's values into practice. As Thomas à Kempis wrote in the early 15th century: "whoever wishes to understand fully the words of Christ must try to pattern his whole life on that of Christ."[83] Accordingly, let us propose that we qualify to be counted as true Christians—true members of the Ekklesia—if we:

- Experience, individually and/or collectively, the divine presence in our lives.
- Draw upon the rich traditions of Christianity as sources of individual and collective inspiration.
- Express the unity of being, the communion of all life, and the universal love of Christ through meaningful forms of worship.
- Work for the healing, wholeness and betterment of humanity, the planet and all realms of life thereon.
- Give expression to the command to love our neighbor as ourselves by paying as much attention to our own weaknesses as to those perceived in others, as much attention to other's strengths as to our own. Our neighbor, as *Luke*'s Samaritan demonstrated, is *everyone*, including those to whom we might not ordinarily be drawn.
- Seek the inner meaning of life, follow truth sincerely and honestly wherever it may lead, and express that truth in love, healing and service.
- Move toward ever-more-perfect states of being, as guided by higher purpose, and ennoble humanity by our lives, relationships, work and play.

What kind of actions would *disqualify* us from membership in the Ekklesia? Jesus Christ probably would not have condemned people for their actions; moved by compassion, he would have hoped for change. But would he have approved of people who, with informed foresight and claiming to act in his name, waged religious war against Arians, Muslims, Cathars, Waldensians, Hussites or Huguenots or who converted Saxons, Jews or Mayans by the sword? Would he have approved of the torture and execution by the most gruesome means of "heretics" and "witches"? Would he approve of terrorism as a tool for social activism?[84] Based on everything we know of Christ, there are types of behavior which, *when proclaimed to be expressions of their religion rather than lapses from it,* persuade us that the perpetrators had forfeited the right to be considered Christian in any legitimate or meaningful sense.

The argument can always be made that Christian values and responsibilities were understood differently in the past. Attitudes have changed, and that itself is a tribute to the steady unfoldment of Christian values. Slavery was commonplace in the first century CE, but we still criticize individuals in the 19th century who quoted the Bible to defend participation in the slave-trade and ownership of slaves. We criticize anyone today who expresses hatred toward other racial, social or religious groups. To hold a belief that others are less blessed by God than ourselves is, from any perspective, un-Christlike. We reluctantly reach the conclusion that major segments of organized "Christianity" have, at times, forfeited their right to be called Christian.

On the other hand, we joyfully suggest that certain groups that the institutional church rejected, persecuted or slaughtered were in fact authentic members of the Ekklesia. May we also suggest that the Ekklesia extends to individuals and groups who never claimed to be Christian but who expressed through their lives the values that Jesus Christ expressed? Jesus would surely have embraced them as his own. In proposing a new universal religion, the Bengali intellectual Keshab Chandra Sen (1838-1884) acknowledged the debt that the Asian religions owed to Christ, adding that "In Christ . . . Europe and Asia will learn to find harmony and unity."[85] Daniel Andreev commented on that passage: "In referring to Christ, Sen clearly meant not the historical figure Jesus, but the Logos, Who found expression chiefly, but not exclusively, in Jesus Christ."[86]

Certainly we should not be so insensitive as to force the "Christian" label onto members of other world religions. But we affirm that the impulse set in motion by the cosmic Christ spread beyond those who trace their inspiration to the historical Jesus or his followers.

Reflections

The concept of an overarching Ekklesia is supported both by scripture and by persuasive theological arguments. It enables us to reconcile the diversity within Christianity with trust that diversity is transcended by a larger reality. Episcopal priest Cynthia Bourgeault glimpsed its meaning:

> The presence of the divine is not "unitive" simply in the sense of dissolving the multiplicity back into the One, but in the sense of seeing the One beautifully and radiantly illuminating the multiplicity, like light pouring through a stained-glass window, present in both the unity and the diversity. This is the particular genius of the Christian path."[87]

In that insight she has given us an appreciation of the "cathedralness" referred to earlier, though perhaps we could suggest "Christian *paths*" instead of "path."

Appreciation of the Ekklesia reassures us of the ultimate validity of Christianity and perhaps can give us a more sympathetic view of the "historical church." We can view the church of history as the imperfect manifestation of a perfect archetype, the creation of human hands struggling to respond to a divine impulse larger than they could understand. Certainly Christianity has fallen short of its ideals, but it has also succeeded in important ways. Again to quote Daniel Andreev:

> [O]ne should gauge the potential of religion as a whole, not by its specific forms. What matters is not how long ago the last major forms emerged but whether the evolution of religion has reached a dead-end; . . . whether there glimmers within such a worldview the possibility of making sense of our experience in the new era, and whether religion will be able to play a real and progressive role in such experience.[88]

We acknowledge with sadness, honesty, and a sense of our own complicity, the imperfections of the past. But we look forward to a more perfect manifestation of the Ekklesia as we learn from our mistakes, focus more clearly on Christianity's mission, and overcome sins of separateness. The historical church will never be more than an imperfect manifestation of its archetype, but the creative tension between them urges the church forward on its evolutionary journey. Karl Barth captured something of that journey to perfection when he contrasted "the Christian community"—his term for the historical church—with the kingdom of God: "The community is not the kingdom of God, nor will it ever be before the kingdom encounters it, and is revealed to it, in its glory at the end of all history. It prays for the coming of the kingdom, that encountering in its true and perfect form it may be directly and universally and definitively revealed."[89]

Some kind of organization may be needed to express the social dimension of the Ekklesia; but no particular structural form is divinely ordained, and forms can be created, modified or dismantled according to the needs of the time. The medieval church and the few large denominations that emerged from it may have been appropriate in their time to wield authority, issue doctrinal and moral dicta, train and appoint clergy, dispatch missionaries, negotiate with secular entities, and oversee the activities of the faithful. Now different organizational forms may be more appropriate; the decline of the institutional church, worrisome as it is to some, can open up exciting new possibilities.

Already we have witnessed a trend away from centralized authority toward congregational autonomy. Also, small communities, resembling those of earliest Christianity, are emerging which may be even more effective. Perhaps, after 2,000 years, we are finally discovering an "apostolic church." The smallness of the new

Christian communities provides flexibility to meet the needs of people of different religious orientations and at different levels of spiritual ability. On the other hand, religious entities on a regional, national or global scale—whether we call them denominations or something else—can offer support and coordinate endeavors beyond the abilities of individual congregations or communities. Moreover, the spiritual integrity of the Ekklesia is of no small importance, and due attention should be paid to the need for a larger Christian communion. Perhaps we need to stop looking for communion in organizational terms and seek it elsewhere. Communion could be sought in subjective unity; it could be expressed through collective worship or service—or even through the combined aspiration of individual Christians.

In an attempt to define "a Christian," we have asked what kind of person would Jesus Christ embrace as his own. Christ applauded faith, in the sense of trust, but he never insisted on a creedal confession; his message was one of love and acceptance. Accordingly, in proposing a tentative definition of a Christian, we have placed emphasis on actions rather than beliefs. On that basis we are forced to conclude that major segments of the historical church—and possibly segments of today's—do not merit the label "Christian." On the other hand we can also conclude that many people "outside the church" deserve to be included.

Our model Christian is on a spiritual journey which may take him or her from one set of beliefs and practices to another or from one denomination or liturgical tradition to another. Where he or she may be at any particular time is of secondary concern; more important are the insights, epiphanies and shared experiences gained along the way. Our Christian may return, enriched by the journey, to traditional Christianity or—with others of like mind—create a new, more meaningful, form of Christianity. The possibilities are endless, and expectations should be unlimited. Humanity is evolving and new religious forms may be appropriate; but it is important to note that people today are not insensitive to the value of tradition. Nor should we accept uncritically those popular stereotypes that cast modern people as materialistic, indifferent, or pleasure-seeking. It is probably fair to say that never before have so many people been motivated to explore the individual and collective dimensions of human spirituality and to reach out to their neighbors.

Whereas the Calvinists spoke of humanity's total depravity, Eastern Orthodox teachers speak of *theosis*, or "deification." Theosis, the spiritual goal of the great saints, is a process of enlightenment brought about by the agency of divine energy; Christ's transfiguration on Mount Tabor is regarded as the supreme example. We can envision, as the Russian theologians did, global theosis as the spiritual goal of Christianity—perhaps even the whole of humanity. For Sergei Bulgakov that global theosis was the final manifestation of Sophia, the Bride of Christ, and the implications for a new appreciation of the Divine Feminine are obvious. Through our individual and collective spiritual growth, perhaps we can glimpse the deification of the church and humanity and the manifestation of Sophia on earth. When that deification is achieved then the historical church—Barth's "community"—will finally be one with the Ekklesia.

---

1. Karl Barth. *The Word of God & the Word of Man*. Harper & Row, 1928, pp. 273-274.
2. Etymologically, *ekklesia* can be broken down into *ek* (ek, "out" or "from") and *kaleo* (kalew, "call" or "summon").
3. *Exodus* 12:6.
4. See the discussion in: Benedict XVI. *Jesus of Nazareth*. (Transl: A. Walker.) Doubleday, 2006/2007, pp. 47-48.
5. *John* 17:21.
6. *Ephesians* 4:5.
7. Ignatius of Antioch. *Epistle to the Smyrnaeans*, 8. (Transl: A. Roberts & J. Donaldson.) Ante-Nicene Fathers, vol. 1, 1867.
8. *The Shepherd of Hermas*, Vision 2, 4(8):1. (Transl. J. Lightfoot.) Early Christian Writings.
9. *2 Clement* 14:1. (Transl: J.B. Lightfoot.) Early Christian Writings. See also: *The Tripartite Tractate*, 1 51, 57. *The Nag Hammadi Library*. Harper-Collins, 1990, p. 63. This latter text further asserts that the Son and the church emanated jointly from the Father.
10. *Ibid.* 14:2-3.
11. *Eugnostos the Blessed*. III, 81. James M. Robinson (ed.). *Nag Hammadi Library*, Revised Edition. Harper-San Francisco, 1988, pp. 231-232.
12. *Proverbs* 8:22-30.
13. It will be recalled that the Gnostics regarded the Logos and Sophia as coupled *aeons*.
14. Pavel Florensky. *The Pillar and the Ground of Truth*. (Transl: B. Jakim.) Princeton University Press, 1997, p. 245.
15. Sergei Bulgakov. *Sophia: the Wisdom of God*. Lindisfarne Press, 1993, pp. 138-139.
16. Daniel Andreev. *Rose of the World*, 1,1. (Trans: J. Roberts.) Daniel Andreev Charity Foundation, 1997. Much of this work was completed while Andreev was in a labor camp.
17. See for example: Mar Melchizedek. "Sobornost, Catholicity and True Salvation." *Theandros*, vol. 3, no. 1, Fall 2005. Also: Nikolai Berdyaev. *The Russian Idea*. (Transl: R. French.) Lindisfarne Press, 1947/1992, pp. 176-181.
18. Nancy Seifer points out that the literal meaning of *sobornost* is "cathedral-ness." But she suggests that it implies "oneness in the presence of God." See: *Russian Odyssey*. Xlibris, 2003, pp. 94, 193.
19. Valdimir Lossky. *The Mystical Theology of the Eastern Church*. St. Vladimir's Seminary Press, 1944/1976, p. 175.
20. Esotericists would insist that the Ekklesia embraces both the soul and monad, the latter being the divine spark and source of life.
21. Center for Progressive Christianity. *The Eight Points*, point 2, 2006.

22. John S. Spong. *Why Christianity Must Change or Die*. Harper-Collins, 1998, p. 189.

23. The author is indebted to Dr. Luke T. Johnson of Emory University for those insights.

24. We must be even more cautious in judging a concept by its dominant expression. See the discussion in: Hans Küng. *On Being a Christian*. (Transl: E. Quinn.) Doubleday, 1974, p. 44.

25. *Unitas Fratrum* was the principal branch of the church founded by Jan Hus, former Catholic priest, who was burned at the stake in 1415 after being lured to the Council of Constance on a false promise of safe conduct. To avoid a similar fate Martin Luther was spirited away from the Diet of Augsburg before sentence could be pronounced on him.

26. Keith Clements (ed.). *Friederich Schleiermacher: Pioneer of Modern Theology*. Fortress Press, 1987, p. 99ff.

27. Eugenia Gourvitch. *Vladimir Soloviev: the Man and the Prophet*. Rudolf Steiner Press, 1992, pp 45-49.

28. Andreev, *Rose of the World*, 1.3. Note that only seven truly ecumenical councils were held before the Great Schism.

29. William Cecil, Baron Burghley. Quoted in: F. Peck. *Desiderata*, vol. 1. London, 1732, p. 44. Burghley was commenting on the impossibility of coexisting Protestant and Catholic faiths in Elizabethan England.

30. Leo XIII. Apostolic letter: *Message to America*. Vatican, September 18, 1895.

31. Leo XIII. Encyclical *Testem Benevolentiae*. Vatican, 1899. "Americanism" also included threats to ecclesiastical authority arising from civil liberties and reliance on individual conscience in moral issues.

32. Mark Noll. "American Lutheranism Yesterday and Today." Richard Cimino (ed.). *Lutherans Today*. William Eerdmans, 2003, pp. 7ff.

33. The history of the World Council provides interesting confirmation of the idea that the motivation for service can become refined and purified as the work proceeds.

34. Source: World Council of Churches.

35. The Vatican sends observers to WCC meetings.

36. Interestingly, the Fellowship's website is *www.sobornost.org*.

37. Second Vatican Council. Decree: *Unitatis Redintegratio*, Ch. 3:15. Vatican 1965.

38. Paul VI. Decree: *Unitatis Redintegratio*, ch. 1, item 4. Vatican, 1964. "Separated brethren" contrasts with the earlier label of "false religions."

39. *Ibid.*

40. The declaration was signed at Augsburg, Germany, on October 31, 1999, the 482nd anniversary of Luther's posting of the 95 Theses.

41. Timothy Ware. *The Orthodox Church*. Penguin Books, 1963/1977, p, 310.

42. *Ibid.*, pp. 318-324.

43. Central Committee. *Final Report of the Special Commission on Orthodox participation in the WCC*. World Council of Churches, Geneva, 2002.

44. Church Council of the Evangelical Lutheran Church in America. *Declaration of the Evangelical Lutheran Church in America to the Jewish Community*. Chicago, April 18, 1994.

45. Traditional Catholics objected to the new view that Jews in general did not bear responsibility for Jesus' crucifixion. See for example: Craig L. Heimbichner. "The Semi-Catholic Catechism of the Catholic Church." *Angelus*, vol. XXIII, no.4, April 2000.

46. Source: United Religions Initiative.

47. Quoted in: Marian Hillar. "Sebastian Castellio and the Struggle for Freedom of Conscience." *Essays in the Philosophy of Humanism*, vol. 10, 2002, pp. 31-56.

48. Central Committee. *Final Report of the Special Commission on Orthodox participation in the WCC*, section B, V: 40. World Council of Churches, Geneva, 2002.

49. Oligopoly refers to a market dominated by a small number of powerful players. Perfect competition refers to one where no buyer or seller is able to exert significant power.

50. In a Gallup Poll taken in the 1990s, 40 percent of Americans claimed to have attended a church or synagogue within the previous seven days. However these claims are thought to be exaggerated. Regular attendance by Protestants may be closer to 20 percent, and by Catholics 28 percent. See: C. Kirk Hadaway and P.L. Marler. "Did You Really Go To Church This Week?" *The Christian Century*, May 6, 1998, pp. 472-475.

51. The three liturgically recognized stages in life are sometimes referred to as "hatching, matching and dispatching."

52. Marriage to someone of a different faith may be grounds for banishment. Also, members—and in notorious cases clergy—who contacted AIDS from tainted blood transfusions have been expelled from fundamentalist congregations. Relatively few denominations or congregations openly welcome homosexual, bisexual or transgendered persons.

53. Richard Cimino. Introduction to *Lutherans Today*. William Eerdmans, 2003, p. xi.

54. In early America a high degree autonomy was almost inevitable in rural areas because of congregations' geographical isolation.

55. Source: Baptist Union of Great Britain.

56. See the discussion on rural Presbyterian churches in: Paul F. Gillespie (ed.). *Foxfire 7*. Anchor Books, 1973, pp. 248-255.

57. Wade C. Roof. *Spiritual Marketplace*. Princeton University Press, 1999, pp. 297-298.

58. *Ibid.*, p. 299.

59. Bernard J. Lee *et al. The Catholic Experience of Small Christian Communities*. Paulist Press, 2000, pp. 103-116.

60. Base communities were discussed in Chapter 19.

61. See the discussion in: Lee *et al., The Catholic Experience of Small Christian Communities*, pp. 4-9.

62. *Ibid.*, pp. 77-103.

63. For example, some communities welcome people of all gender orientations in defiance of denominational policies.

64. Ruth Carter Stapleton. *The Experience of Inner Healing*. Guideposts, 1977, p. 156.

65. An example is the SparrowHawk Village in Oklahoma.

66. Tau Malachi eben Ha-Elijah. *The Secret Gospel of Mary*. Llewellyn, 2006, §65. This delightful book captures the spirit of Mary Magdalene as it emerges from scripture, but it should not be confused with the extra-canonical *Gospel of Mary*.

67. Carol Parrish-Harra. *Sophia Sutras: Introducing Mother Wisdom*. Sparrow Hawk Press, 2006, p. 131.

68. Ambrose A. & Olga N. Worrall. *The Gift of Healing*. Harper & Row, 1965, p. 126.

69. Where the saints' abilities came from is a separate issue. Those who believe in reincarnation would conclude that the saint made exceptional progress in previous lives.

70. William W. How. "For All the Saints." Earl Nelson (ed.). *Hymns for Saint's Days, and other Hymns*, 1864. This processional hymn is usually sung to the 1906 tune *Sine Nomine* by Ralph Vaughan Williams. Some versions have "Yet all are one within your great design."

71. Annie W. Besant. *Esoteric Christianity*. Theosophical Publishing House, 1901/1953, p. 2.

72. Alice A. Bailey. *Discipleship in the New Age*, II. Lucis, 1955, p. 62.

73. Marko Pognačnik. *Christ Power and the Earth Goddess*. Findhorn Press, 1999, p. 48.

74. Belief in reincarnation includes the understanding that individuals evolve over many lifetimes. Slow progress in one lifetime might be compensated for by rapid progress in another.

75. It is an interesting commentary on human behavior to note that scientific materialism, whose proponents complained so bitterly in the 18th century that institutional Christianity was closed-minded and arrogant, quickly embraced some of the same attitudes.

76. A precedent for this source of authority can be found in the doctrine of the "priesthood of all believers," attributed to John Wycliffe and Martin Luther. Baptists have given special emphasis to that doctrine.

77. *Gospel of Thomas*, saying 2. (Transl: S. Patterson & M. Meyer.) Gnostic Society Library.

78. Elaine Pagels. *Beyond Belief: the Secret Gospel of Thomas*. Vintage Books, 2004, pp. 184-185. After being marginalized by the other apostles Thomas set out to preach the gospel to Assyria and India.

79. *Luke* 17:21.

80. Such a measure of inclusiveness is found in Hinduism.

81. *John* 3:16.

82. Charles Sheldon. *In His Steps*, 1896. Sheldon's book became the "bible" of the Social Gospel movement.

83. Thomas à Kempis (attributed to). *Imitation of Christ*. (Transl: unknown.) Bruce Publishing Company, c.1418/1940, p. 1.

84. For example, some "Christian" groups have created an environment that encourages violence, including murder, against family planning clinics. Others have used terrorist tactics to promote environmental causes.

85. Keshab Chandra Sen. Quoted in: Thomas Ebeneger Slater. *Keshab Chandra Sen and the Brahma Samáj: Being a Brief Review of Indian Theism from 1830 to 1884*. Spink, 1884, p. 60. Keshab Chandra Sen was influenced by the writings of Theodore Parker and Waldo Emerson; but he rejected the "Europeanized Christianity" of the missionaries.

86. Andreev, *Rose of the World*, 1,3.

87. Cynthia Bourgeault. *Centering Prayer and Inner Awakening*. Cowley Publications, 2004, p. 72.

88. *Ibid.*, 1,1.

89. Karl Barth. *Church Dogmatics*, book IV, ch. 2. Quoted in: Clifford Green. *Karl Barth: Theologian of Freedom*. Fortress Books, 1989, pp. 253-254.

Chapter 22
The Seven Paths of Christianity

The Ekklesia captures a view of Christianity as the *One*; the seven paths capture the diversity within it, the sense of the *Many*. The Paths of Devotion, Ceremony, Knowledge, Service, Healing, Activism and Renunciation all offer valid ways to express the Christian experience, aspirations, ideals and commitment. They provide opportunities to worship, serve, grow spiritually, and move humanity forward on its journey to perfection. Which path, or paths, we are drawn to will depend on our background, abilities, dedication, and individual preference. We can choose to follow one or more than one. It is unlikely that anyone could do justice to all seven at once; on the other hand to pursue a single path for a lifetime might unnecessarily limit our experience.[1] We are not required to follow the same path or set of paths for our whole lives; we can switch to a different path or paths and perhaps return at some future time. Emphasis is on experience, learning and sharing.

The notion of multiple spiritual paths has many precedents. Matthew Fox identified four paths of Creation Spirituality: his *Via Positiva* incorporated delight, awe, wonder and revelry; the *Via Negativa* darkness, silence, suffering, and letting go; the *Via Creativa* birthing and creativity; and the *Via Transformativa* compassion, justice, healing and celebration.[2] The Vedic scriptures mentioned five yogas, or paths to union with the Divine: *bhakti yoga*, the way of devotion; *jnana yoga*, the way of knowledge; *karma yoga*, the way of service; *raja yoga*, the "kingly yoga;" and *vibhuti yoga*, the way of beauty.[3] Other yogas that developed over the centuries included *mantra* yoga whose emphasis is on chanting. The seven rays of modern esoteric teachings, which among much else identify areas of discipleship work, are: Will or Power, Love-Wisdom, Active Intelligence, Harmony through Conflict, Knowledge or Science, Devotion or Idealism, and Ceremonial Order.

The Hasidic Jewish writer Martin Buber identified ten "rungs" on the ladder to heaven: God and Man, Prayer, Heaven and Earth, Service, Teachings, the Way, Love, Good and Evil, Pride and Humility, and Redemption.[4] Buber may have been aware of the writings of a desert father, preserved in the *Philokalia*, whose ladder began with "purest prayer" and ended with "a step that has no limit."[5] The only cautionary note that needs to be made with regard to "ladder" metaphors is that the paths are not sequentially prioritized but offer parallel choices of comparable merit.

The seven paths express religious options; they are areas of emphasis or directions which Christian seekers can take. Understandably there is overlap among them; after all the Ekklesia is unified. Moreover the breakdown into seven paths is somewhat arbitrary, and we should not insist too strongly on the precise number. Efforts to identify seven sacraments in the 12th century resulted in difficult decisions on which to include and exclude. Nevertheless, there is a strong temptation to call the paths the *seven churches*, recalling the churches or Christian communities of Asia mentioned in *Revelation*;[6] as noted earlier, a number of writers interpreted them as spiritual paths.[7]

Each of the seven paths has strong roots in tradition. However the paths are not denominations or religious identities; nor are they characterizations such as conservative, liberal, fundamentalist, primitive, or new-age. Like the Ekklesia, the seven paths are archetypes; and, as is true of all archetypes, the labels attached to them are no more than a convenient shorthand. "Devotion," for example, is more comprehensive than the term's conventional meaning. The underlying meanings are rich and complex. The paths can be actualized in a variety of ways, some expressing more faithfully than others the perfection of their archetypes. Each path provides opportunities for people at all levels of spiritual ability; and the combination of the paths and different levels of challenge offers a wide range of religious options. At the same time, some paths have potential pitfalls, and we need to be aware and steer clear of them.

Meanwhile, the notion of the spiritual journey itself recalls the medieval pilgrimage and also the *Tao*, "the Way." As noted in the previous chapter, the journey is more important than any simplistic notion of a "destination." We can speak of the paths as being paths to God or Christ, but there is no end-point, at least until we may pass into a completely different state of consciousness; certainly physical death will not be the "end of the road." That observation does not imply that we are under a multi-life sentence; rather it emphasizes that we shall never exhaust the possibilities for adventure and advancement.

Path of Devotion

"Devotion" means dedication, loyalty or love. The Path of Devotion refers to the totality of ways in which human love reaches out to unbounded, divine love. Quoting *Deuteronomy*, Christ exhorted his followers to "love the Lord thy God with all thy heart, and with all thy soul, and with all thy mind."[8] Christian devotion is the response to those words and to the universal love expressed by the life of Christ. It is unshakable dedication and loyalty to Christ.

The Path of Devotion embraces—and what more appropriate word could be used in this context!—awe, humility, loyalty, yearning for relationship, longing to become like the beloved. Commonly it is expressed through prayer; but, recognizing that *Devotion*, in the present context is a broad concept, we note that it can also be expressed through music, art, architecture, poetry, dance and drama. We love what is beautiful, and what we love becomes beautiful. The Path of Devotion is the path trodden by the Assyrian poet Ephrem of Nisibis, the 14th-century Friend of God from the Oberland, spiritual writer Thomas à Kempis, artist Michelangelo, Spanish mystic John of the Cross, Benjamin Keach who published the first Baptist hymnal, architect Christopher Wren, master composer Johann Sebastian Bach, the anonymous pilgrim in *Way of the Pilgrim*, French mystic Thérèse of Lisieux, Russian poet Vladimir Solovyov, Trappist monk Thomas Merton, and the modern English composer John Rutter. It corresponds to Matthew Fox's *Via Positiva*, to the Hasidic rung of prayer, and to the sixth ray of Devotion and Idealism.[9] It corresponds to *bhakti yoga* but also has associations with *raja*, *mantra* and *vibhuti yoga*.

Because it turns our awareness toward a larger, loving reality, devotion helps overcome self-absorption. Under the impulse of devotion desire gives way to aspiration, and consciousness is raised to a level where exercise of the spiritual will and effective action become possible. Love is the strongest motivating force in the universe, and pilgrims on the Path of Devotion can branch off onto other paths. Hildegard of Bingen combined the Paths of Devotion and Healing; Francis of Assisi, Devotion, Service and Renunciation; Leonardo da Vinci, Devotion and Knowledge; and John Koukouzeles, compiler of Byzantine chant, the Paths of Devotion and Ceremony.

Prayer is usually understood as a dialog with God. Prayer—chanted, sung, spoken or unspoken—is one of the oldest and most revered religious practices. Styles of prayer range from the quiet dignity of the Anglican liturgy, to the boisterous praise of Holiness services, the ceaseless contemplation of the hermit, and the quiet recitation of spiritual poetry. Prayer can express thanksgiving, praise or adoration; but prayers of petition may be the most common. Petitionary prayer may seek protection, deliverance from harm, healing, forgiveness, or some higher value such as grace or spiritual growth; in turn it can be broken down into *personal prayer*, for our own benefit, and *intercessionary prayer* for the benefit of others. Petitionary prayer reflects a person's faith, but it can also enhance faith. As one writer observed, prayer can "clarify the dimensions of our own belief;" in particular: "If faith is strong and deep, we cannot ask God to be merciful . . . mindful, patient, forgiving, or gentle. Such a request implies that we doubt the very divinity of Deity."[10] He went on to urge that we seek "that which is not within our own power to know or to accomplish;" it might result in a conversion experience, an epiphany, or an initiation.

The continued relevance of prayer is called into question at a time when many Christians have rejected traditional notions of God or of relationships with God. For example, to pray might suggest belief in an external God; after all, dialogue implies two interacting intelligences; or it might suggest that we believe in a theistic God who sits on a throne to administer justice or mercy—or at least sits across the room from us. Petitionary prayer also raises a number of age-old philosophical issues.[11] The hope that prayers might be answered raises questions about God's immutability or about divine justice and compassion. Why should a God of universal love intervene to help certain individuals but not others? And why would an omniscient, compassionate God wait until we plead for help? Joseph Ratzinger, the future pope Benedict XVI, commented on the tension created by the "synthesis" of an absolute God who nevertheless can enter into relationship with human beings.[12]

Such problems can be avoided by focusing less on intervention and more on the intrinsic power of prayer. An environment of love provides a benevolent medium in which intercessionary prayer produces its own results. From that alternative perspective, God does not intervene; concerned people intervene to help those in need, and under favorable conditions—and perhaps according to universal laws—their efforts produce positive outcomes. Prayer is effective not because God "does something" but because we reach out with loving intent and set beneficent processes in motion.[13] Energy follows thought, particularly when the thought is supported by strong emotion or will. Sustained prayer or the collective prayers of large groups can be expected to have more effect than casual prayers with minimal investment of effort.

Regardless of how we understand the mechanism of prayer, some cautionary words may be in order. Intercessionary prayer should seek the recipient's highest good rather than some specific outcome. We cannot see the whole picture; what we might judge to be a favorable outcome could have negative implications; conversely, what seems to be a distressful situation might be the price paid for some greater advantage. To pray for a person's highest good allows intelligence and wisdom greater than ours to determine what conditions should be remedied, how, and at what time. Where does that intelligence and wisdom reside? Or, to ask a related question: to whom do we pray? Cardinal Ratzinger warned against praying to "the void."[14] The simplest answer is that we pray to entities within the benevolent environment that embody divinity in their own reality as well as in our consciousness. Principal among them, of course, would be the Christ; but angels and saints may also be able to set the processes in motion.[15] Or perhaps we can pray to higher levels of our own being. Dialog between different levels of the self—including a divine level—is perfectly reasonable; indeed it may help to bring the different levels into harmony.[16] Prayer, including petitionary prayer, can retain its validity in the context of belief in an inner, immanent God or in a pantheistic or panentheistic God.

Similar concerns have been voiced about the continued relevance of worship. Does worship imply dutiful homage—or fear—before an external, theistic God? One writer suggested that we should worship the divinity within humanity at large.[17] However, we recognize that a pantheistic or panentheistic God pervades not only humanity but the whole of creation. Is not that God as deserving of worship, or awe, as any "father in the sky"? Belief that we are potentially divine beings does not imply that there is no divinity outside us. Hindus greet one another with *namaste*, which can be translated as "the divinity in me acknowledges the divinity in you."[18] Christ, Mary and the saints express more divinity than we do and merit *latria* or *dulia*, as the case may be.[19]

The Rosary and the *hesychastic* Jesus Prayer resemble mantra yoga in their repetitions of elementary prayers.[20] In "centering prayer," developed in the 1970s by three Trappist monks, the resemblance is even closer.[21] The devotee chooses a mantra, or sacred word, such as "peace," "trust," "Mary" or "Father." In its procedure, centering prayer resembles yogic meditation: withdrawal to a quiet location, sitting in a comfortable position, and stilling the mind; a daily rhythm of meditative prayer is encouraged. Centering prayer was designed to provide a bridge to "contemplative prayer," which goes beyond emotion and mind, beyond words, beyond self.

Contemplative prayer is the prayer of the mystics. It moves "from the frequent vocal prayer to prayers of the mind and from that to prayer of the heart."[22] The "heart," in that context, is more than the physical organ, more even than the seat of emotion; it is the conscious link with the soul—the individual human soul and perhaps also the collective soul of the Ekklesia. Regardless of whether we speak of prayer, meditation or contemplation, the encounter with God becomes more profound as the process grows quieter and deeper. Emphasis is no longer on talking to God but on listening to the "still small voice."[23] Contemplative prayer even moves beyond "listening" to God in any sense of expecting to receive a message. Cynthia Bourgeault described *apophatic* prayer as "prayer that . . . bypasses our capacities for reason, imagination, visualization, emotion, and memory" but makes use of "spiritual awareness."[24] The ego is transcended in a quest for pure union with God. In the words of one writer: "[T]he mystic gazes on the Beatific Vision, . . . the sage rests in the calm of the Wisdom that is beyond knowledge, . . . the saint reaches the purity wherein God is seen."[25]

In their attempts to describe the unquenchable yearning for union with the Divine, many mystics have compared it with yearning for a human beloved. Bernard of Clairvaux wrote no fewer than 86 sermons on the *Song of Solomon*, drawing upon its erotic imagery to describe his mystical experiences. Notwithstanding, Bernard felt compelled to set the desire for God above any human desire. "[W]hat human affections," he asked, "have you ever experienced . . . that are sweeter than is now experienced from the heart of the Most High?"[26] The experience of the mystics is not only one of yearning but also the sense that God fills that yearning.

The Paths of Devotion and Renunciation inevitably intersect. Mysticism requires discipline, almost always demanding withdrawal from the hubbub of everyday life. Most of the best-known Christian mystics lived in monastic environments, though countless others may have encountered God in nature: in wilderness settings, on mountain tops, or by the seashore. An important advantage of private devotion, as distinct from public worship, is avoidance of any overt display of piety. We are reminded of Jesus' parable of the Pharisee who drew attention to himself in the temple.[27] On the other hand, even private devotion does not entirely insulate us from the pitfalls of ego and self-absorption.

Path of Ceremony

The Path of Ceremony is the expression of Christianity through ritual, liturgy, and the sacraments. Ceremony, ritual, liturgy and pageantry are closely related concepts. A religious ritual is a prescribed series of actions with sacred purpose; it is the very embodiment of sacred tradition. Ritual, the oldest known religious practice, dates back far into prehistory; we saw in Chapter 8 that the word "ritual" originally captured the notion of preserving cosmic order.[28] Liturgy (Greek: λειτουργια, "public work") refers to acts of public worship, normally performed according to established ritual. Ceremony is the more general western term denoting either secular or religious activities invested with symbolic importance. Pageantry denotes an elaborate or impressive ceremony. Although "pageant" has acquired secular meaning in modern times, originally it referred to a scene in a mystery play or the stage on which it was performed.[29] In turn, the roots of mystery plays can be traced back to pre-Christian cult dramas.

Countless individuals have participated in the rich tradition of Christian sacred ritual. The Path of Ceremony is the path of every priest baptizing a child or celebrating Holy Communion, every acolyte, every chorister, every actor in a passion play, every performer of a sacred dance. Because the liturgy changed little over the centuries few individuals became famous for innovations. However some individuals whose names are remembered were: Basil of Caesarea and John Chrysostom, who created the liturgy of the Mass; Ambrose of Milan, first of the great compilers of Latin chant; Claudio Monteverdi and George Frideric

Handel, whose mastery of sacred musical pageantry set new standards for the Baroque era and beyond; Bishop Edward King and other "ritualists" of the Oxford movement;[30] Éliphas Lévi, whose lifetime dream was the revitalization of western sacramental ritual; Charles Leadbeater, creator of the liturgy for the Liberal Catholic Church; and Archbishop Marcel LeFevre, leader of the Traditionalist Catholic movement.

The Path of Ceremony is clearly linked to the seventh ray of Ceremonial Order; and we note that the special quality of the seventh ray is the descent of divine energy to the physical level. We are reminded of the Qabalistic notion of the descent of divine force from *Kether* or *Tiphareth* to the everyday—but still divine—level of *Malkuth*/*Shekinah*. Ceremony involves the creation of beautiful forms, and with that perspective we can see a link with *vibhuti yoga* and the fourth ray of Harmony.

Ritual accumulates power through repeated enactments. Performance of a ritual with a definite periodicity—daily, weekly, monthly, annual or otherwise—can be likened to the rhythmic tolling of a bell. Each enactment is a recapitulation, recreating a timeless moment and giving the term "reliving the experience" precise validity.[31] Participants step out of time into the eternal present, absorb timeless energies, and re-emerge refreshed with a sense that their mundane lives are "beginning again."[32] The most highly developed rhythmic pattern may be monks' recitation of the "canonical hours;" but the annual liturgical cycle, with its prescribed scriptural readings, changing vestment colors, and days of penitence and festivity, is more evident to the faithful. Even rituals enacted at irregular intervals, like the installation of a bishop or the coronation or death of a monarch, build upon what has gone before. Although religious ritual is less popular than hitherto, it still plays a part in most religious services;[33] and there is every reason to believe that ritual one day will regain the preeminent place it once occupied in Christian worship.

The rituals of the early church were based on, and drew their power from, antecedents in the Jewish temple and the ancient mystery schools. Early Christian rituals evolved into the familiar sacraments and "sacramentals" of the late Middle Ages. Consecration of the Eucharist, which had antecedents in Judaism, Zoroastrianism and Mithraism, evolved into the elaborate ceremony of the Mass. Catholicism and Eastern Orthodoxy have preserved the sacraments and the Mass from early times. But the Protestant reformers emphasized Bible study, preaching, and congregational hymn-singing in place of ceremony; Protestant communion services still resemble the Mass to some degree, but much of the power has been lost. Traditional disdain for ritual, in Protestant circles, stemmed largely from lack of understanding of its purpose; the dismissal of ritual as meaningless, or "empty," betrayed participants' attitudes as much as critics'.

Efforts by Anglo-Catholics, Neo-Lutherans, Liberal Catholics, and others to restore to pre-Reformation grandeur the sacramental rituals of Protestant Christianity are of major significance. In the eyes of Traditional Catholics, restoration of the pre-Vatican II Latin Mass is equally important. In every case there is recognition of the power and timelessness of sacred ritual.[34] Skillfully choreographed and enacted by dedicated ritualists, religious ceremony can be powerful indeed. The Christmas or Easter High Mass, or the office of *Tenebrae* (Latin: "shadows") performed on Maundy Thursday or Good Friday, surely can compete in psychological impact with the Eleusinian mysteries.

Ritual is a vessel, or form; and as Taoists would be quick to point out, the value of a vessel lies not in the material from which it is made but in the space that it encloses. In a religious ritual, that "space" is filled from above by divine grace and, from below, by participants' intent and reverence. A religious ceremony raises participants' consciousness above the mundane level and focuses it upon the transcendent. Important elements are the liturgical prayers, which convey the ceremony's meaning and purpose, and the environment in which it is performed. Ceremony demands a sacred space, indoors or outdoors. The setting for an elaborate ritual may require careful planning and meticulous preparation.[35] Practitioners' demeanor and the underlying mood may range from exuberant joy to quiet meditation. Ritual gestures should be made with profound feeling, sensitivity and devotion; self-consciousness, boredom or resentment detracts from their effectiveness. Poorly or carelessly performed ritual can easily become "empty" and meaningless; it might even attract negative energies.

Rituals are as important as generations of worshippers choose to make them. Individuals should be allowed to invest in them as much significance as they wish. Evangelical clergy do nobody a favor by repeating traditional warnings that the Eucharist is "purely commemorative." Neither should the Catholic Church insist that everyone embrace a particular interpretation of the real presence. Eastern Orthodoxy wisely preserves a sense of mystery rather than mandating the conceptual formula of transubstantiation. Where the prevailing belief is in the real presence, the Eucharist will obviously take on great significance, and congregations or denominations have the right to restrict access to it; but congregations are to be commended that open the sacrament to all sincere worshippers.

The rituals most obvious to ordinary Christians are those incorporated into regular Sunday worship services. Formats vary widely from denomination to denomination and even within denominations. Many Christians demand overt congregational participation in worship; that desire harks back to the hymn-singing and "Amens" of early Evangelicalism and extends to the hand-waving, clapping, and foot-stomping of modern Pentecostal services. Hunger for experiential worship contrasts with time-honored formats of passive congregations. But not everyone wants to see worship become an opportunity for rock bands to turn up the volume; nor do they all want to clap their hands and dance in the aisles—or in the converted warehouse. The experience implied in "experiential worship" does not necessarily have to be physical. The congregation listening to a gifted orator, a Palestrina motet sung by a professional choir, or a Bach or Saint-Saëns organ composition may have an overwhelming spiritual experience; participants may not move a muscle, but their souls are anything but passive. The solitary worshipper sitting in a gothic cathedral, bathed in light from the stained-glass windows and wisps of incense from the chancel may be transported to heights of ecstasy. The anchorite walled up in a cell, as much as the young person at a praise service, would claim to be participating in experiential worship.

Whatever style of worship is preferred, the liturgy should provide a balance between sensory stimulation and quietude. Just as the liturgical year is divided into periods of anticipation, rejoicing and introspection, the sequence of prayers, music, pageantry, and congregational participation in a worship service should be interspersed by intervals of silence. Those intervals provide the "space" within the ritual vessel. Worship is intended to bring people to God; and it is sad if epiphanies and insights are drowned out by unrelenting noise or compulsive action. Fortunately, periods of silent meditation are becoming more common in worship services. Participants understand that a quiet interlude is not an embarrassing delay in the service but an invitation to turn inward; such interludes recover something of the introspection of the monastic tradition and "a willingness to risk personal depth."[36]

Sacred drama and dance formed part of the ancient mystery tradition and can play expanding roles in a Christianity of the future. Drama has long been used as a teaching or experiential tool, and there is great potential for integrating it into formal worship. Sacred dance has been frowned upon in mainstream Christianity because of negative attitudes toward the human body.[37] But it was practiced by the Quakers; and romantic nostalgia for Quaker simplicity and spontaneity— extending far beyond the Society of Friends—has popularized the Christmas carol *Tomorrow Shall be My Dancing Day*[38] and Sydney Carter's hymn *Lord of the Dance*.[39] Pentecostals often break into spontaneous dance during worship. Dance, choreographed or improvisational, is becoming an important part of the liturgy in progressive Christian communities.

The traditional Christian liturgy may have timeless value; but it may seem irrelevant to people who have become estranged from traditional Christianity or to groups that are alienated from the social milieu in which it evolved. It may also seem foreign and irrelevant to people in societies without historic ties to European civilization. To meet a wider range of needs, rituals can be imported from other traditions or new ones developed. Even in mainstream western society rich potential exists for exploring the use of rituals whose origins lay in indigenous societies or in earth-centered religions. The Creation Spirituality movement encourages familiarity with rituals from extra-Christian traditions. Incorporation into the Christian liturgy may offer a great deal, but it should be approached with caution, sincerity and humility; casual or reckless experimentation can offend rituals' traditional conservators or harm participants by unleashing unwelcome energies. The desire for liturgical reform and innovation needs to be balanced against respect for the unifying power of tradition. Creation of new rituals and improvisation can be refreshing, and all rituals were once new; but it may take time before they acquire significant power.

Anyone can perform a ritual. To light a candle, bless oneself or others, or recite a prayer may require little training; the combination of a meaningful action, personal dedication, and rhythm of enactment creates a worthwhile ritual. But the more powerful types of liturgical ritual require carefully prepared sacred spaces and a priesthood, trained and experienced in invoking and handling the energies involved. Anyone can play with a kitten at home; but nobody but an experienced trainer should play with a grown tiger, and the encounter should take place in a safe environment. As noted Chapter 18, sacramental ritual and ceremonial magic may be more closely related than has usually been acknowledged. The importation of expertise, techniques and insights from Masonic and other esoteric traditions, as has been attempted in the Liberal Catholic Church, clearly must be approached with caution.[40] Conventional seminary training, even in the Catholic and Orthodox churches, may be inadequate; and new forms of training may need to be developed. Approached in a responsible way, however, the cross-fertilization of traditions could have far-reaching potential.

Both men and women should participate in sacred ritual. Gender issues in religion have attracted much attention in recent years, and emotions run high. Women have reacted justifiably against uniformly masculine divine images, the patriarchy of institutional religion, and treatment as second-class Christian citizens. Great controversy has arisen over women's eligibility for ordination. Few people today would doubt women's capability for ecclesiastical administration, pastoral care, Bible study, and preaching.[41] But gender interchangeability in sacramental ritual calls for more careful consideration. The ancient mysteries carefully distinguished rites performed by priests and priestesses; male and female roles were assigned according to the types of energy to be invoked and the deities contacted. When rituals were absorbed into Christianity, only male roles were admitted.[42] Traditional Masonic groups did the same, and they too insist on gender-specific roles.[43]

Charles Leadbeater, bishop in the Liberal Catholic Church, commented thus on the Mass: "this particular type of magic is not adapted to work through the feminine organism"—though he added that Christ could make other arrangements when he returns.[44] Perhaps consecration of the Eucharist is a male role; but neither Leadbeater nor anyone else has yet made a convincing case that it is. Typical arguments for excluding women from the priesthood are almost pathetic: "Women are not called to serve in this way because God has not given this responsibility to women."[45] Whatever the rights and wrongs on that particular issue, traditional Christian rituals are incomplete and unbalanced. There is a pressing need to recover ancient rites in which priests and priestesses played complementary but distinct roles. New rites should also be developed solely for feminine celebrants, and the earth religions may offer worthy guidelines. Great progress has been made in theological studies of the masculine and the feminine aspects of God; and those efforts need to be accompanied by corresponding attention to the liturgy. Christianity can only benefit from a liturgy that expresses complementary masculine and feminine energies. If a balanced liturgy were created, women playing male roles might become as anachronistic as men playing female roles in Shakespearean drama.

Path of Knowledge

The Path of Knowledge encourages study, teaching, and—perhaps most important—reflection on what has been learned. It is the approach to God through the pursuit of truth, the sharing of insights within a supportive community, and the collective transformation made possible. The Path of Knowledge was the path of John the Evangelist, the fourth-century Theodore of Mopsuestia, Augustine of Hippo, Cyril of Thessalonica, Thomas Aquinas, Isaac Newton, Philipp Melanchthon, John Calvin, Jakob Böhme, Friedrich Schleiermacher, Vladimir Lossky, Alice Bailey, and Marcus Borg. Clearly it is linked to the fifth ray of Knowledge and Science. In its teaching aspect it also expresses the second ray of Love-Wisdom; significantly, esoteric Christians refer to Christ—who so strongly expresses second-ray energy—as the "World Teacher."

The Gnostics insisted that the "fall" was a descent into ignorance and that humanity must be redeemed—though they preferred "transformed"—by knowledge. The Path of Knowledge is linked to *jnana yoga*; and both the Gnostics and the jnana yogis stressed that truth is to be gained through intuition and personal insight. The institutional church rejected the Gnostic focus on personal insights in favor of knowledge sanctioned and disseminated by religious authority. It developed a vast body of dogma and established a powerful teaching ministry. In its present form this teaching ministry includes week-by-week preaching by parish clergy, Sunday school programs, church schools, seminaries, and denominationally affiliated universities. It also includes the personal study of countless individuals.

Jesus commanded the apostles to preach, and increased emphasis on preaching was a positive outcome of the Reformation. During most of the church's history preaching was the only source of religious teachings, even the only formal education of any kind, for the masses. Unfortunately, it was often in a language the people did not understand or was mechanical, empty of meaning, and threatening. Clergy are not always good communicators, and even today many are poorly educated. Worse, preachers do not always tell the truth; leading seminaries still advise future preachers to withhold information, like the results of higher scriptural criticism, for fear that it could undermine people's faith. That kind of dishonest paternalism calls the clergy's integrity into serious question. More importantly, withholding knowledge insults those whom the churches are committed to serve. Many members of the laity are highly educated—and no less committed to their faith than their preachers. They struggle with the same issues, with the same sincerity and the same doubts. Moreover, they have access to alternative sources of information and can do their own research. The attitude that ecclesiastical authorities are shepherds protecting their poor sheep from being led astray was resented even in the Middle Ages, and certainly it has no place in today's sophisticated society. The greater danger now is that the churches will lead people astray.

Likewise, the religious education of children must be approached in a spirit of honesty, as well as with openness and joy. Bible stories, those long-time staples of Sunday-school classes, acquaint children with foundations of western culture as well as of Christian religion. Scripture is full of inspiring stories of heroes and heroines who transcended conventional limitations; it can introduce children to the mysteries of God and the universe. Biblical passages should be selected with care, however. Emphasis on the Israelites' indiscriminate slaying of men, women and children or on the misogyny of the Pseudo-Paul is unlikely to nurture commendable moral values.[46] Education in moral precepts should never be linked to fear or guilt; to stress the fires of hell or the physical aspects of Jesus' passion is more likely to create neurosis than successful relationships and lives of loving service.[47] By contrast, religious education that instills joy, compassion, respect for the natural world, and a sense of the sacred can prepare a child for a lifetime of spiritual adventure.

Bible study became of central importance to Protestants when Martin Luther proclaimed the principle of *sola scriptura*. Scriptural study provides endless opportunities for learning, reflection and contemplation by people of all ages and educational levels. The Bible should be read as a set of sacred texts and allowed to speak to the reader on multiple levels; to try to read them as "plain sense" revelation is to mistake their purpose and can only lead to fundamentalism or to a rejection of scripture's true value. Moreover, memorizing "chapter and verse" not only clutters up the mind but encourages use of the Bible as a polemical weapon.[48] In that regard and more generally, the Path of Knowledge is vulnerable to separatism unless it is mediated by love. We noted in Chapter 7 and elsewhere that the major pitfall of the Path of Knowledge is divisiveness.

Revelation is not confined to the Old and New Testaments. Adults can benefit from studying a broader range of scriptures; and an increasing number of churches now include readings from extra-canonical or extra-Christian texts in worship services. The sacred books of the world religions express the wisdom of the ages and speak to us with the power invested in them not only by their authors but by centuries of believers and seekers. The message of world scripture rises above any concerns about historicity, authenticity or literalism. The scriptures capture the mysteries, the myths of their cultures, and the ongoing search for answers to the ultimate questions of human existence. The idioms and images may vary from culture to culture, but universal truths emerge to the discerning mind. Furthermore, God speaks to us through media other that scripture. Who can say that we cannot hear the voice of the Divine in the arts, the sciences, or nature? As scholars from Thomas Aquinas to the authors of the Rosicrucian Manifestos were fond of pointing out, God is revealed through the Book of Nature.

Secular institutions have long recognized that higher education and research are mutually supportive. Lecturers who do not engage in research can become stale, and researchers who never teach lose the benefit of students' insightful—and often penetrating—criticism. Research at seminaries need not be restricted to the traditional areas of biblical exegesis, theology, homiletics, ethics, religious history, and sacred languages. A broad range of topics in the arts and sciences— including the life sciences—as well as topics in education are also appropriate. Church-sponsored universities should encourage research in the whole range of academic subjects.

Religious institutions can no longer claim the best intellects, the most knowledge, or the clearest insights. Secular universities have taken the lead in philosophy and religious studies; even in theology, the most important advances over the last 200 years have been made outside the seminaries. The reasons are not hard to discover. Ecclesiastical authorities too often want apologetics, not scholarship; free inquiry is threatening. As a leading biblical scholar lamented: "The truth may set you free, but it may also make a lot of people extremely annoyed."[49] Such attitudes drive theology further away from its traditional base and away from fruitful contact with the liturgy and pastoral care. If the churches are to regain their leadership position in theological inquiry they need to embrace an unrestricted search for truth. Educational institutions are judged by the stature of their teachers, the quality of their teachings, and the climate of exciting discovery they create. Ecclesiastical sponsors should realize that they have more to gain by being in the forefront of discovery than by fighting rearguard actions to defend failed dogma. To quote esoteric writer Alice Bailey:

> [The churches] must learn to recognize that the Lord is not with them and they too must go forth, as Mary did, and seek him anew. If they will do so, they will surely find Him and again become His messengers . . . [T]he Living Christ will walk among men and lead them onward towards the Mount of Ascension . . . All men will come under the tide of inspiration from on high, and though they may speak with many tongues, they will all understand each other.[50]

Ecclesiastical authorities traditionally have insisted that existing doctrine is complete, infallible, unchanging and unchangeable; but in fact all knowledge is historical. Our understanding of God, Christ and humanity continues to unfold. Epistemological humility demands that we recognize that all truth formulated by the human mind—regardless of its source—is incomplete and provisional, eventually to be replaced by, or incorporated into, larger truths. For Karl Barth, "Theology . . . is a pilgrim venture, always open to revision, a self-critical discipline, ever seeking to give a better account of its subject matter."[51] Knowledge should be allowed to evolve freely; unsupported opinions and false arguments do not need to be suppressed; they will die of their own accord. Contrasting views should be encouraged in the assurance that confrontation between thesis and antithesis can lead to synthesis.[52] Conflicting ideas and temporary inconsistencies are not signs of trouble; they may prompt the emergence of new insights. Differences of interpretation may provide a catalyst for the perception of more comprehensive and inclusive truths.

Even in the 21st century some people want to be told what to believe; but growing numbers want to study, learn, and make their own doctrinal judgments. Today it is not just church officials, clergy and professional theologians who study religious issues; many "laypeople" are interested too, and often they pursue their studies with considerable enthusiasm. One survey indicated that "two-to-three times as many lay Catholics [in America are] enrolled in graduate programs in theology, ministry, and religious studies than . . . seminarians in the four years of theology preparation to ordination."[53] High educational levels, attitudes of intellectual independence, and ready access to books, television documentaries, the Internet, continuing-education courses, and discussion groups combine to make serious study possible to a degree unimaginable even a few decades ago. People are also studying comparative religion, Marxism, Theosophy, Wicca, shamanism, and many other subjects once prohibited.

Not unexpectedly many church leaders are worried about the prospect of an increasingly informed laity. Institutional Christianity's great failure has been to define too much dogma, provide too many simplistic answers, and discourage awkward questions; but a questioning attitude is central to the Path of Knowledge. Instead of promoting dogma, clergy should challenge people to do their own research and gain new insights. We need more clergy like the insightful Episcopal priest who insisted: "We don't seek to answer your questions, we seek to question your answers."[54] Concerns are often expressed that people might "lose their faith;" but losing one's faith may be the very stimulus needed to seek a more durable truth. Some may be led away from Christianity, but many will come to a larger view of it. We should remember that "faith" originally meant "trust"—and trust extends to redeemed humanity's ability to find truth.

Humanity has an insatiable thirst for knowledge. As mental beings, we can either use our God-given intellect to the full or suppress it, with all the implications that would have for our own integrity and our relationship with God. In 1819 William Ellery Channing (1780-1842), father of modern Unitarianism, prayed that "the servile assent, so long yielded to human creeds, may give place to honest and devout inquiry into the Scriptures; and that Christianity, thus purified from error, may put forth its almighty energy, and prove itself, by its ennobling influence on the mind, to be indeed 'the power of God unto salvation.'"[55]

Dominican priest Matthew Fox commented 160 years later on "the immense importance of ideas for people's freedom, integrity, courage, and ecstasy."[56] Situations in which Christian teachings conflict with the legitimate discoveries of physics, biology, psychology, or any other field of scholarship cannot be ignored. To be sure, religion and science address different categories of reality, but there are areas of overlap. In those areas, intellectual integrity demands that we confront inconsistencies and contradictions and strive toward a unified truth. The alternative is for permanently disconnected bodies of religious "truth" and academic "truth" to grow up side-by-side (along with categories like political and marketing "truth"). Claims that Jesus was an Essene, or that he traveled to India during his "silent years," potentially are verifiable or falsifiable through historical research. On the other hand we should pause before dismissing Jesus' miracles as fictional because they conflict with current scientific understanding of reality; today's understanding of the natural order may turn out to be incomplete. Apparent conflicts challenge us to examine both our religious and our scientific beliefs.

Not everything we learn from scripture, traditional Christian teachings, or elsewhere will have lasting value for us. But enduring truth contributes to the edifice of wisdom that we build throughout our lives. We have the opportunity, and the responsibility, to build wisely. Our responsibility is also to put our knowledge to good use as a basis for worthwhile action; otherwise it only satisfies idle curiosity. Truth is to be utilized in love and service.

Emphatically the Path of Knowledge is much more than the mere acquisition and dissemination of facts. Factual knowledge, like ritual, is a vessel into which a higher reality can flow; in this case the higher reality is the insight and intuitive understanding that transcends the intellect. As the Gnostics well understood, *gnosis* transcends the intellect to penetrate and stimulate the higher levels of the psyche. At an intuitive level new wisdom and understanding are possible even though they may no longer be expressible in linear verbal formulas. Also at that level, it may be possible to resolve pairs of opposites or apparent contradictions. How do we reach the intuitive levels? Through quiet reflection, away from the books, the websites, and the classroom. The jnana yogis turned to meditation, and therein we see the confluence of intellect and mysticism.

The Path of Knowledge extends beyond Christianity. Many doctrinal differences between Christians and members of other world religions could probably be bridged. A first step would be to formulate doctrine in more inclusive language. Also, we need to be sensitive to the symbols of other religions; to ridicule the "worship of wooden idols," while we revere symbols in our own churches, is hypocritical as well as offensive. We can learn much from the wisdom of other religious traditions and from the perspectives of people unfettered by our own habits of thought. Concepts that have evolved in non-Christian religions may be highly relevant to our quest.

Path of Service

The Path of Service is dedicated to helping our neighbor and making the world a better place. Christ commanded us to love our neighbor as ourselves.[57] "Love" in the relevant scriptural passages translates the Greek word *agape* (αγαπη) which captured the notion of impersonal, universal love. Agape contrasted with both *philia* (φιλια, "affection") and *eros* (ερως, "erotic passion").[58] We are not expected to feel affection for others; we may not even *like* them; but we treat them with empathy, respect and goodwill. At the same time, Christ's commandment requires an adequate level of self-love to set a standard. Service is an important expression of the second ray of Love-Wisdom and is directly analogous to *karma yoga*.

The Path of Service was the path of the Good Samaritan and the deacons of apostolic times; the path of Clare of Assisi, Vincent de Paul, John Wesley, William and Catherine Booth, Walter Rauschenbusch, and Mother Teresa. It is the path of workers at the soup kitchens, homeless shelters, and domestic violence havens in every city; the path of volunteers at a disaster scene; the path of every person caring for a handicapped child or an aging parent. If devotion is a "vertical" activity, in which we reach out to God, service is a "horizontal" activity in which we reach out to humanity. The juxtaposition of the vertical and horizontal creates the image of the Cross, confirming the central importance of the two paths in the Christian experience. To invoke another image, if the Path of Ceremony provides a vessel for divine grace, and the Path of Knowledge a vessel for the influx of divine light, the Path of Service—together with the paths to be discussed next—provide vessels through which divine love can flow to humanity.

Religion, by its very nature, involves realities that transcend the level of mundane, everyday life; but the relative emphasis is changing. The primarily devotional religion of the past, which emphasized personal sanctity, is giving way to a more grounded religion concerned with improving conditions in the world as much as with preparing for the hereafter. Religion today is concerned more with moving humanity toward perfection, with building the kingdom of God on earth. Spiritual growth, once thought to require escape from the everyday world, now demands involvement in the world—often on very practical levels. The effectiveness of discipleship is measured less by a person' piety than by how much work is done. Service is a response to human need; but it should be a mental rather than an emotional response. To respond emotionally may be understandable, but it may not produce the capacity for useful work; for example, the sheer enormity of a disaster may overwhelm the emotions, whereas a clear head can find a way to alleviate suffering and misery as best we can. Effective discipleship requires training to raise our mental faculties to a position of psychological leadership and to integrate our physical and emotional natures with them.

The priority given to service has varied over time, and from one society to another, as humanity has progressed—unevenly—from tribal consciousness to strong individualism, to group consciousness.[59] During the long phase of tribal consciousness people identified with their extended family or clan and were expected to share resources as needed.[60] A subsequent trend toward individualism was necessary for the development of personal identity; but inevitably it created an impediment to sharing. Herbert Spencer's "social Darwinism" or President Herbert Hoover's "rugged individualism"[61] could easily produce attitudes of selfishness and indifference. In the third phase, uniqueness is affirmed, but separateness has been overcome; we refer to this phase as group consciousness. Sharing again becomes automatic, but now it is based on a compassionate response to the needs of others, whoever they might be. We are willing to share resources beyond the nuclear family, social group, religious affiliation, or nation.[62] We treat everyone as members of the human family, all made in the image and likeness of God and equally deserving of our help. A shrinking world—one where need can be seen in every quarter—makes this selfless attitude more attainable, and more necessary.

The seeds of group consciousness were sown by the Buddha, by the Stoics, and most conspicuously by Jesus Christ. Christianity was the first religion to teach principles of universal love. But those seeds took a long time to germinate and bear fruit. Church father Basil of Caesarea encouraged religious orders to take on service as a kind of specialization: feeding the hungry, nursing the sick, and comforting the afflicted. In an earlier chapter we noted that the 12th-century Slavic king Vladimir Monomachos urged his people: "forget not the poor, and support them to the extent of your means. Give to the orphan, protect the widow."[63] John Wesley and his early followers visited prison inmates. In due course, serving the downtrodden segments of society came to be seen as a broader area of responsibility for lay orders like the Society of St. Vincent de Paul and the Salvation Army. Compassion is now taking hold among Christians and non-Christians on a much-larger scale. Today's world is often criticized for its indifference; but concern for human need has never been greater.

Nobody would claim that service has become a universal priority, but it is embraced as an ideal by virtually all Christian persuasions. Potential areas of service are almost unlimited. Everywhere people are in need: in our own neighborhoods; in the inner cities, prisons, hospitals, disaster scenes; and in Third-World countries on the other side of the world. Many international humanitarian programs are dependent entirely on volunteer support; but the person living across the street may be in as desperate need as someone in sub-Saharan Africa. Large-scale human services and disaster relief may be administered by government agencies. But there is still great need for the kind of ministry that only a Francis of Assisi, a Seraphim of Sarov, a Mother Theresa, or an Abbé Pierre can provide.[64]

Service is a most effective unifying activity, bringing together people who might otherwise have little in common. It can unite members of congregations, congregations with other congregations, denominations with other denominations, Christians with non-Christians. Humanitarian organizations like the Red Cross/ Red Crescent, the United Nations Children's Fund, and Doctors Without Borders[65] may be "secular" but they express ideals that Christ would surely have endorsed. For Christians to participate in their programs can be a way to affirm the broad expression of those ideals. If we have applicable skills we can participate directly. Alternatively we can donate money or participate in fundraising or the collection of other resources. The response to well-publicized disasters may be bountiful; but response to ongoing famine, systemic poverty, or conflicts that escape media attention is often less generous. "Giving fatigue" sets in when disasters drag on too long. We all need to heed Paul's advice: "[L]et us not be weary in well doing . . ."[66]

Addressing structural inequities in wealth, civil rights, and opportunity may be a matter of activism more than service. But it has also become apparent that multiple, small-scale efforts can do much to help disadvantaged people help themselves. Some of the best examples come from the Third World. The successful Heifer Project donates breeding livestock to poor people to provide sustainable food supplies; the program demonstrates how love and sharing can be fostered along with economic aid.[67] Bangladeshi economist Muhammad Yunus established the highly successful Grameen Bank to provide micro-loans to poor people, mostly women, to set up small businesses in underdeveloped countries.[68] Since then micro-loan programs have spread to numerous countries.[69] Small businesses not only support their proprietors; they create jobs, stimulate the economy, and improve social stability.

Similar self-help schemes can be effective in the developed world. An unglamorous but most important area of service addresses poverty and crime in blighted inner-city neighborhoods. Urban ministries provide after-school facilities for children, help the victims of domestic abuse and drug addiction, organize neighborhood-watch programs to combat crime, and refer people to available social-service agencies.[70] They help disadvantaged people secure affordable housing, improve educational opportunities, stabilize families, encourage citizens to vote, and—perhaps most important—gain new hope. Forward-looking churches have turned their under-utilized facilities into business incubators to help new enterprises get established.[71] Disadvantaged people need help to find and retain employment, and this may involve coaching to overcome cultural hurdles.[72]

Who is competent to serve? Should we be nervous about our ability to do useful work? To quote an Evangelical woman who devoted her life to service:

> "Many of us may fear the idea of service because we feel unworthy, inexperienced, ignorant, or untrained. None of these reasons is valid. Who of us is strong enough to serve people as Christ did? We are all weak and inadequate. But God has the wonderful ability to use our weaknesses to help the weak. After our pains and weaknesses have been overcome, we can help others who have been similarly afflicted, without pity or condescension and with understanding.[73]

Why do we serve? People may serve from a sense of obligation or from a desire to heal the world, to work for justice, or to express Christian faith.[74] Ongoing involvement in service is rewarded not only by steadily increasing competence but also by a progressive purification of motives. Initially a person may serve because he or she is paid or receives some other reward, such as college credits.

Later the person may serve in expectation of praise or feelings of satisfaction. Still later the person may view service as a means to spiritual growth; but even that is self-serving, and purification can be taken further. When group consciousness is fully established, service becomes simply a response to need; it arises from overflowing compassion. To quote the Indian spiritual teacher Jiddu Krishnamurti: "[Y]ou must give yourself to the service of the world because you love it, and cannot help giving yourself to it."[75] Jesus would settle for us to serve because we love him; but he would prefer that we help others because we love them.

Promoting Christianity may be a worthy cause, but it is a questionable motive for service. Many Christians regard activities like feeding the hungry as "opportunities for evangelism." But the best way to witness to Jesus Christ is to emulate the life he lived and to serve others in imitation of the way he served: "Let your light so shine before men, that they may see your good works, and glorify your Father which is in heaven."[76] The virtues of Christianity come across naturally if people act in wise, loving ways. If this requirement is met, there is little need to preach; if is not met, preaching is hollow. To those who do not want it, proselytizing is an unwarranted intrusion into their lives and can only be counterproductive.

Path of Healing

The Path of Healing is dedicated to alleviating pain and nurturing the fullness of life. It is a branch of the Path of Service, but it also draws upon sacramental practices from the Path of Ceremony. Notable individuals who trod the Path of Healing were the Roman physician Galen, the deaconess Fabiola, Jerome's friend Paula, Cuthbert of Lindisfarne, Mother Ann Lee, Phineas Parkhurst Quimby, Mary Baker Eddy, William James Seymour, Australian James Moore Hickson, Edgar Cayce, Kathryn Kuhlman, and Ambrose and Olga Worrall. The Path of Healing is the path of every mother cradling a sick child; every physician, nurse, social worker, prison chaplain, pastoral counselor, and practitioner of alternative medicine. It is the path of the peacemakers; the mediators who try to heal domestic, industrial, political and international disagreements, or who reach out to mend the divisions among Christian denominations and world religions. The latter aspects of Healing overlap with the Path of Activism; in faith healer Ruth Carter Stapleton and former president Jimmy Carter, we find siblings who spanned the two paths.

Healing expresses the second ray of Love-Wisdom, the fourth ray of Harmony, and the seventh ray of Ceremonial Order. Christ came to earth as both a teacher and a healer. The redemption was itself a stupendous act of healing. To quote a Church of England report:

> Christ healed because healing itself was central to the proclamation of the new creation (*2 Corinthians* 5:17), into which we are called as we repent

and believe. This is the work of the Holy Spirit, and it is a healing work, the work of redemption.[77]

Christ's concern was for people's wellbeing in this life as well as for their souls. He healed many people of physical and other ailments and charged others to do likewise. In response, we set out as disciples to heal—and to be healed.

In the Orthodox churches an uninterrupted healing ministry has been pursued since apostolic times. But in the west confidence in healing has still not recovered completely from doubts about its propriety. Nevertheless, the various obstacles are slowly being overcome, and once again many churches are offering an active healing ministry. The work seems likely to expand as more people come to understand its relevance and effectiveness.

Jesus' own healing ministry and his charge to the apostles should be understood as part of a more general assertion of humanity's untapped potential: "He that believeth on me, the works that I do shall he do also; and greater works than these shall he do."[78] That potential may be unlimited. Jesus recalled passages in *Psalms* and *Isaiah* when he asked: "Is it not written in your law . . . Ye are gods?"[79] Athanasius of Alexandria is credited with saying: "God became man so that man could become God." Divine potential implies the fullness of health for ourselves and the gift—and privilege—of healing others. Certainly, healing is a blessing to humanity; but the blessing lies in the process, not in divine interventions that violate natural laws. As one renowned practitioner remarked: "I believe that most so-called 'miracles' are not miracles in any accepted sense, but only the working out of . . . immutable universal laws on a higher level of consciousness and being than we know."[80] Healing is a process set in motion by skilled, gifted people working in an environment of compassion.

Healing demands confidence in the possibility of improvement; as Ruth Carter Stapleton commented: "It is important to visualize a positive image in the situation confronted. When group imagination is negative, the first order of business is to bring it to an image of positive faith. Otherwise prayers are an exercise in futility."[81] On the other hand, to foster unrealistic expectations concerning the extent or speed of recovery may be irresponsible. Dramatic healings do occur; cases in which skeletal deformities are reduced, cancers decrease in size, "untreatable" infections clear up, or severe pain is eliminated are well-documented.[82] However healing may be gradual and incremental rather than instantaneous or radical; significant healing may require extended periods of contact between practitioner and patient, just as conventional medicine may require multiple therapy sessions. To attribute "failure" to a patient's lack of faith or "negative thinking" is cruel as well as misguided. Healing is successful even if patients simply feel better or are better able to handle their suffering. "Psychological" or "psychosomatic" conditions may or may not be the most responsive to treatment. But the records show that spiritual healing extends far beyond such conditions.

The Christian healing ministry includes sacramental healing, based primarily on the techniques described in scripture: prayer, anointing, and the laying-on of hands. The laying-on of hands has obvious connections with bio-energetic healing methods such as Reiki.[83] Anointing with oil may have connections to essential-oil and Ayurvedic therapies or to homeopathy. The formal discipline of music therapy may be relatively new, but the therapeutic benefits of music have been recognized since the time of Orpheus in ancient Greece. Chinese medicine dates back at least as far. Rich opportunities exist for incorporating ancient traditions into modern spiritual healing practices.

Clearly the healing ministry overlaps with professional healthcare and should be regarded as supportive of conventional medicine; all forms of healing tap into the same divine power and should be viewed as parts of a single process.[84] Vocations in professional healthcare may be at least as strong as they are in the Christian ministry, and conventional treatments may have, in the words of one commentator, a "sacramental dimension."[85] The healing ministry overlaps even more with holistic healing modalities which address the wellbeing of the whole person: body, soul and spirit.

Within the medical profession a wide spectrum of opinion exists regarding the role of the mind in treatment strategies. Presently, an all-too-common view is that all pathologies, including neuroses and psychoses, can be treated by medication or surgery. Modern psychiatry has become almost totally chemicalized, while psychology has pursued an independent path, not always with the support of the medical profession. Scientific medicine has made great strides; and sadly we acknowledge that some of its greatest advances were made in the face of determined religious opposition.[86] But its very success has led to over-specialization in both diagnosis and treatment. There is now broad awareness of the limitations of specialized medicine and a pressing need for integration. On the other hand, religion's influence on health has long been recognized. Psychologist Carl Jung (1875-1961) commented on the patients he had treated in the latter part of his life: "It is safe to say that every one of them fell ill because he had lost that which the living religions of every age have given to their followers, and none of them has really been healed who did not regain his religious outlook."[87] Some medical professions have acknowledged the power of prayer in healing,[88] though statistical studies have been inconclusive.

The healing ministry includes general care of the sick, pastoral counseling, hospital and prison chaplaincy, and exorcism. The broader aspects of social and global healing will be discussed in the next section. Pastoral counseling is a major component of the Christian healing ministry. Healing is not just about cancer, kidney failure, or psychosis. It is also about depression, grief, addictions, inability to form loving relationships, and the inability to hold down a job or manage money. Problems of that nature extend to all levels of society, including the clergy.[89] Counseling is a demanding service; one commentator describes it as "a unique interdisciplinary ministry that is clinically sensitive and spiritually informed."[90] Unfortunately seminary training in counseling may be inadequate, and lack of expertise is not necessarily compensated for by belief in the guidance of Christ or the Holy Spirit. Patients with deep psychological wounds may need the services of professional therapists outside the religious communities to which they belong.[91]

Building on an age-old tradition of spiritual counseling, the Eastern Orthodox churches have taken a lead in integrating exorcism and psychotherapy.[92] Spiritual counselors perform exorcisms to dispel *logismoi*, or what are variously depicted as demons, elementals, or negative thoughtforms. They recognize that logismoi can cause a variety of psychological conditions from mild neurosis to severe psychosis; in turn psychosis can manifest in physical pathologies. The existence of logismoi has almost entirely been dismissed in the west. To be sure, Jesus and apostles are reported to have driven out "demons;" but modern western scholars have tended to explain them away as figments of ignorant superstition, predisposition to sin, primitive understanding of the cause of sickness, or unspecified mental illness. Similarly, reports that the early desert fathers, like Anthony of Egypt, confronted demons are dismissed as isolation-driven hallucinations or the side-effects of sexual frustration. Eastern Christianity has always taken the existence of demons more seriously, and in consequence its healing ministry is more comprehensive.

Francis MacNutt published an in-depth study of exorcism from a traditionally western standpoint. He discussed demonic possession by "spirits of the occult," "spirits of sin," "spirits of trauma," and "ancestral, or familiar, spirits."[93] Recommended therapies included prayer, the patient's repentance, and the use of blessed objects, oil, salt, and holy water. MacNutt's interest in traditional exorcism is welcome, given western Christianity's reluctance to discuss the subject; but problems of "possession"—however that is interpreted—need to be regarded as more routine. Correspondingly, therapies need to be less dramatic than the stereotypical exorcism and integrated more effectively with pastoral counseling, clinical psychology, and psychiatry.[94]

The methodologies of modern psychotherapy are not entirely different from those of the sacrament of penance, now also known as "repentance" or "reconciliation." As traditionally viewed, the sacrament may have placed undue emphasis on guilt; nevertheless it helped innumerable people unburden themselves; and if medieval theologians interpreted "healing" as the forgiveness of sin, perhaps we can reinterpret absolution as healing. That is not to say that sin is simply another word for sickness; people are capable of the most heinous crimes, and to portray all of them simply as "sick" is to render words meaningless. Notwithstanding, many people really are sick; they engage in destructive or self-destructive behaviors because they are incapable of doing otherwise. Redemption cannot be considered complete unless it offers hope that sick people can be rescued from the conditions that plague them.

The Path of Healing, like other types of service, has rich ecumenical potential. Christians of widely different persuasions can work together without compromising what they perceive as core doctrinal positions.[95] In turn, those doctrinal positions may become less critical as people commit themselves to the alleviation of suffering.

Path of Activism

The Path of Activism seeks peace, justice and dignity for all people. If service and healing are concerned with helping those in need, activism seeks to create an environment in which many of those needs could be avoided. Activism addresses problems of systemic hunger and sickness, degradation, tyranny, repression, inequity and waste. It is concerned with establishing just peace, dismantling structures of injustice, and promoting responsible husbandry of shared resources—including the natural resources of the planet. It is concerned with eliminating abuses within institutional religion and bringing disparate sects into mutual harmony. Exemplars of the Path of Activism—several of whom also graced other paths—were Meister Eckhart, Peter Waldo, John Wycliffe, Jan Hus, Nilus of Sora, the Protestant reformers, Jan Comenius, the Quaker abolitionists, Henry David Thoreau, Theodore Parker, Leo Tolstoy, Karl Barth, Archbishop Óscar Romero San Salvador, Martin Luther King, Jr., Jimmy Carter, Archbishop Desmond Tutu, Lech Wałęsa, and Matthew Fox.

Special mention should be made of Philipp Melanchthon, Martin Bucer, Reginald Pole and Gasparo Constarini who tried to heal the Catholic-Protestant rift in the 16th century and to individuals like Vladimir Solovyov who tried to bring the Catholic and Orthodox churches together. Special mention should also be made of the countless individuals who participated in the civil-rights movement, the recipients of the Nobel Peace Prize, and the signatories to the Kyoto Protocol on Climate Change.[96] The Path of Activism is mirrored in Fox's *Via Transformativa*. It is also mirrored in the first ray of Will, necessarily mediated by the second ray of Love-Wisdom and the fourth ray of Harmony.

Activism can easily evoke a strident image in the popular imagination; angry demonstrators come to mind, shouting and shaking their fists. But the truly great activists, like Jesus, made their points through a combination of mildness and firmness, total fearlessness, and a spirit of self-sacrifice. To quote Mahatma Gandhi:

> Self sacrifice of one innocent man is a million times more potent than the sacrifice of a million men who die in the act of killing others. The willing sacrifice of the innocent is the most powerful retort to insolent tyranny that has yet been conceived by God or man.[97]

The angry zealot may be motivated by Will, but a Jesus or a Gandhi exemplifies the mediation of Will by Love and Wisdom. Another way to view activism is in terms of *social* or *global healing*; and that may soften both its image and the ways we seek to express it. The Paths of Activism and Healing are closely related.

Activism is often regarded as a purely modern activity, and opportunities for bringing about meaningful change may be greater now than they were in the past. But the impulse to redress injustice goes back to antiquity. The prophet Amos berated the ruling establishment of Israel: "Hear this word, ye kine of Bashan, that are in the mountain of Samaria, which oppress the poor, which crush the needy."[98] Sadly, his words went unheeded. The apostle Paul drew comparisons between the sovereignty of God and the claims of the emperor; he was beheaded. Countless others who spoke out against injustice were persecuted or killed. Activism requires not only courage but a measure of empowerment that was rare in earlier times and cannot always be taken for granted today. Can we make a difference? When we look around at the world's problems it would be easy to despair; but the hopelessness of some can be overcome by the hope of others.

Activism has not always been encouraged by institutional Christianity; when Frenchman Alphonse Esquiros (1812-1876) wrote an influential book depicting Jesus as a social reformer,[99] he was imprisoned for "an affront to religion." The churches have tended to embrace the *status quo*, whatever form it might take.[100] As children, we were made to sing: "The rich man in his castle, / The poor man at his gate, / He made them, high or lowly, And ordered their estate."[101] Churches often allied themselves with privileged classes, totalitarian regimes, even organized crime.[102] One critic in the 1990s targeted Catholicism:

> Since the time of Emperor Constantine in the early fourth century, the consistent policy of the Roman Catholic leadership has been to secure special recognition from the state . . . from outright establishment, preferment, and financial support, through various intermediate forms (such as arrangements under which the state and the international headquarters of the church have a symbiotic relationship that allows the state a voice in

naming national church leadership), to several forms of "accommodation" with the state, including participation in "multi-establishments" as in Britain or Germany today.[103]

Perhaps it was unfair to single out the Church of Rome; state-sponsored Protestant churches have done likewise. In any event, Christian activists have too often been shunned by mainstream churches, and it has fallen to courageous people on the fringes of Christianity to support causes that Jesus Christ himself supported.

Vladimir Monomachos, whose plea for charity was mentioned earlier, declared: "permit the mighty to destroy no man."[104] Four centuries later Nilus of Sora became an important social activist in the Russian Orthodox Church. In the west the Quakers were among the first social activists to take up the cause of those downtrodden by the powerful political establishment; they also played a leading role in the abolition of slavery. Unitarian minister Theodore Parker took a strong abolitionist stance, and Transcendentalist Henry David Thoreau is often considered the father of civil disobedience. Anglo-Catholics in the Church of England took a lead in promoting the Christian social conscience. The Liberal Catholic Church has taken a lead in promoting animal welfare, to the point of encouraging vegetarianism. The objectives and work of the Social Gospel movement and Liberation Theology were discussed in Chapter 19.

Racial and gender issues have long been prominent among the concerns of Christian activists, and we have already mentioned the attitudes of major denominations to those issues. The American civil-rights struggle and the campaign against apartheid in South Africa succeeded in dismantling state-sanctioned racial discrimination. But official and unofficial discrimination continues in many parts of the world. State-sanctioned discrimination against women persists in Saudi Arabia, and women's rights are restricted to some degree in most countries. The churches have been slow to admit women to the ministry, and the campaign to secure admission of gays and lesbians to the ministry is still in its infancy. Organizations like Witness Our Welcome and Soul Force are working to remove sexual-orientation restrictions against ordination in all major Christian denominations; their efforts support activism within individual denominations.

Recent decades have seen increasing concern for environmental issues associated with population growth, technology, and demand for resources; those issues range from depletion of the ozone layer to the extinction of animal and plant species. Many fundamentalists oppose environmental activism altogether. They cite biblical passages to dismiss environmental concern; for example: "subdue [the earth] and have dominion over the fish of the sea, and over the fowl of the air, and over every living thing that moveth upon the earth," and "cursed is the ground for thy sake,"[105] Additional resistance comes from fundamentalist beliefs that the end-times are near and environmental concerns, if they exist at all, will be overtaken by the Armageddon.

Notwithstanding, certain religious leaders and groups have given high priority to environmental concerns; and mainstream Protestant denominations, the Church of Rome, and the Eastern Orthodox churches are now joining in the work. Ecumenical Patriarch Bartholomew of Constantinople has earned the nickname "green patriarch" for his efforts, through seminars and symposia, to promote harmony between humanity and nature. His special concerns have been the Danube River, the Black Sea, Adriatic and Baltic. In the west, the Unitarian-Universalist Church and many progressive Christian communities have done much to support environmental causes. The Creation Spirituality movement is concerned with renewing theologies and practices within religion and culture that promote personal wholeness, planetary survival, and universal interdependence.[106] Its founder insisted that respect for the natural environment is firmly based in the teachings of Jesus and the prophets and was reaffirmed by Thomas Aquinas and Meister Eckhart.[107]

A number of national and international Christian organizations have been formed to coordinate environmental initiatives, such as the A Rocha Trust and Target Earth. Groups of Evangelicals founded the Evangelical Climate Initiative and the Evangelical Environmental Network. The latter declares "the Lordship of Christ over all creation," and it calls upon Christians to "[b]uild our Lord's kingdom by active service to restore and renew the works of his hands."[108] The invective hurled at those organizations by hard-line fundamentalists testifies to the good they are doing. On the fringes of Christianity are activists like Andrew Harvey who identified the earth with the Divine Mother.[109] These diverse efforts are all succeeding in raising public awareness of environmental issues. However we cannot support the misguided efforts of environmental extremists for whom violence is justifiable in pursuit of their cause.

Occasionally an individual with burning conviction sets out alone to protest a repressive, unjust, or life-limiting situation. More commonly, activism is a comprehensive process involving substantial numbers of workers to raise public awareness, assure concerned people that they are not alone, and support those who "take to the streets and man the barricades." Work done behind the scenes is not inconsequential and can provide worthy opportunities for Christian congregations or communities to get involved. Large-scale activist campaigns require careful planning and execution. Writing from a jail cell in Birmingham, Alabama, during the civil-rights struggle, Martin Luther King, Jr., listed four necessary steps: "collection of the facts to determine whether injustices exist; negotiation; self-purification; and direct action."[110] He added: "We have gone through all these steps in Birmingham. There can be no gainsaying the fact that racial injustice engulfs this community."

Religious activism inevitably comes into contact with political ideology, but therein lie many pitfalls. For more than a century Christian activists in many countries have formed alliances with pacifist or socialist political parties, labor unions, and other movements for social change. However, to wage political campaigns under the guise of Christian activism can be extremely dangerous.[111] Christians should be encouraged to participate individually and collectively in the political process; indeed it is their civic duty; but they should be clear about their own motives and the issues at stake. Most importantly, Christian activism must be conducted in a spirit of universal love and tolerance and with a sense of proportion.

Christian denominations and congregations should avoid the temptation to become entangled in the affairs of secular government. We are only too aware of the well-financed campaigns mounted by Evangelical fundamentalists to influence elections. Discussion of issues is perfectly appropriate; but denominations that pressure members to vote for particular candidates or support political parties are crossing the line of propriety. Religious parties or state churches and denominations that sponsor political parties have already crossed that line. The Deist founders of the United States wisely provided for what Thomas Jefferson called the "wall of separation" between church and state. Church-state separation was derived at least in part from the teachings of Martin Luther, and the Lutheran Church-Missouri Synod affirmed: "[W]e condemn the policy of those who would have the power of the State employed 'in the interest of the Church' and who thus turn the Church into a secular dominion; as also of those who, aiming to govern the State by the Word of God, seek to turn the State into a Church."[112] Over the years, the wisdom of separation of church and state has become abundantly clear—as have the problems that can occur when the wall of separation is breached.

Path of Renunciation

The Path of Renunciation is the approach to God through self-discipline, reordering of priorities, and alignment with divine will.[113] It would be easy to say that spiritual growth necessarily demands some level of renunciation; but it is equally true that renunciation is a product of growing spirituality. The renunciant turns away from the distractions of everyday life to seek higher consciousness and demonstrate commitment to the spiritual life. Asceticism played a conspicuous role in the early church; but many modern people also feel drawn to self-imposed disciplines to enhance their experience of the divine. Their scriptural inspiration is: "come, take up the cross, and follow me."[114] Notable exemplars of the Path of Renunciation were Anthony of Egypt, Simeon of Antioch, the Manichaean *electi* and Cathar *parfaits*, Bruno of Cologne, Julian of Norwich, Thérèse of Lisieux, Marion Rebecca Hughes, Anne Ayres, and the Padre Pio. The Path of Renunciation, closely related to the Path of Devotion, is linked to raja yoga and to the sixth ray of Devotion and Idealism.

It was a strong impulse that urged the desert fathers to withdraw to the wilderness, the medieval anchorites to their cells, and the contemplatives to the cloister. The great majority of people may feel unable to enter a monastery or take on the more rigorous forms of asceticism; but priorities can still be reordered. The 10th-century abbot, Symeon the New Theologian, told the story of a city-dwelling young man who was "steward of a house, having in his charge slaves and free men and carrying out all the tasks incumbent on such a life;"[115] the man achieved a high degree of sanctity because he "regarded all material things of life with indifference." Possessions need not be distractions from the spiritual life; they offer opportunities for service.[116] Money that would otherwise be spent on luxuries can be used for worthy causes. Christians and indeed all people of goodwill should avoid excess of all kinds, including the unrestrained pursuit of materiality; sufficiency must take precedence over abundance. Awareness of the fragility of the planet and limited resources make that all the more urgent. Only when we live within our collective means can we expect to live in harmony with one another and with the natural world. Herein we see an important link between the Path of Renunciation and environmental activism.

Renunciation involves setting aside fear, anxiety and all the psychological baggage that hinders spiritual development. Our goal should be to become clear channels of grace. We strive for inner purity and rise above attitudes, habits and drives that make it more difficult for divine love to flow through us. Detachment from the things of this world is an obvious requirement; but the religions of Asia also emphasize the need for harmlessness: the resolve to never harm a living being, however lowly. One way to express harmlessness toward other people is to practice truthfulness; bending the truth violates our own integrity as well as the trust others place in us. Harmlessness also involves forgiving others for wrongs suffered and overcoming any harbored ill-will. We must seek forgiveness, if not individually at least in general, for the wrongs we have perpetrated. Correspondingly we need to forgive ourselves for our own failures. We need to put ourselves in right relation to life in all its forms.

Asceticism is found in Catholicism in the spiritual practices of the great mystics. In its early days Evangelical Christianity encouraged puritan values and austere lifestyles. But Martin Luther's devaluation of "good works" launched

Protestantism onto a path that discouraged the forms of self-discipline which produced the great mystics; of the very few mystics who came from Lutheran traditions, Jakob Böhme and Emanuel Swedenborg were ostracized by their churches. However the revival of interest in monasticism within the Anglican and other denominations is a significant development. Equally significant is the growing popularity—among people of many persuasions—of intentional communities, including ecovillages.

The Eastern Orthodox churches expect all Christians to participate in ascetic practices, and as a direct result they have nurtured large numbers of mystics both in monastic institutions and among the laity. The 11th-century Orthodox saint Ilias the Presbyter explained: "The first stage of ascetic practice is marked by self-control and truthfulness; the intermediate stage by moderation and humblemindedness; the final stage by freedom from thoughts and the sanctification of the body."[117] The disciplinary observances of Orthodox Christianity have strong periodicity; fasting on Wednesdays and Fridays, and during Advent and Lent, establish a rhythm that has ritual as well as ascetic quality. Establishing and maintaining rhythm is the key to adherence to ascetic disciplines. If the ascetic is likened to an athlete, rhythmic observances correspond to the athlete's daily training regimen. A similar periodicity once existed in the west, but it has been eroded along with the general encroaching laxity. Whether or not asceticism is mandated by ecclesiastical authority, individuals and groups can voluntarily adopt rhythmic patterns of discipline; and greater merit obviously derives from the lack of coercion.

Orthodox ascetic practices may not be as severe as those of Jainism, but they have much in common with practices in Buddhism, Islam, and Hasidic Judaism.[118] Christians of all persuasions can learn much by studying the principles of yoga outlined by Patanjali whose famous *Yoga Aphorisms* provided a step-by-step method for achieving union with the Divine. Christian Theosophist Geoffrey Hodson intentionally used the word yoga, which he described as "a carefully ordered regime of self-training."[119] Elsewhere he commented:

> The practice of yoga takes one into the heart of Reality . . . The successful yogi and yogini must become ablaze with the Fire of God . . . A kind of divine rest is the real result of yoga, a deepening of consciousness as if a way had been found into the deeper recesses of the Soul into which at any time one could retire.[120]

A major objective of yoga and all ascetic practices is to still the emotions and mind, purify the self, and facilitate a transformation in consciousness that makes union with God possible. The ascetic imitates, in a small way and in "many lesser renunciations," the great renunciation Christ made at the crucifixion.[121] Teachers emphasize the need for consistency, the establishment of rhythm, and cheerful endurance of difficulty and pain.

Throughout history many people have embraced the contemplative life, sometimes, but not necessarily, through total withdrawal from the world. Quakers sit in silent worship, and many people have adopted a discipline of regular meditation. The need for silence has already been mentioned in relation to religious ritual; it also extends to life in general. In the modern world we are bombarded not only by external noise but by the inner "noise" of our own ceaseless thoughts. The contemplative withdraws from the world to escape the former, but he or she is still left with the need to overcome the chattering of the mind. Periods of solitude are necessary, but they do not automatically lead to tranquility. A contemporary monk explained: "The monastic tradition sees any such tranquility as a short-lived consolation to encourage beginners, which will dissipate once the search for God is pursued with real determination and the demons get to work to prevent any further progress."[122] Those demons plagued the desert fathers as they sought to draw closer to God.

The contemplative life is often criticized on the grounds that it is self-serving or escapist. Certainly asceticism should never be a way to escape from the world. Martin Buber pointed out that man "is not required to abandon the external and internal reality of earthly being, but to affirm it in its true, God-oriented essence and thus so to transform it that he can offer it up to God . . . The task of every man . . . is to affirm for God's sake the world and himself and by this very means to transform both."[123] Similarly contemplatives are criticized for not engaging in service; but the author of a Russian Orthodox text made a contrasting point: "The man who lives in silent solitude . . . is in the highest degree active, even more so than the one who takes part in the life of society . . . For he who watches in silence, by communicating his inward experiences . . . promotes the spiritual advantage and the salvation of his brethren . . . His experience and teaching pass on from generation to generation."[124]

Bearing in mind the interconnectedness of all people, all life, spiritual advantage may be gained even if there is no overt communication. Before condemning the contemplative, we ought to ponder whether we have fully understood the richness of service.

We are fond of saying that God is experienced most directly in suffering. The suffering may be personal or vicarious, sharing in another's pain. Few people today advocate the types of self-afflicted pain practiced in the Middle Ages, though we saw in Chapter 20 that such practices persist in our own time. Moreover, notions that the body is evil have no place in a Christianity that affirms the incarnation of Christ and the divinity of all creation. The ascetic life should be aimed at creating harmony between body and soul, between the everyday and the spiritual life, between the self and God.[125] We cannot love our neighbor if we hate ourselves. Anyone plagued by self-hatred requires psychological help rather than encouragement to engage in ascetic practices.

The merits of celibacy continue to be debated, and individuals should feel free to adopt any lifestyle they feel will further their spiritual development. Celibacy is firmly rooted in the monastic tradition; but examples of religious communities that admit families show that alternatives are possible. The imposition of celibacy as a condition for ordination to the secular clergy cannot be supported.

Final Reflections

Whether we feel drawn to traditional or innovative forms of Christianity, we can all find a spiritual path within the Ekklesia. Some persuasions emphasize one path or another, but the seven paths are intrinsically free from denominational or factional associations. Moreover they are open to people at all levels of spiritual attainment and aspiration. Each path offers a distinctive way to express the presence of God and the love of Christ in our lives. Certainly we have acknowledged that the paths have pitfalls; Knowledge and Activism are prone to divisiveness, and Ceremony may be culturally separative. Devotion, Ceremony and Renunciation can ensnare people in pride and self-absorption. But to be aware of the pitfalls gives us the opportunity to avoid them. Service and Healing are not entirely free from pitfalls, but they may offer the strongest affirmation of the unity of the Ekklesia.

Whatever path we are on, and wherever we may be on our journeys, we are united in common ideals. We oppose injustice but aim to heal the world rather than resorting to violence. We seek truth but pause to reflect that what we discover can only be partial and time-dated. We renounce excess in our own lives but value the creation of great works of sacred artistic heritage. We strive to love all whom we meet, no matter how different they may be from ourselves. And we worship God and share in the love of Christ, realizing that both may be known by different names.

Where does the Christian ministry fit into this picture? The ministry is primarily a service function, but its responsibilities extend to all spiritual paths, except perhaps to political activism. A professional clergy has special responsibilities for the Paths of Ceremony and Healing, and we urge that seminary training be strengthened to equip graduates for the more advanced types of work. Where does salvation fit in? Salvation is healing, transformation, enlightenment.[126] It springs from the awareness that something profound happened to human consciousness 2,000 years ago—and is still unfolding. Salvation acknowledges the divine potential that gives meaning to human existence. It acknowledges the healing of the human condition, and affirms our power to heal individual wounds as well as those of a troubled world. Salvation is the confidence that we have personal and collective worth, able to make a difference in this world and worlds to come. Where do heaven and hell fit in? The answer is simple: they need to be abandoned as models of the afterlife not only because they insult divine justice and compassion but also because the very notion of an "end-state" rules out any prospect for further growth toward perfection.[127] More generally, "heaven" and "hell" can describe phases in the human journey, and creating a heaven on earth is the goal of several of the spiritual paths.

Being a Christian is not a destination but an ongoing journey. With 19th-century Unitarian James Freeman Clarke we affirm "the progress of [hu]mankind, onward and upward forever."[128] Our journey is not one that we travel just on Sundays, during the canonical hours, or at times set aside for meditation or study. To be a Christian is a seven-day-a-week, 24-hour-a-day undertaking. As we grow spiritually, distinctions between the "sacred" and the "secular" disappear—not because we descend into a tiresome religiosity but because we joyfully express our ideals through work, play, interpersonal interactions, experiences, and everything else we do, think or feel. Even when our earthly life comes to an end, we can be sure that further opportunities will open up—perhaps greater ones than were possible during physical embodiment.

Christianity is a communion of pilgrims inspired by the love and wisdom of the Christ. We do not march with the army of the Church Militant—and certainly not to the beat of a single drummer. But we do travel our paths with companions, students, teachers, unseen mentors and guides, listening to the sounds of nature, sacred music, and our own inner voices. Each of us is unique, with a different genetic, cultural, economic, social and educational background. We carry with us personal histories, hopes, fears, weaknesses, strengths, successes and disappointments. We have stumbled many times and are familiar with setbacks and disillusionment; but we have also experienced rebirths, epiphanies, and expansions of consciousness. Epiphanies can occur at any time, and opportunities for service are most likely to arise when we are not engaged in "religious" activities. Perhaps a life-changing experience urged us forward onto a new path, gave us courage to meet the next challenge, or opened our eyes to new realities. Perhaps we shall have a life-changing experience tomorrow.

Christianity is a pilgrim on its own journey, ever striving to express its archetype more fully. The history of Christianity could be seen as a series of failures, missed opportunities, and incomplete successes. From another perspective we can see a success story that surpasses any other human creation, with or without divine support. The soul-searching made necessary by conditions in the modern world is giving the churches a new sense of their mission and identity. Christianity's journey is not over. It has a bright future as the subjective union of denominations, congregations, communities and individuals under the leadership of Christ, pursuing their various paths and giving expression to their highest aspirations. We affirm the progress of Christianity onward and upward for ever; the most glorious days lie ahead.

We also affirm that the Ekklesia extends beyond those who may be identified, or who identify themselves, as Christian. All are welcome in the great "Cathedral." Several writers have shared the vision of a new world religion formed by the convergence and synthesis of the religions we know today. Not everybody would view such an eventuality as either possible or desirable; but as Christianity continues to evolve toward greater inclusiveness and perfection its potential to play the leading role in a larger synthesis will become clearer. The emergence of a new global religion would in no way diminish the significance of what Jesus Christ initiated 2,000 years ago; rather, it could be the culmination of his work. The apostles set out to preach the gospel to all nations. For much of the last two millennia, "the gospel" was viewed in narrow, exclusive terms; however the loving impulse of the cosmic Christ—Logos and Sophia—is universal. The collective consciousness continues to expand from the initial divine impulse; it is not our place to limit the ways in which it should be expressed. We joyfully welcome the possibility that humanity could be guided to new harmony and spiritual greatness in the decades and centuries to come.

---

1. To achieve perfection no doubt we shall have to walk all seven paths—from the lowest to the highest levels of challenge. Moreover, each path provides opportunities for people at different levels of ability. But, as believers in reincarnation will understand, many lifetimes will be needed to reach perfection.
2. Matthew Fox. *Sheer Joy*. Tarcher, 1992.
3. See for example: John Nash. *Quest for the Soul*. 1stBooks Library, 2004, pp. 190ff. *Jnana* is the origin of the Greek word *gnosis*, and their meanings are similar.
4. Martin Buber. *Ten Rungs: Hasidic Sayings*. Schocken Books, 1947.
5. Theophanis the Monk. "The Ladder of Divine Graces." *Philokalia*. (Transl: G. E. H. Palmer, P. Sherrard, & K. Ware.) Eling Trust, March 1977, vol. 3, p. 67.
6. *Revelation* 1:11.
7. See for example: Rudolf Steiner. *Christianity as Mystical Fact*. Rudolf Steiner Press, 1914, pp. 113-124. Also: Zachary Lansdowne. *The Revelation of Saint John*. Weiser, 2006, p. 6.
8. *Deuteronomy* 6:5; *Matthew* 22:37: *Mark* 12:30; *Luke* 10:27.
9. We may also see connections with the fourth ray of Harmony through Conflict.
10. Manly P. Hall. *The Mystical Christ*. Philosophical Research Society. 1951, pp. 138, 140.
11. These issues are related to the larger "problem of evil," which has been a topic of centuries of debate: How could an infinitely compassionate God, who is also omnipotent and omniscient, permit human suffering?

12. Joseph Ratzinger. *Feast of Faith*. (Transl: G. Harrison.) Ignatius Press, 1981, p. 18. See also pp. 17-18, 20-23.

13. Scientific studies of collective consciousness lend credence to this possibility. See for example: Attila Grandpierre. "The Physics of Collective Consciousness." *World Futures: Journal of General Evolution*, vol. 48, pp. 1-4, 23-56, 1997.

14. Ratzinger, *Feast of Faith*, p. 14.

15. See the discussion in: Annie W. Besant. *Esoteric Christianity*. Theosophical Publishing House, 1901/1953, pp. 189ff.

16. John Nash. *The Soul and Its Destiny*. Authorhouse, 2004, pp. 192ff.

17. John S. Spong. *Why Christianity Must Change or Die*. Harper-Collins, 1998, especially p. 187.

18. *Namaste* literally means "reverential salutation to your inner."

19. As explained in earlier chapters, *dulia* is reverence for the saints—or in the Orthodox tradition for icons—and *hyperdulia* is the special reverence merited by Mary of Nazareth. *Latria* is worship reserved for God alone.

20. Hesychastic prayer was discussed in Chapter 12.

21. The three were William Meninger, Basil Pennington, and Thomas Keating. For an introduction to centering prayer see: Cynthia Bourgeault. *Centering Prayer and Inner Awakening*. Cowley Publications, 2004. As noted in Chapter 8, the use of mantras was proposed in the west as early as the 14th century.

22. *The Pilgrim Continues his Way*. (Transl: R. French.) HarperCollins, 1991, p. 175.

23. *1 Kings* 19:12.

24. Bourgeault. *Centering Prayer and Inner Awakening*, pp. 32-33. *Apophatic* prayer contrasts with *cataphatic* prayer which is based on mental concepts or language.

25. Annie W. Besant. *Esoteric Christianity*. Theosophical Publishing House, 1901/1953, pp. 201-202.

26. Bernard of Clairvaux. Sermon 52. *Bernard of Clairvaux on the Song of Songs*, vol. 3. Cistercian Publications, 1979, p. 50.

27. *Luke* 18:9-14.

28. "Ritual" is derived from the Sanskrit *rita*, a divine principle that preserved order in the world

29. "Pageant" is derived from the Middle English *pagyn*, or *pagent*.

30. Bishop Edward King of Lincoln was the highest ranking—and last—Anglo-Catholic clergyman prosecuted for conducting Roman-style rituals in the Church of England.

31. Mircea Eliade. *The Myth of the Eternal Return*. Princeton University Press, 1954, pp. 34-35.

32. Mircea Eliade. *The Sacred and the Profane*. (Transl: W. Trask.) Harvest Books, 1957, pp. 80-95.

33. Interestingly, while emphasis on religious ritual has declined, secular ritual has become increasingly popular. Examples can be found at sports events, political conventions, and sales meetings.

34. John Nash. "The Power and Timelessness of Ritual." *Esoteric Quarterly*, Fall 2007, pp. 35-53.

35. *Ibid*. Furnishings, decorations, regalia, symbols, and visual and musical facilities should be appropriate to the purpose of rituals to be performed.

36. See the discussion in: Hal Taussig. *A New Spiritual Home*. Poleridge Press, 2006, pp. 14ff, 56.

37. Participants at Pentecostal services frequently break into dance, but it is spontaneous and unscripted rather than ritualistic.

38. William Sandys. "Tomorrow Shall be My Dancing Day." *Christmas Carols Ancient and Modern*. Richard Beckley, 1833.

39. Sydney Carter. "Lord of the Dance." Stainer & Bell, 1963.

40. Relevant issues are discussed in: John Nash. "The Power and Timelessness of Ritual." *Esoteric Quarterly*, Fall 2007. For warnings against incautious use of ritual see: David Conway. *Ritual Magic: An Occult Primer*. Dutton, pp. 199-201.

41. The Southern Baptist Convention opposes a preaching role for women, based on *1 Corinthians* 14:34.

42. It may be significant that the *priestly* function—as distinct from that of presbyters—was modeled after the Jewish *kohanim* whose specific responsibility was blood-sacrifice.

43. In one tradition the candidate for Master Mason swears that he will not cooperate in the initiation of "a woman, an old man in his dotage, a young man in his nonage, an atheist, a madman, or fool." See: Malcolm C. Duncan. *Masonic Ritual and Monitor*. McKay, 3rd ed., (undated), p. 95.

44. Charles W. Leadbeater. *The Science of the Sacraments*. Apocryphile Press, 1920/2000, pp. 291, 349-350. Interestingly, Leadbeater strongly supported the Co-Masonry movement that admitted women on equal terms to men. See his *Glimpses of Masonic History*. Theosophical Publishing House, 1926, pp. 324-329.

45. A. L. Barry. "The Ordination of Women to the Pastoral Office." Lutheran Church—Missouri Synod, 2006.

46. Much of the misogyny of the "Pauline epistles" is contained in letters Paul never wrote.

47. Churches that stage "Hell House," "Judgment House," and similar fear-filled dramas, bear a grave responsibility for childhood and adult neurosis.

48. Quoting chapter and verse in an argument is equivalent to saying "take that!"

49. John D. Crossman. *A Long Way from Tipperary*. HarperCollins, 2000, p. xiii.

50. Alice A. Bailey. *The Externalisation of the Hierarchy*. Lucis Publishing Co., 1957, p. 471.

51. Clifford Green. *Karl Barth: Theologian of Freedom*. Fortress Books, 1989, p. 22.

52. The notion that thesis and antithesis will be resolved into synthesis was promoted by Georg W. F. Hegel (1770-1831).

53. Bernard J. Lee *et al*. *The Catholic Experience of Small Christian Communities*. Paulist Press, 2000, p. 64.

54. See the reference in: Hal Taussig. *A New Spiritual Home*. Poleridge Press, 2006, p. 69.

55. William E. Channing. "Unitarian Christianity. Sermon delivered at the Ordination of Rev. Jared Sparks in the First Independent Church of Baltimore, May 5, 1819.

56. Matthew Fox. *Passion for Creation*. Inner Traditions, 1980/2000, p. 24.

57. *Matthew* 19:19; 22:39; *Mark* 12:31; *Luke* 10:27; *Romans* 13:9; *Galatians* 5:14; *James* 2:8. The parable of the Good Samaritan explained that our "neighbor" was everyone.

58. The fourth Greek term, *storge* (storge), which captures affection of the parent-child kind, was rarely used in classical or New Testament times.

59. This topic was addressed in much greater detail in: Nash, *The Soul and Its Destiny*, chs. 6, 8.

60. See for example: *Deuteronomy* 15:7-11.

61. Herbert C. Hoover. Campaign speech: New York City, October 22, 1928.

62. See the discussion in: Nancy Seifer and Martin Vieweg. *When the Soul Awakens*. Xlibris, 2007, ch. VII.

63. Quoted in: Timothy Ware. *The Orthodox Church*. Penguin Books, 1963/1977, p. 79.

64. "Abbé Pierre" was originally a pseudonym given to Henri Pierre Groués by the French Resistance. Later, Groués used the name exclusively.

65. Doctors Without Borders, *Médecins Sans Frontières*, was founded in 1971 by a group of French physicians.

66. *Galatians* 6:9.

67. The Heifer Project, founded in 1938, sought to alleviate world hunger. A cow was provided to a poor family with the stipulation that it "pass on the gift" of offspring to another family. The program has now grown to include water buffalo, goats, sheep, chickens, and other livestock. Source: Heifer Project International.

68. Yunus was recognized for his work by award of the 2006 Nobel Peace Prize.

69. For example, the Microcredit Summit, held in Washington, D.C., in 1997 launched a nine-year campaign to reach 100 million of the world's poorest families, especially the women of those families, with credit for self-employment and other financial and business services.

70. See for example: Tony Campolo. *Revolution and Renewal*. Westminster John Knox Press, 2000.

71. *Ibid.*, pp. 127ff.

72. *Ibid.*, pp. 147-150.

73. Ruth Carter Stapleton. *The Experience of Inner Healing*. Guideposts, 1977, p. 149.

74. The author is indebted to the Reverend Susan Crow for these insights.

75. Jiddu Krishnamurti. *At the Feet of the Master*. Theosophical Publishing House, 1908, p. 16.

76. *Matthew* 5:16.

77. Bishop John Perry *et al. A Time to Heal*. Church House Publishing, 2000, p. 18.

78. *John* 14:12.

79. *John* 10:34. See also: *Psalm* 82:6; *Isaiah* 41:23.

80. Ambrose A. & Olga N. Worrall. *The Gift of Healing*. Harper & Row, 1965, p. 17.

81. Stapleton, *The Experience of Inner Healing*, pp. 38-39.

82. Worrall, *The Gift of Healing*, pp. 121-174. Francis MacNutt. *The Power to Heal*. Ave Maria Press, 1977, pp. 35-87.

83. As the term is currently used, bio-energetic healing includes all methods in which energy is directed or channeled to a patient. It may be offered to address physical, emotional or mental conditions.

84. Christian Science teaching that discourages conventional medical care may have been well-intentioned, but it was misguided.

85. Peter Bistolarides. "Regenerating the Heart" a Wholistic Perspective." Stephen Muse (ed.). *Raising Lazarus*. Holy Cross Orthodox Press, 2004, p. 37.

86. An example was religious opposition to the use of anesthetics in the 19th century.

87.   Carl G. Jung. *Modern Man in Search of a Soul*. Harcourt Brace, 1933, p. 239.

88.   See for example: Larry Dossey. *Healing Words : The Power of Prayer and the Practice of Medicine*. Harper, 1885; *Prayer is Good Medicine*. Harper, 1997.

89.   Significant numbers of ordained clergy and other professionals—or their families—are hurting. They may conceal from others, or themselves, alcohol or drug abuse, spiritual crises, or sexual orientations they cannot accept. See the discussion in: John Nash. "Discipleship and Disillusionment." *The Esoteric Quarterly*, Summer 2006, pp. 43-51.

90.   Demetra Jaquet. "Pastoral Psychological Response." Stephen Muse (ed.). *Raising Lazarus*. Holy Cross Orthodox Press, 2004, p. 96.

91.   Separation from the community establishes boundaries for successful therapy.

92.   Jeff Rediger. "Psychiatric Considerations," pp. 61-83; Demetra Jaquet. "Pastoral Psychological Response," pp. 95-112. Stephen Muse (ed.). *Raising Lazarus*. Holy Cross Orthodox Press, 2004. Also: Kyriacos C. Markides. *The Mountain of Silence*. Image Books, 2001, pp. 118ff.

93.   Francis MacNutt. *Deliverance from Evil Spirits*. Chosen Books, 1995, pp. 87-94.

94.   See the discussion in: Ruth Carter Stapleton. *The Gift of Inner Healing*. Guideposts, 1976, pp. 58-63.

95.   Bishop John Perry *et al. A Time to Heal*, p. 75.

96.   Signed in 2006, the Kyoto Protocol to the United Nations Framework Convention on Climate Change called for mandatory emission limitations for the reduction of greenhouse gas emissions. To date, 169 countries and other governmental entities have ratified the agreement. Notable exceptions are the United States and Australia.

97.   Mahatma Gandhi. *Collected Works*, XXVI-141, 1925.

98.   *Amos* 4:1. Samaria, or Shomron, was the capital of the northern kingdom of Israel. Amos warned that God's punishment would be the kingdom's downfall, which occurred when the Assyrians overran Shomron in 722 BCE.

99.   Alphonse Esquiros. *L'Evangile du People*, 1840.

100. It will be recalled that early Christianity suffered greatly under the violent, repressive Roman Empire but made good use of it after the conversion of Constantine.

101. Cecil F. Alexander. "All Things Bright and Beautiful." *Hymns for Little Children*, 1848.

102. The Lateran Treaty and the concordat with Hitler's Germany exposed the Vatican's willingness to deal with repressive regimes. Lutheran authorities supported National Socialism in the 1930s.

103. Edd Doerr. "Vatican Interests Versus the Public Interest—The Political Power of the Catholic Church." *The Humanist*, Sept-Oct., 1993. Parenthesis in original.

104. Quoted in: Timothy Ware. *The Orthodox Church*. Penguin Books, 1963/1977, p. 79.

105. *Genesis* 1:28, 3:17.

106. Matthew Fox. *Creation Spirituality: Liberating Gifts for the Peoples of the Earth*. HarperCollins, 1991.

107. Fox, Aquinas and Eckhart were all Dominicans

108. Source: Evangelical Environmental Network.

109. Andrew Harvey. *The Return of the Mother*. Tarcher/Putnam, 1995.

110. Martin L. King, Jr. Letter from a Birmingham Jail, April 16, 1963.

111. Politico-religious entanglement has become a conspicuous feature of American Evangelical fundamentalism. Moreover, "most Latinos view the pulpit as an

appropriate place to address social and political issues." See: *Changing Faiths: Latinos and the Transformation of American Religion*. Pew Hispanic Center, 2007.

112. Lutheran Church-Missouri Synod. Doctrinal Statement: *Of Church and State*. Concordia Publishing House, 1932.

113. Many people would say "surrender to divine will," but the notion of surrender may suggest unwarranted passivity.

114. *Mark* 10:21.

115. Symeon the New Theologian. "On Faith." *Philokalia*. (Transl: G. Palmer *et al.*) Eling Trust, March 1977, vol 4, pp. 19-20.

116. See the discussion in: Benedict XVI. *Jesus of Nazareth*. (Transl: A. Walker.) Doubleday, 2006/2007, p. 77.

117. Ilias the Presbyter. "A Gnomic Anthology", Part IV, §34. *Philokalia*, vol. 3, p. 52.

118. Jamie Moran. "Spiritual War." Muse (ed.), *Raising Lazarus*, p. 146. Moran even uses the word "union" or "yoke," whose Sanskrit equivalent is *yoga*.

119. Geoffrey Hodson. *Call to the Heights*. Theosophical Publishing House, 1976, p. 77.

120. Sandra Hodson (ed.). *Illuminations of the Mystery Tradition*. Theosophical Publishing House, 1992, p. 218. See also: *Light of the Sanctuary*. Theosophical Publishers, 1988, (numerous references).

121. Alice A. Bailey. *Discipleship in the New Age*, I. Lucis Publishing Co., 1944, p. 312.

122. Christopher Jamison. *Finding Sanctuary: Monastic Steps for Everyday Life*. Liturgical Press, 2006, p. 42.

123. Martin Buber. *The Way of Man*. Citadel Press, 1964, p. 6.

124. *The Pilgrim Continues his Way*. (Transl: R. French.) HarperCollins, 1991, p. 199.

125. Nash, *The Soul and Its Destiny*, pp. 216ff.

126. See: Marcus J. Borg. *The God We Never Knew*. HarperCollins, 1997, pp. 158-167. See also the discussion in Chapter 12 on the Eastern Orthodox view of salvation.

127. The notion of heavens and hells of our own making is viable.

128. James F. Clarke. *Vexed Questions in Theology*. Harvard University Press, 1886.

Index to Volume 2

Q

R

7758669R00207

Printed in Great Britain
by Amazon.co.uk, Ltd.,
Marston Gate.